Alterations
of
Consciousness

Alterations
of
Consciousness

AN EMPIRICAL ANALYSIS
FOR SOCIAL SCIENTISTS

Imants Baruš

AMERICAN PSYCHOLOGICAL ASSOCIATION
WASHINGTON, DC

Second Printing, December 2010
Published by
American Psychological Association
750 First Street, NE
Washington, DC 20002
www.apa.org

To order
APA Order Department
P.O. Box 92984
Washington, DC 20090-2984
Tel: (800) 374-2721
Direct: (202) 336-5510
Fax: (202) 336-5502
TDD/TTY: (202) 336-6123
Online: www.apa.org/books/
Email: order@apa.org

In the U.K., Europe, Africa, and the Middle East, copies may be ordered from
American Psychological Association
3 Henrietta Street
Covent Garden, London
WC2E 8LU England

Typeset in Goudy by World Composition Services, Inc., Sterling, VA

Printer: Edwards Brothers Inc., Ann Arbor, MI
Cover designer: Berg Design, Albany, NY
Project Manager: Debbie Hardin, Carlsbad, CA

The opinions and statements are the responsibility of the author, and such opinions and statements do not necessarily represent the policies of the American Psychological Association.

Library of Congress Cataloging-in-Publication Data
Barušs, Imants, 1952–
    Alterations of consciousness : an empirical analysis for social scientists / by Imants Barušs.—1st ed.
        p. cm.
    Includes bibliographical references and index.
    ISBN 978-1-55798-993-2 (alk. paper)
    1. Altered states of consciousness.   I. American Psychological Association.   II. Title.

    BF1045.A48 B37 2003
    154.4—dc21   2002038313

British Library Cataloguing-in-Publication Data
A CIP record is available from the British Library.

Printed in the United States of America
First Edition

CONTENTS

Preface vii

Acknowledgments xi

Chapter 1.   Introduction 3

Chapter 2.   Wakefulness 25

Chapter 3.   Sleep 51

Chapter 4.   Dreams 79

Chapter 5.   Hypnosis 107

Chapter 6.   Trance 135

Chapter 7.   Psychedelics 161

Chapter 8.   Transcendence 187

Chapter 9.   Death 211

Chapter 10.   Conclusion 233

References 241

Index 279

About the Author 291

PREFACE

Throughout my academic career, I have been interested in fundamental questions about the nature of reality. As a doctoral student in psychology, I wanted to get at the essence of the human psyche. But how was I to proceed in a manner that was compatible with the scientific orientation of the discipline of psychology? The study of consciousness, I thought, could be the right approach, and thus I found my specialty. On completing my studies, I was fortunate to find a school looking for someone with my expertise, and I have been teaching courses in consciousness to undergraduate students for more than 15 years.

At one point in my teaching, I split off the material about altered states of consciousness into a general course that was open to students across the university. Having put in place the course, I needed a textbook for it. However, although there have been advances in recent years in knowledge concerning separate altered states of consciousness—such as sleep, hypnosis, and experiences associated with death—there was no contemporary overview of altered states that was suitable for use as a textbook. Thus I took it on myself to fill a need in the literature by writing a book that I could assign to the undergraduate students in the altered states course.[1]

But I kept in mind readers other than my students as I was writing. In the last half-decade of the twentieth century there was an explosion of academic interest in consciousness, so I have also written this book as an

---

[1] I have also compiled a wealth of instructor resources that are available to instructors at www.apa.org/books/resources/baruss. Please consult this for supportive material if you wish to use this book as a classroom textbook.

introduction to altered states of consciousness for researchers who may be coming to the subject matter without any background in it. Because it is an introduction, I have included much well-known material, such as William James's characterization of thinking and the Good Friday experiment in which divinity students were given psilocybin before a Good Friday service. For the sake of readers with some familiarity with the subject matter, I have tried to cover such ground in a fresh manner—for example, by reflecting James in contemporary cognitive science and discussing the experiences of one of the participants in the Good Friday experiment based in part on my conversations with him.

The public has long had an interest in altered states of consciousness, and so I wrote this book with the general reader in mind as well. No previous knowledge of psychology or physiology is necessary. I have tried to keep the language as simple as possible, introducing technical terms only when they are commonly used or necessary and defining them explicitly when their meanings are not transparent from the context. I have tried to include descriptions of technical material, such as the activity of neurotransmitters, in a way that will allow readers to visualize that which is being described in sufficient detail without unnecessarily complicating matters. At the same time, I have tried not to simplify in such a way as to misrepresent that which is complex in reality.

One of the exciting aspects of the study of consciousness has been its multidisciplinary nature. The contemporary study of consciousness has drawn, for example, on psychology, cognitive science, philosophy, neuroscience, religious studies, medicine, anthropology, and physics. Methods of inquiry vary with the disciplines, so that a physiologist often proceeds quite differently from an anthropologist. Although there has been considerable research, information concerning consciousness remains patchy and disputed, so that there are numerous questions with few answers. I have tried to evaluate the knowledge that is available in the various disciplines and integrate it into a coherent whole that I think sits comfortably within the discipline of psychology. Indeed, I hope that psychologists will take up the task of synthesizing the results of research concerning consciousness from other disciplines and guide a research agenda for greater understanding of its nature.

I had to decide what to include and what to leave out of a brief overview of altered states of consciousness. A standardized list of topics has not yet been developed, so there was considerable latitude for choice. Some topics clearly needed to be included, such as sleep, dreaming, hypnosis, and psychedelic drug use. Then there were some topics it was reasonable to consider, such as daydreaming, sensory restriction, meditation, mystical experiences, and near-death experiences. But I also included some puzzling states that clearly involve alterations of consciousness, although we do not usually discuss them in the context of the psychology of consciousness—namely, shamanism, possession, dissociative identity disorder, alien abduction experiences, and experiences associated with death. I have left out a number of alterations of consciousness, including most psychopathological states, drug-induced states other than those induced by psychedelics and similar drugs, and perceptual anomalies such as synesthesia and blindsight.

My approach to each subject area has been to try to characterize its essence while avoiding some of the unfruitful lines of investigation that have been followed in the past. Let me give an example: There was great excitement in the 1970s regarding the fact that small asymmetries existed between the cerebral hemispheres of the brain, so that left-brain and right-brain streams of consciousness were proposed, and explanations of psychological events were given in terms of left-brain and right-brain processing styles. By the 1980s it had become clear that the implications of the small lateral asymmetries had been overstated given that in the intact brain, behaviors such as language were not cleanly lateralized to a single hemisphere, the cerebral hemispheres did not function as units, no differences in cognitive processing style between hemispheres could be found, and the assignment of psychological functions to one or the other hemisphere had little explanatory value. Thus I have not summarized the efforts that have been made at explaining some alterations of consciousness in left-brain/right-brain terms. I have included a few twists and turns that were perhaps unnecessary to include but that have been of considerable historical significance, such as Freud's dream theory. In general, however, I have summarized the most significant knowledge in each subject area, sometimes from a historical point of view but always in as straightforward a manner as possible.

If it is not already apparent, it will become so quickly in chapter 1 that much of the material in this book is controversial, particularly that which concerns anomalous experiences. Rather than trying to avoid the controversy, I have tried to reflect in an evenhanded manner the main positions that have been taken and to follow as much as possible the evidence wherever it may lead. In writing, rather than belaboring the use of the word "purported" when dealing with anomalous phenomena, I have often left it out when referring to people's experiences—for example, to alien abduction experiences—which occur however we may end up explaining them, or when there are reasonable scientific grounds to suppose that the phenomena in some sense really did occur, such as some cases of anomalous information transfer. What we think is true today may no longer be regarded as true tomorrow, whatever the truths we may be discussing, so it seems beside the point to belabor the tenuousness of knowledge concerning anomalous phenomena in particular.

Finally, in keeping with my interest in the fundamental questions about reality, I have made a point of raising existential, ontological, and similar questions whenever they surface in the context of altered states of consciousness. Indeed, 10 thematic threads based on such questions are introduced in chapter 1, woven throughout the text, and then gathered up in the conclusion in chapter 10. I hope that these threads inspire the reader and ignite a sense of wonder about the nature of consciousness and reality.

ACKNOWLEDGMENTS

I thank the following scholars for reading selected chapters and providing me with comments during the writing of the manuscript: Lynne Jackson, Chris Burris, Eric Klinger, Peter Suedfeld, Mary Carskadon, Charles George, Stanley Krippner, Donald Gorassini, John Mack, Nicholas Cozzi, Lester Grinspoon, Kym Dawson, Ron Leonard, and Bruce Greyson. I also thank Ian Brown, Ranjie Singh, Isabella Colalillo-Kates, Norm Thomas, and Saguenay Baruss for reading the entire manuscript. None of these readers are responsible for any errors that may yet remain in the book, nor do they necessarily endorse the ideas that I express. Indeed, I tried to choose at least some readers with whom I expected to disagree to take into account viewpoints contrary to my own. I also appreciate the supportive comments and helpful suggestions made by four anonymous reviewers.

I am grateful to all the people who have told me about their altered states experiences and, in some cases, helped me to collect additional data about them. Four of those accounts have made it into this book: Isabella Colalillo-Kates provided the example of contemporary North American channeling, discussed in chapter 6; Mike Young provided comments about his experiences in the Good Friday experiment, described in chapters 7 and 8; Allan Smith provided reflections on his experience of cosmic consciousness, discussed in chapter 8; and Lydia Bristow provided the report of an out-of-body experience, discussed in the beginning of chapter 9.

I am grateful to King's College for a paid sabbatical leave and research funds that allowed me to write this book. I thank my research assistants Lisa Van Dyk and Elizabeth Russell for unearthing, retrieving, and organizing a large collection of library resources. I appreciate the outstanding enthusiasm, effort, and cooperation of the publication staff at the American Psychological Association, particularly Susan Reynolds, Mary Lynn Skutley, Kristine Enderle, Phuong Huynh, Jennifer Macomber, Kristen Sullivan, Christina Davis, Russ Bahorsky, and Debbie Hardin. I thank Charles Tart and Stanley Krippner, who have championed my explorations into consciousness, and C. D. B. Bryan, Ann Thomas, Katie Paterson, and Robyn Howard, who have all contributed in their own way to this book, as have my students and colleagues with whom I have had the opportunity to discuss alterations of consciousness. Finally, I thank Michelle Cobban, who encouraged my writing and assisted with research, editing, and proofreading.

Alterations
of
Consciousness

1

INTRODUCTION

We are used to the everyday world being there for us while awake, day after day, and we know from its [...] is real and what is not. At night, perhaps we dr[...] and while we dream, we think we know that what we dr[...] is real, but on waking, we realize that it is not. And sometimes, while [...] disappears, and what we thought was real is gone, and we are confronted with that which is not supposed to be [...] ward, perhaps we come to think that that which is not supp[...]ed to be real really is real, or we no longer know what is real and what [...]

What is real? What is imaginary? What is true? Alterations of consciousness pose fundamental questions that can challenge our ideas about the nature of reality.

Handwritten note: McKenna – 2 weeks after / Psychedelic drugs / – see a UFO / – formed waterspout in clouds / – vacuum cleaner end cap.

An Example of Altered Consciousness

Terence McKenna had an unusual experience at dawn after a night of rumination while sitting on a flat stone by a river at La Chorrera in the Amazon. He noticed a mist at some distance from him that "split into two parts" (McKenna, 1993, p. 157) with each of those parts splitting again so that he was "looking at four lens-shaped clouds of the same size lying in a row and slightly above the horizon, only a half mile or so away" (McKenna, 1993, p. 157). Then they coalesced in reverse of the manner in which they had divided. "The symmetry of this dividing and rejoining, and the fact that the smaller clouds were all the same size, lent the performance an eerie air, as if nature herself were suddenly the tool of some unseen organizing agency" (McKenna, 1993, pp. 157–158). The clouds grew darker, swirled inward, and formed what appeared to be a waterspout. McKenna "heard a high-pitched, ululating whine come drifting over the jungle tree tops" (McKenna, 1993, p. 158). He tried to shout but no sound came out as he was gripped by fear. And then everything seemed to speed up as the cloud formed into "a saucer-shaped machine rotating slowly, with unobtrusive, soft, blue and orange lights" (McKenna, 1993, p. 158).

The flying saucer pass[...] identical in appearance to [...] assumed to be a picture of [...] "in a form that [cast] doul[...] McKenna off more than it [...] completely convincing" (N[...] did not know what to thi[...] After all, this early mornin[...] delic drugs. But what he [...] hallucinated imagery" wit[...] suggested, what he saw w[...] which in that instance c[...] which could have appear[...] something's omniscient control over the world of form and matter" (Mc-Kenna, 1993, p. 159).

Hallucinations are perceptions that do not correspond to physical reality (cf. Bentall, 2000; R. K. Siegel, 1975). But can such misperceptions nonetheless occasionally be perceptions of possible nonphysical dimensions of reality? Ordinarily we are locked into a particular way of thinking about our experience. Our everyday world seems so real to us. Alterations of consciousness can open us to something unusual. As McKenna has suggested, sometimes, perhaps, to something deeper that lies underneath the surface of life.

I have deliberately chosen an example of an experience in altered states of consciousness whose meaning is ambiguous. There will be other examples of experiences that appear to be clearly products of the imagination and still others that are arguably veridical. What does the reader think? Was McKenna's a true hallucination or perception of something that truly exists? McKenna had recently used psychedelic drugs; he was sleep-deprived and emotionally aroused; he had been absorbed all night in his own thoughts; and perhaps he had entered a trance of some sort. But are the psychological events that occur in such alterations of consciousness the sources of unusual experiences, or do they form a doorway into a reality that is ordinarily hidden from us? Conversely, are the psychological events that occur in the ordinary waking state reliable mechanisms for encountering that which is real, or are they the source of experiences that obscure the real? This book is about alterations of consciousness, the vistas that they open for us, and the questions that they raise.

CONSCIOUSNESS

Let us begin by setting the framework for a study of alterations of consciousness. What does the expression "alterations of consciousness" mean, and how does it differ from "altered states of consciousness"? In fact, what are we talking about when we talk about "consciousness"? We also need to clarify the conflation of alterations of consciousness with psychopathology. But before we do any of that, let us consider the perspectives that have been adopted in discourse about consciousness.

Perspectives on Consciousness

There are three perspectives from which consciousness can be approached: the physiological, the cognitive, and the experiential (cf. Baruš, 2000a). Each of these perspectives not only defines a domain of inquiry but is usually associated with particular ways of thinking about consciousness. The *physiological* perspective is concerned with the physiological processes involved in consciousness as studied usually within neuroscience using methods appropriate for the biological sciences. Questions have also been raised about possible direct relationships between consciousness and subatomic aspects of the brain, bringing ideas from physics, particularly quantum mechanics, to bear on discussions of consciousness (e.g., Baruš, 1986; Lockwood, 1989; Walker, 2000).

The *cognitive* perspective is concerned with cognitive processes involved in consciousness such as perception, thinking, memory, decision making, and creativity. This perspective falls largely within cognitive science and the disciplines of psychology, philosophy, and computer science, whereby knowledge of cognitive events is acquired through the observation of behavior, including verbal behavior, as well as through rational inquiry.

The *experiential* perspective is concerned with the conscious experiences that a person has for herself. This is also known as a phenomenological perspective in that phenomena are considered as such without reification into some other way of conceptualizing them. This perspective toward consciousness has sometimes been taken in psychology, philosophy, anthropology, and religious studies, and it depends on *introspection*, a person's examination of her own experiences, as its primary method of investigation (cf. Baruš, 2000a).

But such a tripartite division of discourse concerning consciousness raises questions. How do specific experiential events occur as cognitive processes? In turn, what are the physiological mechanics corresponding to specific cognitive processes? There are obviously interconnections. For example, marijuana affects a person's brain, which in turn affects cognition and experience. But these interconnections can be quite complex given that, for example, some seasoned marijuana users can experience the effects of marijuana intoxication from smoking marijuana cigarettes that have had the main psychoactive ingredient removed (Jones, 1971). A person's belief that she is smoking a marijuana cigarette appears to be enough to provide her with an appropriate experience of marijuana intoxication. But in that case what exactly is happening in the brain? The problem is that there are explanatory gaps between the three perspectives so that it is not clear how these interconnections actually occur (cf. Chalmers, 1995; Jackendoff, 1987; Shear, 1996).

I think that it is important to engage all three perspectives, including their associated research strategies, as much as possible when trying to understand consciousness. Hence all three appear throughout this book. However, the physiological perspective is somewhat downplayed because it requires for its full development more knowledge of physiology than that assumed on the part of readers, and the experiential perspective is emphasized to document the varieties of altered-states experiences and to open up a discussion of fundamental questions concerning their meaning, epistemology, and ontology.

Definitions of Consciousness

We use the word "consciousness," but what do we mean by it? There are four common meanings of the word, which I will distinguish primarily by numbering them with subscripts. Thus, $consciousness_1$ refers to the registration of information and acting on it in a goal-directed manner; *behavioral* $consciousness_2$ refers to the explicit knowledge of one's situation, mental states, and actions demonstrated behaviorally; *subjective* $consciousness_2$ refers to the experiential stream of events that occurs subjectively for a person; and $consciousness_3$ refers to the sense of existence of the subject of the experiential stream (Baruss, 1987). Let us look more closely at each of these definitions in turn.

Sometimes we are interested in distinguishing between an unresponsive state of an organism and one in which it is functioning normally within its environment. Such normal functioning is characterized by the ability to make discriminations among various stimuli, to process that information, and, at least minimally, to act in a goal-directed manner. That is the meaning of $consciousness_1$. To avoid arguments about how minimal or extensive the processing should be, let us say that the referent of the term $consciousness_1$ is a variable, of which there can be more or less. There is also no reason to restrict the term to biological organisms, so let us apply it also to computers, mechanical contrivances, and anything else that meets the criteria (Baruss, 1987). This definition is most closely associated with both the physiological and cognitive perspectives on consciousness.

If the processing of information is so sophisticated that an organism demonstrates substantial explicit knowledge of its own situation, internal states, and actions, then we say that it has behavioral $consciousness_2$. Ordinarily, this would apply to human beings but eventually could also apply to computers. However, this definition stems from an effort to capture from the outside the events of the experiential stream that occur on the inside, as it were, for individuals. Thoughts, feelings, and sensations occur for us in a stream-like manner within the confines of our subjective experience, as noted by William James, one of the founders of modern psychology, whose ideas we will consider in chapter 2. Subjective consciousness$_2$ refers to that experiential stream. Even though, for historical reasons, I have designated both of these definitions of consciousness as consciousness$_2$, the referent of the behavioral definition does not necessarily coincide with that of the subjective one. In particular, it could be possible for a computer to demonstrate behavioral consciousness$_2$ but not to have subjective consciousness$_2$. The behavioral and subjective definitions belong, respectively, to the cognitive and experiential perspectives, thereby providing another way of characterizing the two sides of the explanatory gap that exists between those perspectives (Barušs, 1987, 2000a).

The meaning of consciousness$_3$ is the most difficult to conceptualize. The word "consciousness" is sometimes used to try to capture the inimitable quality of being that one may have for oneself. This is a feeling of existence associated with being oneself that accompanies the contents of one's experience. The point is that this feeling is precisely not a feeling in the sense of being a content of one's experience but rather of being a precursor for the possibility of there being any experience at all (Barušs, 1987). This referent of consciousness belongs to the experiential perspective on consciousness.

To illustrate the meanings of the word "consciousness," we can imagine that we are driving a car when a traffic light turns red. Noticing the changed light and stopping the car would be consciousness$_1$. If we demonstrated that we explicitly realized that the light had turned red and that we had stopped the car, for example, by saying that the light had turned red and that we have moved our foot from the gas pedal to the brake pedal, then that would indicate the presence of behavioral consciousness$_2$. Whatever is going on in our experiential stream at the time would be subjective consciousness$_2$. Perhaps we are thinking about the changed light and the pedals. Or perhaps we are having a conversation and thinking about what we are talking about, not about the light or the pedals. Consciousness$_3$ refers to the fact that we experience an experiential stream at all, irrespective of what we are thinking about.

Altered States of Consciousness

But what about altered states of consciousness? How are they to be defined? Altered states of consciousness have been studied for more than a generation by Charles Tart, whose edited book *Altered States of Consciousness* has become a classic in the psychology of consciousness (Tart, 1972a). Tart (1975) has pointed out that we know what it is to be conscious in our everyday waking state. But suppose now that we were to fall asleep, or become hypnotized, or ingest psychoactive drugs, or meditate, or almost die. Our neurophysiology could change, our thinking could change, and our experience could be quite different from what it is in our everyday state. From the point of view of the person for whom it occurs, an *altered state of consciousness* is "a qualitative alteration in the overall pattern of mental functioning, such that the experiencer feels his consciousness is radically different from the way it functions ordinarily" (Tart, 1972c, p. 1203; see also Ludwig, 1966). From the point of view of an external observer, the presence of a radical shift of consciousness would have to be inferred from changes to a person's physiology and behavior (cf. Tart, 1972b).

We can define altered states of consciousness more generally by specifying changes to the ordinary waking state along any number of dimensions. Given that we have introduced three perspectives concerning consciousness, we can say that altered states of consciousness are stable patterns of physiological, cognitive, and experiential events different from those of the ordinary waking state. We can also use our definitions of consciousness to say that altered states of consciousness are changes to the registration of information and acting on it in a goal-directed manner (consciousness$_1$); the explicit knowledge of one's situation, mental states, and actions (behavioral consciousness$_2$); the stream of thoughts, feelings, and sensations that one has for oneself (subjective consciousness$_2$); and the sense of existence of the subject of mental acts (consciousness$_3$).

Based on responses from participants in a study who had been asked how they identified a state of consciousness in which they found themselves, Tart (1975) organized the resultant "experiential criteria for detecting an altered state of consciousness" (Tart, 1975, p. 12) into 10 categories such as sensing the body, time sense, and interaction with the environment. There have also been proposed, among others, a "componential analysis of consciousness" (Hobson, 1997, p. 383) consisting of 10 components, phenomenological mapping whereby altered states of consciousness are to be compared along 12 dimensions (Walsh, 1995), a phenomenological inventory for measuring changes to consciousness along 12 dimensions (Pekala, 1991), and a list of 14 dimensions of consciousness within which are included attention, perception, imagery, inner speech, memory, decision making, problem solving, emotions, arousal, self-control, suggestibility, body image, personal identity, experience of time, and meaning (Farthing, 1992). Given that there is no standardized set of dimensions that is used for characterizing altered states of consciousness, in this book I will use whichever dimensions seem most appropriate for the phenomena that we are discussing.

Alterations of Consciousness

Sometimes I will want to emphasize the stability and distinctiveness of specific patterns of physiological, cognitive, and experiential events, in which case I will use the term "altered states of consciousness." Often, however, there is some question regarding the identification of a specific pattern of psychological functioning, or the distinctions between apparently different states of consciousness disappear. For example, is hypnosis a phenomenon in which there is a definite switch into a special state or does it lie on a continuum with phenomena in the ordinary waking state (Woody, Drugovic, & Oakman, 1997)? In what state is a person who is asleep according to physiological measures but aware that she is asleep and able to communicate through observable behavior with those watching her (LaBerge & Gackenbach, 2000)? What of John Wren-Lewis (1988), who inadvertently ate poisoned candy, went into a coma, almost died, and has subsequently been in an almost continuous transcendent state of consciousness? Was his a drug-induced, near-death or transcendent state? And what of McKenna's account given at the beginning of this chapter? In what state was he?

There is also a problem with the baseline for altered states. What is the ordinary waking state against which changes take place? If we accept Tart's definition of an altered state as subjectively different from a person's ordinary experience, then one person's ordinary waking state could be someone else's altered state. Wren-Lewis's transcendent state of consciousness is his ordinary state of being. The experiences of whole societies of people may be quite different from the experiences familiar to the Western intellectual tradition. Such may have been the case, for example, with the native people who were living in parts of what are now Mexico and Central America before contact with Europeans (cf. Tompkins, 1990). We can also think of the ordinary waking state as the state of mind usually experienced in Western societies while awake. It turns out, however, that that state itself is not homogeneous but varies, sometimes dramatically, along the same dimensions that have been proposed for identifying altered states of consciousness (cf. Roger Broughton, 1986). This leads to questions about whether alterations in the flux of waking consciousness, such as strong emotions or daydreaming, should be considered altered states of consciousness (cf. Farthing, 1992). In other words, the state of consciousness that is to be taken as the baseline is neither universal nor uniform but could itself be conceptualized as a collection of altered states.

It should be noted as well that the moniker "altered state" is not an explanation for psychological events but a short-hand description of the complexity of psychological processes characterizing any given altered state.

In other words, the discussion is about psychological events anyway, whether or not they are labeled as "altered," so that the use of the term "altered state" is not essential.

For the reasons given, it seems to me that it is not always necessary to try to identify discrete states but enough to just talk about *alterations of consciousness*. Sometimes I will use the term "altered state" to emphasize the distinctiveness and stability of a pattern of psychological functioning and "alteration" when the pattern of psychological functioning is more amorphous.

Altered States and Psychopathology

There has been a tendency in the past, in the Western culture, to regard the ordinary waking state as the optimal state and all other states, except for that of sleep, as a form of mental illness (cf. Baruš, 2000b; Tart, 1972b). Certainly some alterations of consciousness, such as those that occur in the mental disorder schizophrenia, fall within the pathological range, but that is quite a different matter from regarding alterations of consciousness themselves as symptoms of schizophrenia. For example, a shaman in an indigenous culture may undertake a soul journey to resolve a problem in her community. Her journey may involve the deliberate cultivation of an altered state of consciousness, separation from her body, traveling in a world different from that of ordinary reality, encountering spirits, searching for information or power that can resolve the problem, reentering her body, and implementing the results of her journey in the community (Walsh, 1995)—or at least, that is how the shaman would describe the events of her journey. We might say that these events transpire within the realm of her imagination. But in the past, we have gone further and labeled the shaman's experiences as symptoms of schizophrenia. However, as we shall see in chapter 6, careful comparisons between schizophrenia and soul journeying reveal that they are not the same.

Analysis of autobiographical accounts of experiences in schizophrenia, psychedelic drug intoxication, mystical experiences, and the ordinary waking state reveal that they are more different from one another than alike and that, whereas "the description of the schizophrenic experience points to a devalued, negative sense of self, both of the other 'altered states' are associated with a vocabulary connoting a sense of self-enhancement" (Oxman, Rosenberg, Schnurr, Tucker, & Gala, 1988, p. 406). As we examine different alterations of consciousness in the course of this book, we will frequently consider the extent to which they are pathological.

That experiences in altered states of consciousness are not to be regarded as necessarily pathological does not mean that they cannot, nonetheless, disrupt a person's life. For example, disruption often occurs after near-death experiences, which are events sometimes reported by a person to have occurred around the time that she was close to death. She may report having experienced a feeling of peace, separation from her body, witnessing of events occurring within the vicinity of her body, encounters with deceased relatives or spiritual beings, the presence of a loving light, and a panoramic life review. Subsequently a person may come to believe that death is not the end of life, that our usual concerns about our material well-being are unimportant, and that the purpose of life is to love one another. Despite the positive nature of most near-death experiences, a person may experience anger and depression at having been brought back to life, career interruptions, fear of ridicule and rejection, alienation from her relatives and acquaintances, and broken relationships, including divorce. Many of these problems appear to result from the experiencer's inability to reconcile her altered sense of reality and changed values with the materialistic concerns of the people with whom she must interact (Greyson, 2000).

BELIEFS ABOUT CONSCIOUSNESS AND REALITY

The dilemma encountered by someone who has had a near-death experience reveals the importance of a person's beliefs about consciousness and reality for making sense of alterations of consciousness. This applies not only to experiencers but also to researchers who study consciousness. In this section we will consider beliefs about consciousness and reality and the challenges posed to materialism by anomalous phenomena that occur in alterations of consciousness.

Material Versus Transcendent Beliefs

Robert Moore and I found in an empirical study that there is a material-transcendent dimension within the Western intellectual tradition. The *material* pole is represented by the notion that reality is entirely physical in nature, apparently in the sense that the world is essentially a machine that functions in a deterministic manner. For the materialist, all phenomena, including consciousness, result from physical processes. The *transcendent* pole, on the other hand, consists of the notion that consciousness is ontologically primitive and that the physical world is a byproduct of consciousness. Between these two poles are various gradations of dualist thought whereby reality is considered to consist of both physical and transcendent aspects. Materialists, those who believe that the world is a physical place, would likely be interested in the physiological and cognitive aspects of consciousness and would think of consciousness as an emergent property of the brain or as information in an information-processing system. Dualists, those who maintain what could be called a conservatively transcendent position, tend to emphasize the subjective, experiential aspects of consciousness and believe that consciousness gives meaning to reality and provides evidence of a spiritual dimension. Those identified with the extraordinarily transcendent position at the transcendent extreme of the scale are more likely to believe that they have had unusual experiences and to emphasize altered states of consciousness. For them, not matter but consciousness is the fundamental reality to be understood through a process of self-transformation (Baruš, 1990; Baruš & Moore, 1989, 1992, 1997, 1998).

Moore's and my use of the word *materialist* to designate a particular empirically derived cluster of beliefs is consistent with the use of that term in philosophy (e.g., Lycan, 1987). Sometimes I think materialists conceptualize the world as made up of tiny colliding particles that behave in predictable patterns like billiard balls on a billiard table and believe that everything can ultimately be explained by such interactions. Such a conceptualization is *mechanistic* and *deterministic*. Others, who could be called *physicalists*, maintain that everything is physical in whatever way physicists will eventually determine that to be. Usually, I think, there is the accompanying assumption that what physicists will find will not depart too greatly from one's usual conceptions of what it means for something to be physical. A materialist position is *reductionistic* in that psychological phenomena, such as consciousness, are considered to be ultimately dependent on physical processes even if the details of such reductions, in principle, remain opaque to the investigator. These are also the *conventional* ways of thinking about the nature of reality that are widely accepted within science (cf. Baruš, 1996, 2001b). In this book, although one or another of these more specific expressions will be used when such precision is necessary, in general the term "materialist" will be used to designate the belief that the world is ultimately physical in nature, whatever the details of that conceptualization may be.

But is materialism not correct? Is there any reason to belabor the existence of transcendent beliefs if they are misguided? Why are we even raising these questions? It turns out that there are a number of problems with a materialist interpretation of reality that must at least give us pause. First, it turns out that matter, at subatomic levels, violates our everyday intuitions about its nature and does not behave in the mechanical fashion that we might suppose that it would (Baruš, 1996). In an odd reversal of character, "the universe begins to look more like a great thought than like a great machine" (Jeans, 1937, p. 186). Second, there is a philosophical problem. All that we can ever know directly are our experiences, which appear to go on for us within our subjective domains. From our experiences, we must infer the independent existence of an objective world if materialism is to be correct. And such an inference is not automatic. Third is a problem that we will encounter repeatedly in this book: the need for any materialist theory to adequately account for anomalous phenomena (Barušs, 1993), a problem about which there has been considerable controversy (e.g., Richard Broughton, 1991; Cardeña, Lynn, & Krippner, 2000; Irwin, 1994; Kurtz, 1985; Radin, 1997; Zusne & Jones, 1989). To illustrate the problem posed by anomalous phenomena, let me use as an example a series of studies that was done to try to detect the presence of the transfer of information through some mechanism other than sensory perception—in other words, to try to find extrasensory perception.

Anomalous Information Transfer

A series of studies was conducted over the course of 6½ years in which a method, called the *ganzfeld procedure*, was used to try to demonstrate the existence of extrasensory perception. Suppose that extrasensory perception consists of the mental detection of a weak signal that is ordinarily masked by internal somatic and external sensory stimulation. The idea behind the ganzfeld procedure is to seek to minimize the somatic and sensory noise. This is done by having a participant in the study, the receiver, recline in a chair in an acoustically isolated, electrically shielded room. "Translucent ping-pong ball halves are taped over the [receiver's] eyes and headphones are placed over [her] ears" (Bem & Honorton, 1994, p. 5). A red floodlight is directed toward her eyes and white noise is played through the headphones to produce a visually and acoustically "homogeneous perceptual environment that is called the *Ganzfeld*" (Bem & Honorton, 1994, p. 5). Before turning on the floodlight and noise, the receiver is led through a 14-minute relaxation exercise whose purpose is to lower internal somatic stimulation. Then the receiver is subjected to the ganzfeld stimulation for 30 minutes while she reports aloud her thoughts and images to the experimenter who is in the room together with her. In the meantime, there is a sender in a separate acoustically isolated, electrically shielded room, in many cases a friend of the receiver brought along to the experimental session for the purpose of acting as sender.

Before the beginning of this series of ganzfeld experiments, 160 potential targets had been prepared, 80 of which were still pictures and 80 of which were video segments with sound of about 1 minute in duration. The groups of static and dynamic targets had each been arranged in 20 sets of four in such a way as "to minimize similarities among targets within a set" (Bem & Honorton, 1994, p. 9). At the time of a ganzfeld session, a controlling computer randomly selected a target from one of the 40 sets of targets and repeatedly presented it "to the sender during the ganzfeld period" (Bem & Honorton, 1994, p. 9). Following the ganzfeld period, the computer randomly ordered the four potential targets in the set from which the actual target had been drawn and presented them to the receiver on a television monitor to be judged by her with regard to their resemblance to the thoughts and images that had occurred for her during the ganzfeld period. Once the receiver had judged the images, the sender came into the receiver's room and "revealed the identity of the target to both the receiver and the experimenter" (Bem & Honorton, 1994, p. 10).

The experiments have been designed in such a way that there is no possibility that either the receiver or the experimenter could know the identity of the target that has been used, or even the target set from which it has been drawn, until the actual target has been revealed to them at the end of the ganzfeld period by the sender. Several dozen researchers, including known critics of this type of research, have examined the automated ganzfeld protocol and "expressed satisfaction with the handling of security issues and controls" (Bem & Honorton, 1994, p. 10). In addition, two magicians who specialize in the simulation of psychic phenomena have examined the automated ganzfeld system and declared that it was secure from deception by research participants. In a review of methodological issues in a number of research areas, the ganzfeld studies were found to "regularly meet the basic requirements of sound experimental design" (Bem & Honorton, 1994, p. 9). In other words, whatever the results that may be found, they should not be attributed to inattention to proper experimental procedures.

In the series of ganzfeld studies that we have been discussing, there were 240 receivers, 140 women and 100 men, with a mean age of 37 years, who participated in a total of 354 sessions of which 329 were used for the primary data analyses. Whereas one would expect about 25% of the targets to be correctly identified by chance, that is to say, about 82 targets, in fact 106 targets were correctly identified giving a statistically significant hit rate of 32%. Dynamic targets proved to be more effective than static ones with hit rates of 37% and 27% for the dynamic and static targets, respectively. In 20 sessions, 20 undergraduate students in drama, music, and dance from the Juilliard School in New York City correctly identified 10 of the 20 targets for a hit rate of 50%, thereby suggesting the presence of a relationship between creativity or artistic ability and performance on extrasensory perception tasks. The 32% overall hit rate is just below the postulated level at which a careful observer could see the effect with the naked eye without recourse to statistical analyses. It corresponds to an observer witnessing a correct identification about every third session rather than about every fourth session as would be the case if the results were occurring by chance. These results demonstrate the high probability of the presence of anomalous information transfer—that is to say, extrasensory perception—when using the ganzfeld procedure (Bem, 1994; Bem & Honorton, 1994).

Despite the apparent care with which this series of studies was carried out, the conclusions drawn from it as well as from other ganzfeld studies have been contested on various grounds (e.g., Hyman, 1994; Milton, 1999; Milton & Wiseman, 1999). But the objections to the conclusions have also been contested (Bem, 1994; Storm & Ertel, 2001). I leave it to the interested reader to consult the details of the arguments and to make up her own mind. If the results are sound, as indeed they appear to be, then they need to be explained, and they pose, by their nature, a challenge to the materialist interpretation of reality. If the results of these studies can be safely discounted, then we are back where we started, not knowing whether such anomalous information transfer occurs or not.

Anomalous Phenomena

The thrust in the past has been to characterize those who believe in the reality of anomalous events as cognitively inferior to disbelievers. However, in a recent study in which undergraduate university students were required to critically evaluate favorable or unfavorable study reports of extrasensory perception, researchers found that "those participants who received a report which challenged their own *a priori* beliefs rated the study as of poorer quality than did those whose beliefs were in sympathy with or neutral towards the paper's conclusions" (Roe, 1999, p. 92). There was no support for the contention that believers are less proficient at critical thinking than nonbelievers.

One of my students found some evidence to suggest that, among university undergraduate students, transcendent beliefs are associated with a personality characteristic called "understanding" that is essentially concerned with interest in the pursuit of rational knowledge about the world. Furthermore, she found that those who tend toward a conservatively transcendent position are "more curious about the world, more open to experience, strive more conscientiously toward goals in life, and are less concerned about what others think of them than those with materialist beliefs" (Jewkes & Barušs, 2000, p. 97), whereas those tending toward an extraordinarily transcendent position "are not only more curious, open to the world, and unconcerned about others' perceptions of them, but they also tend to be unorganized, adventurous, and spontaneous" (Jewkes & Barušs, 2000, p. 97). A correspondence between transcendent beliefs and understanding was again found in a replication study at another university, although the results were weaker and were found only for a sample of undergraduate students and not for another set of participants solicited through the Internet (E. James, 2001). At the least, these data show that undergraduate students with transcendent beliefs are not necessarily cognitively inferior to those with materialist beliefs.

Anomalous events are often reported to occur in the context of altered states of consciousness. It has been suggested that the apparent occurrence of extrasensory perception may be related to relaxation, a passive state of mind, decreases in externally directed attention, and openness to others, which could occur in various altered states of consciousness such as dreaming, hypnosis, or meditation (Honorton, 1974). It may be that anomalous events are facilitated by the disruption of ordinary states of consciousness or that "altered states function as a means of psychophysiological noise reduction" (Krippner & George, 1986, p. 352), allowing a more subtle level of reality to manifest, as theorized in the ganzfeld studies.

To explain higher than average rates of professed paranormal experiences among those reporting childhood physical or sexual abuse, it has been proposed that paranormal experiences are an expression of the capacity for a psyche's functions to dissociate, so that healthy individuals with dissociative tendencies, as well as those who have been traumatized, would be more prone to report paranormal experiences (Ross & Joshi, 1992). The possibility that anomalous events could be facilitated both by healthy and pathological conditions is reflected in the psychological characteristic of *transliminality*, an openness to images, ideas, and feelings arising from within the mind or the world outside the mind, which has been found to be common to a number of psychological variables such as "alleged experience of the paranormal, creative personality, mystical experience, . . . history of manic-like experience . . . and attitude toward dream interpretation" (Thalbourne, 1998, p. 402). Increased prominence of mental imagery, changed levels of arousal, increased expectations of anomalous experiences, and favorable characteristics of self-selected participants in altered states research have been proposed as explanations for the increased occurrence of anomalous experiences in altered states of consciousness (Krippner & George, 1986). Whatever the reason for their presence, the academic literature concerning alterations of consciousness is sprinkled with reports of anomalous experiences.

THE SCIENTIFIC STUDY OF CONSCIOUSNESS

I have been setting the stage for a discussion of alterations of consciousness first by defining key terms and then by indicating the important role played by beliefs about consciousness and reality in the investigation of consciousness. But this book is an empirical analysis for social scientists, and hence we must also consider the study of consciousness as a scientific enterprise. What happens when science encounters consciousness? And what are we to do as scientists when we encounter anomalous phenomena that do not readily fit a materialist interpretation of reality?

The Nature of Science

Science has three aspects—an essence, methodology, and world view—and two modes of practice—the inauthentic and authentic. The inauthentic mode, called *scientism*, resembles the practice of a religious faith. The world view of scientism is that of materialism, and it drives the kinds of data that can be collected. After all, there is no point in collecting data about extrasensory perception if one already believes that extrasensory perception cannot exist. The methodology of scientism consists of an idealized set of procedures based on the use of the sensory modalities for making systematic observations of objective events and drawing conclusions from those observations using one's rational faculties. This scientific method is thought by some to be complete in that nothing is thought to exist in nature that cannot in principle be explained by its application. A rigid set of procedures that can guarantee the acquisition of truth is necessary for scientism given that the essence of science is perceived to consist of the accumulation of facts, and it is important that the collection of facts not become contaminated with falsehoods (Barušs, 1996, 2001b).

In its *authentic mode*, the essence of science is not the accumulation of objective information but the acquisition of knowledge for someone. One seeks to deepen one's understanding through open-ended investigation. The methods that one uses follow from the questions that one asks, so that one is not restricted in one's epistemological approach. The results of one's investigations form the basis for one's world views. In other words, an authentic scientist seeks knowledge through open-ended investigation and forms theories on the basis of the resultant data. It is important to note that authentic science can include the collection of information, the use of specific traditional scientific methods, and the development of materialist theories as explanations for one's data. The point is that science is supposed to be authentic science, a genuine quest for truth, rather than scientism, the dutiful adherence to proscribed ideas about the world and the manner in which it is to be known (Barušs, 1996, 2001b).

This brief characterization of science does not do justice to the heterogeneity of the scientific enterprise or the ways in which science is conceptualized by scientists, but it does give us a heuristic for identifying problems with the scientific study of consciousness. Thus, adherence to rigid rules, although applicable in many cases, such as the ganzfeld studies, may, in other situations, result in the failure to acquire knowledge that may otherwise be available. In particular, to the extent that consciousness consists of that which can only be privately observed by an individual for herself, as denoted by subjective consciousness$_2$ and consciousness$_3$, it cannot meet the requirement of public observability, which is thought to be required in science.

Introspection, the method of investigation associated with the experiential perspective, has had a rocky history since it was proposed as a way of studying consciousness in psychology toward the end of the 19th century and has finally, supposedly, disappeared as a legitimate method of investigation (Lyons, 1986). However, given that 93% of 212 respondents to a survey at a major international scientific consciousness conference agreed that "introspection is a necessary element in the investigation of consciousness" (Baruš & Moore, 1998, p. 486), it would appear that introspection needs to be readmitted in some form as part of a more flexible approach to the study of consciousness.

Methodological Flexibility

But what does the freedom of methodological flexibility do for us? To begin with, we can consider the possibility of each person developing her own ideas about the nature of consciousness on the basis of observations from her own experience. This is a strategy that has been recognized by some consciousness researchers (e.g., Dennett, 1978; Mandler, 1985). Indeed, this is what already happens, for example, when those who have had near-death experiences change their ideas about the nature of reality on the basis of what they have experienced. In a similar vein, it has been suggested that research concerning alterations of consciousness be carried out by those who have developed the relevant skills necessary for accessing and making observations in specific altered states of consciousness (Baruš, 2001b; Tart, 1972c). In fact, some states of consciousness may remain inscrutable unless a person enters those states herself to understand them. For example, transcendent states of consciousness have been alleged to be ineffable and must occur for a person to be known (Wulff, 2000). Furthermore, it may not be enough for us to remain as indifferent observers of transcendent states, but we may need to become active participants if we are to know such states (Merrell-Wolff, 1994). It is also possible that we may have available to us latent faculties of knowledge that could become activated through a process of self-transformation (Baruš, 1996). At the previously mentioned consciousness conference, 69% of 212 participants agreed with the statement that "there are modes of understanding latent within a person [that] are superior to rational thought" (Baruš & Moore, 1998, p. 486). We may have noetic resources available to us in addition to sensory perception and rational thinking with which to develop our understanding of alterations of consciousness.

But have we not now gone too far? By throwing open the epistemological doors, have we not simply encouraged "free-floating uncritical fantasies about mental life" (Hilgard, 1980, p. 15)? We need to be careful. "The difficulty with studying [altered states of consciousness] by simply experiencing them is that we run as much risk of systematizing our delusions as of discovering 'truth'" (Tart, 1972b, p. 5). Whatever process of self-transformation a person may undertake for the exploration of consciousness will need to include training, to the extent that it turns out to be possible, in the ability to discriminate between that which is real and that which is delusional (Baruš, 1996). But the notion of self-transformation is not as radical as it may seem given that some self-development is already implied in becoming an authentic scientist. To understand new knowledge, a scientist must be able to set aside her preconceptions in order to follow the evidence wherever it may lead. Not surprisingly, that is not as easy to do as it may seem (Baruš, 1996; see also Olson & Zanna, 1993), so that a process of self-examination and psychological adjustment on the part of a scientist may be required (Baruš, 2001b). It should be noted that viewing self-transformation as necessary for understanding consciousness happens to be associated with the extraordinarily transcendent position of beliefs about consciousness and reality (Baruš, 1990).

We may also be aghast at the relativism implied by the prospect of unbridled self-exploration. It is one thing to criticize the fallacies of the scientific method but quite another to dispense with the notion of a shared body of knowledge agreed on by a community of scientists (cf. Bauer, 1992). However, the situation may not be as dramatic as it seems, given that those able to enter specific altered states of consciousness may be able to verify characteristics of reality found by others who have also entered those same states (Tart, 1972c). In that sense, knowledge, although individual, can nonetheless be at least potentially consensual. However, because altered states may be radically different from the ordinary waking state, those exploring such states may end up developing *state specific sciences* in that what is known about the nature of reality may depend on the state of consciousness in which a person finds herself (Tart, 1972c, 2000).

The point to emphasize is that we are not dismantling any of the strategies that are currently available for seeking knowledge in psychology but trying to expand the repertoire to access the phenomena that may be of interest to us. Indeed, as much as possible, it is beneficial to use all the methodological resources available in science when approaching alterations of consciousness. For example, in many studies of consciousness, productive use has been made of the conventional experimental format in psychology of using experimental and control conditions. Participants are randomly assigned either to an *experimental group* whose members are exposed to the *experimental condition*, which is a condition of interest to the researcher, or to a *control group*, whose members are exposed to a *control condition*, for which the condition of interest is missing but which otherwise imitates as much as possible the experimental condition (cf. Shaughnessy & Zechmeister, 1994). For example, we will consider the Good Friday experiment in chapter 7, in which participants randomly received either the psychedelic drug psilocybin or the nonpsychedelic drug nicotinic acid before a Good Friday service. We shall see variations on this design in the course of this book with sometimes a number of experimental or *comparison conditions* being used as alternatives to single experimental and control conditions. What are needed in research concerning consciousness are more studies in which such designs are used when it is possible to use them because they allow for the ability to discriminate between contributing factors to a phenomenon.

The Politics of Science

Materialism, as the starting point of investigation for scientism, presents an obstacle to the study of consciousness. I have already noted some of the problems with materialism, described a series of studies concerning anomalous information transfer, and mentioned the ubiquity of reports of anomalous phenomena in alterations of consciousness. In other words, there are challenges to materialism that appear to become particularly pronounced with the study of consciousness. Hence it seems ill-advised that a discussion of alterations of consciousness begin with the assumption that materialism is the correct interpretation of reality.

However, what I have found in my experience is that some scientists have appeared to be unduly attached to materialism. This may in part be a result of the *politics of science* (cf. Kellehear, 1996), whereby "major segments of public and private policy and expenditure for research, development, construction, production, education, and publication throughout the world" (Jahn, 2001, p. 24) are controlled by those who are "consumed with refinements and deployments of mid-20th century science" (Jahn, 2001, p. 24) so that, among other things, conventional interpretations of data are encouraged. Indeed, I myself have felt pressure to conform to materialist beliefs so as not to jeopardize my career as a scientist. It seems to me that in spite of political pressure to do so, it is counterproductive to insist that phenomena associated with consciousness always be reified in physical terms.

The point is that we cannot have a balanced discussion of alterations of consciousness if we begin with the assumption that people's experiences cannot possibly be what they appear to be whenever they fail to conform to our beliefs about the world. That applies also to materialist beliefs. Some version of materialism may yet turn out to be correct, but such an explanation has to follow from the data and cannot be determined a priori. We need to set aside personal predilections and political pressures so that we can objectively examine the evidence. The purpose in this book is not to convince the reader of any particular interpretation of reality, but rather to present for her consideration a variety of phenomena that occur during alterations of consciousness along with some of the explanations, materialist and transcendentalist, that have been proposed for them.

OVERVIEW OF THE BOOK

We now have the context for our empirical investigation of alterations of consciousness. Before getting started on them, let me briefly give an overview of the topics that we will consider and introduce 10 thematic threads that run through the material in this book.

Outline

We started out in this chapter by discussing the study of consciousness and circumscribed the subject area of alterations of consciousness. We noted that consciousness researchers range along a material–transcendent dimension of beliefs about consciousness and reality. Problems with materialism, including challenges posed by anomalous phenomena such as apparent anomalous information transfer in the ganzfeld studies, remind us that we need to remain open-minded when considering alterations of consciousness as required in the practice of authentic science.

In chapter 2 we will consider the ordinary waking state, starting with the question of access and then working our way deeper and deeper into the nature of the experiential stream of consciousness. Thus, we will start by revisiting introspection, then discussing the characteristics of thinking, definitions of daydreaming, uses of the imagination, and the pronounced interior experiences of sensory restriction. In the process of examining the ordinary waking state we will see that it already embodies some alterations and presages phenomena found in altered states. In chapter 3 we will consider the prototypical altered state of consciousness, namely sleep, beginning with physiological and phenomenological descriptions of the sleep stages, and then go on to discuss sleep need, the possible purposes of sleep, the effects of drugs on sleep, and some of the sleep disorders. The study of sleep itself is relatively uncontroversial. However, such is not the case with the study of dreams, the subject matter of chapter 4. In our discussion of dreams we will consider dream theories, dream research, working with dreams, lucid dreaming, and precognitive dreams. In fact, much of the material in this book is controversial, both because of issues that are specific to individual altered states as well as those that are shared.

The second half of the book is concerned with particularly controversial alterations of consciousness starting with chapter 5, hypnosis. We will consider what it is like to be hypnotized, research concerning hypnosis, theories of hypnosis, the apparent hypnotic enhancement of memory, and practical applications of hypnosis. Some of the phenomena associated with hypnosis are found again in shamanism, possession, dissociative disorders, and alien abduction experiences, discussed in chapter 6. In chapter 7 we will consider drug-induced alterations, particularly those induced by the psychedelics, and some of the drawbacks and benefits of their use. At the end of chapter 7 we will also discuss the Good Friday experiment, which will lead into various accounts of events in transcendent states of consciousness in chapter 8, along with some explanations for them and methods such as meditation aimed at inducing them. In chapter 9, after considering alterations of consciousness associated with death, such as near-death experiences, past-life experiences, and mediumship, we will consider the possibility of the survival of consciousness after death. In chapter 10 we will have an opportunity to reflect back on the phenomena discussed in the earlier chapters, to draw any conclusions, and to indicate directions for further research.

Thematic Threads

There are 10 *thematic threads* running through the book associated with fundamental questions about the nature of reality, some of which reflect the controversies concerning alterations of consciousness. We have already considered a few of these thematic threads. The first is concerned with the perspective taken when approaching consciousness, whether that is *physiological, cognitive,* or *experiential.* The second is that of *material versus transcendent* beliefs about consciousness and reality. Both of these threads pervade the discussions of various altered states. The third is concerned with the question of whether events that occur in alterations of consciousness are *delusional* or *veridical.* For example, was McKenna hallucinating or did he see something that was really present? The fourth thread is related to the third in that it is concerned with whether a phenomenon is actually *mundane or extraordinary* in nature. Are near-death experiences interesting but ultimately mundane in nature or is there something extraordinary about them?

The fifth thread is concerned with whether or not a phenomenon is *meaningless or meaningful.* This applies, for example, to the question of dreams: Are dreams meaningful? But then, if some events are meaningful, are they meaningful in the same manner as meaningfulness is established during the ordinary waking state, or is there an increased depth of meaning such as that which apparently occurs during transcendent states? We will refer to these two dimensions constituting the sixth thematic thread as *lateral versus vertical.* Using the example of shamanism, we have already considered the question of whether experiences that occur during alterations of consciousness are pathological or normal. But they could also be instances of exceptional well-being. Thus we have the seventh thread of *psychopathology versus well-being* concerning the degree of psychopathology, normality, or exceptional well-being associated with specific experiences. Related to the seventh thread is the eighth, concerning the extent to which alterations are *dangerous versus beneficial*. Are some altered states dangerous, such as intoxication with psychedelic drugs, whereas others are beneficial, such as sleep? The ninth thread is concerned with the *nature of the self*. For example, is the self homogeneous as we ordinarily think of it, or fragmented as it appears to be in some dissociated states? Finally, the tenth thread is concerned with whether or not the psyche is *open or closed*. The ganzfeld studies, among others, raise the question of whether consciousness is skull-bound or not.

These 10 thematic threads, sometimes identified as such, will recur as we make our way through the material in this book. My thesis is that paying attention to such fundamental questions about alterations of consciousness forces us to reconsider our ideas about the nature of consciousness and reality. Perhaps the world is a more interesting place than we usually think. Or perhaps not.

2

WAKEFULNESS

In this chapter we will briefly examine the ordinary waking state of consciousness. It is something that we take for granted, but do we know what it is really like? What is the nature of our ordinary waking consciousness? Perhaps that is too broad a question. We would have to summarize considerable tracts of current psychological research to answer it, because the ordinary waking state is implicitly the subject matter of much of the discipline of psychology. Perhaps we can ask the more circumscribed question of what it is that goes on for us in our experiential stream. What are the contents of subjective consciousness$_2$? I suppose we could say that the answer is thinking, as the activity of our experiential stream has often been characterized (cf. Holyoak & Spellman, 1993; Markman & Gentner, 2001), although our experiential stream encompasses more generally thoughts, perceptions, feelings, emotions, imagination, and so on.

Let us start by examining the method of access to our experiential stream—namely, introspection. Then we will go back to the late 19th century to look at what introspection apparently revealed to William James about the characteristics of thinking. From there we will keep pursuing the breadth and depth of our inner experience through contemporary studies of thinking, daydreaming, the use of the imagination, and finally, states of sensory restriction in which our ordinary waking consciousness reveals itself, perhaps most purely. Or perhaps that is not quite the way to think about it. On examination, the richness of our inner life becomes revealed, and we may come to see that increased engagement of the imagination can already result in alterations of consciousness so that there is nothing ordinary about the waking state. Clusters of our thematic threads surface in this chapter, at one point when considering the relationship of the imagination to immune function and, at the end, in a discussion of sensed presences. As we shall see, challenging questions about consciousness and reality are raised even without entering the dramatic altered states of consciousness considered in later chapters of this book.

INTROSPECTION

Introspection has had a long and troubled history as a method for studying the mind. Let us go not too far back, to the time of the founding of psychology and the modern beginnings of introspection, then consider the more recent deconstruction of introspection by computationalists, and end with some practical ways in which introspection may be used in the investigation of consciousness.

Modern Beginnings

Wilhelm Wundt, a German professor with a background in physiology, has often been touted as the founder of psychology as a laboratory science in the late 19th century. Although Wundt recognized that the data of science about objective phenomena were derived from the experiences of scientists, he rejected the notion that scientists could understand experience itself through the unaided self-observations of others. Rather, his procedure of "experimental introspection" (Hilgard, 1987, p. 44) was confined to research concerning sensation and perception, in which laboratory instruments were used to vary the stimuli. The result was that the stimulus conditions were so controlled and the demands on the observer so limited that the process of observation "came to resemble in all important respects external, ordinary perception" (Lyons, 1986, p. 4). In practice, for example, Wundt would present a participant in a study with a simple colored shape using a tachistoscope, a device for presenting visual stimuli for brief time periods, and ask questions about the shape's size, intensity, and duration.

The method of introspection used by Wundt was a version of what Franz Brentano had called *inner perception*, the discrete noticing of what was happening to mental events as they occurred without interfering with them. Mental events, so it was believed, "by their very nature forced themselves into our notice" (Lyons, 1986, p. 4). The idea was to perceive indirectly, out of the corner of one's mental eye as it were, "mental phenomena as they went about their business" (Lyons, 1986, p. 4). The alternative to inner perception was *inner observation*, the direct focusing on one's inner mental life. This, according to Brentano, would not work because attention would be drawn away from the "mental life of thoughts, feelings, and volitions" (Lyons, 1986, p. 4), thereby devitalizing or destroying the very mental events that one was trying to observe.

But not everyone was enthusiastic about such a constrained research program. "There is little of the grand style about these new prism, pendulum, and chronograph–philosophers," said William James (1890/1983, p. 192). He accused the experimentalists of being boring. For James, "*Introspective Observation is what we have to rely on first and foremost and always. The word* introspection need hardly be defined—it means, of course, the looking into our own minds and reporting what we there discover" (W. James, 1890/1983, p. 185). No mere noticing for James, but looking. However, James was not insensitive to the various problems associated with inner observation, so he ended up with the notion that mental states could only be examined and reported once they had already occurred. In other words, James's introspection was *retrospection*, whereby a person examines her memory of that which has previously transpired (Lyons, 1986). James acknowledged that such a method was "difficult and fallible" but maintained that "the difficulty is simply that of all observation of whatever kind" (W. James, 1890/1983, p. 191, emphasis removed).

There were other approaches to introspection at the time but, in psychology, the whole discussion about introspection was extinguished in the early part of the 20th century with the rise of behaviorism. Psychologists became interested in the behavior evoked in an organism by specific stimulus situations and the manner in which stimulus–response associations could be changed (Hilgard, 1987). In his 1919 book, John Watson has said that "the reader will find no discussion of consciousness" (Watson, 1919, p. viii) nor reference to any mental activity given that Watson had found that he could "get along without them both in carrying out investigations and in presenting psychology as a system to [his] students" (Watson, 1919, p. viii). Until the 1950s and, in many cases until much later, psychologists by and large dismissed consciousness and introspection as myths or, at least, regarded them "as items that were not amenable to investigation by a scientific psychology" (Lyons, 1986, p. 47). Philosophers continued to discuss introspection as a process by which one part of the brain scans another, for example, but the theories that they advanced were also not without problems.

The Computational Approach

The development of information theory and the advent of computing machines in the 1950s brought new ways of thinking about the psyche that revitalized psychology (Hilgard, 1987). It was thought that just as a computer can process information on its hardware, so too the human brain can process information on its wetware. Thus, *mental processes* were conceptualized as operations on *mental representations*, the information that is in the brain (Jackendoff, 1987). Although such a computational approach brought renewed interest in memory, language, problem-solving, and other cognitive processes (Hilgard, 1987), consciousness initially failed to be readmitted into mainstream psychology (Natsoulas, 1983a). Furthermore, in "a review of the evidence bearing on the accuracy of subjective reports about higher mental processes" (Nisbett & Wilson, 1977, p. 233), the authors concluded that introspection was not possible. That conclusion has subsequently been challenged (White, 1988), but the idea has persisted that what we come up with when we believe that we are introspecting is not any actual knowledge about our mental life but an imaginative reconstruction of what we think our mental life should be like based on perceptions of our own and others' behavior (cf. Lyons, 1986). Despite this conclusion, at the close of the 20th century there was an explosion of academic interest in consciousness along with, as already mentioned, the assertion that introspection needs to be used as a means for its investigation. Indeed, although it does not need to be so, the computational model of the psyche underlies the cognitive perspective of consciousness.

Although the computational approach has been productive, particularly for research concerning human cognition, aspects of the psyche that cannot readily be conceptualized as calculations, such as the imagination or emotions, have been downplayed (Aanstoos, 1987; Hilgard, 1987). Furthermore, despite its overall utility, there have been problems with the computational interpretation of psychological events given that it is unlikely that the brain actually instantiates formal logical states as does a properly programmed computer (Barwise, 1986). Nor is it clear how information processing can give rise to subjective experience (Chalmers, 1995; cf. Eccles, 1966). Hence, to the extent that computation is an account of cognition, we have the presence of explanatory gaps between the physiological, cognitive, and experiential perspectives of consciousness. Computation has alternatively been conceptualized as proceeding in an idealized network of processing units (Rumelhart, Hinton, & McClelland, 1986), although that approach comes with its own difficulties and also does not solve the problem of the explanatory gaps (cf. Hanson & Burr, 1990; Smolensky, 1988). Nonetheless, a computational way of thinking about the mind has remained dominant in psychology and hence will recur throughout this book as a possible rationale for the phenomena associated with alterations of consciousness.

Practical Applications

In the end, then, what are we to make of introspection? As we can see from our selective overview, introspection seems to refer to a number of somewhat different putative processes. At the most basic level, the question is, can we simply tell what is happening in our minds? From a computational point of view, whereby our minds consist of the churning of computing machinery that occasionally crosses a threshold into awareness, the prospects do not look good. What we end up having to do is determine the scope of *metacognition*, our ability to know something of our own cognitive processes (cf. Metcalfe & Shimamura, 1994). However, switching from the cognitive to the experiential perspective, the answer to the question of whether we can know something of our minds appears to be, obviously, yes. Consciousness, in the sense of subjective consciousness$_2$, is awareness. Suppose I imagine unicorns frolicking in a sunlit meadow, unaware perhaps that my mind has drifted and that I am fantasizing. Wait a minute, I think, I am supposed to be writing a book, not thinking about unicorns. If you were to ask me what I had just been thinking about, I would give a verbal report and say that I had just been thinking about unicorns. I would report the contents of my experience as I recall them in memory. This notion of introspection appears to encompass the experimental introspection of Wundt as well as the introspective observation of William James. All that we have is experience of various sorts that goes on for us. Normally, it just goes on, but some of the time the contents of our experience can refer to previous contents as having been experiences for us. Thus, introspection is part of the normal process of our consciousness whereby we explicate what it is that is occurring in our awareness (cf. Howe, 1991a, 1991b).

Even this experientially straightforward version of introspection is not without potential problems. Although it seems self-evident, I cannot be certain that I had really been thinking about unicorns. Perhaps I have incorrectly recalled what occurred. Rather than imagining playful unicorns I may have been actually seeing sinister extraterrestrials, but the truth was so awful that I hid it from myself behind a screen memory of playful unicorns. In that case, do I know that I thought that I had been thinking about unicorns? The point is that our experience is precisely that of which we are aware, so that introspection, to the extent that it involves knowing what is happening in our minds, is just the awareness of our own experience. It is possible that there is imaginative reconstruction of our experience and difficulties with making verbal reports of our experience, but these problems are usually thought not to be prohibitive (Farthing, 1992; Pekala & Cardeña, 2000). Or at least, it can be argued that these problems are not greater than those associated with scientific data collection in general, given that empirical observation ultimately depends on scientists' reports of their experiences, as noted previously with regard to Wundt.

At any rate, from a practical point of view, people are asked to report what goes on for them as a matter of course in psychology. Any time someone is asked to respond to the perception of a sensory stimulus, to report one's experience, or to fill out a questionnaire about oneself, introspection is involved. In the *experience sampling method*, participants wear an electronic pager that goes off at random intervals as they go about living their lives. When the pager goes off, participants "give a high-resolution description of their mental states right as these are happening" (Csikszentmihalyi & Csikszentmihalyi, 1988, p. 253) by filling out a self-report booklet in which information is collected about the "main dimensions of consciousness" (Csikszentmihalyi & Csikszentmihalyi, 1988, p. 253), such as affect and intrinsic motivation, as well as "the main contextual dimensions that influence the state of consciousness" (Csikszentmihalyi & Csikszentmihalyi, 1988, p. 253), such as "where a person is [located], with whom, [and] doing what" (Csikszentmihalyi & Csikszentmihalyi, 1988, p. 253). Indeed, much of our understanding of thinking comes from studies using some variation of the experience sampling method.

Filling out a questionnaire about oneself is probably more problematic than reporting what goes on in one's mind when a beeper goes off. How well do people really know themselves? How good are people's judgments about their own natures? To what extent do self-deception and deliberate self-presentation play a role? To illustrate the type of problem that exists, let us consider four metaphors that have been used to characterize the manner in which people's perceptions of themselves function. The *scientist* metaphor refers to a person's "dispassionate search for accurate self-knowledge" (Robins & John, 1997, p. 659), constrained only by actual "perceptual and informational limitations" (Robins & John, 1997, p. 659). The scientist is the truth seeker. The motivation of the *consistency seeker* is to reduce inconsistency by selective remembering of life events, reconstruction of the past, seeking out and creating contexts in which one's ideas about oneself are confirmed, and distorting or discounting inconsistent information, even when one's self-views are negative. The *politician* defines, constructs, and negotiates her self-concept through interaction with others in such a way as to create favorable impressions on others and to gain their approval. The premise of the *egoist* metaphor is that people are motivated toward self-enhancement, that "people want to like themselves and will adopt cognitive and interpersonal strategies to create and maintain a positive self-image" (Robins & John, 1997, p. 665). Each of these metaphors emphasizes a different aspect of the self-perception process, although the balance between them differs among people. For example, in a number of studies "only about 35% of the subjects show a clear self-enhancement bias, whereas about 50% are relatively accurate and about 15% actually show self-diminishment bias" (Robins & John, 1997, p. 669).

The matter of introspection becomes even more muddied if we ask not about access to the contents of people's experiences but about the structure and dynamics of their minds. Can we determine, for example, what it was that led us to the solution of a puzzle (e.g., Nisbett & Wilson, 1977)? Or how an object of perceptual awareness can have presence to our consciousness (cf. Natsoulas, 1999)? Or whether and how pure consciousness without contents is possible (e.g., Shear, 1996)? And what about our convictions? The feelings of knowing that accompany some mental events, particularly those that occur in altered states of consciousness? What are these feelings of knowing and how well do they affirm the correctness of what we think we know? Can we determine through introspection the correctness of our judgments about correctness (cf. Koriat, 2000; Metcalfe, 2000; Rosenthal, 2000)? Here we are in a more difficult situation. We do not know the answers to these questions. But to rule out the possibility of answering any of them because that seems implausible is contrary to the spirit of scientific investigation. The task becomes one of determining the extent to which and the means whereby answers may become possible as suggested in the discussion in chapter 1 about the need for greater methodological flexibility. It may yet be possible to introspect in such a way as to know the underlying ground of consciousness (Shear, 1996). This is an area of inquiry in which further research is needed. In the end, however, because we can question anything, including the self-evidence of objective existence, complete certainty may elude us anyway (cf. Metcalfe, 2000). We may always be left with judgments about relative truths. In the meantime, in this book we will report straightforward accounts of experiential contents as a matter of course but exercise caution with regard to more extensive introspective claims.

THINKING

I have found that sometimes there is an expectation that those who profess to know something about consciousness be familiar with the writings of William James, so let us briefly consider James's (1890/1983) influential characterization of thinking from his famous textbook *The Principles of Psychology*. James's ideas are reasonably consistent with more recent computational views (Flanagan, 1992), so that it is also reasonable to use them as a starting point for our discussion. Then we will skip forward to Eric Klinger's contemporary characterization of thinking derived from empirical investigations. These two descriptions of thinking provide us with a framework for deepening our understanding of waking experience as this chapter progresses.

The Stream of Consciousness

James has listed five characteristics of thinking, the first of which is that "every thought tends to be part of a personal consciousness" (W. James, 1890/1983, p. 220). For James, thoughts do not float freely but are always owned by someone, thereby presupposing the experienced presence of a personal self implied in consciousness₃. But after emphasizing the "*existence of personal selves*" (W. James, 1890/1983, p. 221), James has gone on to deconstruct the self until the self ends up being interpreted as a passing thought that appropriates previously aggregated ideas about what one is like. In contemporary cognitive science, the self is the biological organism that a person actually is along with the mental representation of the biological organism and its attributes within a person's information processing system. The sense of self arises from the use of that mental representation. There are no other referents of the word "self" in reality (cf. Flanagan, 1992; Natsoulas, 1983b). We can, of course, question such an interpretation and, indeed, one of the threads running through this book is concerned with the nature of the self.

"Within each personal consciousness thought is always changing" (W. James, 1890/1983, p. 220). For James, *"no state once gone can recur and be identical with what it was before"* (W. James, 1890/1983, p. 224). The things that we think about may be similar to things we have thought about in the past, but the brain changes as a result of experience and hence is not the same at the time of a later event as it was at the time of an earlier one. Changes in the brain translate into changes in experience. "For to every brain-modification, however small, must correspond a change of equal amount in the feeling which the brain subserves" (W. James, 1890/1983, p. 227). That is probably overstated. "There are almost certainly neural changes that do not affect either nonconscious or conscious mental functioning (in any interesting way)" (Flanagan, 1992, p. 161). The converse is generally accepted as true in cognitive science—namely, that "any change at the level of consciousness must be explicable in terms of changes at the neural level" (Flanagan, 1992, p. 161). However, if brain changes were to be insufficient to change thoughts, does that mean then that mental states can recur? Furthermore, there appears to be an implicit understanding of the nature of time underlying the changing of thoughts. But what if time itself appears to change in alterations of consciousness, as we shall see, for example, in the case of some psychedelic drug-induced experiences? What then happens to thoughts?

"Within each personal consciousness thought is sensibly continuous" (W. James, 1890/1983, p. 220). Consciousness spans time gaps in the sense that thoughts that follow a time gap feel as though they belong together with those that preceded it. Furthermore, James has argued at length that differences in content between successive thoughts are no more breaks in thinking than the joints in bamboo are breaks in the wood. Consciousness "is nothing jointed; it flows. A 'river' or a 'stream' are the metaphors by which it is most naturally described. *In talking of it hereafter, let us call it the stream of thought, of consciousness, or of subjective life"* (W. James, 1890/1983, p. 233). This metaphor has become so pervasive in our culture that we have already been using it in this book as a characterization of subjective experience.

According to James, the stream of consciousness has both substantive and transitive parts such that an object about which one thinks constitutes the substantive part, and a *"fringe of relations"* (W. James, 1890/1983, p. 249) of that object to other objects constitutes the transitive part within which the substantive part is embedded. Although a succession of words and images may be discrete, the fact that such contents of thought are "fringed" (W. James, 1890/1983, p. 262), according to James, means that our thoughts are continuous. In other words, the substantive and transitive elements of thinking combine to form a stream. The problem is that the investigation of thinking, for example, by analyzing the verbal output of participants who have been asked to think aloud, has revealed that thinking can reliably be broken down into identifiable segments (Klinger, 1971, 1999). Where, then, does the continuity lie, if it is not apparent in the content? But if consciousness feels continuous experientially does it matter that the content is discontinuous or if, from a computational point of view, the underlying cognitive processes giving rise to consciousness are themselves discrete (cf. Flanagan, 1992)? And what happens to continuity in alterations of consciousness in which the contents of thought apparently disappear "leaving *consciousness* alone by itself" (Shear, 1996, p. 64)?

Pure consciousness without contents poses a problem also for James's fourth assertion that thought "always appears to deal with objects independent of itself" (W. James, 1890/1983, p. 220). The first part of this characterization, that thought appears to deal with objects, is the contention that consciousness is structured in such a way as to be about something. This quality of aboutness, whereby mental phenomena exhibit the property of having "a direction upon an object" (Brentano, 1874/1960, p. 50), has been called *intentionality*. This use of the word "intentionality" should not be confused with the more common usage of "intentionality" as deliberateness (cf. Dennett, 1978).

The second part of James's fourth characteristic of thinking is the contention that the things about which we think appear to have an existence independent of our thoughts themselves. In other words, it appears that there is a real world out there that we can encounter in our thoughts. That seems obvious from our everyday way of thinking about reality but becomes problematic on reflection. What makes us think that there really is anything out there? James has noted that the recurrence of some object of thought leads us to "take the object out of [our past and present thoughts] and project it by a sort of triangulation into an independent position" (W. James, 1890/1983, p. 262). The repetitive presence of objects of thought is not enough to prove the existence of an objective reality, but, for all practical purposes, it can suffice for us to act as though there were an objective reality until the ontological status of objects of thought can be settled (cf. Lipson, 1987). James, it appears, grew skeptical of the existence of an independent material reality and dropped this fourth characteristic of thought from his 1892 version of the book (Taylor, 1981). Of course, the independent existence of a material reality is a cornerstone of materialism. Is it possible that there are objective realities that are not material (cf. Mavromatis, 1987b)? Or is there anything objective about reality at all, in which case what is the nature of objects of thought?

"[Thought] is interested in some parts of these objects to the exclusion of others, and welcomes or rejects—*chooses* from among them, in a word—all the while" (W. James, 1890/1983, p. 220). We selectively attend to some parts of objects rather than to others, and emphasize and unite some impressions but not others, so that we are always in a process of choosing between alternatives and, in doing so, leaving behind the alternatives not chosen. "The mind, in short, works on the data it receives very much as a sculptor works on his block of stone" (W. James, 1890/1983, p. 277). Indeed, given that the senses act as a data-reduction system and that, furthermore, we are conditioned by cultural influences and, of necessity, choose to direct our attention toward some objects and not others, "ordinary consciousness is an exquisitely evolved personal construction" (Ornstein, 1972, p. 45).

Dimensions of Thinking

What can we add to James's description to further understand the waking state of consciousness? Let us turn to a contemporary characterization of thinking by Eric Klinger and his colleagues, who have studied thinking using a version of the experience sampling method in which participants were asked to record the last thoughts that went through their minds whenever a beeper went off at irregular intervals as they were going about their everyday lives (Klinger, 1990; Klinger & Kroll-Mensing, 1995). As a result of these studies, a number of dimensions have been identified along which thinking can vary.

To begin with, thinking can be deliberate or spontaneous. *Deliberate thinking* (Klinger, 1990) is thinking that consists of specific content that is intentionally directed toward the attainment of certain goals (Klinger & Kroll-Mensing, 1995). Conceptually related to deliberateness is *controllability*, so that thinking can be "accompanied by a sense of volition, [be] checked against feedback concerning its effects, [be] evaluated according to its effectiveness in advancing particular goals, and [be] protected from drift and distraction by . . . deliberately controlling . . . attention" (Klinger, 1978, p. 235). *Spontaneous thinking* consists of thoughts that "just pop into our minds" (Klinger, 1990, p. 76). Klinger and his colleagues have found that "about two thirds" (Klinger, 1990, p. 78) of their participants "rated a majority of their thoughts as mostly deliberate, but nearly a third rated a majority of their thoughts as mostly spontaneous" (Klinger, 1990, p. 78). Overall, about one third of a person's thoughts are more spontaneous than deliberate.

Thinking can be either externally or internally focused. That is to say, we can be either *externally focused*, paying attention to what is going on in the environment around us, or we can be *internally focused* on thoughts away from what is happening in our environment. About one third of the time our thoughts are "focused on another place or on the past or future" (Klinger, 1990, p. 80). There can, of course, be combinations of deliberate versus spontaneous and externally versus internally focused thoughts. Suppose that I were listening to a song on my sound system. Trying to make out the lyrics of the song would be an example of deliberate, externally focused thinking. Realizing that it is difficult to figure out the lyrics would be an example of spontaneous, externally focused thinking. Trying to remember the name of an actress in a movie while listening to the music would be an example of deliberate, internally focused thinking. And worrying about an exam the following day while hearing the song would be an example of spontaneous, internally focused thinking.

Our thoughts can be *strange* along one of three dimensions. First, thoughts can be *fanciful* or *realistic*. Fanciful thoughts are ones in which "important social role expectations or current versions of natural laws" (Klinger, 1978, p. 241) are violated. Imagining that I am sailing my bicycle over the rooftops of the neighborhood houses would be an example of a fanciful thought. About 21% of thoughts depart at least to some degree from being physically possible (Klinger, 1990). Second, thoughts can also inexplicably jump from one to another so that nearly half the time participants in Klinger's (1990) studies rated their thoughts as being at least somewhat *disconnected*, calling into question the degree to which thinking is continuous. Third, thoughts can be either *well-integrated* or become *degenerated* as they do in dreams, whereby "images often flow without respect to beginnings or endings, shift gears drastically in the middle, interweave different concerns with one another, and offer images that seem to be the fused representatives of different basic ideas or forms" (Klinger, 1978, p. 241). In one of the thought-sampling studies, about 25% of thoughts contained "at least a trace of dream-like mentation" (Klinger & Cox, 1987, p. 124). Thus, thoughts can be strange in that they can be fanciful, disconnected, or degenerated.

Using the beeper methodology, Klinger and his colleagues have found a number of other characteristics of thoughts. The single most common feature is the presence of *self-talk*. We are silent in only about a quarter of our thoughts, and half the time we converse with ourselves in "fairly complete statements or running commentaries" (Klinger, 1990, p. 69). Visual imagery, at least in fragmentary form, occurs in two thirds of our thoughts, and half the time visual elements that usually include some color and movement are prominent. "About half of our ... thoughts include some sound apart from our own voices" (Klinger, 1990, p. 70). About one quarter of the time we think "about other people and relationships" (Klinger, 1990, p. 85). And 3% of the time "we focus on anxiety-provoking or worrisome thoughts" (Klinger, 1990, p. 85).

Emotions are often part of our multidimensional subjective experiences either accompanying or triggering thoughts. For example, we may feel shame on remembering our reprehensible behavior toward someone or recall thoughts of being given flowers by someone we love because of the positive emotions that were associated with that event (Klinger, 1990). In explanations of them, theorists have often regarded emotions as being made up of components. Thus, emotion experience itself can be thought of as consisting of what it is like to have a particular emotion and that of which one is aware during an emotion. This could be thought of as a distinction between consciousness$_3$ and subjective consciousness$_2$ applied to emotions. The level of a person's physical arousal and her bodily location in a spatial environment are other components of emotions, as are feelings of pleasure or displeasure and tendencies to take action. Cognitive components could include appraisals of emotion triggers, evaluations of one's situation, and plans for action, which could proceed at the level of consciousness$_1$ or consciousness$_2$ (cf. Lambie & Marcel, 2002). For example, an encounter with an extraterrestrial alien in one's bedroom could trigger fear and an effort to escape. Reappraisal of the situation could lead one to conclude that escape is impossible, that one is actually dreaming, or perhaps that the alien is just a figment of one's imagination. In fact, as this example suggests, changes of emotional expression can be associated with alterations of consciousness (Ludwig, 1966).

Sometimes we suppress our thoughts in the sense of trying not to allow them to be part of the stream of subjective consciousness$_2$. However, studies have shown that we appear to monitor how well we are able to keep unwanted thoughts outside of our awareness so that, ironically, the suppressed thoughts have not disappeared but, indeed, surface again when we cease to try to suppress them or when there are multiple demands being made on our cognitive resources. Thus, suppression of pain can result in greater pain, suppression of substance cravings can increase them, suppression of awareness of one's unwanted personal characteristics can lead to projection of those characteristics on others, and trying not to be like someone else can result in becoming like them. It has also been found that "relationships that remained a secret were more likely to occupy a person's attention than previous public relationships" (Wenzlaff & Wegner, 2000, pp. 78–79) and that "individuals who suppress thoughts on a chronic basis show a pattern of physiological responses that [is] consistent with anxiety" (Wenzlaff & Wegner, 2000, p. 76). *Thought suppression* appears to be a clumsy way of managing our thoughts and raises the question of the degree to which more effective means could be used for mental control. Some forms of meditation, considered briefly in chapter 8, for example, have had as their purpose the control of the mind.

• DAYDREAMING

There appears to have been a tendency in our Western culture to conceptualize our subjective life as consisting of rational thinking devoted to mentally solving problems by carefully following the rules of classical logic with, perhaps, an occasional unfortunate lapse into irrationality. However, as we have seen thus far, our subjective life does not conform to such a preconception but is richly varied. In fact, using an experience sampling method, Klinger and his colleagues found that participants in one study were engaged in "active, focused problem-solving thought" (Klinger, 1990, p. 91) only 6% of the time. It would make more sense to say that our subjective life consists of irrational thinking with occasional patches of reason. Or to put it another way, we could say that daydreaming is a substantial part of our experiential stream. Let us shift our attention to the daydreaming aspects of thinking.

First, we have to realize that there have been different definitions of daydreaming, which we can clarify with reference to the dimensions of thinking. Thus, for William James, "the essence of daydreams [was] their spontaneity" (Klinger, 1990, p. 81). In other words, we can think of daydreams as those thoughts that are spontaneous rather than deliberate. Sigmund Freud, founder of psychoanalysis at the beginning of the 20th century, used the criterion of fancifulness: Daydreams were those thoughts that violated the rules normally imposed on us by reality. For Jerome Singer, "the pioneer of modern daydreaming research" (Klinger, 2000, p. 437), daydreams were thoughts that did not pertain to the daydreamer's immediate environment (Klinger, 1990; Klinger & Cox, 1987). Thus, for Singer, daydreams were internally focused rather than externally focused thoughts. As we have seen, each of these dimensions of thinking is "largely independent of the others" (Klinger, 1990, p. 81). If we accept a definition whereby daydreams are thoughts by any of these criteria, then 70% of our thoughts would be considered to be daydreams. If we restrict ourselves, as Klinger has done, to defining *daydreams* as thoughts that are spontaneous or "at least partially fanciful" (Klinger, 1999, p. 43), then about 50% of our thoughts would be daydreams. If we insist on all of the criteria being met simultaneously, then only about 3% of our thoughts could be considered to be daydreams (Klinger, 1990).

As suggested by the apparent exaltation of rationality, daydreaming, however it may have been defined, has largely been ignored and denigrated until recent scientific interest has uncovered its benefits. What, then, are some of those benefits? Daydreaming, in Klinger's sense of spontaneous or fanciful thoughts, is an integral part of our psychological nature and hence fits with the brain processes, emotions, motives, actions, and more deliberate and realistic thoughts that make up our psyche (Klinger, 1990). We have *current concerns* that are issues relevant to goals that are present for a person from the time she commits herself to those goals until such time as those goals have been attained or abandoned (cf. Klinger, 1978), and daydreaming helps to keep us organized by reminding us of the current concerns that are emotionally most important to us. By replaying events from the past, daydreaming allows us to learn from them, while anticipating and rehearsing possible future scenarios enables us to better prepare for and make decisions regarding the future. "Daydreaming is a channel of information about our-selves to ourselves" (Klinger, 1990, p. 7) in that it helps us to know what we want, what we fear, and, sometimes, what we do not want to know. Daydreaming can be used to assist with personal growth and to contribute to creative expression. "Finally, daydreaming can serve as a way to change our moods—to relax and to entertain ourselves, providing a way to have fun with life" (Klinger, 1990, p. 8). In other words, rather than being unfortunate lapses, daydreams are important ingredients of our subjective lives.

Daydreaming Styles

When defined as stimulus-independent or task-irrelevant thoughts, using questionnaires that had been developed for that purpose, often given to college students, Singer and his colleagues found three different *daydreaming styles*. Those who score high on *Positive–Constructive Daydreaming* become absorbed in frequent, vivid, playful, and wish-fulfilling fantasies that are accepted, enjoyed, and used for problem solving. These are the happy day-dreamers (Klinger, 1990; Singer & Antrobus, 1972; Zhiyan & Singer, 1997). Those having a *Guilty–Dysphoric Daydreaming* style tend to repeat "a small number of themes of a somewhat bizarre nature often emerging with a near hallucinatory vividness" (Singer & Antrobus, 1972, p. 200) that have to do with ambition, heroic deeds, fear, failure, regrets, hostility, aggression, and guilt. Their mood is dysphoric. Those inclined toward *Poor Attentional Control* have difficulty concentrating and are anxious, distractible, easily bored, and unable "to sustain an elaborate fantasy" (Zhiyan & Singer, 1997, p. 401; see also Klinger, 1990; Singer & Antrobus, 1972). Their emotions can be unpleasant or pleasant.

Daydreaming styles are a private part of more general personality tendencies. Five dimensions of personality have emerged from a number of different studies supporting a *five-factor model of personality*. The first dimension, Extroversion, is concerned with a person being "sociable, lively, and outgoing" (Sternberg, 1995, p. 624) in contrast to being "quiet, reserved, and generally unsociable" (Sternberg, 1995, p. 624). The second dimension is that of Agreeableness, with a person tending toward being humane, altruistic, caring, nurturing, and emotionally supportive, or tending toward self-centeredness, indifference toward others, spitefulness, jealousy, and hostility. The Conscientiousness dimension captures a person's degree of self-control, will to achieve, and dependability. Neuroticism refers to poor versus good emotional adjustment (Digman, 1990), reflecting "the tendency to experience psychological distress in daily life" (Zhiyan & Singer, 1997, p. 401). The fifth dimension of personality is Openness, the degree to which a person is "imaginative, intelligent, curious, artistic, . . . aesthetically sensitive" (Sternberg, 1995, p. 626), and open to experience (Digman, 1990). Not surprisingly, the last three of these personality traits turn out to be particularly relevant to daydreaming styles, with Openness correlated with Positive–Constructive Daydreaming, Neuroticism with Guilty–Dysphoric Daydreaming, and both Neuroticism and the negative pole of Conscientiousness with Poor Attentional Control (Zhiyan & Singer, 1997, pp. 404–406).

It will also not come as a surprise to learn that patterns of behavior can change daydreaming styles. A study was conducted with 744 3rd- and 5th-grade Dutch children to determine what changes in daydreaming styles would occur over the course of a year as a result of viewing different types of television programs. Program types were identified as "violent dramatic programs, . . . nonviolent dramatic programs, . . . [and] nonviolent children's programs" (Valkenburg & van der Voort, 1995, p. 277). In the children's version of the daydreaming questionnaire that was used, the three daydreaming styles were identified as a *positive–intense daydreaming* style, which is "a pleasant, childlike, and fanciful style of daydreaming about things that could never happen or exist" (Valkenburg & van der Voort, 1995, p. 271); an *aggressive–heroic daydreaming* style, which is "characterized by daydreams about heroes and about the things one would like to do to a disliked person" (Valkenburg & van der Voort, 1995, p. 271); and a *dysphoric daydreaming* style, which consists of "unpleasant daydreaming about the things that could happen to oneself or one's family" (Valkenburg & van der Voort, 1995, p. 271). The researchers found that watching nonviolent children's programs increased positive–intense daydreaming, watching nonviolent dramatic programs inhibited aggressive–heroic daydreaming, and "watching violent dramatic programs inhibited positive–intense daydreaming" (Valkenburg & van der Voort, 1995, p. 285) and stimulated aggressive–heroic daydreaming. These are changes in the styles of daydreaming in which the children were engaged and not changes in the overall frequency of daydreaming. There were no statistically significant effects of television viewing on the dysphoric daydreaming style.

Imagination

Even though the imagination is an implicit part of waking consciousness, there has been little understanding of it in psychology (cf. Giorgi, 1987), with discussions about the imagination getting deflected to discussions about imagery and with the use of the verb "imagine" getting replaced with the noun "image" (Aanstoos, 1987). One way of conceptualizing imagery from a computational point of view is to think of it as an expression of nonverbal mental representations that occur as if one were metaphorically perceiving something with one's mind's eye. Such imaginative perception could occur in any of the sense modalities, although we usually associate imagery with vision (Paivio & te Linde, 1982). Although imagery has primarily been linked with memory and pattern recognition (Aanstoos, 1987), the notion of *imagination*, more generally, implies the presence of a creative aspect of mind that can give rise to mental imagery, however such a creative aspect may be conceptualized (cf. Giorgi, 1987).

We noted earlier that daydreams can be used to assist with personal growth. How could that be done? One way would be to harness our imagination in the form of *guided imagery*, a process of actively directing images in a symbolically meaningful sequence. The visualization of symbols has been extensively used in a form of psychotherapy called *psychosynthesis* that was developed by Roberto Assagioli beginning in 1910 with a critique of Freud's psychoanalysis (Hardy, 1987). According to Assagioli, nonconscious aspects of our psyche include not only a *subconscious*, which is the source of primitive drives and residue from past events, but also a *superconscious*, which is the source of ethical imperatives, altruistic love, inspiration, and genius (Assagioli, 1965). One way of accessing the superconscious was thought to be through the use of guided imagery such as the following inner dialogue exercise.

Imagine yourself in a meadow on a warm, sunny morning. Become aware of the environment around you—the whispering of the breeze in the grass and its touch against your face, the fragrance of flowers, the sight of the sky, blue, above you. Now imagine that there is a majestic mountain rising in front of you. You decide to climb it and set out on a path into a forest at the foot of the mountain. You feel the coolness of the shade among the trees and hear the sound of a stream beside the path. The path leaves the forest and begins to rise steeply. The ascent becomes arduous as you use your hands as well as your feet to climb. The air has become rarefied and invigorating. As you pass through a cloud you can barely make out your hands on the rocks in the mist. You emerge from the cloud with the sun shining brightly above. Climbing feels easier as you near the summit. You emerge on a plateau at the top of the mountain. There is perfect silence around you. In the distance you see a luminous point that takes on the shape of a person as it approaches you. You find yourself face to face with a loving and wise being. You can talk about anything you wish and listen to anything that the wise being has to say in turn. Perhaps the wise being has a gift to give you before you leave to come back down the mountain (cf. Ferrucci, 1982).

The idea in this exercise is to try to create a psychological effect through the use of symbolic imagery. Ascending a mountain represents a refinement of consciousness, and encountering a wise being is a personification of whatever latent wisdom we may possess. Deliberate thinking is involved in the directed sequence of specific images, with spontaneous thinking supplying the details of those images and any apparent response on the part of the wise being. But, getting back to one of our thematic threads, does any of this play of the imagination actually mean anything? Are we accessing a superconscious or just fooling ourselves? Indeed, we may end up with spontaneous images that are fragmented, self-deprecating, and meaningless—that is to say, images that have nothing wise about them. However, at other times the spontaneous images may be accompanied by a sense of rightness, understanding, and joy, even though the presence of such qualities does not guarantee that they are objectively true or necessarily wise (cf. Ferrucci, 1982). Although some research has been done to determine the effectiveness of the use of guided imagery (e.g., Feinberg-Moss & Oatley, 1990), more research is needed to determine the extent to which it is meaningful and useful. For now, we can see that imagining a wise being can be a way of trying to generate some interesting ideas, and techniques such as the inner dialogue exercise can be means of attempting to harness our daydreams for creative expression, problem-solving, and personal growth.

Psychoneuroimmunology

Whether or not we can create psychological effects as a result of working with imagery, it appears that sometimes our thoughts can have effects on our immune systems as found in a field of investigation that has come to be known as *psychoneuroimmunology* (O'Regan, 1983). In one study, rats were given a novel-tasting drink 30 minutes before being injected with a drug that suppresses the immune system. Subsequently, these same animals, when given the novel-tasting drink alone, had suppressed immune functioning even though they were no longer receiving any immunosuppressive drugs (Ader & Cohen, 1975). In other words, an association had been formed between the way something tasted and the activity of the immune system. Other studies have confirmed links between a variety of stimuli and physiological processes (Ader & Cohen, 1982, 1993). These results carry over to humans with associations between psychological parameters and measures of immune functioning having been demonstrated (Adler &

Matthews, 1994). For example, in one study, participants who had been asked to suppress their thoughts had significantly decreased levels of white blood cells (Petrie, Booth, & Pennebaker, 1998).

Other studies have shown that thoughts can have positive physiological effects. John Schneider and his colleagues did a series of 10 studies in which they examined the effects of guided imagery on the immune system, with particular interest in white blood cells known as *neutrophils*. Neutrophils have a property called *adherence*, which is capable of being increased and which has been hypothesized to be related to their ability "to migrate from the blood stream to a particular [site] of infection" (Schneider, Smith, Minning, Whitcher, & Hermanson, 1990, p. 181). In one of the studies, 16 healthy students "who believed they could influence their immune function" (Schneider et al., 1990, p. 182) were recruited from classes at a medical school and given a lecture and slide presentation about "neutrophils and their function in the immune system" (Schneider et al., 1990, p. 184) and "two two-hour imagery training sessions" (Schneider et al., 1990, p. 184). The participants were asked to imagine that their neutrophils were responding as if there were a crisis so that the neutrophils would be expected to increase their adherence and migrate out of the blood stream to the site of the imagined crisis. Blood was taken from the participants before and after the experimental condition, and changes in the total white blood cell count, neutrophil count, and adherence were measured. The investigators found a significant 60% drop for the number of neutrophils but not for other white blood cells and, contrary to expectation, they found a significant decrease in the adherence of the neutrophils. The investigators also found correlations between the immune system changes and the participants' self-reported effectiveness of their imagery along various dimensions.

Although the decrease in neutrophil count had been expected in the imagery study, what was troubling to the investigators was that the adherence of the neutrophils had decreased and the size of the decrease had been greater precisely for those participants who had rated their imagery as having been more effective. Was it possible that so many neutrophils had left the bloodstream that only those with low adherence remained in the bloodstream to be counted? To check this possibility, the experiment was repeated with 27 medical and graduate students who were asked to keep the neutrophils in their bloodstream while increasing their adherence. This time there was no change in the white blood cell count, but there was a significant increase in the adherence of the neutrophils and a positive correlation between increased neutrophil adherence and quality of imagery ratings (Schneider et al., 1990).

What has been demonstrated in Schneider's studies has been the ability of a specific type of white blood cell to conform to imagined changes. If the immune system can be affected by guided imagery in healthy people, this raises the question of the scope of the power of the mind to create physiological and psychological changes also in cases of illness. For example, an effort has sometimes been made to use guided imagery in the treatment of cancer (e.g., Baron, 1989). Not unexpectedly, this area of research has been controversial, particularly when the healing intentions occur in someone other than the person being healed, a situation analogous to that in the ganzfeld studies (e.g., Bengston & Krinsley, 2000; Dossey, 1992; Greyson, 1996; Krippner & Achterberg, 2000). More research is needed in this area to follow up on the work that has already been done and to identify the variables that contribute to healing effects. As it stands, the results of research in psychoneuroimmunology suggest that there is a more intimate connection between the physiological, cognitive, and experiential aspects of our nature than we might suppose.

SENSORY RESTRICTION

Normally our ordinary waking state of consciousness includes sensations of the environment around us as reflected in the external versus internal dimension of thought so that we can pay attention to what is going on around us or to what is going on in our minds. But what would happen if we were to restrict sensory input either by attenuating it or by substantially removing the variability of sensory stimuli? What if we were to force attention, in a sense, to the internal aspects of the stream of consciousness? What would happen? We already saw an example of sensory restriction with the ganzfeld technique described in chapter 1. In that case, sensory restriction was thought to promote the possibility of anomalous information transfer. What we find more generally is that some of the phenomena associated with the more dramatic alterations of consciousness already occur with sensory restriction, making it valuable not only as perhaps the most pronounced expression of ordinary waking consciousness but, paradoxically, as an example of an altered state of consciousness.

Early Research

John Lilly wanted to know what would happen if sensory input were to be reduced as much as possible. He thought about all of the ways in which sensory variations are created in the body and came up with the idea of using water flotation as a way of minimizing them. He devised an underwater breathing mask and rubber supports to hold up his arms and legs in the water while being "minimally stimulating to the skin" (Lilly, 1978, p. 102). One day in 1954, he put on the mask and the arm and leg supports and immersed himself in a tank filled with tap water that was situated in a dark, soundproof room. He discovered that "this environment furnished the most profound relaxation and rest that he had ever experienced in [his] life" (Lilly, 1978, p. 103) and claimed "that two hours in the tank gave him the rest equivalent to eight hours of sleep on a bed" (Lilly, 1978, p. 103). He found, furthermore, "that there were many, many states of consciousness, of being, between the usual wide-awake consciousness of participating in an external reality and the unconscious state of deep sleep" (Lilly, 1978, p. 103) and that he could experience events in his fantasy that seemed so real that "they could possibly be mistaken for events in the outside world" (Lilly, 1978, p. 103). Over the years Lilly improved the flotation tank technique of sensory restriction and then, one day, injected himself with 100 micrograms of LSD before getting into the tank. But that is a story for chapter 7.

Lilly's positive experiences in the tank were at odds with much of the research concerning sensory deprivation in the 1950s and 1960s when participants often reported feelings of anxiety, cognitive inefficiencies, restlessness, and other symptoms of distress. Many of these effects appear to have been associated with prolonged confinement rather than just sensory restriction (Zuckerman, 1969). In some studies, for example, participants spent a week in a coffin-like box with straps and a head retainer restricting their movements and with their visual and auditory perceptions confined using ganzfeld procedures similar to the one described in chapter 1 (Zubek, Bayer, Milstein, & Shephard, 1969). A summary of the early results ended with the conclusion that without "a changing sensory environment . . . the brain ceases to function in an adequate way, and abnormalities of behavior develop" (Heron, 1957, p. 56). Perhaps it was because of such adverse publicity surrounding them that participants entered sensory deprivation studies with feelings of anxiety, thereby contributing to their experience of distress (Suedfeld & Coren, 1989; Zuckerman, 1969).

To demonstrate the effects of anticipated anxiety on results, in one study, on arrival for the experiment, participants in the experimental group were exposed to a stressful environment whereas participants in the control group encountered a more relaxed atmosphere. In the experimental condition the experimenter was dressed in a white coat, a medical history of the participants was taken, "a tray of drugs and medical instruments . . . labeled 'emergency tray' was in full view" (Orne & Scheibe, 1964, p. 5), and inside the isolation room was "a red pushbutton mounted on a board and labeled 'Emergency Alarm' " (Orne & Scheibe, 1964, p. 6). These and other anxiety-provoking elements of the situation were missing for participants in the control condition who were told that they were in "a control group for a sensory deprivation experiment" (Orne & Scheibe, 1964, p. 6). Participants in either group were subsequently confined to a well-lit room for 4 hours that was not soundproofed and in which they could freely move around. "The room, it should be pointed out, could hardly be construed as a sensory deprivation environment" (Orne & Scheibe, 1964, p. 6). Yet after 4 hours of confinement, the participants in the experimental group had greater decrements in cognitive and perceptual performance and more frequently reported intellectual dullness and restlessness than did participants in the control group. In considering this result, however, it should be noted that there were some problems with the manner in which the data were collected (Zuckerman, 1969).

As we shall see a number of times in this book, the social situation associated with alterations of consciousness often has a substantial impact on subsequent altered-states experiences. In the restricted stimulation situation, however, the effect of contextual cues disappeared in a replication study more than 25 years later, presumably because the overall public attitudes had changed considerably since the time of the original study (M. Barabasz, Barabasz, & O'Neill, 1991).

Types of Sensory Restriction

Lilly continued his flotation research and, in the 1970s, invented a flotation tank in which a person could float in a "warm solution of Epsom salts" (Suedfeld & Coren, 1989, p. 20) for the purposes of relaxation. Around the same time it was found that "stimulus reduction, either alone or combined with other techniques, was a highly effective treatment in habit modification" (Suedfeld & Coren, 1989, p. 20) such as smoking cessation. As a result, among investigators, sensory restriction began to shed its image as a form of torture, and increased research was undertaken to explore its additional therapeutic applications to habit modification. What had been known as perceptual isolation or sensory deprivation was reconceptualized as *restricted environmental stimulation technique* and *restricted environmental stimulation therapy*, depending on the context and, in either case, abbreviated as *REST*.

Two versions of REST have been used. In *flotation REST* a person floats on her back in a pool or tank of water filled with enough Epsom salts so that the face and surface of her body are above the waterline. Substantial effort is required to turn over, with the result that she can daydream or sleep without being concerned about her safety. The pool or tank is itself in a dark and quiet room with an intercom connecting the person with a monitor. The usual length of time spent in a flotation tank is about 45 minutes, although a participant can leave at any time before then. In *chamber REST* a person lies on a bed in a completely dark room with reduced sound for a number of hours, with 24 being a frequently used time period. "Food, water and toilet facilities" (Suedfeld & Borrie, 1999) are available inside the room. Again, there is an intercom that "permits a monitor nearby to respond to questions or requests, and to help the subject leave the chamber before the scheduled end of the session if desired" (Suedfeld & Borrie, 1999, p. 546).

Effects of Sensory Restriction

As expected, REST has provided relief from the stressors in a person's environment with increases in relaxation found on physiological and self-report measures "from before to after flotation sessions" (Suedfeld & Borrie, 1999, p. 553). Participants have sometimes indicated that the time spent in REST was an opportunity for them "to think more deeply than usual" (Suedfeld & Borrie, 1999, p. 557) about their life problems and to come up with solutions that were successfully implemented afterward. These solutions have included subsequent increased health-related behaviors such as initiating exercise programs or reducing the intake of unhealthy foods, as well as improved interpersonal relations with family members and colleagues at work. In some cases of serious self-examination, participants could uncover disturbing aspects about themselves such as self-destructive patterns of behavior. Although such discoveries can be distressing, they can also be therapeutically productive. Sometimes individuals who are depressed may not benefit from REST because it provides them with an opportunity to ruminate about their woes if they tend to have self-deprecating thoughts. In general, however, participants appear to experience an improvement in mood, particularly with flotation REST.

It has been thought by some that it is reduced rigidity of thinking and behaving that has been at the root of successful habit modification with REST. The idea is that sensory restriction provides an opportunity to develop flexibility of mind with regard to the "thoughts, emotions, motivations, and behaviors supporting [a] habit" (Suedfeld & Borrie, 1999, p. 552), thereby creating the possibility for new psychological patterns to emerge that are consistent with a participant's desire to change. In the treatment of smoking addiction, a 12- to 24-hour chamber REST session in complete darkness and silence has sometimes been combined with another proven smoking cessation method such as self-management training, hypnosis, or counseling, creating an additive effect of the benefits of either method used alone. What is particularly significant is that the addition of REST to the treatment program dramatically decreases the probability of relapse. In one study, in which "hypnotherapy and counseling with an experienced clinician were combined with 1–3 very brief chamber REST sessions" (Suedfeld & Borrie, 1999, p. 552), 47% of participants were abstinent at a 19-month follow-up compared with 4% to 36% abstinence for hypnosis only or hypnosis combined with other methods and 6% for an untreated control group (A. Barabasz, Baer, Sheehan, & Barabasz, 1986). It is possible that in this study, the results could be attributed, in part, to the increased suggestibility and hypnotizability of participants found during and immediately following REST (cf. Suedfeld & Borrie, 1999).

A not unexpected effect of sensory restriction is *stimulus hunger*, the tendency after 24 or more hours in a dark, silent room to "respond positively to information or stimulation that breaks the sameness of the environment" (Suedfeld & Borrie, 1999, p. 550). For example, participants will request to hear boring materials and will comply with "counter attitudinal behavior in order to obtain information" (Suedfeld & Borrie, 1999, p. 550), although unpredictable and cognitively challenging stimuli are preferred. The presence of stimulus hunger as a result of sensory restriction has been used for treating people with phobias. In one study, participants with a fear of snakes were placed in a REST chamber for 5 hours. At the end of this time, they could push a button that allowed them to view slides of snakes of varying degrees of realism. Subsequently, participants demonstrated diminished fear of snakes compared to a control group that had seen the slides but had not experienced REST. In keeping with the affinity for the unpredictability of sensory information during sensory restriction, it was found that random presentation of the slides of snakes with regard to their realism was more effective for diminishing fear than any other order, including a hierarchical order from least to most realistic that would be used in traditional therapeutic treatments of phobias.

REST has not only been shown to be effective in a variety of clinically relevant situations (e.g., M. Barabasz, Barabasz, & Dyer, 1993; Harrison & Barabasz, 1991; Ruzyla-Smith & Barabasz, 1993) but has also been demonstrated to contribute to enhanced performance in other areas of life such as athletic performance. Collegiate basketball playing, tennis playing, and rifle marksmanship have all improved subsequent to the use of REST (A. Barabasz, Barabasz, & Bauman, 1993; McAleney, & Barabasz, 1993; McAleney, Barabasz, & Barabasz, 1990; Wagaman, & Barabasz, 1993; Wagaman, Barabasz, & Barabasz, 1991). For example, in a study of 22 college basketball players, the participants who experienced flotation REST for six sessions in addition to imagery training had better game performance than players who experienced only imagery training (Wagaman et al., 1991).

Sensed Presences

Lilly (1978) became concerned about his exploits in the flotation tank when "he realized that there were apparent presences" (Lilly, 1978, p. 103) of people "who he knew were at a distance from the facility" (Lilly, 1978, p. 103) and "strange and alien presences with whom he had had no known previous experience" (Lilly, 1978, p. 103). He subsequently came to believe that he had established contact with an alien civilization made up of solid state beings. A *sensed presence* is a feeling that another being is present when no other being is actually physically present. In addition to deliberately induced sensory restriction, sensed presences have been known to occur in situations of social isolation such as solitary sailing, polar exploration, and mountain climbing, as well as during religious rituals and traumatic events (cf. Suedfeld & Mocellin, 1987). Charles Lindbergh sensed presences during his pioneering solo transatlantic flight from Boston to Paris in 1927. Even though they seemed to be behind him, Lindbergh said that he could see them because his skull was "one great eye, seeing everywhere at once" (Lindbergh, 1953, p. 389). The presences appeared and disappeared from the cockpit of his airplane and spoke to him above the engine's roar, encouraging him and advising him regarding his flight. In one study, sensed presences were evoked in participants by stereo-acoustic stimuli, suggesting to the researchers that transient brain activity may give rise to the phenomenon (Johnson & Persinger, 1994). However we may account for them, sensed presences can play a constructive role in one's life as we have previously noted with regard to the wise being of the inner dialogue exercise and as was apparently also the case with Lindberg. As we shall see, alien presences show up in a number of alterations of consciousness, often with their ontological status not quite as firmly established as we might suppose.

We started this chapter by considering the manner in which a person can come to know something of her subjective consciousness, namely through various introspective activities. What, then, does introspection of some form or other appear to reveal about subjective experience? James identified five characteristics of thought, and Klinger found three dimensions of it. Furthermore, one's inner life appears to be a mixture of perceptions, thoughts, images, self-talk, emotions, and other events that occur in one's experiential stream. In exploring more deeply the nature of waking consciousness, we shifted attention to the imaginative aspects of the stream and considered daydreaming and the uses of the imagination both for psychological and physiological benefit. We ended this chapter with an examination of sensory restriction and its practical applications.

There is need for research throughout this material. The disparate ideas about introspection need to be consolidated, and research needs to be undertaken to determine its scope. The characteristics of thought identified by James need to be more closely examined. How does the sense of ownership of thoughts arise? Is thinking really continuous, or is it discrete? The manner in which different psychological components contribute to the flux of the stream of consciousness needs to be established. The links between the mind and biology, including the mechanisms by which they operate, need to be revealed. The positive potential of sensory restriction needs to be mined, and the conditions under which it could be dangerous must be identified. With regard to sensed presences, is there anything truly meaningful about them? Could they be external to the experiencer as they appear to be? What is really happening when experience goes on for us? Can an adequate explanation be found in physiological and cognitive terms, or do we need new ways of thinking about the experiential stream that are not restricted by contemporary beliefs about the nature of the mind? As we can see, there are a number of fundamental questions about the nature of consciousness and reality that are raised by a consideration of the ordinary waking consciousness.

3

SLEEP

Although the ordinary waking state is the state against which all other states are compared, sleep is the prototype of an altered state. Clearly there are physiological, cognitive, and experiential changes associated with sleep. Indeed, the stages of sleep are defined by some of the physiological changes that occur during sleep, so we will pay more attention to the physiological perspective in this chapter than we have previously. But for all that it is familiar, just as with the ordinary waking state, the history of sleep research has revealed sleep to be a varied phenomenon. Although fundamental questions about the nature of consciousness and reality surface less often with the study of sleep than with other alterations of consciousness, there are other provocative questions specific to the subject matter. What happens to the body during sleep? What happens to consciousness during sleep? How do different drugs affect sleep? Why do we sleep? What are some of the ways in which sleep becomes disordered? What happens during sleepwalking? Should we be held accountable for actions that we commit while asleep? The answers, to the extent that they are available, may surprise us, so that by the time we get to the end of this chapter and through most of the next one concerning dreams, we will see that some of the fundamental distinctions between wakefulness and sleep have disappeared.

SLEEP PHYSIOLOGY AND BEHAVIOR

Let us start at the beginning—not the historical beginning this time, as in chapter 2, but the biological beginning, with the brain. That will allow us to describe the physiological changes that occur during sleep.

The Nervous System

The brain is made of particular types of cells called *nerve cells*. There are lots of other types of cells in the brain as well as open spaces filled with fluid. But it is the nerve cells in which we are interested because they are

51

the ones that are associated with the processing of information. Extending from the brain is the *spinal cord*, which is made up of nerve cells inside the backbone. Or we can think of it the other way around. The spinal cord, on its way into the head, widens to become the *brainstem*, the top of which is a structure called the *thalamus*, located in the center of the head, which in turn opens up into the multiply folded *cerebral cortex* that wraps around the lower parts of the brain.

This is how the system works. Your cat snuggles up against your hand; a message travels along peripheral nerve cells to the spinal cord, up the spinal cord, through the brainstem into the part of the cortex that maps the sensation of touch in your hand, then into the rest of the brain where higher levels of processing take place; you decide to pet your cat; the motor part of the cortex sends a message back down through the brainstem, the spinal cord, and peripheral nerves to the arm and hand; and then you stroke your cat. There are a number of other aggregates of nerve cells attached to this central corridor but they will not concern us in this book. We should note, though, that the brain is bilaterally symmetrical, in that structures laterally away from the midline come in pairs. That applies also to the cerebral cortex that has a *left hemisphere* and a *right hemisphere* connected by a number of bundles of nerve cells (Carlson, 1994; Netter, 1986). Much is known about the higher levels of processing in the brain, but there is considerable controversy concerning the manner in which sensations become conscious perceptions, how consciousness arises in the brain, how volition plays a role in cognitive processing, and whether, indeed, human experience can be explained entirely in terms of brain processes (Libet, Freeman, & Sutherland, 1999; Searle, 2000; Shear, 1996).

Messages travel from one nerve cell, or *neuron*, to the next. The neuron's *cell body*, along with branching projections called *dendrites*, is the receiving end of the neuron, while a branching projection from the cell body, called an *axon*, is the transmitting end. Messages along neurons are actually changes in the electrical potentials across the cells' walls created through electrochemical processes. Communication between nerve cells in human beings takes place through the release of chemicals called *neurotransmitters* into the intercellular fluid from various locations on the axon of one cell and the attachment of the chemicals to *receptor sites* on the dendrites or cell bodies of subsequent cells, thereby activating electrochemical processes that can inhibit or enhance a subsequent cell's ability to send a message. After binding to receptor sites for a while, neurotransmitters are taken up by the cell from which they came or broken down and flushed away in the intercellular fluid (Carlson, 1994).

Historically, it was thought that nothing happened in the brain unless it received stimulation through the senses, so sleep was considered to be the result of a dormant brain (Dement, 2000). In fact, this was a hypothesis that Lilly tested by climbing into the isolation tank. As he found out, removal of almost all sensory stimulation did not inevitably cause sleep (Lilly, 1978). Nor, as we shall see, is the brain dormant during sleep. A fair amount of spontaneous electrochemical activity goes on at all times. Not all of the activity is excitatory. Many neural circuits are inhibitory in that they attenuate the activity in other neural circuits including those that bring sensory messages from the periphery. There are also groups of nerve cells known as *pacemakers* in various parts of the brain that synchronize the electrochemical activity of other groups of nerve cells (Steriade, 2000).

Polysomnography

If the electrochemical activity of groups of cells can become synchronized, is it possible to measure any resultant collective voltage changes? Yes, some voltage changes can be measured. Electrodes attached at various locations on the scalp can detect changes in electrical potential across the dendritic membranes primarily of a layer of large neurons in the cortex (Aldrich, 1999). In other words, there is electrochemical activity throughout the brain, including the rhythmic activity of pacemakers that entrain whole groups of cells. If we stick electrodes on the head of a person, we can pick up changes in electrical activity of groups of cells that are not too far from the electrodes. The observed changes of electrical potential over time look like waves, which can be recorded using an *electroencephalograph (EEG)*. More sophisticated methods of imaging brain activity have been developed in recent years (Lester, Felder, & Lewis, 1997), but the EEG is the primary instrument that has been used for defining the physiological changes associated with sleep (Rechtschaffen & Kales, 1968).

Some of the patterns of voltage changes over time that are seen with an EEG can be classified into frequency bands. Waves of frequency greater than 13 cycles per second (cps) are called *beta waves*, those 8 to 13 cps are *alpha waves*, those 4 to 7 cps are *theta waves*, and those less than 4 cps are *delta waves* (cf. Aldrich, 1999; Carskadon & Rechtschaffen, 2000; Walter & Dovey, 1944). In general, shorter, more rapid waves tend to be of lesser amplitude, whereas longer waves of lower frequency tend to be of greater amplitude. Delta waves, for example, can exceed amplitudes of 200 microvolts (μV) from trough to peak (e.g., Rechtschaffen & Kales, 1968). Other more specific waveforms with regard to frequency and amplitude have also been identified, as we shall see.

In addition to an electroencephalograph, two other electrical devices have been used for defining the course of sleep. One of these is the *electrooculograph (EOG)*, which is used for detecting eye movements through electrodes taped close to the eyes. The other is the *electromyograph (EMG)*, which measures muscle tension through electrodes placed beneath the chin

(Carskadon & Rechtschaffen, 2000). The recordings made by an EEG, EOG, or EMG are also abbreviated as EEG, EOG, or EMG (Carlson, 1994). A number of other devices can be used to measure physiological events of interest such as heart rate, oxygen content of the blood, breathing difficulties (Kryger, 2000), penile circumference (Ware & Hirshkowitz, 2000), and motor movements (Spielman, Yang, & Glovinsky, 2000). The simultaneous recording of various physiological measures during sleep is called *polysomnography* (Aldrich, 1999).

Traditionally, polysomnography has been carried out in a sleep laboratory associated with a university or a clinic. A participant would spend one or more nights sleeping in a bed in a room in the sleep laboratory while being monitored. A paper copy of the sleep record would be obtained by printing the output from the different channels of the polysomnograph on continuous sheets of paper using recording pens. The sleep record would then be scored for sleep stages and other features of sleep through visual inspection. With the availability of computing devices, *computerized polysomnography* has been developed so that sleep events can be recorded, scored, and summarized by computer. With increasing miniaturization of electronics, *portable computerized polysomnography* has become feasible, so that sleep records can be obtained from people sleeping at home in their own beds. This has the advantage of collecting data in a naturalistic setting in which sleep cannot be disturbed by the strangeness of sleeping in a laboratory. The concern with computerized polysomnography is that the quality of the sleep record and its analysis be comparable to that obtained by technicians inspecting paper recordings made in a sleep laboratory (cf. Hirshkowitz & Moore, 2000).

Sleep Stages

Using the physiological measures of EEG, EOG, and EMG, a number of *sleep stages* have been found to recur during a night's sleep. Given that there are variations in the physiology of sleep with age, it should be noted that the following description of sleep stages pertains to young adults. During waking in the ordinary waking state, the EEG reveals beta activity with some intermixed alpha activity and occasional theta. The EOG shows rapid eye movements and eye blinks, and the EMG indicates "high levels of muscle activity" (Aldrich, 1999, p. 10). For 85% to 90% of people, relaxing and closing their eyes results in the occurrence of alpha rhythm. The onset of sleep is indicated by the attenuation of alpha and the predominance of theta (Aldrich, 1999), so that the EEG pattern of stage 1 sleep has been described as "relatively low voltage, mixed frequency EEG" (Rechtschaffen & Kales, 1968, p. 5). *Vertex sharp waves* consisting of sharp negative peaks with amplitudes occasionally reaching 200 μV (Rechtschaffen & Kales,

1968) can occur in isolation or in groups (Aldrich, 1999) during the latter part of stage 1 (Rechtschaffen & Kales, 1968). "Slow, often asynchronous eye movements" (Carskadon & Dement, 2000, p. 16) occur during the transition from wakefulness to stage 1 sleep, their onset usually preceding the beginning of sleep by 1 or 2 minutes, although the lead time can be as long as 15 minutes. In general, there is no discrete change in muscle tension at the point of transition to sleep; however, there could be a gradual diminution of EMG amplitude within moments of sleep onset (Carskadon & Rechtschaffen, 2000).

Stage 1 sleep lasts for 1 to 7 minutes before giving way to stage 2 sleep (Carskadon & Dement, 2000), which is characterized by the presence of K complexes and sleep spindles against a "background of mixed frequencies predominantly in the theta range" (Aldrich, 1999, p. 11). A K complex is a waveform lasting for at least .5 seconds that consists of a sharp negative component "several hundred microvolts" (Aldrich, 1999, p. 12) in amplitude immediately followed by a "positive slow wave" (Aldrich, 1999, p. 12) of smaller amplitude (Aldrich, 1999). About one to three K complexes per minute would occur during stage 2 in young adults (Carskadon & Rechtschaffen, 2000). A sleep spindle is a brain wave of about 12 to 14 cps in frequency (cf. Aldrich, 1999; Hirshkowitz, Moore, & Minhoto, 1997; Rechtschaffen & Kales, 1968), lasting .5 to 1.5 seconds, that often waxes and wanes in amplitude. About three to eight spindles per minute would occur during stage 2 sleep in normal adults and "spindle rate appears to be a fairly stable individual characteristic" (Carskadon & Rechtschaffen, 2000, p. 1203). Slow eye movements "may infrequently and only very briefly persist after the appearance of sleep spindles and K complexes" (Carskadon & Rechtschaffen, 2000, p. 1204). The EMG is "generally at a low amplitude relative to wakefulness" (Carskadon & Rechtschaffen, 2000, p. 1204).

As stage 2 sleep deepens, high amplitude delta waves become more frequent. When delta waves slower than 2 cps of at least 75 μV occupy more than 20% of the sleep record, we say that the sleeper is in stage 3. If such slow, high-amplitude delta waves occupy more than 50% of the sleep record, then she is in stage 4 sleep (Rechtschaffen & Kales, 1968). Both K complexes and sleep spindles can occur in stages 3 and 4, although they may be difficult to differentiate from the predominant delta activity. Some individuals experience a pattern of sleep called alpha-delta sleep, which consists of relatively large-amplitude alpha rhythms that are 1 to 2 cps slower than waking alpha occurring throughout stages 1 to 4 (Carskadon & Rechtschaffen, 2000), with the greatest amount found during stages 3 and 4 (Aldrich, 1999). Stages 3 and 4 of sleep are sometimes collectively referred to as slow-wave sleep (SWS; Carskadon & Dement, 2000). During slow-wave sleep there are no eye movements and, while muscle tension is still present, the levels are low (Carskadon & Rechtschaffen, 2000). In the course of its first occurrence after falling asleep, stage 2 has a duration of about 10 to 25 minutes, stage 3 usually lasts only a few minutes, and stage 4 persists for 20 to 40 minutes (Carskadon & Dement, 2000).

About 80 minutes from sleep onset, there is a change in the polysomnograph, indicating a transition to yet another sleep stage (Aldrich, 1999). The delta activity declines, there may be a few minutes of stages 3, 2, or 1 (cf. Aldrich, 1999; Carskadon & Dement, 2000), and then a "low voltage, mixed-frequency" (Rechtschaffen & Kales, 1968, p. 7) rhythm occurs that resembles that of stage 1 "except that vertex sharp waves are not prominent" (Rechtschaffen & Kales, 1968, p. 7). There may, however, be alpha activity that is about one to two cps slower than waking alpha and *sawtooth waves* of 2 to 6 cps occurring intermittently, "usually in runs lasting 1 to 5 seconds" (Aldrich, 1999, p. 14). These changes in EEG are accompanied by changes in EOG and EMG. Sometimes the eyes move sporadically in a jerky manner during this stage, giving rise to the moniker *rapid eye movement (REM)*, although the rapidity of eye movements is not greater than that during waking (Aserinsky, 1996; Aserinsky & Kleitman, 1953). The rapid eye movements "occur singly or in bursts" (Aldrich, 1999, p. 14), often accompanied by sawtooth waves and brief episodes of facial muscle activity (Aldrich, 1999). Because of the presence of rapid eye movements during this sleep stage, it has been named *REM sleep*, whereas stages 1 to 4 are often called *non-REM (NREM) sleep* (Carskadon & Dement, 2000).

Within REM sleep, the periods of time when there is "muscle twitching with bursts of eye movements" (Aldrich, 1999, p. 14) have often been "referred to as *phasic REM sleep*" (Aldrich, 1999, p. 14), whereas periods of time during REM sleep when there are "few or no eye movements and muscle twitches" (Aldrich, 1999, p. 14) have been "referred to as *tonic REM sleep*" (Aldrich, 1999, p. 14). The muscle twitches during REM sleep are short-lived events against a background of muscle atonia, which consists of the "suppression of skeletal muscle tone and reflexes" (Carskadon & Rechtschaffen, 2000, p. 1205) to levels below those of the other sleep stages (Carskadon & Rechtschaffen, 2000). Characteristic also of REM sleep are penile erections in men and "changes in erectile tissue" (Aldrich, 1999, p. 19) in women that begin "within a few minutes of the onset of REM sleep and [persist] throughout the REM period" (Aldrich, 1999, p. 19). Whereas NREM sleep has been characterized as "a relatively inactive yet actively regulating brain in a movable body" (Carskadon & Dement, 2000, p. 15), REM sleep has been described as "a highly activated brain in a paralyzed body" (Carskadon & Dement, 2000, p. 16). Because of the presence during sleep of brain activity comparable to that of waking, REM sleep has also been known as *paradoxical sleep* (Jouvet, 1993/1999). The first REM sleep period lasts from a few minutes to about 15 minutes (cf. Aldrich, 1999; Carskadon & Dement, 2000).

Patterns of Sleep Stages

The cycling of NREM and REM sleep is repeated throughout a night's sleep, with the average length of the first cycle being about 70 to 100 minutes, increasing to about 90 to 120 minutes in the second and later cycles so that there would be a total of four to six NREM–REM sleep cycles a night. The amount of time spent in slow-wave sleep decreases in the second cycle, and SWS "may disappear altogether from later cycles, as stage 2 sleep expands to occupy the NREM portion of the cycle" (Carskadon & Dement, 2000, p. 20). Meanwhile, "the duration of REM sleep periods tends to increase with each successive cycle" (Aldrich, 1999, p. 14), so that the average period of REM sleep ends up being about 22 minutes long (cf. Carskadon & Dement, 2000). Brief arousals and awakenings can occur from any of the sleep stages (Aldrich, 1999). The term *sleep latency* refers to the time that it takes to fall asleep; *sleep efficiency* refers to "the ratio of actual time spent asleep to time spent in bed" (American Psychiatric Association, 2000, p. 598); and *sleep continuity* refers to "the overall balance of sleep and wakefulness during a night of sleep" (American Psychiatric Association, 2000, p. 598), with better continuity indicating "consolidated sleep with little wakefulness" (American Psychiatric Association, 2000, p. 598). "Wakefulness within sleep usually accounts for less than 5% of the night" (Carskadon & Dement, 2000, p. 20). Stage 1 sleep constitutes 2% to 5% of sleep, stage 2 is 45% to 55%, stage 3 is 3% to 8%, stage 4 is 10% to 15%, and REM sleep constitutes 20% to 25% of a night's sleep (Carskadon & Dement, 2000).

The proportions of different sleep stages as a percentage of a night's sleep given in the previous paragraph are those for young adults. Whereas "no consistent male versus female distinctions have been found in the normal pattern of sleep in young adults" (Carskadon & Dement, 2000, p. 19), as mentioned at the outset, there are differences in the physiological patterns of sleep associated with age. Although the alteration of NREM sleep and REM sleep is present in newborn infants, it has a period of only 50 to 60 minutes (Carskadon & Dement, 2000). Infants often enter the cycle through REM sleep, which "constitutes approximately 50% of the sleep period" (Hirshkowitz et al., 1997, p. 22) and declines until adolescence when it stabilizes at adult levels, which are "maintained well into healthy old age" (Carskadon & Dement, 2000, p. 21). The EEG patterns of NREM sleep emerge "over the first 2 to 6 months of life" (Carskadon & Dement, 2000, p. 21), with slow-wave sleep being "maximal in young children" (Carskadon & Dement, 2000, p. 21) and decreasing "markedly with age" (Carskadon & Dement, 2000, p. 21). Indeed, slow-wave sleep may no longer be present by age 60, with women maintaining slow-wave sleep later into life than men (Carskadon & Dement, 2000). "Total sleep time declines throughout the life span, and after middle age, wakefulness intermixed with sleep . . . begins to increase in many individuals" (Hirshkowitz et al., 1997, p. 25). Variability in the characteristics of sleep increases in late adulthood, so that it is difficult to make "generalizations such as those made for young adults" (Carskadon & Dement, 2000, p. 21).

SLEEP MENTATION

An understanding that sleep is neither a passive nor a homogeneous physiological process means that we need to consider mental activity during sleep in the context of the sleep stages in which it occurs. In this section, we shall consider arousal from sleep, some states of diminished mental functioning, and begin a discussion of dreaming that we will continue in chapter 4.

Arousal

The possibility of being aroused from sleep by external stimulation depends on the sleep stage and the meaningfulness of the stimulus. It is easiest to awaken someone from stage 1, most difficult from stage 4, with the difficulty of waking someone from REM sleep being variable (Aldrich, 1999). In particular, "it is nearly impossible" (Carskadon & Dement, 2000, p. 21) to awaken young children from the slow-wave sleep of the "night's first sleep cycle" (Carskadon & Dement, 2000, p. 21). In some studies, "using meaningless stimuli" (Roger Broughton, 1986, p. 464), it has been found that the thresholds for awakening from REM sleep were higher than those for awakening from stages 3 and 4 of NREM sleep. However, in other studies it has been shown that individuals can be easily awakened from REM sleep by stimuli that are significant to them. "An example of a particularly effective stimulus is the playing of a tape recording of her infant's crying to a sleeping mother" (Roger Broughton, 1986, p. 464). In general, meaningful stimuli are more effective than meaningless stimuli in evoking K complexes. Both K complexes and sleep spindles have been characterized as "incomplete arousal responses" (Roger Broughton, 1986, p. 464) and thought by some investigators to represent the activity of mechanisms that serve to keep a person asleep (Carlson, 1994). There are other event-related wave forms corresponding to the automatic detection of changes in sound whose presence has been used to infer that auditory stimuli are processed without awareness in REM sleep (Nashida et al., 2000). What these data collectively suggest is that we monitor at least some sensory stimuli while we sleep and wake up if they are too intense or of sufficient significance to us (Roger Broughton, 1986).

Coma is an altered state of consciousness "in which awareness of self and environment is lost and there is no meaningful response to external stimuli or inner needs" (Aldrich, 1999, p. 16). In other words, coma is a condition in which there is neither consciousness$_1$ nor behavioral consciousness$_2$ and in which the presence of subjective consciousness$_2$ and consciousness$_3$ cannot be tested. Although there are superficial similarities between sleep and coma, coma is associated with decreased cerebral metabolic activity and an inability to arouse someone through the use of stimulation, whereas in sleep the brain metabolism is only slightly altered and a person can be aroused from sleep with appropriate stimulation except perhaps during slow-wave sleep or in some cases of "severe sleep deprivation" (Aldrich, 1999, p. 16). Unlike coma, sleep is natural, transient, periodic, and reversible. Coma may be followed by *persistent vegetative state* in which physiological functions concerned with maintaining the body are preserved, including sleep–wake cycles, "but there is no evidence of awareness or cognition, and cerebral metabolism is markedly reduced" (Aldrich, 1999, p. 16). Sleep–wake cycles are also preserved in the related condition of *akinetic mutism*, in which, during wakefulness, those with the condition "maintain an alert appearance, but they do not exhibit signs of awareness or cognition" (Aldrich, 1999, p. 16). Normal sleep is clearly distinguishable from these pathological conditions.

Dreaming

Of course, when we think of sleep, we usually think of dreaming, the experiences that go on for us as we sleep. In other words, even with diminished consciousness$_1$ and usually absent behavioral consciousness$_2$, there are still subjective consciousness$_2$ and consciousness$_3$, which go on, at least for some people, some of the time. But how is dreaming related to the sleep stages? In Eugene Aserinsky's initial sleep laboratory studies, when participants were awakened from REM sleep, 20 of 27 times (74%) they reported "detailed dreams usually involving visual imagery" (Aserinsky & Kleitman, 1953, p. 273), whereas when they were awakened from NREM sleep only 2 of 23 (9%) reported such dreams, with two others reporting having had " 'the feeling of having dreamed,' but with inability to recollect any detail of the dream" (Aserinsky & Kleitman, 1953, pp. 273–274). For a while, dreaming became identified with REM sleep (Foulkes, 1996). More careful investigation, however, has revealed that the distinction between NREM and REM sleep mentation is not so clear-cut. For example, using a portable computerized "sleep monitoring system" (Stickgold, Pace-Schott, & Hobson, 1994, p. 16) called "Nightcap" (Stickgold et al., 1994, p. 17), which participants use while sleeping in their own beds at home, a study was made of dream reports following spontaneous awakenings. In this case, 88 of 149 reports (59%) were from REM sleep awakenings, whereas 61 of 149 reports (41%) were from NREM sleep awakenings. The REM sleep dream reports were significantly longer than the NREM sleep reports, with a median length of 148 words for REM sleep reports "compared to 21 words for NREM reports" (Stickgold et al., 1994, p. 24). However, not all NREM sleep reports were short, with 17% of reports longer than 100 words resulting from NREM sleep awakenings. However, "the longest NREM reports . . . were obtained within the first 15 [minutes] of NREM periods" (Stickgold et al., 1994, p. 25). In other words, it is possible that the NREM sleep reports resulted from transitional periods of sleep in which "some aspects of REM physiology [continued] to exert an influence" (Stickgold et al., 1994, p. 25) or that "reports given early in NREM periods actually reflect sleep mentation from the preceding REM period" (Stickgold et al., 1994, p. 25).

Some of the ambiguities of NREM sleep were addressed in a sleep laboratory slow-wave sleep dream study in which participants "were awakened after 10 minutes of continuous delta sleep . . . provided that at least 30 minutes from the initial sleep onset had elapsed" (Cavallero, Cicogna, Natale, Occhionero, & Zito, 1992, p. 563), or they "were awakened during the second REM period, 10 minutes after the appearance of the first clear burst of rapid eye movements" (Cavallero et al., 1992, p. 563). The first night in the sleep laboratory was an adaptation night, then participants were awakened in each of the conditions as indicated, once per night, on two nonconsecutive nights. If no dream was reported on awakening, they would return to the sleep laboratory to try again. After repeated attempts, 10 of 60 participants were unable to report a dream in the slow-wave sleep condition. The average dream recall rates for all 60 participants was 89% for REM sleep and 65% for slow-wave sleep. Excluding 10 participants who could not recall a slow-wave sleep dream, a comparison was made of the slow-wave sleep and REM sleep dreams of the remaining 50 participants. The researchers found that REM sleep dream reports were significantly longer, had more characters other than oneself as well as having more undefined characters such as groups of people, and contained more emotion than SWS dream reports (Cavallero et al., 1992).

Why have fewer dreams been reported from NREM sleep than REM sleep? Is it that dreams are present only occasionally during NREM sleep or that NREM sleep is such that whatever dream activity is present, it is easily forgotten on arousal? The investigators in the slow-wave sleep dream study advanced two arguments in favor of the latter hypothesis. First, they said that "some of the NREM reports of our subjects [were] practically indistinguishable from typical REM dreams" (Cavallero et al., 1992, p. 565) and, second, that even when they could not recall a dream on awakening from SWS, participants would frequently make comments such as "definitely there was something going on, but now it is gone" (Cavallero et al., 1992,

p. 565). The investigators offered the suggestion that "mental activity is continuously present during sleep and that cortical activation (even if synchronized as in SWS) is a sufficient condition for dream production" (Cavallero et al., 1992, p. 565). However, the degree to which that mental activity is elaborated is loosely correlated "with the level of cortical activation of each particular sleep stage" (Cavallero et al., 1992, p. 565). In particular, during SWS memory resources are at low levels of activation, whereas during REM sleep they are high. Greater access to memory in REM sleep means that a greater number of associated memory elements, such as those of people and emotions, can be present, resulting in longer, more narrative dream reports. These ideas support a cognitive theory of dreaming that we shall briefly consider in chapter 4.

THE PURPOSE OF SLEEP

For all the time that we spend in sleep, it is not at all clear why we sleep. In this section we will first consider the research demonstrating the need for sleep and then examine some explanations for the occurrence of sleep.

Sleep Need

That there is an apparent sleep need has been established in both human and animal studies. The most obvious consequence of total sleep deprivation is sleepiness (Bonnet, 2000), with marked decreases in cognitive performance being more insidious (Everson, 1997). Initially, poor task performance can be overcome by motivation, but after about 48 to 64 hours of total sleep deprivation "poor performance cannot be overcome by motivational forces" (Everson, 1997, p. 38). Longer periods of sleep loss have greater impacts on task performance than shorter periods, with "speed of performance" (Bonnet, 2000, p. 53) being more affected than accuracy. Tasks that are most affected by sleep loss are "long, monotonous, without feedback, externally paced, newly learned, and [contain] a memory component" (Bonnet, 2000, p. 58). Mood appears to be more strongly affected than cognitive ability, which in turn appears to be more strongly affected than motor activity (Bonnet, 2000). Mood changes can occur after a single night of sleep loss, "worsen as the sleep deprivation is prolonged" (Everson, 1997, p. 39), and result in "emotional instability" (Everson, 1997, p. 39) during the time of sleep loss. Misperceptions and hallucinations, "primarily visual and tactile" (Everson, 1997, p. 39), are commonly reported, sometimes after only 48 hours of total sleep deprivation, although they become more intense as sleep loss progresses. In one study, after 205 hours of total sleep deprivation, the participants experienced lapses in alertness, which sometimes consisted of transient periods of disorientation ending in confusion, amnesia, or reports of dreams (Everson, 1997). In studies of partial sleep loss, investigators have found rapid functional impairment with nightly sleep periods of 5 hours or less and the possibility of measurable decrements following 6-hour sleep periods (Bonnet, 2000).

The long-term effects of sleep loss could be serious. In studies in which rats have been deprived of sleep, the animals "developed a characteristic appearance including disheveled, clumped fur; skin lesions on tail and paws; and weight loss" (Bonnet, 2000, p. 60) in spite of "large increases in food intake" (Bonnet, 2000, p. 60). Meanwhile, body temperature dropped "by as much as 2°C" (Bonnet, 2000, p. 60), and all of the rats "died (or were sacrificed at imminent death) within 11 to 22 days of deprivation" (Bonnet, 2000, p. 60). It is possible that the deterioration of functioning seen in human participants is an initial psychological and physiological breakdown that, if allowed to continue, would progress to death (cf. Everson, 1997).

With the ability to monitor sleep stages, it is possible to deliberately deprive someone of a particular stage of sleep without changing the total sleep time. This has been done numerous times with REM sleep with a participant in a study being awakened every time she would enter REM sleep. What researchers have found is that the proclivity to enter REM sleep increases with REM *sleep deprivation*, so that the number of awakenings has to increase every night of the study to maintain the deprivation. Furthermore, a REM *sleep rebound* is found during undisturbed recovery sleep, with increased amounts of REM sleep for three recovery nights found in one study. Less frequently, participants have been selectively deprived of stage 4 sleep. As with REM sleep deprivation, there is pressure to enter stage 4 sleep and a subsequent *stage 4 rebound*. However, stage 4 sleep is only increased on the first recovery night, whereas REM sleep, for which there has not been deprivation, is increased on the second and third recovery nights, according to the same study in which REM sleep deprivation was investigated. Recovery from stage 4 sleep deprivation is similar to the pattern of recovery from total sleep deprivation (Bonnet, 2000). These findings suggest that there is a homeostatic process that seeks to restore through SWS and REM sleep whatever it is that becomes depleted during waking. In other words, there must be a purpose served by sleep (cf. Benington, 2000).

There is another factor that plays a role in the length and timing of sleep stages—namely, the presence of biological rhythms. *Circadian rhythms* are approximately 24-hour cycles generated by an internal *circadian pacemaker system* that constrains a multiplicity of physiological and behavioral events including sleep and waking, "endocrine secretions, body temperature regulation, sensory processing, and cognitive performance" (Mistlberger & Rusak, 2000, p. 321). It has been proposed that sleep is regulated by both homeostatic and circadian processes. During the day and subsequently as long as waking continues, sleep need increases and with it the homeostatically regulated pressure for slow-wave sleep. The circadian process increases the propensity for sleep during the night and decreases it during the day. Thus, the circadian rhythm helps to maintain sleep during the night as sleep pressure from the homeostatic process declines, and it helps to maintain alertness during the day as sleep pressure escalates (Borbély & Achermann, 2000; see also Aldrich, 1999).

Explanations for Sleep

But why do we need to sleep at all? Perhaps the most intuitive explanation is that sleep has a biologically restorative function. The brain seems to be resting, at least during slow-wave sleep. The presence of delta waves corresponds to lowered brain activity as evidenced by cerebral metabolic rates and blood flow rates that, in stage 4 sleep, are 75% of what they are during waking (Carlson, 1994). The activity of the sympathetic division of the autonomic nervous system, a subsystem of the nervous system that induces physiological activation in the body (cf. Carlson, 1994), is decreased by about 30% to 50% during slow-wave sleep compared to wakefulness (Aldrich, 1999). A restorative function for sleep has been suggested by "increased rates of cerebral protein synthesis" (W. Schwartz, 1997, p. 5) during slow-wave sleep. Slow-wave sleep has also been associated with the secretion of growth hormone, which, because of its particular importance for stimulating children's growth, may explain why "SWS is high during children's peak developmental years and declines (or can even disappear) with advancing age" (Hirshkowitz et al., 1997, p. 31). Because SWS appears to be "linked with cerebral recovery" (Horne, 1988, p. 312) and because it occurs predominantly during the beginning of a night's sleep, it has been suggested that the first three cycles of sleep be considered to be *core sleep* that is necessary for restoration of the brain and the remainder of the sleep cycle be thought of as *optional sleep* whose purpose is to occupy unproductive hours of the night (Horne, 1988).

The suggestion that there is an optional component to sleep that is behaviorally determined is consistent with adaptive theories in which sleep is considered to be an adaptive response to environmental conditions developed in animals over the course of evolution. After all, why not be asleep, conserving energy, rather than stumbling around in the dark getting eaten by animals with better night vision? The problem with this theory is that sleep persists in species even when they would be better off without it. For example, "the Indus dolphin . . . has become blind, presumably because vision is not useful in the animal's environment" (Carlson, 1994, p. 260). It is forced to constantly keep swimming "because of the dangerous currents and the vast quantities of debris carried by the river" (Carlson, 1994, p. 260), so one would expect it to lose sleep as well as sight, yet it sleeps for "a total of 7 hours a day, in naps of 4–60 seconds each" (Carlson, 1994, p. 260). As another example, for both the bottlenose dolphin and the porpoise, the "cerebral hemispheres take turns sleeping, presumably because that strategy always permits at least one hemisphere to be alert" (Carlson, 1994, p. 260). Although sleep may be adaptive in some situations, there are others in which it is not, so it appears that there must be other reasons for it.

Maybe the purpose of sleep has to do with the maintenance of cognitive processing. Perhaps neural circuits are restructured during REM sleep as a result of experiences acquired during the day, which could explain why infants spend so much time in REM sleep (Carlson, 1994, p. 265). A number of possibilities have been proposed. Perhaps "the synapses being strengthened are those which had been activated during previous waking" (Benington, 2000, p. 964; see also M. A. Wilson & McNaughton, 1994). Or perhaps, during sleep, those synapses that "are not adequately stimulated during the neuronal activity of waking" (Benington, 2000, p. 964) get a workout so as not to be lost. Or perhaps the reverse takes place, that the neuronal activity in REM sleep "may weaken synaptic connections that are now no longer needed" (Benington, 2000, p. 962). In animal studies, it has been shown that REM sleep increases above baseline levels following successful learning (C. Smith, 1996). In a study with college students, an increase in the number of rapid eye movements was found three to five days "after the end of their examinations" (C. Smith, 1996, p. 54) relative to when they were not taking courses (C. Smith & Lapp, 1991). On the other hand, when participants were deprived of REM sleep the first or second night following the acquisition of a complex logic task, then there was memory loss for the task (C. Smith, 1995). In other words, REM sleep appears to facilitate retention of learning even if the actual neuronal processes by which that occurs are not known.

Using a computer analogy, it has been suggested that the brain goes "off line" during sleep to do whatever work it has to do on itself as evidenced by a diminished ability to remember what goes on during sleep (W. Schwartz, 1997). In one study, participants monitored with a polysomnograph were presented with word pairs at 1-minute intervals through speakers located by the bed in which they were lying and "were requested to repeat each word pair aloud . . . after hearing it" (Wyatt, Bootzin, Anthony, & Stevenson, 1992, p. 113). In the course of this task, participants fell asleep and were subsequently awakened after either 30 seconds or 10 minutes of sleep. When asked to recall the word pairs, participants who had been awakened after 10 minutes of sleep showed impaired performance for the word pairs presented within 3 minutes before sleep onset. The same decrement in performance was not noted for those who were awakened after only 30 seconds of sleep (Wyatt et al., 1992). It may be that sleep interferes with the consolidation of short-term memory into long-term memory. Whatever the explanation, we are unlikely to remember what happened during the few minutes before falling asleep after having slept for about 10 minutes. This memory impairment includes the inability to remember the moment of falling asleep, forgetting conversations that occurred in the middle of the night, and having difficulty remembering dreams (Carskadon & Dement, 2000). We cannot remember what goes on for a few minutes before sleep; we often have difficulty remembering what, if anything, happened during NREM sleep; and sometimes we cannot remember our experiences during REM sleep. It appears that we periodically lose subjective consciousness$_2$ during sleep so that some necessary activity can take place. But we still do not know exactly what that activity is that could not take place in the presence of awareness. We still do not know the purpose of sleep.

THE NEUROBIOLOGY OF SLEEP

Let us turn our attention to the neurobiology of sleep by briefly considering the neural mechanisms that govern the sleep stages and the effects of drugs on sleep. What happens in the brain when we sleep? What is the underlying neural activity of the sleep stages? What happens to sleep under conditions of intoxication with drugs such as opium or caffeine? In addition to providing us with some interesting information, answers to these questions will give us a feeling for the manner in which the characteristics of alterations of consciousness can be modulated by biological processes.

The Neural Mechanisms of Sleep

Changes in the EEG from waking to sleep and between sleep stages reflect changes in underlying patterns of neuronal activity. Some regions of the brain become more active, whereas others become more passive. In one sleep laboratory study, the cerebral blood flow of 11 participants was measured during REM sleep, then the participants were awakened and questioned about whether or not they had been dreaming. In all cases, they reported having had dreams. The investigators found a 4% increase in blood flow in the "associative visual area" (Madsen et al., 1991, p. 503), which is toward the back of the cortex, and 5% to 9% decreases in blood flow in "lower frontal cortical areas" (Madsen et al., 1991, p. 504). The relative activation of the associative visual area while dreaming during REM sleep is not surprising given that the associative visual area is known to be correlated with the processing of "complex visual material" (Madsen et al., 1991, p. 506). The lower frontal cortical areas appear to be involved in the management of emotions and motivation, the suppression of "interference from internal and external stimuli" (Madsen et al., 1991, p. 506), and "the temporal organization of behavior and cognition" (Madsen et al., 1991, p. 506). Thus, some of the unique features of dreams, such as frequent temporal changes, may reflect the relatively decreased functioning of the lower frontal cortical areas of the brain. Similar results were found in another study in which the authors postulated that the "brain mechanisms subserving REM sleep" (Braun et al., 1998, p. 91) formed their own processing system dissociated from both actual sensory input and high-level organizational control.

The regulation of circadian rhythms and sleep is carried out by the brain through intricate interactions of groups of nerve cells. These interactions include a decrease during NREM sleep of the activity of neural circuits originating in the brainstem that normally increase alertness and organismic activity (Carlson, 1994). In addition, unlike waking and REM sleep, during NREM sleep, the transmission of sensory information is strongly reduced by the thalamus (Steriade, 2000). Thus the physiology of NREM sleep is consistent with decreased arousal and decreased responsiveness to environmental stimuli irrespective of their significance to the sleeper. REM sleep is largely controlled by neural mechanisms also located within the brainstem (Carlson, 1994). It turns out that the neural pathways involved in turning the components of REM sleep on and off are partially separable so that, for example, it is possible to have *REM sleep without atonia* (J. M. Siegel, 2000) or its opposite, muscle atonia in the absence of REM sleep. Dysfunction of specific pathways appears to lead to variations in waking and sleep events, as we shall see later. Sensory information is inhibited from reaching awareness during REM sleep, not through blocking of the incoming signal at the thalamus but by discriminative processing in the cerebral cortex (Oswald, Taylor, & Treisman, 1960) with the result, as we have already noted, that a sleeper can sometimes awaken from REM sleep in response to a meaningful stimulus.

Sleep and waking are affected by a variety of neurotransmitters found in the neural pathways of the brain. For example, levels of the neurotransmitters *noradrenalin* and *serotonin* decrease during NREM sleep to minimum values for REM sleep in groups of synapses associated with arousal. These decreases allow the executive mechanism for REM sleep, which uses the neurotransmitter *acetylcholine*, to become active (Carlson, 1994). There are, of course, other neurotransmitters involved in complex interactions of numerous neural pathways to bring about the physiological events associated with waking and sleeping (Aldrich, 1999).

It is important to note these biological changes during sleep to realize that differences in patterns of neural functioning could be associated with phenomena occurring during other alterations of consciousness. If areas of the brain are activated during REM sleep, thereby creating compelling visual images while other areas necessary for editing and making sense of those images are simultaneously somewhat deactivated, could something similar be occurring in alterations of consciousness such as shamanic journeying, in which events apparently seem so real yet contain unusual elements? Similarly, if the blocking of incoming sensory information can occur during NREM sleep, could it not occur as well under other conditions such as during hypnosis? If a change in the balance of neurotransmitters can activate a pattern of neural activity associated with REM sleep, could changes to the neurochemistry of the brain by exogenous substances such as psychedelic drugs create stable patterns of neural activity with their own phenomenology that are rarely experienced otherwise? In fact, would there not be neural mechanisms, not necessarily the same ones as those involved in sleep, that would correspond to the various characteristics of the different alterations of consciousness? Probably yes. But is that necessarily always true? Is that true, for example, in the case of near-death experiences?

The Effects of Drugs on Sleep

If there is chemical interference of neuronal activity in the brain, then we would expect sleep and waking to be affected. The use of *amphetamine* potentiates the effects of noradrenalin and serotonin through a number of mechanisms, so it is not surprising that its use is associated with "arousal and sleeplessness" (Carlson, 1994, p. 279). While intoxicated, sleep latency is increased, sleep continuity is worse, there are more body movements, the total amount of sleep is reduced, and there are decreases in SWS and REM sleep. During withdrawal from chronic amphetamine use, there is excessive daytime sleepiness, night-time sleep is prolonged, and there may be both SWS and REM sleep rebound (American Psychiatric Association, 2000).

Cocaine slows down the reuptake of noradrenalin (Carlson, 1994), thereby increasing its activity and producing insomnia followed by excessive sleep during withdrawal from a binge. The total amount of sleep can be "drastically reduced" (American Psychiatric Association, 2000, p. 658) during acute intoxication, "with only short bouts of very disrupted sleep" (American Psychiatric Association, 2000, p. 658).

Opioids are drugs such as opium, morphine, and heroin that are derived from the poppy plant and synthetic substances such as methadone whose effects are similar to those of the naturally derived drugs. They have multiple effects in a complex network of neural systems (Gillin & Drummond, 2000), including the stimulation of *opiate receptors* implicated in analgesia and the activation of neurons using the neurotransmitter *dopamine* that are associated with the experience of pleasure (cf. Carlson, 1994). Initially, opioids "reduce total sleep time and REM sleep" (Gillin & Drummond, 2000, p. 1192), but then tolerance develops so that, for example, "the REM suppressing effects to morphine are lost within a week ... although the arousing effects may persist" (Gillin & Drummond, 2000, p. 1192). The initial REM-sleep-suppressing effects of morphine may result, in part, from the inhibition of acetylcholine in brain mechanisms regulating REM sleep (Gillin & Drummond, 2000).

There are drugs that affect sleep without having a direct effect on sleep mechanisms using the neurotransmitters noradrenalin, serotonin, and acetylcholine. *Caffeine* is a drug found in coffee, tea, cola, chocolate, pain relievers, "cold remedies, and stimulants" (Gillin & Drummond, 2000, p. 1187), which can cause insomnia apparently by blocking the action of *adenosine*, which may function as a sleep-promoting substance in the brain (Gillin & Drummond, 2000). Under the effects of caffeine, it may take longer to fall asleep, there may be increased wakefulness, and decreased slow-wave sleep (American Psychiatric Association, 2000).

Alcohol is known to have multiple effects in the body, including ameliorating anxiety by apparently sensitizing a subtype of receptors of a receptor complex that uses yet another neurotransmitter, *gamma-aminobutyric acid (GABA)*, which is used in neural pathways that have widespread inhibitory effects on other neural networks in the brain (Carlson, 1994). Alcohol also increases the activity of some dopaminergic neurons associated with the experience of pleasure and "destabilizes the [membranes] of cells, interfering with their functions" (Carlson, 1994, p. 589). In nonalcoholics, ingestion of four or five drinks of alcohol "in the hours before bedtime" (Gillin & Drummond, 2000, p. 1180) decreases the length of time it takes to fall asleep, increases NREM sleep, and decreases REM sleep during the early part of the night. However, as alcohol concentrations in the blood diminish during the night, the previously inebriated individual "is likely to be in withdrawal and to experience shallow, disrupted sleep, increased REM sleep, dream recall or nightmares" (Gillin & Drummond, 2000, p. 1180), and general physiological arousal that can include increased heart rate and sweating. Alcoholics, on the other hand, have "long sleep latencies; poor sleep efficiencies; and decreased total sleep, slow-wave sleep (SWS), and REM sleep" (Gillin & Drummond, 2000, p. 1181).

Of course, drugs can be used to try to improve sleep, in which case they are called *hypnotics*. The drugs of choice, such as *benzodiazepines*, activate *benzodiazepine receptors* on the GABA receptor complex, thereby increasing inhibition in the brain. These drugs "hasten sleep onset, reduce wakefulness after sleep onset, and reduce the amount of light (Stage 1) sleep" (Roehrs & Roth, 1997, p. 342). Withdrawal symptoms such as insomnia and nightmares as well as more serious problems such as seizures and death can occur on discontinuation of high-dose use of hypnotics. Discontinuation of low-dose use of benzodiazepines can cause problems during withdrawal such as "anxiety, agitation, insomnia, nightmares" (Gillin & Drummond, 2000, p. 1186), heart problems, loss of appetite, "muscle spasms, increased sensitivity to light and sounds" (Gillin & Drummond, 2000, p. 1186), and abnormal sensations, which "can last for months and can be severe and disabling" (Gillin & Drummond, 2000, p. 1186).

There is a class of drugs known as *selective serotonin reuptake inhibitors (SSRIs)* used in the treatment of depression, whose primary effect is to block the reuptake of serotonin so that it cannot be taken back up into the cell from which it was released. The result is that serotonin remains in the synapses longer, continuing to stimulate the next cell in the communication sequence. Because levels of serotonin must decrease during sleep and, in particular, decrease for the acetylcholinergic pathways associated with REM sleep to become activated, we would expect that SSRIs would interfere with sleep. And that is indeed what has been found, although the mechanism is not necessarily the obvious one. SSRIs worsen sleep, generally increase wakefulness, and decrease total sleep time (Schweitzer, 2000).

A number of detrimental effects on sleep have been attributed to an SSRI called *fluoxetine*. In one study 41 clinical outpatients with depression were evaluated for nocturnal eye movements and muscle tension in a sleep laboratory before and after four to five weeks of daily treatment with 20 milligrams of fluoxetine. "Every subject showed increased activity from baseline in at least one measure of oculomotor activity" (Armitage, Trivedi, & Rush, 1995, p. 161). Fourteen participants had increases in eye movements and muscle tone in all sleep stages, 29 had an increased number of eye movements, 30 had increased size of eye movements, and 33 had increased muscle tension. "The eye movements induced by fluoxetine are not classic, binocularly symmetrical, rapid eye movements" (Armitage et al., 1995, p. 163) but "are better characterized as medium to fast eye movements" (Armitage et al., 1995, p. 163). Fluoxetine intoxication leads to increased eye movements even in sleep stages 2 to 4 of NREM sleep (Armitage et al., 1995). In another study, the polysomnographic records of 9 depressed hospital inpatients being treated with 10 to 80 milligrams of fluoxetine who were complaining of insomnia and fatigue were compared with 6 depressed inpatients not being treated with fluoxetine but also complaining of insomnia and fatigue. Those being treated with fluoxetine had worse sleep efficiency, a greater number of eye movements during stages 2 to 4 of NREM sleep, and took longer to enter REM sleep (Dorsey, Lukas, & Cunningham, 1996).

The detrimental effects of fluoxetine extend to disturbing muscle activity. *Periodic limb movements* are "four or more" (Montplaisir, Nicolas, Godbout, & Walters, 2000, p. 744) movements of the legs and sometimes arms (Aldrich, 1999), each of which lasts from .5 to 5 seconds and is separated by an interval of 4 to 90 seconds from temporally adjacent ones (Montplaisir et al., 2000). Periodic limb movements are found most frequently during stages 1 and 2 of NREM sleep, less frequently during SWS, and are "generally absent" (Aldrich, 1999, p. 177) from REM sleep. *Periodic limb movement disorder* is diagnosed if there are more than five periodic limb movements an hour for each hour of sleep (cf. Montplaisir et al., 2000). In the study with depressed hospital inpatients, 4 of the 9 participants being treated with fluoxetine had "clinically significant" (Dorsey et al., 1996, p. 440) periodic limb movement disorder. "Some aperiodic leg movements also were observed" (Dorsey et al., 1996, p. 440) in the fluoxetine group, and "elevation of overall muscle tone was apparent in all fluoxetine recordings" (Dorsey et al., 1996, p. 440).

Results somewhat similar to those just described were found in a study of 6 children and adolescents with an average age of 12 years tested before and after about 11 months of using 10 to 20 milligrams of fluoxetine daily. The percentage of stage 1 sleep almost doubled, the number of arousals increased, the number of eye movements during REM sleep increased, and there were five times as many leg movements with four of the six children meeting criteria for periodic leg movement disorder (Armitage, Emslie, & Rintelmann, 1997). Much as it looks as though that should be the case, it is not clear whether these effects of fluoxetine can be attributed directly to the potentiation of serotonin in neural pathways regulating sleep or whether the effects are, in fact, more indirect—for example, through serotonergic effects on dopaminergic pathways (Armitage et al., 1995).

SLEEP DISORDERS

If sleep disruptions from drug use, either through intoxication or withdrawal, cause "clinically significant distress or impairment in social, occupational, or other important areas of functioning" (American Psychiatric Association, 2000, p. 660), then they would be classified as a *substance-induced sleep disorder*. In the *Diagnostic and Statistical Manual of Mental Disorders* (*DSM-IV-TR*; American Psychiatric Association, 2000), there have also been listed sleep disorders due to a general medical condition, sleep disorders related to another mental disorder, and primary sleep disorders. *Primary sleep disorders* have been presumed to be caused by "abnormalities in sleep–wake generating or timing mechanisms" (American Psychiatric Association, 2000, p. 597) and have been themselves divided into *dyssomnias*, "characterized by abnormalities in the amount, quality, or timing of sleep" (American Psychiatric Association, 2000, p. 597), among which have been included primary insomnia, narcolepsy, and breathing-related sleep disorder; and *parasomnias*, "characterized by abnormal behavioral or physiological events occurring in association with sleep, specific sleep stages, or sleep–wake transitions" (American Psychiatric Association, 2000, p. 597), among which have been included nightmare disorder, sleep terror disorder, and sleepwalking disorder.

Narcolepsy

One of the oldest known sleep disorders is *narcolepsy* (Dement, 2000), a condition in which an individual experiences irresistible sleep attacks of "unintended sleep in inappropriate situations" (American Psychiatric Association, 2000, p. 610). One moment, a person will be talking to someone or driving a car, the next, she will fall over sound asleep (American Psychiatric Association, 2000). After a few minutes to possibly more than an hour, she wakes up relatively refreshed with "a refractory period of 1 to several hours before the next episode occurs" (Guilleminault & Anagnos, 2000, p. 677). Varying degrees of daytime sleepiness can also be present that cannot be entirely eradicated no matter how much sleep a person gets (Aldrich, 1999). *Cataplexy* is a second symptom of narcolepsy. During a *cataplectic attack* there is bilateral muscle weakness that can range in severity from fleeting sensations of weakness throughout the body, to "a slight buckling of the knees" (Guilleminault & Anagnos, 2000, p. 677), stuttering, or clumsiness, to "a complete loss of muscle tone" (Guilleminault & Anagnos, 2000, p. 677), possibly leading "to total body collapse and the risk of serious injuries" (Guilleminault & Anagnos, 2000, p. 677). Cataplectic attacks can occur apparently spontaneously or can be brought on by emotions such as laughter or anger, "stress, fatigue, or heavy meals" (Guilleminault & Anagnos, 2000, p. 677) and can last a few seconds to 30 minutes. Perhaps it is becoming clear what happens in narcolepsy. As a person falls asleep, not exclusively but often, she goes directly into REM sleep rather than going through the NREM stages of sleep. Cataplexy occurs when the mechanisms for muscle atonia become activated without the person even having fallen asleep (cf. Carskadon & Dement, 2000).

A third possible symptom of narcolepsy that can result from a disconnection of REM sleep components is sleep paralysis. *Sleep paralysis* is "partial or total paralysis lasting a few seconds or minutes that occurs during transitions between sleep and wakefulness" (Aldrich, 1999, p. 155). What happens in sleep paralysis is similar to what happens in cataplexy except that it happens immediately before or after sleep. Sleep paralysis can also occur outside the context of narcolepsy, with 40% to 50% of individuals in the general population having experienced at least a single episode of sleep paralysis at some time in their lives (American Psychiatric Association, 2000). Sometimes associated with sleep paralysis in the context of narcolepsy while at other times occurring independently of it at the interface of sleep and waking (Aldrich, 1999), there can be vivid images that are called *hypnagogic* when they occur on falling asleep and *hypnopompic* when they occur on awakening. They are usually visual but can also be auditory or kinesthetic (American Psychiatric Association, 2000). There may be impressions of being rubbed or touched, "changes in location of body parts" (Guilleminault & Anagnos, 2000, p. 676), and *exosomatic* experiences—that is to say, experiences that appear to occur outside of one's body, including seeing one's body lying some distance below oneself (cf. Guilleminault & Anagnos, 2000). The prevalence rate of hypnagogic and hypnopompic images among the general population is approximately 10% to 15% (American Psychiatric Association, 2000). We shall return to a discussion of hypnagogic and hypnopompic images in chapter 4. In some cases of narcolepsy, sleep can be so disrupted that those with narcolepsy feel that "they spend the entire night drifting in and out of sleep with nightmares, intermittent hallucinations, and episodes of paralysis" (Aldrich, 1999, p. 156).

Both behavioral and drug treatments have been used for narcolepsy. Behavioral treatment strategies consist of 15- to 20-minute naps every four hours during the day and good sleep hygiene, which is briefly characterized in a subsequent section about insomnia. Drug treatments can include the use of stimulants such as amphetamines to offset daytime sleepiness and medications such as fluoxetine to counteract the muscle atonia associated with cataplexy (Guilleminault & Anagnos, 2000). Indeed, such use of fluoxetine is an example of a drug whose side-effects for one condition become the curative effects for another, highlighting the question of the relative dangers and benefits of drugs.

Sleep Apnea

Another long-standing sleep disorder is *obstructive sleep apnea syndrome* (Dement, 2000), a form of *breathing-related sleep disorder* in which a person cannot sleep and breathe at the same time, resulting in a poor night's sleep and daytime sleepiness. What happens is that a person falls asleep, her muscles relax, and the upper airway becomes blocked so that she cannot breathe (American Psychiatric Association, 2000). While she is not breathing, the level of carbon dioxide in the blood increases until the increase is registered by the nervous system, which wakes the person up enough to restore muscle tension, thereby opening the upper airway and allowing her to breathe (cf. Carlson, 1994). From what we have said previously regarding memory for events before sleep onset, such transient arousals are unlikely to be remembered by a person in the morning. However, someone present while the person is sleeping could hear "loud snores or brief gasps that alternate with episodes of silence that usually last 20–30 seconds" (American Psychiatric Association, 2000, p. 616) but can be "as long as 60–90 seconds" (American Psychiatric Association, 2000, p. 616), terminated by "snores, gasps, moans or mumbling, or whole-body movements" (American Psychiatric Association, 2000, p. 616). The throat does not always fall completely shut, causing apnea, but may close only partially, as evidenced by snoring, in which case the condition is called *hypopnea* (American Psychiatric Association, 2000). Sometimes neither apnea nor hypopnea occur, nor does a drop in the oxygen content of the blood that usually accompanies them, it is just that upper-airway resistance is increased, leading to "sleep fragmentation" (Sanders, 2000, p. 879).

Sleep apnea can have serious consequences. In one study, participants with severe sleep apnea had 13.0 motor vehicle accidents per million kilometers whereas for those with milder sleep apnea that number was 1.1, and for those in a control group without sleep apnea it was 0.8 (Horstmann, Hess, Bassetti, Gugger, & Mathis, 2000). More generally, sleep apnea has been associated with decreased quality of life (Yang et al., 2000).

There is a noninvasive method of treating breathing-related sleep disorders, known as *continuous positive airway pressure*. If the problem is a collapse of the upper airway, increasing the pressure against the walls of the airway should open it. In using this treatment, someone with obstructive sleep apnea, hypopnia, or upper-airway resistance would wear a mask over her nose, providing pressurized air to the upper airway, thereby keeping the airway open and allowing her to breathe. Indeed, this is often an effective form of therapy, with SWS and REM sleep rebound being seen during the first week of use (Grunstein & Sullivan, 2000).

Insomnia

Insomnia refers to sleeplessness, difficulty falling asleep, nighttime awakenings, and early morning awakening (Partinen & Hublin, 2000). "Insomnia is the most common sleep–wake-related complaint, and sleeping pills are among the most commonly prescribed drugs in clinical practice at the primary health care level" (Partinen & Hublin, 2000, pp. 558–559), with the incidence of long-standing insomnia in middle-aged adults being about 10%, with women one and a half times more likely to be affected than men (Partinen & Hublin, 2000). Although individual sleep needs differ (Carlson, 1994), insufficient sleep or sleep of insufficient quality leads to daytime sleepiness (Roehrs, Carskadon, Dement, & Roth, 2000) and can be accompanied by subjective feelings that one has slept poorly and wakened unrefreshed, deterioration of mood and attentional ability, and increased complaints of daytime fatigue (American Psychiatric Association, 2000).

Daytime sleepiness, in and of itself, need not be a sign of insomnia. In some cases, sleepiness is simply the result of chronically insufficient sleep, in which case there may be reports of sleeping about an additional two hours on weekend nights compared to weekday nights and polysomnographic evidence of unusually high sleep efficiency (Roehrs et al., 2000). There appears to have been a historical trend toward "voluntary curtailment of sleep" (Bliwise, 1996, p. 462) in that men in 1980, when compared to men in the 1930s, "were more likely to report fatigue and tiredness, although they were no more likely to report disturbed nocturnal sleep" (Bliwise, 1996, p. 462). Sometimes subjective complaints of insomnia are not borne out by objective measures, in which case the condition is classified as *sleep state misperception*. In one study, participants with subjective complaints of insomnia without objective evidence for them were found to have a higher percentage of slow-wave sleep relative to participants with objectively verified insomnia and those without complaints, suggesting that the sleep of those with sleep state misperception is better rather than worse than that of others (Dorsey & Bootzin, 1997). In some cases, sleep state misperception may be the result of dreaming all night that one is awake, trying to fall asleep (Carlson, 1994). In general, people underestimate the amount of sleep obtained when compared with polysomnographic recordings so that, in a sense, sleep state misperception is a matter of degree, with those identified as having sleep state misperception representing the extreme manifestation of this phenomenon (Hauri, 2000).

In addition to the other drugs we have already considered as having an effect on sleep, smoking tobacco has been associated with "difficulty initiating and maintaining sleep, as well as having increased daytime sleepiness" (Sanders, 2000, p. 881). It has been found that "people who smoke on a regular basis sleep poorly, and when they abruptly stop smoking, their sleep improves moderately" (Kales & Kales, 1984, p. 149). In part, the effect appears to result from the stimulation by nicotine in tobacco of acetylcholinergic neurons (Carlson, 1994; Zarcone, 2000). In addition, it is possible that difficulty sleeping that is associated with smoking is breathing-related. "Smokers have a four- to five-fold greater risk than those who never smoke of having at least moderate sleep-disordered breathing" (Sanders, 2000, p. 881). Cigarette smoking may irritate the walls of the throat, leading to "increased upper airway resistance" (Sanders, 2000, p. 881), thereby contributing to poor sleep. For those who imbibe all three before going to sleep, there can be a synergistic arousing effect from caffeine, alcohol, and nicotine once the initial sedation associated with alcohol has worn off (Zarcone, 2000).

Poor sleep hygiene can contribute to insomnia. Staying away from caffeine, alcohol, and nicotine before bedtime can improve sleep. It is also important to recognize the presence of a homeostatic drive and circadian rhythms so that, for example, regular bedtimes would contribute to better sleep. Potential sources of arousal in the sleep setting should be avoided. Thus, the sleep setting should be quiet and dark with minimum interruptions by people and pets. Clocks can be turned to face away from the sleeper so that she is less likely to worry about how little time is left in which to sleep. Ideally, the bedroom should be used only for sleeping. Engaging in other activities in the bedroom can lead to an association of the bed with arousal, so that when it is time to sleep, the arousing associations can keep one from falling asleep (Zarcone, 2000). In fact, lying in bed trying to fall asleep can itself create sufficient stress about the inability to fall asleep so as to cause arousal.

In *psychophysiological insomnia,* a person who sleeps "poorly during a period of stress" (Hauri, 2000, p. 634) can become worried about her inability to sleep and come to associate going to bed with "frustration and arousal" (Hauri, 2000, p. 634). Paradoxically, the harder she tries to sleep, the more she becomes tense, and the less she can sleep (Hauri, 2000). One strategy that is sometimes successful with insomnia is to get out of bed after 15 to 20 minutes of sleeplessness and to do something relaxing to break the association between worrying and being in bed (Aldrich, 1999). Often there is an inability to create psychological distance between daily concerns and sleep. "Any sort of bedtime ritual that breaks the connection between psychological stressors of the preceding day and the sleep period is to be encouraged" (Zarcone, 2000, p. 659). Such rituals can include various techniques of relaxation or stress management, such as making up a "list of the psychological stressors that have occurred during the preceding day, along with the plans to deal with each the next day" (Zarcone, 2000, p. 659).

"Approximately 15%–25% of individuals with chronic insomnia are diagnosed with *Primary Insomnia*" (American Psychiatric Association, 2000, p. 601, emphasis added), a narrow diagnostic category used when insomnia cannot be classified as any of the other sleep disorders (American Psychiatric Association, 2000). Psychophysiological insomnia, discussed in the previous paragraph, is an example of primary insomnia, as is *idiopathic insomnia* in which there is "a lifelong inability to obtain adequate sleep" (Hauri, 2000, p. 636). Idiopathic insomnia may be result from a chronically aroused state or "an abnormality in the neurological control of the sleep–wake system" (Hauri, 2000, p. 636). The mechanism for it is not understood and there is no standard treatment (Hauri, 2000).

Parasomnias

About 50% of adults have at least occasional nightmares. However, the repeated presence of nightmares, occurring usually in the second half of the night during REM sleep, from which a person awakes fully alert, would be classified as *nightmare disorder* provided that the nightmares cause "significant distress" (American Psychiatric Association, 2000, p. 630) or occupational or social disruption (American Psychiatric Association, 2000).

The NREM sleep version of nightmares are *sleep terrors*, which "consist of sitting up during sleep, emitting a piercing cry, and showing behavioral features of acute terror" (Roger Broughton, 2000, p. 696) lasting about 30 seconds to 5 minutes (Roger Broughton, 2000). Physiological arousal is present, although the person may be difficult if not impossible to awaken and may remember nothing on awakening except perhaps single images (American Psychiatric Association, 2000) of "suffocation, burial, impending death, or monsters" (Aldrich, 1999, p. 262). "The medieval interpretation was that something, usually the devil, was pressing on the chest of the sleeper, causing feelings of suffocation and terror" (Roger Broughton, 2000, p. 697). Sleep terrors usually begin in SWS and appear to occur as "incomplete cortical activation in response to an arousal stimulus" (Aldrich, 1999, p. 263).

Various degrees of behavioral activity are possible during incomplete arousal from SWS. At one end of the spectrum are *confusional arousals* in which a person is markedly confused on awakening from sleep "but without the occurrence of any expression of terror or of leaving the bed and walking away" (Roger Broughton, 2000, p. 694). During sleep terrors, a person will sit up in bed and scream (American Psychiatric Association, 2000), possibly also try to "leave the bed or the room . . . jump from windows . . . react violently to attempts to restrain [her]" (Aldrich, 1999, p. 262). Sometimes her behavior will progress to sleepwalking (Roger Broughton, 2000). *Sleepwalking* usually begins with quiet motor activity such as sitting up in bed, looking around "with a relatively blank facial expression" (Roger Broughton, 2000, p. 701), and perhaps picking at the blankets or "rearranging the pillows" (Roger Broughton, 2000, p. 701). A person may then leave her bed and walk around in a manner that is more clumsy than during waking. There may be vocalizations or even conversations and engagement in complex behaviors such as cooking or cleaning the house. A person who is sleepwalking is relatively unresponsive to efforts at communication or awakening (Roger Broughton, 2000). After several minutes to a half hour the sleepwalker wakes up, or lies down in bed or elsewhere to continue her sleep (American Psychiatric Association, 2000).

Sleepwalking is "common in young children" (Roger Broughton, 2000, p. 701), with 15% to 30% "of healthy children" (Roger Broughton, 2000, p. 701) having had at least one episode and 3% to 4% of children having had frequent episodes. Sleepwalking is heritable in that "about 80% of sleepwalkers have an immediate family history of either sleepwalking or sleep terrors" (Roger Broughton, 2000, p. 700). A number of treatment strategies have been used, including drugs, the avoidance of any known predisposing factors (Roger Broughton, 2000), and waking the sleepwalker "about 15 to 30 minutes before the usual time" (Frank, Spirito, Stark, & Owens-Stively, 1997, p. 349) of her episodes for one month.

A criminal incident occurred just up the road from the university at which I teach that resulted in a landmark decision of the Supreme Court of Canada concerning sleepwalking. Parks, a young married man experiencing a great deal of stress was having difficulty sleeping. One night he fell asleep "on the couch of his living room" (McCall Smith & Shapiro, 1997, p. 41). In the "early hours of the morning" (McCall Smith & Shapiro, 1997, p. 41) he "got up from the couch, put on shoes and a jacket" (McCall Smith & Shapiro, 1997, p. 41), got in his car, and drove 33 kilometers "along a busy road" (McCall Smith & Shapiro, 1997, p. 41) until he got to "the home of his parents-in-law" (McCall Smith & Shapiro, 1997, p. 42). He took a tire iron from the car, entered the house, got a knife from the kitchen, "went into the bedroom" (McCall Smith & Shapiro, 1997, p. 42), and "inflicted a series of knife wounds on both the father-in-law and the mother-in-law" (McCall Smith & Shapiro, 1997, p. 42), killing them both. Parks maintained that he had been asleep and that, therefore, he was not responsible for his behavior. His actions were judged to be "noninsane automatism" (McCall Smith & Shapiro, 1997, p. 45), and he was completely acquitted. The court agreed with expert medical testimony presented at the trial that this was a case of somnambulistic homicide.

Cases of sleepwalking, such as that of Parks, raise questions about our ability to carry out complex behaviors without any apparent awareness of them. In other words, a disconnection occurs between consciousness$_1$ and consciousness$_2$ that is instructive to remember when we consider other alterations of consciousness in which aspects of the psyche appear to become dissociated from one another. What happens in such cases? Should a person be held accountable for behavior that appears to occur without any awareness on her part? One of our thematic threads recurs again as well, in that even though sleep is a naturally occurring altered state, in the form of sleepwalking, it can be dangerous. In other words, it is not only contrived alterations of consciousness such as drug-induced states that can be dangerous.

We started this chapter by considering the physiological activity of the brain and then using some of that information to identify the stages of sleep as measured with a polysomnograph. In particular, we distinguished between NREM and REM sleep, each of which is associated with somewhat different sleep mentation and different apparent purposes. We noted some of the physiological bases of sleep and the effects of drugs on sleep before concluding the chapter with a discussion of sleep disorders.

There has been considerable sleep research in the past, and an area of medicine is devoted to the identification and treatment of sleep disorders, yet basic questions about sleep remain. Why does sleep occur, anyway? Why do the sleep stages take the form that they do? More specifically, why does the brain become activated as it does in REM sleep? Does the purpose of any of what happens during sleep have to do with the presence of sleep mentation? Do dreams mean anything? Ah, yes. There is a fundamental question to occupy our attention. Let us turn, then, to a consideration of dreams.

4

DREAMS

When we are asleep, we dream. Perhaps we dream all the time without later remembering that we have been dreaming; perhaps not. What we do know is that most of us dream some of the time that we are asleep. A distinction is usually made between studying *dreaming* as the process by which dreams arise and studying *dreams* as the content and potential meaning of dreams (Haskell, 1986). Formally, the study of dreams is known as *oneirology* (Stevens, 1995) and is usually subdivided into dream analysis and dream interpretation. *Dream analysis* is concerned with the manner in which social psychological realities such as cultural values are reflected in dreams, whereas *dream interpretation* is concerned with the potential meanings of dreams (Haskell, 1986). Do dreams mean anything? If so, what do they mean? This thematic thread runs through the disparate material in this chapter. And, in fact, we will plunge in directly by reviewing some of the main theories of dreaming and dreams. Then we will consider the content of dreams, lucid dreams, and precognitive dreams. Whereas we were on reasonably solid footing with sleep in chapter 3, we find ourselves on shifting sand quite quickly this time, and by the end of the chapter we are no longer in touch with the ground. Lucid dreams challenge our notions of what it means to be asleep, and precognitive dreams challenge our notions of intentional agency and time. Oneirology is controversial, but if we can manage to withhold judgment, it can provide us with some interesting questions about the nature of consciousness and reality that will surface again in other alterations of consciousness.

DREAM THEORIES

In surveying some of the theories of dreaming and dreams, let us start with those in which dreams are regarded as meaningless and work our way toward those in which dreams do have some meaning. This will take us through physiological, cognitive, psychoanalytic, and Jungian theories. Which theory is correct? The reader can judge for herself. However, toward the end of the subsequent section, I will offer what I consider to be a practical approach to dream interpretation.

Physiological Theories

Throughout history, people have been fascinated with dreams and have attributed various meanings to them. For example, in classical Greece, people would come to the "temples sacred to Asklepios, the Greek god of healing" (Stevens, 1995, p. 24), undergo purification rituals, be given a sleeping potion to drink, and then be left to sleep. The idea was that Asklepios would appear in their dreams with messages of healing. Against the context of a rich variety of ways of thinking about dreams (Stevens, 1995), in the 18th and 19th centuries, "the rise of rationalism led to a new theory that dreams were merely meaningless random expressions of physiologic activity during sleep" (Aldrich, 1999, p. 83). In other words, according to this point of view, dreams do not mean anything. With increased knowledge concerning the physiology of sleep, physiological theories have been advanced with considerable technical detail. One example of such a theory is the *activation–synthesis hypothesis* proposed by Allan Hobson and Robert McCarley (1977).

According to Hobson and McCarley, there are two components to the dream process. The first of these is *activation*, whereby, as a result of the activity of brainstem mechanisms during REM sleep, the brain becomes activated, sensory impressions are reduced, and motor movements inhibited. But the brain, activated without sensory input or feedback from motor movements, does the best that it can to inject meaning into random signals by constructing dreams from images retrieved from memory. This is the second component of the dream process, *synthesis* (Hobson, 1990; Hobson & McCarley, 1977; Hock, 1999; see also Hobson, Pace-Schott, & Stickgold, 2000). Hobson has maintained that dreams have five cardinal characteristics: intense emotions, illogical content, apparent sensory impressions, uncritical acceptance of dream events, and difficulty in being remembered (Hobson, 1988). In other words, while dreaming, we are "formally delirious and demented" (Hobson, 1988, p. 9) so that "the study of dreams is the study of a model of mental illness" (Hobson, 1988, p. 9). Given that dreams are simply "unwilled natural phenomena . . . [it] may thus be as unwise as it is unnecessary to regard their nonsensical aspects as hypermeaningful, and as unhealthy as it is unscientific to indulge in symbol interpretation" (Hobson, 1988, p. 11). This is not to say that occasional valuable insights may not occur as the result of fortuitous combinations of "disparate cognitive elements" (Hobson, 1988, p. 18) as a byproduct of the synthesizing activities of the brain.

There are a number of questions that can be raised about the activation–synthesis hypothesis. To begin with, as we have seen, dreaming does not occur only during REM sleep but also throughout the sleep stages, irrespective of whether or not the brain is highly activated. How do NREM dreams arise? Second, if there is a sense in which the brain injects meaning into its activities during waking, then could meaning not also be present in dreams, perhaps in ways that are different from those of waking? Could the process of synthesis not be one of giving *existential coherence* to the brain's random activity (Bulkeley, 1999)? Third, why cannot the brain events proposed by Hobson and McCarley simply be regarded as the physiological mechanism associated with the production of dreams, which are meaningful in their own right? And finally, to what extent is this dream theory a reflection of belief in a reductionistic interpretation of reality (cf. Bulkeley, 1999)?

There has been a recent outgrowth of the activation–synthesis hypothesis in terms of chaos theory. The premise of the theory is that the brain is not a machine that lies dormant for indefinite periods of time but a self-organizing and self-creative system that is critically poised to respond to small perturbations (Kahn, Krippner, & Combs, 2000). Excitation of the brain leads to *stochastic resonance*, a condition in which excitation "keeps the system in motion" (Kahn et al., 2000, p. 6), so that it can effectively follow "inherently natural patterns of activity" (Kahn et al., 2000, p. 6) without getting stuck. During waking, "the sensory regions of the brain are critically poised to respond robustly and in an ordered fashion to even the smallest stimulation" (Kahn et al., 2000, p. 6). During REM sleep, however, the self-organizing brain is "not constrained by sensory input" (Kahn et al., 2000, p. 6), so that the stochastic resonance reveals the natural contours of cortical activity "shaped by the emotional and cognitive influences present at each moment" (Kahn et al., 2000, p. 8). An analogy used for understanding this process has been that of sand, sprinkled on a drum, settling into a configuration revealing the contours of the drum when the drum is repeatedly tapped. Furthermore, "abrupt alterations in dream experiences" (Kahn et al., 2000, p. 8) might result from shifts in the patterns of activity expected in a self-organizing system under conditions of continuous excitation. Although the authors of this study have been silent regarding the question of meaning, they have suggested the possibility of the occurrence of meaningful insights as the self-organizing brain relaxes into its naturally harmonious patterns of functioning (Kahn et al., 2000).

But perhaps the self-organizing brain can be viewed somewhat differently. Here is a system that is critically poised to respond to perturbation. During sleep, the system is protected from sensory stimulation. However, rather than just revealing the contours of its own activity, perhaps it is being prompted by something else, something that shapes dreams into meaningful events. The analogy that comes to mind is that of a symphony orchestra on the evening of a concert. Before the entrance of the concert master, orchestra members take the opportunity to individually warm up their instruments and practice difficult passages. The result is a cacophony of sound that reveals the acoustic qualities of the various instruments as they fade in and out of the random playing. However, once the concert begins under the baton of a conductor, the musicians follow a score that is musically meaningful. The suggestion in the theories that we have considered thus far is that, while awake, the orchestra plays whatever music is handed to it, but, while asleep, it is forever warming up. Is it possible that there is also music to be played while asleep?

Cognitive Theories

David Foulkes (1966, 1985, 1990) has argued against physiological accounts of dreaming such as the activation–synthesis hypothesis and proposed a cognitive model instead. Thus, rather than being properly explained in physiological terms, dreaming is to be understood as thinking, and hence is not unrelated to what happens during waking, particularly during day-dreaming (Foulkes, 1985). According to Foulkes, what gets activated while asleep is memory. However, unlike typical waking memory, its activation during dreaming is diffuse rather than directed, as evidenced by weak relationships between dream images and "odd fusions and juxtapositions of knowledge in dream imagery" (Foulkes, 1985, p. 145). The insistence and widespread occurrence of the activated memories "calls up the interpretive machinery of the dream-production system" (Foulkes, 1985, p. 145), a nonconscious process that works by using the memory of the actual "characteristics of life experiences" (Foulkes, 1985, p. 176) to simulate waking experience. According to Foulkes, "there is no meaningful plan underlying the construction of particular dream imagery or of its narrative sequence" (Foulkes, 1985, p. 165). Thus, dreams do not mean anything, although, as productions of a computational system, they could incidentally reveal something of the "character of the person" (Foulkes, 1985, p. 204) who does the dreaming.

Dreams are not, however, viewed as meaningless in all cognitive theories. Clara Hill (1996) has proposed a *cognitive–experiential theory* in which dreams are considered to be meaningful. According to Hill, during REM sleep there is a nonconscious effort on the part of the dreamer to incorporate waking events into the cognitive framework used for making sense of reality that is already stored in memory. This occurs by weaving together waking life events with memories from the past into a story. Problems occur when there are waking events, such as traumatic events, for which the existing cognitive framework is inadequate, thereby giving rise to recurrent dreams or nightmares. Dreams can be interpreted by finding meanings for dream events that make sense to the dreamer. There is some empirical support for the therapeutic effectiveness of such dream interpretation as a psychotherapeutic intervention (C. Hill & Rochlen, 1999).

Psychoanalytic Theory

If we are going to discuss the meaningfulness of dreams, then we should backtrack to 1900 with the publication of Freud's *The Interpretation of Dreams* (1900/1950). For Freud, "dreams do really possess a meaning" (Freud, 1900/1950, p. 32)—namely, that of wish-fulfillment. By Freud's own admission, this was not a new idea; others had noticed that dreams could be fulfillments of wishes. Freud, however, insisted that all dreams be considered the result of wish-fulfillment even when they do not appear to be. How could this be so? For Freud, every dream has not only a *manifest content,* which is just the apparent content of a dream, but also a *latent content,* which is what a dream is really about (Freud, 1900/1950). What a dream is really about, according to Freud, is our repressed wishes that he believed to be "infantile in origin and usually sexual in nature" (Stevens, 1995, p. 46). Unknown to us, these disturbing feelings are repressed from entering our dreams during sleep by a part of our psyche that Freud called the censor. But that is not the end of the forbidden impulses. They cleverly disguise themselves through a process "which Freud called the *dream work*" (Stevens, 1995, p. 38) to sneak by the censor and appear in symbolic form as manifest content. Indeed, the purpose of dreams is to protect us from disturbing impulses so that we can sleep (Stevens, 1995). The task of dream interpretation is to proceed backward to identify the symbols of the manifest content and to translate them into the latent content of the actual dream thoughts (Freud, 1900/1950). And when we do that, according to Freud, we find repressed infantile wishes.

How did Freud know that this was the correct explanation for dreams? He has credited his insight that dreams result from wish fulfillment to a dream that he had had in 1895 that appeared, on examination, to be a dream about the fulfillment of hidden wishes in a professional matter. But just because he had had a dream that he interpreted as arising from wish fulfillment, why should he have assumed that all dreams, dreamed by everyone else, are necessarily the result of wish fulfillment? And why always find the origins of those wishes in infancy, particularly when he was unwilling to do so in his own case? Although it is conceivable that our psyche could sometimes play a game of fool the censor, to use that as an explanation for all dream content appears contrived. Indeed, when people reported to Freud dreams whose contents were clearly contrary to their wishes, Freud interpreted those dreams as fulfillment of the wish to prove him wrong. Freud had a "tendency to impose his theories in an arbitrary and authoritarian manner" (Stevens, 1995, p. 50) and to accuse those who disagreed with him of avoiding "true ideas" (Stevens, 1995, p. 48) because they found them to be threatening. In other words, once stated, Freud's theory was seemingly impervious to change because of the presence of an implicit heuristic to invalidate all challenges. Given the unreasonableness of such a strategy, it is tempting to clean the slate and begin again, perhaps by starting with the physiology of sleep, rather than by trying to overwrite Freud's theory.

Jungian Theory

One person who did advance a method of dream analysis that was, in some respects, an outgrowth of Freud's theory was Carl Jung, a Swiss psychiatrist who maintained a 6-year relationship with Freud until Freud's refusal to tolerate Jung's criticisms of his theory led to Jung going his own way. Jung, as well, had dreams that contributed to his understanding of dreaming. In one of his dreams Jung found himself in "a mountainous region on the Swiss-Austrian border" (Jung, 1965, p. 163) at evening time. A stooped, elderly man with a peevish expression dressed "in the uniform of an Imperial Austrian customs official" (Jung, 1965, p. 163) walked by. Someone present in the dream said that it was "the ghost of a customs official who had died years ago" (Jung, 1965, p. 163). Then Jung found himself around midday in a city "bathed in an intense light" (Jung, 1965, p. 164). In the midst of a crowd of people streaming home for dinner "walked a knight in full armor" (Jung, 1965, p. 164) wearing a "white tunic into which was woven, front and back, a large red cross" (Jung, 1965, p. 165). Jung asked himself in the dream the meaning of the apparition and was told that "the knight always passes by here between twelve and one o'clock, and has been doing so for a very long time . . . and everyone knows about it" (Jung, 1965, p. 165).

According to Jung, while some dreams are "lightning impressions" (Jung, 1965/1969, p. 294) and others are "endlessly spun out [dream-narratives]" (Jung, 1965/1969, p. 294), a four-part structure similar to that of a drama "can be perceived" (Jung, 1965/1969, p. 294) in "a great many 'average' dreams" (Jung, 1965/1969, p. 294). Such dreams begin with an *exposition* that sets the place, introduces the characters, and sometimes states the time. The exposition is followed by a *development* of the plot in which "the situation is somehow becoming complicated, and a definite tension develops because one does not know what will happen" (Jung, 1965/1969, p. 295). Then there is a *culmination* whereby "something decisive happens or something changes completely" (Jung, 1965/1969, p. 295). Finally, there is a "*solution* or *result* produced by the dream-work" (Jung, 1965/1969, p. 295), which is at the same time a "final situation"

(Jung, 1965/1969, p. 295) and "the solution 'sought' by the dreamer" (Jung, 1965/1969, p. 295). For example, the second part of Jung's dream follows this structure. The urban midday state of affairs is the exposition, the crowd streaming home for dinner is the development, the presence of the knight is the culmination, and the stated meaning of the dream is the solution (Stevens, 1995).

In Jungian dream interpretation, dream images are *symbolic*. They are symbolic, not in the Freudian sense of admitting a direct translation of one meaning into another, such as a tree being a penis and a cave being a vagina (J. A. Hall, 1977), but as meaningful images compounded of the unconscious and conscious (Stevens, 1995) that are the best possible formulations of "relatively unknown [facts]" (Jung, 1921/1971, p. 474). Dream interpretation depends on the ability to find meaningful parallel ideas to the symbols found in dreams. In his dream, Jung interpreted the dead customs inspector to be Freud, and the knight, which he associated with the beginning of alchemy and the quest for the holy grail, suggested "something still unknown which might confer meaning upon the banality of life" (Jung, 1965, p. 165). For Jung, dreams arise from the unconscious to compensate the conscious attitude of a person for the sake of providing balance to the personality (J. A. Hall, 1977). In this case, the dream's message for Jung was to correct his "conscious high opinion and admiration" (Jung, 1965, p. 164) of Freud and "to go on like the knight . . . supported only by his own 'inner light' and the few congenial souls he was able to collect at his own Round Table" (Stevens, 1995, p. 62).

When Jung worked at the Burghölzli Hospital in Zürich, he was struck by the similarities that the "delusions and hallucinations" (Stevens, 1995, p. 51) of schizophrenic patients had, not only to one another but also to the "myths and fairy tales derived from peoples all over the world" (Stevens, 1995, pp. 51–52). These observations led him to believe that there was a "universal substratum" (Stevens, 1995, p. 52) of the mind underlying "human experience and behaviour" (Stevens, 1995, p. 52), which he called the *collective unconscious*. The "essential psychic characteristics" (Stevens, 1995, p. 52) of the collective unconscious "that distinguish us as human beings" (Stevens, 1995, p. 52) he called *archetypes* and said that they could give rise "to similar thoughts, images, and feelings in people, irrespective of their class, creed, race, geographical location, or historical epoch" (Stevens, 1995, p. 52). Manifestations of archetypes include variations on the relationship between male and female, the conflict between good and evil, the course of the human life cycle, and the ordeals encountered in life. For example, life's tribulations could be represented by "negotiating a maze or a labyrinth" (Stevens, 1995, p. 182). Archetypes surface as symbols in culturally shaped forms in myths, legends, and fairy tales as well as in dreams. In Jung's dream, the Christian knight was an archetypal figure of the warrior following "a destiny which he has no choice but to fulfil" (Stevens, 1995, p. 60), just as Jung was to feel compelled to pursue his ideas about the human psyche.

DREAM CONTENT

Are we getting anywhere? Is Jung's theory any closer to the truth about dreaming? Are dreams compensations of waking experiences? Are they continuations of a day's events? From where does dream content come? How would we know, anyway? We have already considered some of the research concerning dreaming and dreams in chapter 3 in the context of sleep. A number of methods have been used for gathering dream data. Dreams have been collected from participants awakened in a sleep laboratory, from clients receiving psychotherapy who have reported their dreams in the context of a psychotherapeutic relationship, from studies of dream journals, and from participants anonymously completing forms in group settings (Domhoff, 2000). Recently, as we saw in chapter 3, home dreams have been gathered while sleepers have been monitored using portable computerized polysomnography. In addition, as we have seen in the case of Freud and Jung and as was true also of Hobson (1988), data about one's own dreams have been used by dream researchers for understanding their nature.

Let us begin a discussion of dream content by reviewing some of the research concerning the incorporation of stimuli in dreams before returning to a discussion of hypnagogic and hypnopompic imagery, which was introduced in chapter 3. Then I will tackle directly the question of meaningfulness in dreams, provide a practical approach to dream interpretation, and indicate how dreams could possibly be used for solving problems.

Stimulus Incorporation in Dreams

In dreams collected in a sleep laboratory, not surprisingly perhaps, the sleep laboratory itself has showed up in the dreams of participants. In one study, 112 REM-sleep dreams obtained from 20 participants, each spending two nights in a sleep laboratory, were analyzed. It was found that 52% of those dreams had at least some incorporation of the laboratory situation in them. Most frequently, the experimental situation showed up "in individual dream scenes; next came dreams which used the dream experiment as a major theme; about every tenth dream contained only isolated elements of the experiment, scattered among dream events" (Strauch & Meier, 1992/ 1996, p. 172). Realistic inclusion of actual "experiences from the preceding evening" (Strauch & Meier, 1992/1996, p. 172) was rare, so that, "for the most part, the laboratory situation was transformed in an alienated fashion"

(Strauch & Meier, 1992/1996, p. 172). A dreamer in another study found herself in the sleep laboratory in her dreams. She dreamt that she was unable to fall asleep so she "went outside to go sledding"(Strauch & Meier, 1992/1996, p. 171) with her boyfriend, intending to come back in time to be awakened. She "suddenly had a small motorbike" (Strauch & Meier, 1992/1996, p. 171) but got lost, "and it simply got too late" (Strauch & Meier, 1992/1996, p. 171).

Deliberate efforts to introduce stimuli into dreams, in many cases, have been less successful than the natural incorporation of activities in the sleep laboratory itself (De Koninck, 2000). Early studies demonstrating that pre-sleep thoughts about desired personality characteristics would show up in dreams could not be replicated in some subsequent similar studies. As well, having independent judges identify the incorporation of an "increasing and decreasing sound of a jet fighter or the weepy sobbing of a person" (Strauch & Meier, 1992/1996, p. 177) played to participants 5 minutes after the onset of REM sleep led to inconclusive results. Some "common everyday activities" (De Koninck, 2000, p. 503) such as "reading, writing, and counting" (De Koninck, 2000, p. 503) are "seldom incorporated into dreams"(De Koninck, 2000, p. 503).

Incorporations of stimuli in dreams, when they can be identified, are usually indirect rather than direct. In particular, it has been found that indirect incorporations of nouns spoken during REM sleep can include not only incorporations based on associated meanings, but also on similarity of sound so that, for example, the spoken word "Gillian" (De Koninck, 2000, p. 503) has apparently been transformed to "Chilean" (De Koninck, 2000, p. 503) in a dream. There is also a *dream lag effect,* so that "47% of waking incorporations identified by a group of subjects came from the preceding day, 19% from the preceding week, and the remaining 33% from earlier experiences" (De Koninck, 2000, p. 503). There is some evidence that dreams from NREM sleep "contain more day residues than dreams from REM sleep" (De Koninck, 2000, p. 504). And, as the night progresses and REM sleep increases, "dreams refer to events further in the past of the dreamer's life" (De Koninck, 2000, p. 504). Clearly, "dreams are not simply a replay of waking activity and concerns but . . . draw on these experiences in ways that are complex and little understood" (De Koninck, 2000, p. 504). A dream "keeps its own counsel on whether to respond to a suggestion or signal, and if it does take them into account, it remodels them in unpredictable ways and places them into a different frame of reference" (Strauch & Meier, 1992/1996, p. 239).

Unlike everyday events, whose dream incorporation is inconsistent, are events that occur in the course of traumas (Antrobus, 2000) such as natural disasters, criminal violence, and war. One third to more than one half of individuals who have experienced traumatic events end up with posttraumatic stress disorder, whereby a person suffers from persistent anxiety stemming from a traumatic event (American Psychiatric Association, 2000). Among the most common symptoms of posttraumatic stress disorder are nightmares and recurrent dreams. At first, the "dreams are fairly close to a literal reenactment of the trauma, sometimes with the twist that an additional horror, averted in real life, is added to the dream reenactment" (Barrett, 1996c, p. 3). Eventually the trauma is portrayed more symbolically and interwoven "with concerns from the dreamer's daily life" (Barrett, 1996c, p. 3). In one long-term study of "women with a documented history of childhood hospital visits for sexual abuse" (Barrett, 1996c, pp. 3–4), it was found that "a significant proportion of them repressed and then later remembered the abuse" (Barrett, 1996c, p. 4), with dreams being "one of the modes in which these memories first returned" (Barrett, 1996c, p. 4). In some cases those who have received transplanted organs perceive ghosts or perceive themselves as ghosts in their dreams, perhaps reflecting their previous critical situation or that of the donor. In addition, the exultation and horror of being an organ recipient as well as the transformation of self-identity necessitated by being a transplant recipient can be played out in dreams (Bosnak, 1996).

Do dreams compensate for waking activities? For all the difficulties with that line of research, it appears that dream content is usually more continuous with waking content than compensatory (De Koninck, 2000). In fairness to Jung, however, the compensatory character of dreams has less to do with the simple presence during sleep of opposites to waking experiences and more to do with revealing to a person a direction for her psychological growth by pointing out, dream by dream, that which is missing. But it is only in the analysis of series of dreams, sometimes perhaps of hundreds of dreams, that "a planned and orderly process of development" (Jung, 1965/1969, p. 289) becomes apparent. This could not be determined by isolated sleep laboratory studies but would require studying dream journals or documenting series of dreams recounted during psychotherapy. For example, the transformation over time of traumatic events in dreams speaks to this possibility.

Hypnagogic Imagery

To help us to understand the content of dreams, let us return to a consideration of hypnagogic and hypnopompic imagery, the imagery that occurs on falling asleep and waking up. Although there are differences between the psychological states in which such imagery occurs (Ahsen, 1988), Andreas Mavromatis (1987a) has introduced the term *hypnagogia* to collectively refer both to the states in which hypnagogic and hypnopompic imagery occur and to the phenomena, such as the imagery, that occur in those states. A number of methods have been used for studying hypnagogia. One technique consists of a researcher sitting upright in a chair at times when she is drowsy and paying attention to her mental events. As she enters sleep, her head starts to fall over and she wakes up, at which time she can recall and record her observations. Before "beginning a series of observations" (Nielsen, 1995, p. 76), she would establish an "observational intent" (Nielsen, 1995, p. 76) to direct observation to specific features of interest as she falls asleep. For instance, she may have an observational intent to pay attention to the colors of images (Nielsen, 1995). Questionnaires have also been used on which participants have been asked to retrospectively report their experiences (e.g., Cheyne, Newby-Clark, & Rueffer, 1999; Cheyne, Rueffer, & Newby-Clark, 1999; Glickson, 1989).

There is a variety and richness of hypnagogic imagery from the "faintly perceptible to concrete hallucinations" (Mavromatis, 1987a, p. 14), which can include formless images made up of colors and clouds, geometric designs including spirals, "faces, figures, animals, objects, . . . nature scenes" (Mavromatis, 1987a, p. 25; emphasis removed), people, and printing and writing. Faces seem to be particularly prevalent among adults, often taking shape out of "misty stuff" (Mavromatis, 1987a, p. 25). For example, in one case, faces would "come up out of the darkness, as a mist, and rapidly develop into sharp delineation, assuming roundness, vividness, and living reality" (Mavromatis, 1987a, p. 17). Then they would fade, making way for others. At first these faces had been diabolical in appearance but over the years they had become "exquisitely beautiful" (Mavromatis, 1987a, p. 17). Most visual hypnagogic images appear to be external to the viewer, vivid, sharp, and detailed. The capacity for detail has been characterized by one person as the ability to "see *into* the material without its being made coarser as it would appear through a magnifying glass" (Mavromatis, 1987a, p. 29). Indeed, for some people hypnagogic images have evoked "feelings of *heightened reality*" (Mavromatis, 1987a, p. 30). Whereas visual images appear to predominate in hypnagogic states, auditory phenomena can also occur such as hearing "one's name being called" (Mavromatis, 1987a, p. 34) or hearing the ringing of a doorbell. There can also be olfactory, gustatory, or somatic sensations such as a sense of falling (Mavromatis, 1987a).

An observation that has been made regarding hypnagogic imagery is that it can be *autosymbolic* in the sense that the images that occur during the hypnagogic state may be symbolic representations of immediately preceding thoughts of one's mental condition in the hypnagogic state or of somatic sensations. Mavromatis has described one of his autosymbolic experiences. He was "lying in bed with eyes shut, half asleep, . . . thinking of the difficulties of trying to remain awake in hypnagogia" (Mavromatis, 1987a, p. 59), when he had a visual image of a man "rolling a stone bigger than [himself] up a small conically shaped hill and trying to place it on its tip" (Mavromatis,

1987a, p. 59). If he could make it to the top, then he could see all around. But the best that the man could do was to "get to just below [the tip] and then keep going round the tip trying to stop [the stone] from rolling away" (Mavromatis, 1987a, p. 59). Mavromatis interpreted this image as a symbolic depiction of his "thoughts about the difficulties of maintaining waking awareness during hypnagogia" (Mavromatis, 1987a, p. 59). Mavromatis has argued that such symbolization during hypnagogia argues for the presence of a cognitive capacity that is separate from that of ordinary waking thought.

Hypnopompic Imagery

In many cases, as one would expect, hypnopompic images appear to be continuations of dream imagery into the waking state. In other cases, however, hypnopompic images appear to be discontinuous with dreams. For example, "one may wake and see visions of people in [one's] room which one takes for real and thus resort to shouting and calling for help" (Mavromatis, 1987a, p. 39). Again, as with hypnagogic images, hypnopompic experiences that "are not continuations of dreams" (Mavromatis, 1987a, p. 41) can "involve any of the sense modalities" (Mavromatis, 1987a, p. 41) and can include "hearing knocks on the door or one's name being called" (Mavromatis, 1987a, p. 41).

Some of the most interesting cases of hypnopompic images are those in which a person receives a warning or finds a solution to a problem (Mavromatis, 1987a). "Perhaps the single most often cited example of unconscious functioning in scientific discovery" (Harman & Rheingold, 1984, p. 42) is the chemist Kekulé's finding of the benzene molecule's circular structure. One evening as he was riding the bus, Kekulé "fell into a reverie" (Japp, 1898, p. 100) and saw atoms "gambolling before [his] eyes" (Japp, 1898, p. 100) as he had seen on previous occasions. This time, however, the "diminutive beings" (Japp, 1898, p. 100) formed various configurations that he subsequently sketched. Some years later, Kekulé fell asleep in his chair before a fire. Again, he saw the atoms, this time "twining and twisting in snakelike motion" (Japp, 1898, p. 100) until "one of the snakes had seized hold of its own tail, and the form whirled mockingly before [his] eyes" (Japp, 1898, p. 100). He awoke "as if by a flash of lightning" (Japp, 1898, p. 100) and realized that benzene was a circular molecule (Harman & Rheingold, 1984). It is difficult to know from his account whether Kekulé's insightful images were hypnagogic, hypnopompic, or simply dreams. Whatever the case may be, experiences such as Kekulé's speak to the suggestion that sleep may be an alteration of consciousness in which insights concerning life may become available that are not as readily available during the ordinary waking state. We will keep that in mind as we turn to consider in more detail the possibility that dreams really are meaningful.

Meaningfulness of Dreams

Are dreams meaningful? Within the Western culture, particularly science and academia, meaningfulness in general has largely been defined in terms of rationally coherent statements. In particular, statements that can be explicitly written in words on paper. Furthermore, there is an assumption, usually made without explicit acknowledgment, that classical formal logic is the correct type of logic to use when thinking. Indeed, computer analogue computational theories of mind are based on such logical systems. In such theories, the assumption is made that all mental events, including perception, emotions, and consciousness, are byproducts of formal classical logical processes (cf. Hofstadter, 1979). But classical logic is not the only kind of logic that exists (e.g., Goldblatt, 1979; Mac Lane & Moerdijk, 1992), nor is it likely to be the correct logic of the mind (Barwise, 1986). And, as we have already suggested in chapter 1, there may be modes of understanding other than, and perhaps superior to, rational thought. Modes of understanding, perhaps, in which symbols play a role. In other words, meaning could be present in forms other than those in which it is usually recognized.

As he was preparing to write a book about dreams, Anthony Stevens (1995) had a dream. In the dream, two of Stevens's mentors and "some sort of scientist or laboratory technician . . . were arguing over a piece of apparatus . . . that . . . must be an EEG machine" (Stevens, 1995, p. 1; emphasis removed). However, one of his mentors called the apparatus a "poetry machine" (Stevens, 1995, p. 1; emphasis removed), and Stevens was "moved by the simple beauty of [a] song" (Stevens, 1995, p. 1; emphasis removed) being sung by a young woman in the next room. For Stevens, the scientist represented "a modern 'hero' figure . . . determined to advance the frontiers of knowledge through a single-minded application of experimental method and the use of logical deduction based on reproducible and verifiable facts" (Stevens, 1995, p. 4). The "scientist considered dreams to be meaningless charades" (Stevens, 1995, p. 5), whereas his mentors were reminding Stevens "that the creator of dreams is a poet" (Stevens, 1995, p. 2) and his anima, an archetypal feminine aspect of himself, underscored that message with her song. Let us use the term *intuition* to refer to the understanding of poetry, music, and apparent nonconscious communication, without commitment to any specific notions of what intuition may turn out to be (cf. O. Hill, 1987). Using this terminology, Stevens's dream can be interpreted to mean that there exist intuitive aspects of our minds that must not be neglected in favor of the rational.

From a psychodynamic point of view represented by Freud, Jung, and Assagioli, unconscious material can become conscious whenever we relax our rational grip on our experiences. Such irruption could occur through accidental occurrences such as inadvertently saying something we had not planned to say, responding to ambiguous stimulus situations such as inkblots, free drawing whereby we draw whatever inspires us, and dreaming (Ferrucci, 1982). It is as though there were a communications device that allowed the unconscious to become conscious. The problem is that unconscious material is often found in symbolic form. In dreams, for Freud, such symbols were to be translated into unconscious wishes; for Jung, symbols had depth of meaning that revealed what it was that we needed to become whole; and for Assagioli, symbols were tools that allowed us to understand and work with psychological realities, including the superconscious, that may initially be inaccessible to us otherwise (Assagioli, 1965). It has been suggested that, by being concerned with the differences between waking and dreaming, we have drawn the line in the wrong place. Where we need to draw the line is "between symbolic consciousness manifested as such in emergent, creative imagination versus consciousness subordinated to the pragmatic demands of constructing and maintaining the everyday common sense world, a distinction cutting across both dreaming and wakefulness" (Hunt, 1986, pp. 216–217). Dreaming provides an opportunity for the emergence of another, more intuitive, mode of knowing—one that functions through the use of symbols. And, once understood, perhaps, rather than being obscure, dreams may "express the truth even more bluntly" (Stevens, 1995, p. 75) than we may encounter it in waking life (Ullman, 1999). Nor should we suppose that sleep is the only alteration of consciousness in which other modes of knowing could emerge. Daydreaming, trance, psychedelic experiences, transcendent experiences, and experiences associated with death could all be conducive to the presence of more intuitive knowledge, if indeed such knowledge is possible.

Practical Dream Interpretation

If dreams are potentially meaningful, from a practical point of view, how could a person go about interpreting them? Let me answer this question from the literature as well as from my own experience of working with my dreams and helping others to work with theirs. At the outset, a person needs to record and keep track of her dreams. For someone interested in knowing about herself, it is helpful to keep a journal that functions both as a record of significant psychological events and as a workbook. Dreams can be written into the journal while lying in bed after awakening or at the first opportunity after arising. It is helpful to review dreams immediately on awakening, before moving, to be better able to remember them. One can also record dreams on audiotape and write them out later, although one has to be careful not to leave the writing so long that the details become forgotten. In recording a dream, its different dimensions can be described, such as settings, characters, events, and mood (cf. Stevens, 1995).

After having written out a dream, the dreamer can ask herself what associations are called forth, not just from the dream as a whole but also from the various elements in the dream. As she investigates possible associations, meanings may suggest themselves. There are two levels of associations. One of these is personal, the other cultural. For example, I play ice hockey regularly throughout the year, and playing some version of hockey occasionally shows up in my dreams. I have come to associate academic publication with scoring goals and the manner in which they are scored while playing hockey in my dreams. Playing hockey is a personal symbol. For most people neither hockey nor academic publication has anything to do with their lives. On the other hand, we share cultural symbols. A common symbol for the personality is a house with the basement related to the lower unconscious, the main floor with the conscious, and upper floors and attic to the higher unconscious and spiritual aspirations. Events that occur in the house could symbolize the occurrence of psychological events (e.g., D. Baker & Hansen, 1977). One has to "be willing to ransack the libraries of mythology, folklore, and comparative religion" (Stevens, 1995, p. 231) to find cultural associations of events in dreams. Sometimes it is helpful to share dreams with others and to solicit their associations to dream images (Ullman, 1986). We may be unable to perceive uncomfortable associations that disinterested others may see more readily (Barušs, 1996; Stevens, 1995). Indeed, it is often advisable to find an "experienced helper" (Stevens, 1995, p. 233) because "working with dreams on one's own is a precarious business" (Stevens, 1995, p. 233).

An additional way of working with dreams while awake is to use the imagination to interact with dream images. For example, one can engage a dream character in dialogue to ascertain the meaning that that character had in a dream (Stevens, 1995). The process can also be turned around. Rather than just seeking to determine the meaning of a dream, one can use the images in the dream as a way of creating changes in oneself. In keeping with ideas presented in chapter 2, symbols may have some ability to restructure a person's psyche when those symbols representing desired changes are visualized (Ferrucci, 1982). Empirical research could be carried out to determine if such symbolic visualization of psychological changes derived from dream imagery can beneficially affect one's psyche.

Although dreams can sometimes be quite directed, they need not have a single meaning but can be layered so as to be concerned with various issues in one's life. Sometimes dreams are about one's psychological life, sometimes about a situation in which one finds oneself, sometimes about planetary events, and sometimes perhaps about all of those at once. Sometimes dreams can be overly dramatic and exaggerate reality to draw attention to something that needs to be rectified. One of the benefits of keeping track of dreams over time is to learn which dreams are meaningful, if they are meaningful, what it is that they are concerned about, and what the meanings are of different dream images.

But this practical matter of dream interpretation sounds vague, and there appears to be enough room to come up with whatever meanings one wants. Perhaps. The degree to which useful meanings can be found in dreams depends on the care and ingenuity with which the dream interpreter proceeds. But science is often regarded as being literal in nature. Something either is or is not a certain way, and one can maintain that the determination of which way it is in reality has to be unambiguous. And one can insist that something be tested through sensory observation to determine its truth value. And one can refuse to consider the possibility of modes of knowledge other than the rational inference of information from sensory data. In that case, one's knowledge would always be confined to that which is literal and, as Hobson and Foulkes have maintained, dreams would be essentially meaningless. There would be no messages in dreams from the subconscious, the superconscious, or anywhere else for that matter. But if we set aside the compulsion for certainty and pay attention to the unknown, perhaps we can encounter something unexpected.

Using Dreams for Solving Problems

Whatever one's theoretical disposition with regard to their meaningfulness, dreams have sometimes been the apparent source of creative production (Krippner, 1981; Krippner & Dillard, 1988). However, as in Kekulé's case, gleaning insights from a dream may require the interpretation of symbols. Douglas Baker has employed the analogy of using a typewriter to characterize the process of communication between the intellect and a wiser part of ourselves. If the typewriter has "insufficient keys" (D. Baker, 1977, p. 30), then it will be unable to "transmit a coherent message" (D. Baker, 1977, p. 30) from the superconscious. The keys for the typewriter are furnished by enriching the intellect with "visual images and their myriad associations of symbols and analogies with which . . . inner communications may be decked out so that they become comprehensible" (D. Baker, 1977, p. 28). These images can then appear in dreams where they become available for interpretation. "It takes years to separate the real from the unreal in dream experience" (D. Baker & Hansen, 1977, p. 64), but by keeping track of symbols from one dream to another, their meanings can gradually be established. "Later, much later, each individual learns his own dream symbol associations so accurately that [dream] interpretation can be made in a flash" (D. Baker, 1977, p. 23). Baker has said that it took him 25 years of attention to his dreams before he was able to synthesize an effective keyboard. Even then, when considering symbolic experiences a decade after their occurrence, latent meanings could sometimes be found in symbols that could not have been understood at the time of the experiences (D. Baker, 1977).

A person does not have to wait for meaningful dreams to occur spontaneously but can deliberately seek answers to questions in dreams by writing the questions in her diary and posing them to herself in her mind as she falls asleep. She can then pay attention to her dreams, particularly dreams that occur just before awakening. The idea is that answers to her questions can occur in dreams, if not on the first then possibly on subsequent nights on repetition of the process (cf. D. Baker, 1977; D. Baker & Hansen, 1977).

The psychiatrist Judith Orloff has found a technique similar to the one just described to be useful for the clients in her psychiatric practice. According to Orloff (1996), at one time, a "successful child psychologist . . . had grown dissatisfied with her work" (Orloff, 1996, p. 219). She was not attracted to any alternative career choices, either. Orloff suggested that the child psychologist, every evening, write out a request for discovering, in her dreams, a meaningful career direction. The child psychologist kept track of her dreams for weeks, but there seemed to be no answer. However, "apparently unrelated, tagged onto each dream" (Orloff, 1996, p. 220) were whimsical phrases such as "an upside-down sky" (Orloff, 1996, p. 22). It turned out that the child psychologist had always had an interest in unusual words. "Combining her skill as a child psychologist and her flair for words, she began to weave together stories, which later became a delightful children's book" (Orloff, 1996, p. 221).

Those who think that dreams are meaningless might deride the persistence on the part of the soft-headed to seek meaning in meaningless events and consider Orloff's anecdote itself a children's story. Those with psychoanalytic beliefs might see infantile regression. Jungians would see the compensatory quality of dreams. And psychosynthesists may think of the whimsical phrases as expressions of the superconscious. The woman whose dreams are at issue may not care which of the interpretations is correct. She is probably just happy that the examination of her dreams allowed her to find greater satisfaction in her life. Although the ontological question concerning the source of helpful information in dreams has not been settled scientifically, this does not preclude the constructive use of dream imagery in practical situations.

LUCID DREAMING

In chapter 1 I indicated that a number of different aspects of subjective experience have been proposed along which alterations of consciousness can occur. There are three such dimensions that are particularly relevant when considering dream experiences. The first is that of *discrimination*, the degree to which a person recognizes the state in which she finds herself. The second is that of *control*, the degree to which a person has apparent control over the events occurring within her experience. The third is that of *sense of reality*, the degree to which experiences that are occurring for a person seem to be real. This last is not the ability to discriminate between events that are objectively real in the normal sense and those that are subjective, that ability being included in the first dimension, but rather the sense of how real one's experiences seem to be, irrespective of their objectively determined ontological status. In that sense, the third dimension is related to consciousness$_3$.

Characteristics of Lucid Dreams

A number of differences between waking and dreaming have been noted, including, usually, the lack of critical reflection while dreaming, so that the dreamer fails to realize that she is dreaming in spite of various absurdities that could be present in her dreams (Aldrich, 1999). In some cases, however, the dreamer is aware of her actual situation—namely, that she is dreaming. She may also be more likely to act deliberately (LaBerge & Gackenbach, 2000) and to feel that what is happening is as real as waking experience (LaBerge & Rheingold, 1990). Dreams with such qualities are known as *lucid dreams* (e.g., van Eeden, 1913), although, in keeping with contemporary scientific usage, we shall adopt a broad definition of lucid dreams as any dreams in which one knows that one is dreaming (LaBerge & Gackenbach, 1986).

In the tradition of dream researchers, let me give some examples of my own dreams for illustrative purposes, the first of which is a lucid dream.

> In the continuation of a nonlucid dream that I was having, I floated out of a building through the front door and was looking for my car. As I was going through a parking garage, I realized that I was dreaming. I do not know why that realization occurred to me; perhaps I subconsciously had noticed that I was floating. At any rate, the contents of my dream imagery became more solid. In fact, I went over to a wall and tested it. It was solid. Even though I knew that I could do anything I wanted to do because it was a dream, that did not appear to be true. With some effort, I eventually managed to penetrate through the ceiling. That had an odd effect, as though everything, including myself, were made of some sort of rubbery liquid so that I experienced a pleasing satisfaction as I scrunched through the ceiling and came up out of the floor of the level above. I decided to visit my girlfriend, thinking that my intentions would be enough to make that occur, but nothing happened. I

was stuck by myself inside the empty rooms in some sort of building. Eventually I was able to rise until I ended up in a tower that was open to the night sky. There was an angel with me, a chubby sort of fellow, who turned out to be Cupid. Then I lost my lucidity.

How are lucid dreams different from nonlucid dreams? That depends on the amount of experience with lucid dreaming that the dreamer has had. Lucid dreaming is a skill that can be learned with a variety of techniques available for inducing lucidity. Among those inexperienced with them, lucid dreams "are more similar than dissimilar to nonlucid dreams" (LaBerge & Gackenbach, 2000, p. 155). This was the conclusion reached in a study of the differences in content between nonlucid and lucid dreams collected mostly "from dream diaries [and] from questionnaires" (LaBerge & Gackenbach, 2000, p. 155). There were, nonetheless, "more auditory and kinesthetic sensations" (LaBerge & Gackenbach, 2000, p. 155) as well as a greater "sense of control" (LaBerge & Gackenbach, 2000, p. 155) in lucid dreams than in nonlucid dreams. Greater differences between lucid and nonlucid dreams were found in a study of members of an organization devoted to lucid dreaming, who would have been "more likely to use specialized techniques for lucid dream induction, control, and stabilization" (LaBerge & Gackenbach, 2000, p. 156). For the experienced lucid dreamers, "compared with nonlucid dreams, lucid dreams had significantly higher levels of control, more positive emotions, and higher levels of visual vividness, clarity of thinking, physical activity, and changes of scene" (LaBerge & Gackenbach, 2000, p. 156). It would appear that the development of lucid dreaming leads to enriched dream experiences.

Stephen LaBerge, a pioneer in lucid dream research, along with his colleagues, found that some dreamers, while asleep, can indicate the onset of lucidity with "eye movements and fist clenches" (LaBerge, 1990a, p. 110) that could be observed on a polysomnograph in a sleep laboratory. This led them to a series of experiments concerning lucid dreaming. In one study they found that "76 signal-verified lucid dreams" (LaBerge, 1990a, p. 112) from 13 participants all occurred during REM sleep, with 5 to 490 seconds "of uninterrupted REM sleep" (LaBerge, 1990a, p. 112) following the lucid dream signals. A comparison of physiological data for 5 minutes before and 5 minutes following "the initiation of lucidity" (LaBerge, 1990a, p. 112) revealed "highly significant increases in physiological activation during the 30 [seconds] before and after lucidity onset," indicating that the onset of lucid dreaming occurs during phasic REM sleep. In other studies, they have shown that lucid dreaming is more likely to occur during later rather than earlier REM sleep periods. They have also found that "time estimates during . . . lucid dreams [are] very close to the actual time" (LaBerge, 1990a, p. 119) and "that there is a very direct and reliable relation between the gaze shift reported in lucid dreams and the direction of [polysomnographically] recorded eye movements" (LaBerge, 1990a, p. 199). Results such as these suggest that, contrary to the assumptions of some sleep theorists, cognitive activity during lucid dreaming is comparable to waking cognitive activity, at least in those dreamers who are capable of signaling while asleep.

Lucid Dream Induction

There are two ways that a person can try to induce lucid dreams: She can try to add dreaming while she is awake or add wakefulness while she is dreaming. In other words, she can seek to retain continuity of consciousness while falling asleep or she can seek to become aware while dreaming that she is dreaming. One way of retaining consciousness while falling asleep is to pay attention to "the hypnagogic imagery that accompanies sleep onset" (LaBerge & Rheingold, 1990, p. 96). The idea is to "observe the images as delicately as possible" (LaBerge & Rheingold, 1990, p. 98), "without attachment or desire for action" (LaBerge & Rheingold, 1990, p. 99). As "the imagery becomes a moving, vivid scenario" (LaBerge & Rheingold, 1990, p. 99), a person can become "passively drawn into the dream world" (LaBerge & Rheingold, 1990, p. 99) while remembering that she is dreaming. The dreamer is advised against trying to thrust herself into the dream imagery and against becoming lost in the apparent realness of the dream, in which case she could lose her reflective awareness. Other techniques for trying to retain awareness while falling asleep have in common vigilance to a repetitive mental task, such as counting, that is carried on while "perception of the environment diminishes" (LaBerge & Rheingold, 1990, p. 106). The "body falls asleep while the cognitive process carries [the] conscious mind along with it into sleep" (LaBerge & Rheingold, 1990, p. 106). Retaining consciousness throughout the NREM sleep stages at the beginning of the night is difficult, so that wake-initiated lucid dreams are most likely after brief arousals from REM sleep when the sleeper quickly reenters REM sleep after falling asleep again (LaBerge & Rheingold, 1990).

Dream-initiated lucid dreams are more frequent than wake-initiated lucid dreams (LaBerge & Rheingold, 1990) and can be brought about by a variety of methods. One technique is to try to remember to notice events in dreams that could not occur during the waking state and then make the critical judgment that such inconsistencies indicate that one is dreaming (LaBerge & Gackenbach, 1986). A person can, in fact, keep track of events in her dreams that are contrary to ordinary physical reality, what LaBerge has called "*dreamsigns*" (Laberge & Rheingold, 1990, p. 41; emphasis added) and then look for them in subsequent dreams. Floating or flying, such as in the example of my dream given above, is a dreamsign. In some cases, a dreamer may simply note that events are "dreamlike" and hence that she must be dreaming (LaBerge & Gackenbach, 1986). However, a person can try to develop a critical faculty that can alert her when she is dreaming. This critical faculty can be exercised while awake by asking oneself some 5 to 10 times a day: "Is this a dream?" It is important at that point not to reflexively assume that one is awake but to scrutinize one's experience "for any oddities or inconsistencies that might indicate . . . dreaming" (LaBerge & Rheingold, 1990, p. 62). The point is to have access to such a critical faculty while dreaming so as to be able to notice unusual dream events when they occur.

Because presleep thoughts and stimuli can carry over into dreams, appropriate presleep mentation should increase the probability of lucid dreaming. In training himself to have lucid dreams, LaBerge developed a mnemonic method for the induction of lucid dreams (LaBerge & Gackenbach, 1986). The *modified mnemonic method for the induction of lucid dreams* involves two activities to be done as one is falling asleep. First, a person is to "concentrate singlemindedly on [her] intention to remember to recognize that [she is] dreaming" (LaBerge, 1990b, p. 7) and to try to feel that she really means it. If her thoughts stray from this intention, they are to be returned to it. Second, she is to imagine herself back in a recent dream, with the difference that she imagines herself recognizing that it is a dream. The recalled dream is to be examined critically for dreamsigns, identified as a dream, and continued in fantasy with whatever actions she would like to perform while lucid dreaming. These two activities are to be repeated in such a way "that the last thing in [her] mind before falling asleep is [her] intention to become lucid in [her] next dream" (LaBerge, 1990b, p. 7). Two requirements for learning this technique are high motivation and the ability to recall at least two or three dreams per night (LaBerge & Gackenbach, 1986).

Nightmares can induce lucidity. Events in dreams can be so terrifying that the only way for a person to deal with them is to realize that she is dreaming. Once lucid, she may be able to exercise some degree of control, although less control has been reported in nightmare-induced lucid dreams than in lucid dreams induced by the dreamlikeness of a dream (LaBerge & Gackenbach, 1986). Lucid dreaming can also be cultivated as a treatment for nightmares. In addition to learning to induce dream lucidity, a person can practice, while awake, replacing thoughts of being a victim of her dreams with thoughts of empowerment over them. Then, just as in the modified method for the induction of lucid dreams, she can imagine herself in a previous nightmare, confronting rather than avoiding that of which she is afraid and "creating a better outcome" (Levitan & LaBerge, 1990, p. 11).

As we have seen, even though the threshold for perceiving external stimuli is increased in sleep, sensations can sometimes still occur and be incorporated, often in modified form, in one's dreams. On this basis, LaBerge has developed devices that can present cues to the sleeper while she is dreaming. One such device, called the "DreamLight" (LaBerge & Rheingold, 1990, p. 88), is a mask containing miniaturized electronic equipment with an attached computer that can detect the wearer's eye movements and turn on flashing lights directed at her eyes while she is in REM sleep. On going to sleep at night, a person would put on the mask and intend to be on the lookout for light in her dreams. In one study, those using a mnemonic method for the induction of lucid dreams together with a DreamLight had "five times as many lucid dreams as those not using any lucid dream induction technique" (LaBerge & Rheingold, 1990, p. 89). Sometimes the light has the same appearance in a person's dreams as it does during waking. "However, 80 percent of the time the light takes on aspects of the dream world, becoming . . . seamlessly woven into the fabric of the dream" (LaBerge & Rheingold, 1990, p. 89).

The transformation of light in dreams is illustrated by a dream that I had one night when I was wearing a NovaDreamer, a device that is essentially the same as the DreamLight. In my dream I was walking along a somewhat darkened city street when suddenly a nuclear bomb went off some four or five blocks ahead of me. I was terrified. I had forgotten all about the NovaDreamer and did not realize that the nuclear bomb was my cue that I was dreaming. At other times, the light can be recognized, but our penchant "to rationalize rather than think logically" (LaBerge & Rheingold, 1990, p. 89) can result in the conclusion that we are awake. If a dreamer wonders whether or not she is awake, there is a reality test button mounted in the center of the mask that can be used to check if she is dreaming. When the button is actually pushed, the lights flash once, indicating to a person that she is awake. If a person tries to push the button during a dream, on the other hand, all sorts of interesting things can happen. Thus, if the lights do not flash when the button is pushed, a person can conclude that she is dreaming. One night while I was asleep, I saw the lights flash in my dreams and recognized them for what they were. I was sure that they had awakened me. I pushed the reality test button anyway and nothing happened. "Darn," I thought, "I can't believe that the batteries are already dead." In the morning, when I was really awake, to my surprise, there was nothing wrong with the batteries, and the NovaDreamer worked just fine.

A dream in which a dreamer has raised the question of whether or not she is dreaming without drawing the correct conclusion is called a *prelucid dream* (LaBerge & Gackenbach, 1986). Having raised the question, however, there are a number of things that a person can do to try to reach a correct conclusion if she does not have a device with a reality test button. She can hop in the air, for example, and try to fly. Or she can pay attention to something, such as a page of writing, turn away from it, then look at it again to see if it has changed in unusual ways (LaBerge & Rheingold, 1990).

However, "while awake we almost never doubt whether we are awake or not" (LaBerge & Gackenbach, 1986, p. 162), so if we find ourselves questioning "whether or not we are dreaming, we probably are" (LaBerge & Gackenbach, 1986, p. 162).

Implications of Lucid Dreaming

In a somewhat ironic twist on Freud's theory, lucid dreaming offers an opportunity for deliberate wish fulfillment, including the fulfillment of one's sexual fantasies if one were to be so inclined. We have also seen a somewhat more serious potential use for lucid dreaming in alleviating nightmares. And the same flexibility of mind that can be developed for confronting frightening dream characters can be carried over into wakefulness. Indeed, lucidity allows dreaming to become an opportunity to develop adaptive behaviors for waking life more generally. For example, a person can practice skills such as sporting or social skills in her dreams. We have also seen that nonlucid dreams have been used as sources of insight for problem solving. But lucid dreaming can possibly be used even more effectively in creative endeavors. For example, a dreamer could design a whole mental workshop, complete with necessary paraphernalia and wise beings as helpers, in which to seek solutions to particular problems. And if one is tired of all else, lucid dreams can be used as a venue for seeking the meaning of life and pursuing one's spiritual aspirations (LaBerge & Rheingold, 1990; see also Walsh & Vaughan, 1992).

The nature of lucid dreaming raises the question of what it means to say that a person is asleep while she is lucid dreaming. Some critics have argued that lucid dreamers are actually awake, that "they are merely absorbed in their private fantasy worlds" (LaBerge, 1990a, p. 111). As mentioned in chapter 3, there can be numerous brief awakenings during a night's sleep. Perhaps "lucid dreaming occurs during . . . microawakenings" (LaBerge, 1990a, p. 117) within REM sleep. The data, however, suggest that, while "a minority of lucid dreams . . . are initiated from these moments of transitory arousal [they] continue in subsequent undisturbed REM sleep" (LaBerge, 1990a, p. 117). And, during lucid dreaming, although dreamers know where they are because they can remember where they went to sleep, they "report total immersion in the dream world and no sensory contact with the external world" (LaBerge, 1990a, p. 111). According to LaBerge, "the evidence is clear: Lucid dreaming is an experiential and physiological reality; though perhaps paradoxical, it is clearly a phenomenon of sleep" (LaBerge, 1990a, p. 111), yet one in which a person is fully cognizant of her situation.

Perhaps the most interesting implications of lucidity are for the waking state. If we are normally unaware of our lack of awareness of the state of affairs while asleep, could the same also be true of waking existence? Could it be that our everyday consciousness is in some sense analogous to that of being asleep and that we need to wake up (LaBerge & Rheingold, 1990; Malamud, 1986; Tart, 1993; Walsh & Vaughan, 1992)? And just as we need to use specific techniques for becoming lucid on demand while dreaming, could not the development of appropriate strategies also be necessary for becoming lucid while awake? If it turns out that waking life is as much a dream as is sleep, then perhaps we can learn from sleep to wake up from waking life.

PRECOGNITIVE DREAMS

As we have seen, dreams turn out to be more interesting than they at first appear to be when we take some time to look at them. They can be sources of symbolic meaning for some people, solutions to problems, venues for fantastic adventures in full awareness, and an impetus for reexamining the nature of waking reality. But what about one of the most basic assumptions of most dream theories—that dream content is basically a mixture of material dredged up from memory even if recast in meaningful form? What about the future? Could some of the stuff of dreams be from the future? From a materialist viewpoint, that is not even a question that we are supposed to ask. "Yet stubbornly, persistently, exasperatingly, people have reported precognitive dreams in all ages and cultures that we know" (Ullman & Krippner, 1973, p. 175). Let us define *precognitive dreams* as dreams in which there are "meaningful coincidences" (Houran & Lange, 1998, p. 1411) between dream contents and actual future events, whatever explanation there may end up being for such coincidences. Let me give an example of one of my precognitive dreams.

An Example of a Precognitive Dream

Some years ago I had submitted the manuscript for an academic book to a publishing house in another city for consideration for publication. The director of the press had sent it to two reviewers who had made sufficiently favorable comments about it. A meeting of the editorial board of the publishing house was to be held in order to determine the fate of my manuscript. The day before the meeting I had talked to an editor who had told me that a decision would be made at the meeting whether or not to proceed with publication. The night before the meeting I had the following dream:

> I was in a schoolyard playing road hockey. I had the ball. In front of
> me were two players from the opposite team. I realized that I was far
> away from the net, so I headed toward it, managing to get past the two
> players to the front of the net. I crossed in front of the goalmouth from

left to right. The goalie moved with me but not quickly enough. There was some space between his left leg and the goalpost. I took a back-handed shot but the ball turned into a wad of paper and missed the post by several inches. No goal. The game was over. It had ended in a tie. But the next thing I knew, I was standing in the schoolyard with a group of other players. Another game was about to begin. There was going to be another chance to win.

I had been paying attention to my dreams for about 25 years by the time in my life that I had that hockey dream. I do not know whether the explanation for precognitive dreams is mundane or extraordinary. All I know is that I have found a sufficiently reliable meaningful coincidence between dreams that appear to be precognitive and subsequent events so as to be concerned when such dreams occur. When I awoke in the morning, I immediately identified this as a precognitive dream. As I said previously, scoring goals while playing hockey represents academic publication for me. This dream, it seemed, was about the publication of my manuscript. The two defendants on the other team in the dream corresponded to the two reviewers in real life. I had managed to get past them. That part of the dream had to do with events that had already transpired. The problem, as I saw it, was that in the dream I failed to score the goal. The game had ended in a tie. Now that part of the dream, I had to admit, did not fit well with reality. There could be no tie. I had been told that a decision was to be made one way or the other regarding publication. Likewise, the part about the new game made no sense. What I did know was that I had failed to score a goal, indicating to me that the book was not going to be published. Somewhat dejected, I went to school and related my dream to a colleague.

I eventually found out what had happened at the meeting of the editorial board that was held the day after my dream. Matters had been going along well until one of the board members had begun to question the appropriateness of publishing a book containing such controversial subject matter as mine. The discussion deteriorated until it was decided that the manuscript would be given to a third reviewer to make a judgment about the suitability of its publication by the press. The meeting ended without a decision regarding publication after all, just as the game in my dream had ended in a tie. And the manuscript was to be sent out to a new reviewer for assessment, just as in my dream, a new game was starting with a fresh opportunity to win.

Empirical Studies of Precognitive Dreams

I want to emphasize that I have provided the preceding example for illustrative purposes rather than as evidence of actual foreknowledge of future events. However, two systematic studies to test precognition in dreams were carried out at the Maimonides Medical Center in Brooklyn, New York, where Montague Ullman was the director of the Maimonides Community Mental Health Center and Stanley Krippner was the director of the Dream Laboratory. The participant in both studies was Malcolm Bessent, who appeared to have had previous precognitive experiences (Richard Broughton, 1991). In the first study, the idea was to provide Bessent with a multisensory experience in the morning on awakening and to see whether his dreams of the previous night could anticipate the contents of that experience. On eight nonconsecutive nights, Bessent slept in the sleep laboratory, where he was awakened during the night for dream reports. In the morning, after the tape of Bessent's dreams had been mailed out to be transcribed, a target was selected using a random number system and a multisensory experience prepared for Bessent (Richard Broughton, 1991). "Three outside judges would compare each night's [dream reports] to each of the eight target experiences on a 100-point scale" (Ullman & Krippner, 1973, p. 177).

For the first session, the target that ended up being randomly selected was the word "corridor" (Ullman & Krippner, 1973, p. 178). Krippner, who had had "no contact with Bessent or his dreams" (Ullman & Krippner, 1973, p 177) and whose task it was to make up the multisensory experience, chose as the theme the painting "Hospital Corridor at St. Remy" (Ullman & Krippner, 1973, p. 179) by Van Gogh, in which a lone figure can be seen "in the corridor of a mental institution" (Ullman & Krippner, 1973, p. 179). In the morning, Bessent was addressed as "Mr. Van Gogh," was "led through a darkened corridor of the lab" (Ullman & Krippner, 1973, p. 179), was "given a pill . . . and a glass of water" (Ullman & Krippner, 1973, p. 179), was " 'disinfected' with acetone daubed on a cotton swab" (Ullman & Krippner, 1973, p. 179), was shown slides of "paintings by mental patients" (Ullman & Krippner, 1973, p. 179), and was played eerie music and hysterical laughter. Bessent's dreams of the previous night had included the presence of doctors and medical people who had expressed hostility toward him, a "large concrete building" (Ullman & Krippner, 1973, p. 177), a "concrete wall" (Ullman & Krippner, 1973, p. 178), and a patient who was escaping (Ullman & Krippner, 1973). Subsequently, the judges matched the previous night's dreams with the target "corridor," so this session was considered to be a direct hit. Altogether, there were five of eight direct hits, and the probability of the overall results occurring by chance was calculated to be 1 in 5,000 (Krippner, 1993; Ullman & Krippner, 1973). It could be argued that the direct hit of the first night was not surprising given what we know about the incorporation of presleep stimuli in dreams. However, the relative influence of presleep stimuli was tested in the second experiment in which a comparison was made of the incorporation of the target in dreams before and after the participant had been exposed to it.

Bessent was the participant again in the second experiment. This time he was presented with a slide show that had "an accompanying sound track" (Richard Broughton, 1991, p. 97) on the evening after having reported his dreams in the sleep laboratory. Then he would try to dream about the slide show on the following night. In this way a comparison could be made between the incorporation of the stimulus in dreams that occurred before and after its presentation (Richard Broughton, 1991). Again, there were eight targets but this time 16 nights of dream reports. EEG technicians from outside who knew nothing about the design of the experiment were brought in to ensure that those gathering the dream reports would not favor either the precognitive or postcognitive dreams. Again, the dream reports were scored by three outside judges on a 100-point scale for similarity to the eight targets without knowing the order in which the dreams had occurred (Ullman & Krippner, 1973).

The highest score for a dream report and target pair was 98. This was for a precognitive night on which Bessent dreamed repeatedly of the color blue, water, and themes concerning birds. He said, in fact, "I just have a feeling that the next target material will be about birds" (Ullman & Krippner, 1973, p. 184). And it was. The target was a slide show about birds. The following night he dreamed about a secretary going for dinner to a restaurant at the top of a high building but not about birds. The correspondence between the bird target and the following night received a rating of 18 out of 100 by the judges. Overall, for "seven of the eight pairs of nights the precognition night had greater correspondence to the experience than the post-experience nights" (Ullman & Krippner, 1973, p. 184). The probability that the results had occurred by chance was about 1 in 1,000 (Ullman & Krippner, 1973).

Unfortunately, studies concerning anomalous psychological phenomena have sometimes been misrepresented and falsified in secondary descriptions of them in the psychological literature. For example, some critics have described the multisensory experience associated with the target "corridor" as having occurred before Bessent reported his dreams rather than after he had reported them, as was actually the case (Krippner, 1993). Those reading such descriptions would be likely to reach the conclusion that "the researchers were completely incompetent" (Child, 1985, p. 1228), instead of appreciating the possibility of the occurrence of an interesting psychological phenomenon.

What if we were to take the results of the Maimonides dream experiments seriously in the same way that we would take the results of other scientific experiments seriously, particularly considering that these results are consistent with other studies of anomalous precognitive perception during the waking state (Jahn & Dunne, 1987)? Is it possible that, in addition to being fanciful productions of an experience-generating system, dreams can sometimes be meaningful? That not only can they sometimes be meaningful, but that they can also provide us with knowledge about ourselves and the world around us? What if dreams sometimes facilitate access to a level of reality from which we are ordinarily excluded in our ordinary waking state? What if alterations of consciousness as such can sometimes let us see underneath the surface of life?

Well, these are largely empirical questions. There is some meaningfulness as we ordinarily understand it in lucid dreams insofar as we can rationally make judgments in lucid dreams about events that occur in them. But research that takes into account the manner in which symbols appear to occur in dreams is needed to establish whatever additional meaningfulness there may be in dreams. In particular, the nature of dream insights needs to be established, including those that appear to pertain to the future. There is much empirical work that can be done to better understand the possible meanings of dreams.

5

HYPNOSIS

As I was preparing to write this chapter, I had a dream. In my dream I was looking at my face in a mirror and realized that my face looked dramatically different from the way that it normally does. It was somehow rounder, softer. Odd, I thought, that I should look like that. I assumed that my facial appearance had somehow changed. It did not occur to me to recognize this improbable circumstance as a sign that I was dreaming.

Shortly before going to bed the night before my dream, I had read an article about a study in which the researchers had suggested to participants a change of sexual identity following a hypnotic induction. Eighteen participants who were "hypnotic virtuosos" (Register & Kihlstrom, 1986, p. 84), those extremely susceptible to hypnosis, all "responded positively to the sex change suggestion" (Noble & McConkey, 1995, p. 71). The researchers later confronted the participants by requesting them to look at a video image of themselves and asking them to tell the researcher what they were experiencing as they looked at themselves on the screen. Eleven of the 18 virtuosos "continued to maintain their positive response to the suggestion" (Noble & McConkey, 1995, p. 72). During a postexperimental inquiry, 7 of the 18 virtuosos "said that the image on the screen was not them" (Noble & McConkey, 1995, p. 72), and six others said that they were "confused because what they were feeling conflicted with what they were seeing" (Noble & McConkey, 1995, p. 72).

In my dream, I had looked at a distorted image of myself and assumed it to be real, even though it did not coincide with what I knew to be my appearance, whereas in the hypnotic sex change study, some virtuosos looked at a true image of themselves and assumed it to be incorrect because they were convinced that they were the opposite of their actual sex. In both cases, there was an inability to properly reconcile perception of oneself with one's self-identity.

Similarities have historically been noted between sleep and hypnosis (Hilgard, 1987), with hypnotists sometimes using the terminology of sleep in the context of hypnosis (H. Spiegel & Spiegel, 1978). Indeed, the word *hypnosis* itself has apparently been derived from the Greek word for sleep

(Braid, 1842–1883/1960). However, we have to be careful not to overstate the similarities to sleep (H. Spiegel & Spiegel, 1978), which just raises the question of what, really, is hypnosis. In what sense is hypnosis an altered state of consciousness? Or is there anything altered about it at all? In fact, one of our thematic threads runs throughout much of this chapter—namely, is there anything extraordinary about hypnosis, or is it just a mundane phenomenon?

Questions concerning the nature of hypnosis are more difficult to answer than it seems that they should be. And something with which we have quickly become familiar in this book, there is little agreement among researchers concerning the phenomena and theories of hypnosis. Since the beginning of its modern history with the study of animal magnetism by Franz Anton Mesmer in the 18th century (Hilgard, 1987), hypnosis has been both enigmatic and controversial. In chapter 1 we considered various psychological dimensions that could be used for defining altered states of consciousness, including dimensions of changes to body image and personal identity. Hence, from the earlier example of the hypnotically suggested sex change, we can see that at least in some cases hypnosis can be considered to be an alteration of consciousness. Of course, to say that hypnosis is an alteration or an altered state of consciousness is to classify rather than explain it (Kirsch & Lynn, 1995). But is even that minimal classification undue glorification of what may be nothing more than the expression of thoughts and behaviors appropriate to a social situation that is defined as hypnosis (Spanos, 1982, 1986, 1991)?

The phenomena associated with hypnosis are themselves elusive. "Hypnosis, like a chameleon, seems to take on the beliefs and characteristics of the particular experimenter or laboratory in which it is being studied" (Watkins & Watkins, 1986, p. 135). Furthermore, not only is there a variety of hypnotic experiences (Krippner, 1999), but they also apparently blend into other related psychological experiences as we shall see in chapter 6. How then are we to come up with a definition of hypnosis? A practical way of proceeding has been to define a "*domain of hypnosis*" (Hilgard, 1973a, p. 972) consisting of the topics that are studied in hypnosis research. In other words, we can delimit the range of psychological phenomena that are to be considered as being hypnosis. Let us therefore start by looking at hypnotic phenomena, then consider susceptibility to hypnosis, theories, memory enhancement, and, finally, some clinical applications of hypnosis.

HYPNOTIC PHENOMENA

How does hypnosis occur? What does someone do who has been hypnotized? We will consider the process of becoming hypnotized, and then indicate some of the suggestions that could be given to a person who has been hypnotized and the responses to them that she might make.

Hypnotic Induction

When there is an effort to produce it deliberately, hypnosis starts with an *induction* that could proceed as follows. A *hypnotist* speaks while a person being hypnotized, called a *hypnotic subject* listens. (I am continuing the convention of using the word "subject" to refer to a person who gets hypnotized because such a person appears to lose her capacity for self-determination, although, as we have already seen, the matter may not be nearly so straightforward.) The hypnotist begins by telling the hypnotic subject to close her eyes, to pay attention to the hypnotist's voice, and to relax. The hypnotist assures her that hypnosis is safe. Then the hypnotist may tell her that she is sleepy and that she will go into a deep sleep in which she will be able to do what the hypnotist tells her to do. The hypnotist counts from 1 to 10, telling the individual that, with each count, she is going into a deep sleep. After having counted to 10, the hypnotist tells her that she will respond to suggestions to be made by the hypnotist. At that point, various suggestions may be made. A hypnotic session ends with the hypnotist indicating to the individual that the session is over, for example, by counting backwards from five to one, telling the individual that she will be more fully awake with each count (cf. Spanos, Radtke, Hodgins, Bertrand, et al., 1983; Spanos, Radtke, Hodgins, Stam, & Bertrand, 1983).

There are many variations of the hypnotic induction. Hypnotic subjects can be hypnotized individually or in groups (Shor & Orne, 1962). The induction may be done in person or previously recorded and played on a cassette recorder. *Self-hypnosis* is possible in which a person listens to a taped induction or actively plays the role of both hypnotist and subject (Kelly & Kelly, 1995). Subjects may be asked to close their eyes, as in the example above, or to look at a target such as a button or tack (Weitzenhoffer & Hilgard, 1962). One induction technique includes having hypnotic subjects roll their eyes upward and then close their eyelids. An induction can be leisurely or abrupt. One hypnotist, in the middle of a tussle with a man who was trying to kill him, claims to have hypnotized his adversary by telling him to "Look at that ink bottle and keep looking at it!" (H. Spiegel & Speigel, 1978, p. 24). An induction does not have to be characterized in terms of sleep. In one study, suggestions of alertness were substituted for suggestions of drowsiness, and increased effort substituted for relaxation in the usual induction protocol. Participants pedaling a stationary bicycle "received suggestions that the pedaling would not seem difficult and would be without discomfort, that the room would seem bright, and that alertness would be increased as the pedaling went on" (Hilgard, 1979, p. 148). This is an example of *active-alert hypnosis* of which there also have been other variations (Alarcón, Capafons, Bayot, & Cardeña, 1999).

There does not seem to be anything particularly compelling about a hypnotic induction. Indeed, in many cases an induction is simply a guided imagery exercise that is used in a situation that has been labeled as hypnosis. Why should we suppose that that would be enough to cause a person's consciousness to change in a fundamental way? And indeed, often a person's consciousness does not change. One way of conceptualizing what is happening is to think of a person as entering a special state of trance. Trance is an older and broader concept than hypnosis and subsumes a variety of different psychological phenomena. The word *trance* has approximately been used to refer to states of consciousness in which the appearance of awareness is present but that are actually sleep-like states characterized by involuntary behavior and decreased environmental responsiveness (Pekala & Kumar, 2000). The point of an induction, therefore, is to do whatever it takes to try to get a person into the state of trance. Some individuals may be able to enter trance spontaneously, and some may be manipulated into it, whereas others may be impervious to the changed state. Another way of conceptualizing what is happening during hypnosis is to think not of "special psychological states or processes" (Spanos, 1991, p. 324) but of social situations in which individuals "generate experiences and enact behaviors in order to meet what they tacitly understand to be the requirements of the . . . [situations]" (Spanos, 1991, p. 325). We shall interweave these two points of view as we proceed to consider the phenomena associated with hypnosis.

Hypnotic Suggestions

Following an induction, a hypnotic subject would normally be given *suggestions*. The degree to which a subject is responsive to suggestions is called *hypnotic susceptibility* (Bowers, 1976). A subject may be asked to extend her arm in front of her at shoulder height and told that it is being filled with air like a balloon. That it feels lighter and lighter. The arm may rise noticeably. A subject may also be challenged by first being told that her arm is rigid and then asked to try to bend it (cf. Spanos, Radtke, Hodgins, Bertrand, et al., 1983; Spanos, Radtke, Hodgins, Stam, et al., 1983). There are a number of suggestions such as these that can involve making or not making appropriate motor movements in response to imagined situations. There are also more difficult items, less likely to evoke an appropriate response, consisting of cognitive suggestions involving changes in perception, thought, and memory (Weitzenhoffer & Hilgard, 1962). For example, in a hallucination suggestion, a subject could be told that a cat has crawled on her lap and be asked to look at the cat and to pet it. An amnesia suggestion could be given whereby a subject would be told she would forget the previous suggestions that had been given and then subsequently challenged to write them down (cf. Spanos, Radtke, Hodgins, Bertrand, et al., 1983; Spanos, Radtke, Hodgins, Stam, et al., 1983). The sex change suggestion mentioned at the beginning of this chapter is also a cognitive suggestion. Suggestions, known as *posthypnotic suggestions*, can be given during hypnosis to take effect after it has been terminated. For example, in one study, during hypnosis, it was suggested that for the subsequent 48 hours every time a participant heard the word "experiment" she would touch her forehead with her right hand (Bowers, 1976).

Suggesting to a hypnotic subject the presence of something that is not objectively real, such as the hallucinated cat of the previous paragraph, is known as a *positive hallucination* (Bowers, 1976). Let us consider the following study by Martin Orne (1959) in which a positive hallucination was suggested. A collaborator of the experimenter sat within eyesight of a hypnotic subject in a room together with the experimenter and the subject. Once the subject's eyes were closed, the collaborator got up quietly and stood behind the subject. Subsequently, the subject was told to open her eyes and a positive hallucination of the collaborator sitting in the chair was suggested to her. Then the subject was told to turn around and asked who that was standing behind her. In such a case, a subject will typically look back and forth between the collaborator and the empty chair and say that she was "perceiving two images of the same person" (Orne, 1959, p. 296). The "ability . . . to mix freely . . . perceptions derived from reality with those that stem from . . . imagination" (Orne, 1959, p. 295) was called *trance logic* by Orne and considered by him to be one of the "principal features of the hypnotic state" (Orne, 1959, p. 297). Not only could a hypnotist suggest a positive hallucination, she could also suggest a *negative hallucination*, the absence of something that is objectively real. For example, it could be suggested to a hypnotized subject that she will not see "a chair that is in the middle of the room" (Bowers, 1976, p. 103). However, if then asked to walk around the room with eyes open, the subject "will not bump into the chair" (Bowers, 1976, p. 104; emphasis removed). This is again an example of "the ability to tolerate logical inconsistencies" (Orne, 1959, p. 297) during hypnosis.

One of the early uses of hypnosis, during the 19th century, before the invention of chemical anesthetics, was to use *mesmerism*, as it was then called, to suggest a negative hallucination of the absence of pain during major surgery (Hilgard, 1987). Since then, in spite of continuous controversy about the nature of hypnosis, analgesic effects of hypnosis have been demonstrated in both clinical and laboratory settings (J. Barber, 1998a; Dinges et al., 1997; Knox, Morgan, & Hilgard, 1974; Lambert, 1996; Mauer, Burnett, Ouellette, Ironson, & Dandes, 1999; M. F. Miller, Barabasz, & Barabasz, 1991; Montgomery, DuHamel, & Redd, 2000; J. T. Smith, Barabasz, & Barabasz, 1996).

Although not particularly representative, the following study of hypnotic analgesia serves an illustrative purpose. A surgeon hypnotized himself before performing "liposuction surgery of his upper and lower abdomen and flank areas" (Botta, 1999, p. 299). Being uncertain of what to expect, the surgeon used a number of techniques to suggest analgesia. For example, "the areas of the abdomen and flanks were dissociated as if they were another patient's body parts and not the surgeon's own" (Botta, 1999, p. 300). The surgical procedure was performed in a standing position over the course of four hours. This case illustrates hypnotic analgesia particularly well given "the fact that the skin is inundated with cutaneous nerve endings" (Botta, 1999, p. 301), which would ordinarily result in "a continual bombardment of nerve stimulation" (Botta, 1999, p. 301) during liposuction. This case also illustrates the ability to carry out highly skilled cognitive and manual tasks while in a sufficiently deep trance so as to experience analgesia (Botta, 1999). Normally, attempting to do something else during self-induced hypnotic anesthesia would "likely cause loss of the anesthesia" (Ewin, Levitan, & Lynch, 1999, p. 302). In this case, the surgeon was able to dissociate what should have been his experience of pain from his ability to perform the surgery. It is also interesting to consider the extent to which dissociation that occurs in a case such as this is similar to dissociation during sleepwalking as discussed in chapter 3. Indeed, apparently "some early forms of hypnosis resembled sleepwalking" (Bowers, 1976, p. 41).

On rare occasions, a hypnotic subject spontaneously cannot remember what happened during hypnosis. It is also possible to give a posthypnotic suggestion to a subject to the effect that she will forget everything that transpired during hypnosis until she is given a cue from the hypnotist to remember it. On receiving the cue, an awakened subject "suddenly remembers—often with apparent amazement—what he had forgotten up to that moment" (Bowers, 1976, p. 41). But in what sense has information been forgotten in cases of hypnotic amnesia? In one study, individuals were chosen for participation if they could not remember a 7-digit number that they had previously learned after having received "a suggestion that the number had faded away" (Goldstein & Sipprelle, 1970, p. 213). They were then awakened from hypnosis and given an opportunity to learn to reproduce a random color sequence of five blue and five white poker chips. Then, if they were in an experimental group, they were hypnotized, given the suggestion that they would forget the color sequence, and given three opportunities to reproduce it. If the hypnotic subjects had had no memory of the correct sequence, or pretended that they had no memory, then about 15 of the 30 chips should have been placed in incorrect positions. In fact, only an average of 7 errors were made, indicating that subjects did remember the sequence at some level. These results suggest that hypnotic amnesia is neither simply an ablation of memory nor pretending to forget (Goldstein & Sipprelle,

1970). Similar effects have been found for posthypnotic amnesia (Bowers, 1976).

In chapter 2 ironic processes were described whereby efforts to suppress thoughts have the opposite effect of occupying a person's attention. A study was done in which participants "were asked to name a favorite automobile that they would really like to own but could only afford to fantasize about" (Bowers & Woody, 1996, p. 382). Then they "were instructed . . . to prevent any thoughts or mental pictures of their favorite automobile from coming to mind by keeping their mind completely blank" (Bowers & Woody, 1996, p. 382) for two minutes. However, if during that time they did have intrusions of their favorite automobile, they were to push a button for the length of time that those intrusions were present. Participants were then hypnotized and the thought suppression procedure repeated. Then, while still hypnotized, a suggestion was given to subjects that they would forget about their favorite automobile and they were again asked to press the button if any intrusions occurred. What happened? Good hypnotic subjects pushed the button an average of almost five times in the waking condition, an average of only twice in the hypnotic blank-mind condition, and an average of once in the hypnotic-amnesia condition. These results suggest that hypnotic amnesia is not just a matter of thought suppression (Bowers & Woody, 1996).

HYPNOTIC SUSCEPTIBILITY

One of the core features of hypnotic phenomena is the suggestibility of individuals as gauged by their responsiveness to hypnotic suggestions. In fact, the presence of increased suggestibility following hypnotic induction has sometimes been taken as the definition of hypnosis (Hilgard, 1979). Of course, hypnosis is only one context in which suggestibility can occur (cf. Cialdini, 1988), raising the question of whether there is anything unique about hypnotic susceptibility, or whether the behaviors associated with it are responses to the demands of a particular type of social situation. What is the nature of suggestibility in the context of hypnosis?

Hypnotic Susceptibility Scales

The predominant line of contemporary research concerning hypnosis has been defined by the measurement of hypnotic susceptibility based on the use of a small number of similar scales (Woody, 1997). The first of those scales was the *Stanford Hypnotic Susceptibility Scale (SHSS)* developed by Ernest Hilgard and André Weitzenhoffer (Hilgard, 1987; Bowers, 1976). Although the SHSS was designed for individual administration, the *Harvard Group Scale of Hypnotic Susceptibility (HGSHS)* was adapted from one of the forms of the SHSS for group administration (Bowers, 1976; Shor & Orne, 1962). Participants in studies of hypnosis would first be given a standardized induction and then a series of suggestions. The induction and suggestions of arm levitation, arm rigidity, hallucinated cat, and amnesia, described previously, are similar to the protocol of the *Carleton University Responsiveness to Suggestion Scale* (CURSS), in which a total of seven suggestions are used (Spanos, Radtke, Hodgins, Stam, et al., 1983). If an individual responds as suggested, then she is said to have passed that item. The total number of items passed results in a score of hypnotic susceptibility. Using these types of scales most individuals end up being moderately hypnotizable because they would "pass most of the easier items and few of the really difficult ones" (Bowers, 1976, p. 63). Individuals who are particularly unresponsive would be classified as *low* on hypnotic susceptibility, those particularly responsive as *high* (Bowers, 1976), and those who score perfect or almost perfect on susceptibility scales would be classified as *virtuosos* (cf. Register & Kihlstrom, 1986), a term that we have already used to designate the extremely susceptible.

Is hypnotic susceptibility really the sort of psychological characteristic of which there can be more or less? That is to say, is hypnotic susceptibility a dimension or a type? Scales used previous to the SHSS had resulted in the observation that "most people have little or no hypnotic ability" (Woody, 1997, p. 233), so Weitzenhoffer and Hilgard had added easy items to their scales to get a healthy number of midrange scores. In that regard, it is notable that four of the seven items on the CURSS involve making or inhibiting motor movements, whereas only three are cognitive (Spanos, Radtke, Hodgins, Stam, et al., 1983). In favor of the notion that hypnotic susceptibility is categorical are the results of analyses from hypnosis scale data indicating that there are two types of people: those who are responsive to hypnosis and those who are not. It appears that hypnosis is a type rather than a dimension, in spite of the use of susceptibility scales in which it is treated as a dimension (Woody, 1997).

Although the question of whether hypnotic susceptibility is dimensional or typological is theoretically significant, it has had less importance methodologically because often only those scoring high and low on susceptibility scales have been chosen to participate in research (Woody, 1997). Indeed, a common protocol in hypnosis research, suggested by Orne (1959), has been to compare the behavior of hypnotized participants to that of nonhypnotized participants who have been instructed to pretend that they are hypnotized. Orne's idea behind such a strategy was to determine how much of what happened during hypnosis was a result of hypnosis rather than the implicit demands placed on a subject in a hypnotic situation. Differences in behavior between real and simulating participants could be attributed to hypnosis, whereas the status of behavior that was similar would remain indeterminate because such behavior could be a result of hypnosis by the hypnotized participants and successful faking by the simulators. When Orne tried this method, he was surprised to find that "most of the simulating [subjects] did not differ behaviorally from those in deep trance" (Orne, 1959, p. 294). The problem is that simulators could end up being inadvertently hypnotized unless they are low in hypnotizability and impervious to the hypnotic induction. For that reason, high hypnotizable individuals are usually used as reals and low hypnotizable individuals as simulators (Bowers, 1976). This paradigm is not a foolproof method of determining the characteristics of hypnosis because real subjects could also be actually faking, with differences in performance between reals and simulators resulting from differences in task demands.

Differences in Hypnotic Responding

To see the effects of the real versus simulator protocol, let us consider some of the previously mentioned studies. In the sex change study at the beginning of the chapter, 100% of simulators, 89% of high hypnotizable participants, and 100% of the virtuosos "responded positively to the sex change suggestion" (Noble & McConkey, 1995, p. 71). When confronted with an image of their actual appearance, 41% of simulators, 0% of highs, and 73% of virtuosos "continued to maintain their positive response to the suggestion" (Noble & McConkey, 1995, p. 72).

A group of simulators was used in the study in which participants were given a posthypnotic suggestion to touch their foreheads with their right hands every time they heard the word "experiment" within the following 48 hours. To remove the influence of participants' expectations of being evaluated, a laboratory secretary included the word "experiment" three times in her dialogues with participants "in circumstances that permitted the recording of the subjects' responses to the cue word" (Bowers, 1976, p. 19). Under these conditions, simulators responded to the cue 8% of the time, real subjects responded 30% of the time, and a subgroup of real subjects who had passed all of the items on a hypnotic susceptibility scale touched their foreheads 70% of the time (Bowers, 1976).

In Orne's study, the concurrent appearance of a positive hallucination of the experimenter's collaborator and the collaborator's actual presence was apparently accepted by real subjects. Simulators, on the other hand, after having had a positive hallucination induced and then having been asked to turn around to look at the collaborator, "in most cases, either refused to see anyone behind them, or claimed that they could not recognize the person" (Orne 1959, p. 296). What we see in each case is the persistence of suggested behaviors on the part of those who are high or very high on hypnotic susceptibility in a manner that is not matched by those who are simulating hypnotic behavior.

To see how the subjective experience of hypnotized individuals can differ depending on their degree of hypnotic susceptibility, let us consider a study in which participants were required to rate the extent to which they were experiencing what the hypnotist was asking them to experience. The rating was done by having each participant turn a dial to indicate her experience, with the leftmost position corresponding to "not at all experiencing the suggestion" (McConkey, Wende, & Barnier, 1999, pp. 27–28) and the rightmost position corresponding to "completely experiencing the suggestion" (McConkey et al., 1999, p. 28). The participants were 33 high, 47 medium, and 28 low hypnotizable undergraduate students, none of whom was asked to simulate hypnosis. Participants were tested for three suggestions: arm levitation, arm rigidity, and anosmia, which is the inability to smell something that is actually present. The anosmia suggestion was tested by placing oil of wintergreen under a participant's nose and asking her to indicate what she could smell. The investigators found "a strong concordance between subjects' behavioral responses and their subjective responses (as indexed by the dial method)" (McConkey et al., 1999, p. 29).

There were also some interesting differences between groups in the subjective rating study. Only 7 of the 28 low hypnotizable participants passed arm rigidity, but those who did "made very low ratings of their experience" (McConkey et al., 1999, p. 31), in contrast to the medium and high hypnotizable participants. In other words, low hypnotizable participants behaved as though their arms were rigid without feeling that they were, whereas medium and high hypnotizable participants behaved as though their arms were rigid and indicated that they felt that they were. High hypnotizable participants who failed the anosmia item had the same subjective ratings as high hypnotizable participants who passed this item until the response was tested, at which point the ratings of the highs who failed the test decreased, whereas the ratings of the highs who passed the test increased and did not diminish when the hypnotist gave an explicit instruction to cancel the suggestion. This pattern was not found for the medium hypnotizable participants who failed or passed the anosmia item. What these results suggest is that the positive experience of the high hypnotizable participants "during the test of anosmia enhanced and encouraged the intensity of their experiential involvement, and this intensity was not diminished by an explicit instruction from the hypnotist that was intended to cancel their experience" (McConkey et al., 1999, p. 34). Moreover, "across the items, the offset of the experience progressed relatively slowly" (McConkey et al., 1999, p. 34), making it inappropriate to assume "that the cancellation of a hypnotic experience is easy and instantaneous" (McConkey et al., 1999,

p. 35). Overall, what this study shows is that the subjective experience of responding to suggestions is more complex than behavioral tallies of passed items on hypnotic susceptibility scales would indicate. Indeed, the complexity of subjective hypnotic experience will become further compounded in the next section.

EXPLANATIONS OF HYPNOSIS

We have now considered some of the phenomena to which the term "hypnosis" has been applied and the nature of hypnotic susceptibility, so we have some feeling for what we are talking about. But are we any further in our understanding of hypnosis than we were when we started? Are we just seeing ordinary behavior triggered by specific social situations, or are we seeing a special state of trance? Is hypnosis mundane or extraordinary? Let us next look at some explanations of hypnosis, starting with a theory that hypnosis is mundane, then consider some evidence to suggest that there may be something interesting about hypnosis after all, and finally discuss a tripartite theory in which hypnotic events are conceptualized as being extraordinary at least some of the time.

A Sociocognitive Theory of Hypnosis

Nicholas Spanos has maintained that hypnotic phenomena can be explained in the same terms as social behaviors without recourse to any additional psychological constructs (Spanos, Cross, Menary, Brett, & de Groh, 1987). According to the *sociocognitive theory* (Spanos, 1991), "responsive hypnotic subjects retain control of their behavior and guide it strategically in order to meet implicit and explicit role demands as these become regnant in the hypnotic test situation" (Spanos et al., 1987, p. 381). Individual behavior of hypnotic subjects results from "the interactive contribution of numerous variables such as attitudes and expectations concerning hypnosis and the interpretational stance taken toward suggestions" (Spanos et al., 1987, p. 381). There really is nothing left over once the social psychological aspects of the hypnotic situation have been removed, so that differences between simulating lows and real highs are a result of differences in the demands placed on subjects in these two conditions.

Hypnotic susceptibility has been shown to be a stable trait in naive subjects. But what if lows could be made into highs? And indeed, there are a number of ways in which susceptibility can be increased, among them cognitive skills training programs that include teaching individuals how to interpret suggestions and how to use imagery to experience responses to suggestions, demonstrating responses to hypnotic suggestions, and providing opportunities for practicing hypnotic responding (Spanos et al., 1987). In one study the use of cognitive skills training resulted in more than half of the low susceptibles and more than two thirds of the medium susceptibles becoming high susceptibles. Furthermore, the created high susceptible participants "failed to differ significantly from a comparison group of natural high susceptibles on subjective aspects of susceptibility" (Gorassini & Spanos, 1986, p. 1011). If hypnotic responding can be improved through cognitive skills training, then is it necessary for us to look beyond the social–cognitive aspect of psychological functioning for an explanation of hypnosis?

Physiological markers of hypnosis have been sought in a number of studies (e.g., A. Barabasz, 2000; A. Barabasz et al., 1999; De Pascalis, 1999; Graffin, Ray, & Lundy, 1995; Grond, Pawlik, Walter, Lesch, & Heiss, 1995; Schnyer & Allen, 1995; Szechtman, Woody, Bowers, & Nahmias, 1998), sometimes with the idea that a challenge would be posed to the sociocognitive theory if meaningful physiological events could be found that occur during hypnosis but not in its absence. For example, *event-related potentials (ERPs)* are EEG waveforms that follow on the presentation of a series of stimuli. The amplitudes of waveforms occurring 200 to 500 milliseconds after stimulus presentation are thought to be affected by cognitive factors so that, "for example, stimuli that are rare, that require a response, or that demand conscious attention tend to produce larger positive amplitudes" (D. Spiegel, Bierre, & Rootenberg, 1989, p. 749).

In a study by Arreed Barabasz (2000), five high susceptible and five low susceptible participants were selected based on earlier screening of hypnotic susceptibility. An EEG was used to measure ERPs in two conditions while subjects listened to series of "25 tone pips . . . presented at 1 second intervals" (A. Barabasz, 2000, p. 166). In the first condition, both low and high susceptible participants were told to imagine foam earplugs in their ears that would reduce the volume of the sound. Following the first condition, low hypnotizable participants were instructed to simulate hypnosis and both low and high susceptible participants were exposed to an alert hypnotic induction. The same suggestion was then given in the second condition as had been given in the first condition followed by the series of 25 tone pips "while EEG data were collected" (A. Barabasz, 2000, p. 167). Subsequently the suggestion was reversed and "an independent post experimental inquiry was conducted to determine strategies employed by participants in response to the alternative conditions" (A. Barabasz, 2000, p. 167). The question is whether there are physiological differences between just imagining having earplugs and imagining having earplugs while hypnotized. What did Barabasz find?

In his study Arreed Barabasz (2000) found that there were no differences in the amplitudes of ERPs between the nonhypnotic and hypnotic conditions for those who were low in hypnotic susceptibility. However, there was a significant decrease in the average amplitude of ERPs from the nonhypnotic to the hypnotic condition for the high susceptible participants, suggesting that the hallucination of the presence of ear plugs while hypnotized was associated with altered perception of the auditory stimulus. Four of the five high hypnotizable participants "showed attenuation of their average ERPs in the hypnosis condition of at least 50% in contrast to the suggestion only condition" (A. Barabasz, 2000, p. 167). One of the high hypnotizable participants "demonstrated virtually identical ERPs between the two conditions" (A. Barabasz, 2000, p. 167). During the postexperimental inquiry, this participant said that when he had been spanked by his father as a child, he "could turn off the pain like just going to another place" (A. Barabasz, 2000, p. 168) and that he had done what he had learned to do as a child on being given the initial suggestion to place earplugs in his ears and then again when given the same suggestion in the hypnosis condition. "This response appears to be a classic example of spontaneous hypnosis with apparent dissociation" (A. Barabasz, 2000, p. 168). The results of this study appear to show that there are physiological differences in perception associated with hypnosis, although it is not clear exactly what cognitive processes are subserved by the ERP changes.

Involuntary Volition

As we have seen, the subjective experience of a person who is hypnotized is often different from that of someone who has not been hypnotized. Perhaps the most characteristic subjective feature of hypnosis is the *classic suggestion effect* (Kihlstrom, 1985), whereby "hypnotic responses are experienced as occurring involuntarily" (Kihlstrom, 1985, p. 388). First time hypnotic subjects are typically "surprised because they do not experience themselves as making the behavior happen; instead, they experience the behavior as happening to them" (Bowers, 1976, p. 116). However, according to the sociocognitive approach, hypnotic behavior is not involuntary but "purposeful, goal-directed action that can be understood in terms of how the subjects interpret their situation and how they attempt to present themselves through their actions" (Spanos, 1986, p. 449).

The issue of volition has been a tangled one in the history of contemporary thought (Libet et al., 1999), and it is not clear to what extent it can be untangled in the context of hypnosis. From a materialist point of view, the world is a completely determined system in which events follow invariable cause–effect sequences without the intervention of free will or any nonphysical agency. This includes all phenomena associated with consciousness. By this account, feelings of having free will, believing that one is determining one's own actions, and debates about the presence or absence of volition are all already completely determined events. Even if, after lengthy philosophical and scientific investigation, it were to be found that free will really did exist, that too would just be part of the ongoing fully determined chain of physical events. In other words, the conclusion that free will existed would be erroneous but predetermined. All behavior is involuntary, and whether or not we think of it as such is just more involuntary behavior (cf. Libet et al., 1999). From a deterministic point of view, therefore, it makes no sense to insist that hypnotic behavior is purposive because, in a broader sense, there is no purposiveness. Indeed, a materialist could say that hypnotic subjects have a more, rather than less, accurate assessment of their actual situation with regard to volitional acts.

Suppose that we adopt a more *"libertarian* conception of free will" (Libet et al., 1999, p. xiv) and posit that we really can take consciously chosen actions that are not entirely constrained by internal and external forces. It is reasonable to do so given that "there really is no evidence available to draw [the] strong conclusion" (Libet et al., 1999, p. xxi) that free will does not exist. It is the libertarian conception on which "the entire religious, ethical, cultural and legal system of the western world is based" (Libet et al., 1999, p. xxi). In that case, why is it not possible that in some situations we may perceive to have carried out actions that we did not consciously choose to take? An argument from chapter 2 about a practical approach to introspective knowledge can be adapted to these situations. If we are not conscious of having taken an action, then that action was not consciously taken. Using the terminology of chapter 1, we can note the dissociation between experiences that occur as consciousness$_2$ and nonconscious processing that proceeds as consciousness$_1$. Some hypnotic subjects, according to their introspected accounts, do not consciously$_2$ decide to respond to hypnotic suggestions that appear to proceed consciously$_1$. Thus, those actions are involuntary, and it is not clear what is gained by insisting that they are really voluntary.

What, then, are we to make of the sociocognitive approach? Orne's surprise that simulators were as successful as they were in producing hypnotic phenomena and the inability of experimenters to detect simulators in studies using the simulator–real paradigm (e.g., A. Barabasz, 2000) indicates the extent to which hypnotic behavior can be imitated by trying to behave as though one were hypnotized. In general, such imitation is possible for tasks that have been tested in the laboratory but unlikely for extreme situations found in clinical practice, such as physical pain resulting from surgery or serious burns (cf. Graham, 1986). Furthermore, for many hypnotic phenomena, the differences between not being hypnotized and being hypnotized lie not in the behaviors themselves but in a subject's experience of the behaviors. We have seen, for example, that low hypnotizable individuals can comply behaviorally with an arm rigidity challenge while indicating that they are not experiencing the suggestion whereas medium and high subjects who pass an arm rigidity challenge indicate that they are experiencing the suggestion. It is not unreasonable to suppose that some hypnotic responsiveness, particularly for easy items by those who are not susceptible to hypnosis, may be entirely the result of strategic social behavior consistent with a sociocognitive approach. But does that account for all of hypnosis, particularly in the case of good subjects?

A Tripartite Theory of Hypnosis

Let us consider a contention proposed by Theodore Barber (1999) that "hypnosis continues to baffle investigators because it has three separate dimensions" (T. Barber, 1999, p. 21). One of these dimensions, consistent with the sociocognitive view, is embodied by the *positively set person*. Responsiveness to suggestions of a positively set person is not a result of any extraordinary personal characteristics but of a "favorable collocation of 'ordinary' social psychological variables such as attitudes, motivations, and expectancies toward the situation; relationship with the hypnotist; and readiness to think with and not contradict the hypnotist's suggestions" (T. Barber, 1999, p. 27). Such hypnotic subjects have a positive attitude toward the hypnotic situation, are motivated to follow the suggestions that are made, and expect to be hypnotized and to "experience the suggested effects" (T. Barber, 1999, p. 28). They apparently succeed by devising various cognitive strategies that allow them to respond appropriately to hypnotic suggestions.

Another type of excellent hypnotic subject is a *fantasy-prone person* (T. Barber, 1999; Lynn, Pintar, & Rhue, 1997; Lynn & Rhue, 1988). This is someone with "an overriding extreme involvement in *fantasizing per se*" (S. C. Wilson & T. Barber, 1981, p. 134) who is "able to 'hallucinate' at will" (S. C. Wilson & T. Barber, 1981, p. 134) in all of her sensory modalities. For such a person, "fantasy appears to be as vivid as reality" (S. C. Wilson & T. Barber, 1981, p. 134), and what is fantasized appears to be experienced in the same way as reality (S. C. Wilson & T. Barber, 1981), even though the nature of the imagery of such subjects has not been shown to be different from that of other people (Council, Chambers, Jundt, & Good, 1991). During childhood, the fantasy-prone person "typically lived in a make-believe world" (T. Barber, 1999, p. 22) that included her dolls, imaginary companions, angels, and other beings. As an adult she retains vivid memories of her life, including apparent memories of events before age 3. Almost all fantasy-prone people are convinced that they have had paranormal experiences such as "premonitions; telepathic impressions; precognitive dreams; out-of-body experiences; and contact with spirits, ghosts, or apparitions" (T. Barber, 1999, p. 23), and some have reported having had "intense religious experiences or exceptional abilities as healers" (T. Barber, 1999, p. 23). There is an evident connection between mental and bodily events. For example, 75% of women who are fantasy-prone can reach orgasm without tactile stimulation during sexual fantasies. A fantasy-prone person is often highly susceptible to hypnosis, not needing a hypnotic induction in order to respond to hypnotic suggestions (T. Barber, 1999). Some studies have found only a modest correspondence between fantasy-proneness and hypnotic susceptibility, perhaps because of the need for a positive set toward hypnosis even for those who are fantasy-prone (T. Barber, 1999; Lynn & Rhue, 1988).

There is also a third dimension of hypnosis. Deirdre Barrett (1996b) conducted a study with 34 participants who scored perfect or almost perfect on two scales of hypnotic susceptibility. They were split into two groups on the basis of those who could enter hypnosis quickly without a formal induction and those who could not. On investigation, 19 participants who could enter hypnosis quickly turned out to be characterized by "vividness of fantasy processes" (Barrett, 1996b, p. 124) and hence were identified as *fantasizers*—that is to say, as being fantasy-prone. The other 15 participants tended to be amnesic and dissociative and were referred to as *dissociaters* (Barrett, 1996b).

Barrett (1996b) found that dissociaters had difficulty remembering the content of fantasies, and what content they did remember was mundane compared to that of the fantasizers. "Dissociaters experienced dramatic psychophysiological reactions even more extreme than those of fantasizers" (Barrett, 1996b, p. 127), such as some of them, for example, being able to feel pain experienced by other people who had been traumatized. However, none of the dissociaters could achieve an orgasm simply on the basis of fantasy as the fantasizers could. In fact, some of the dissociaters "knew that they had sexual fantasies but usually couldn't remember them afterward" (Barrett, 1996b, p. 127). Fewer dissociaters than fantasizers believed that they had had psychic experiences, and for many of those who had such beliefs, those experiences "were confined solely to altered states of consciousness" (Barrett, 1996b, p. 127) such as "dreams . . . , automatic writing . . . , and trance-like seance phenomena" (Barrett, 1996b, p. 127). Whereas fantasizers tended to have difficulty with amnesia suggestions during hypnosis, "amnesia was consistent and total for [dissociaters] whenever it was suggested, and it sometimes persisted even once removal cues had been given" (Barrett, 1996b, p. 129). Dissociaters had more difficulty than fantasizers distinguishing suggested hallucinations from reality. For example, one dissociater "remained convinced" (Barrett, 1996b, p. 129) that, by coincidence, when a hallucination of a fly was suggested, "a real fly happened to begin to buzz around him" (Barrett, 1996b, p. 129). Whereas fantasizers were immediately alert on awaking from hypnosis, dissociaters "looked confused at first" (Barrett, 1996b, p. 129) and in some cases appeared to be disoriented (Barrett, 1996b). Theodore Barber has used the term *amnesia-prone* (T. Barber, 1999) to refer to excellent hypnotic subjects who are dissociaters.

Dissociation

The concept of dissociation has had a troubled history that goes back to the late 19th century when the terms *disaggregation* and later, *dissociation,* were introduced to refer to the fragmentation of personality elements, which was believed to be the cause of hysteria. The idea was that the psychological integrity of a healthy individual was maintained by associative mechanisms. However, in some individuals, those who are so predisposed, there is insufficient energy to bind the ingredients of the personality so that those parts of the personality that have resulted from the occurrence of some trauma could remain outside of consciousness (Hurley, 1985e; Woody & Bowers, 1994). By the turn of the 20th century, "the concept of dissociation was so familiar that it was a term of the common vocabulary" (Hilgard, 1987, p. 308). However, with a decline in "interest in the kinds of problems that dissociation was designed to explain" (Hilgard, 1987, p. 309), the term dissociation fell into relative disuse.

The notion of dissociation was revived in the 1970s by Ernest Hilgard, who proposed a *neodissociation theory* of hypnotic phenomena (Hilgard, 1973b) as a result of finding that some hypnotic subjects who responded positively to hypnotic analgesia could nonetheless "reveal that some pain had actually been felt" (Hilgard, 1987, p. 309) when it was suggested to them during hypnosis that there was a hidden part of themselves that knew what was happening to their bodies (Bowers, 1976). According to the neodissociation interpretation, there is a *hidden observer* present within a person when she is hypnotized, experiencing pain in a dispassionate manner when she is subjected to painful procedures, in spite of the analgesia experienced consciously during hypnosis (Hilgard, 1973b). The idea was that hypnosis introduces an *amnesic barrier* between a person's higher level cognitive functions from which reports of subjective experiences are normally made and sensory subsystems in which painful stimuli are processed (cf. Hilgard, 1973b, 1987). Of course for sociocognitive theorists there is no amnesic barrier, with hidden observer reports capable of being explained as enactments on the part of hypnotic subjects to meet the expectations of the hypnotist (Spanos, 1986). A more recent *theory of dissociated control* has been proposed by Kenneth Bowers and his colleagues whereby hypnotic induction is thought to weaken control by higher level cognitive systems of lower level cognitive subsystems, allowing "the subsystems to be invoked directly by suggestion" (Kirsch & Lynn, 1995, p. 853; see also Bowers, 1992; Woody & Bowers, 1994; Woody & Sadler, 1998). This is not as unreasonable as it may seem, given that shifts in processing occur in other conditions such as NREM sleep in which, as we saw in chapter 3, sensory stimulation is largely blocked from awareness.

In contrast to using the notion of dissociation for explanatory purposes, it may be more prudent for us to use the term *dissociation* in a descriptive sense to refer to any functional disconnection between elements of a person's psyche (cf. MacMartin & Yarmey, 1999), irrespective of what the psychological or physiological mechanism of that disconnection may turn out to be. For example, we have said that there is dissociation between the previously described surgeon's ability to perform surgery on himself and his inability to feel the pain that would normally occur in such circumstances. In the same way, we can talk freely about dissociation being a third dimension of hypnosis alongside positivity and fantasy-proneness.

Complexity of Hypnotic Experiences

Ronald Pekala and his colleagues have developed a *Phenomenology of Consciousness Inventory (PCI)* with which to measure changes in subjective experiences associated with alterations of consciousness. Participants in an altered state of consciousness of interest to an investigator would be asked to experience the state in which they find themselves, and would be given a few minutes in which to do so. Subsequently they would have an opportunity to fill out the 53 items of the PCI. The PCI would be scored along 12 dimensions and 14 subdimensions such as "Positive affect . . . Altered time sense . . . Altered meaning . . . Visual imagery . . . Attention . . . Internal dialogue . . . [and] Volitional control" (Pekala, 1991, p. 133). For example, "altered time sense addresses the extent to which 'the flow of time changed drastically' or whether it seemed to 'speed up or slow down' " (Pekala, 1991, p. 132).

When the PCI has been given to hypnotic subjects, a number of individual differences in hypnotic experiences have been distinguished. In particular, it has been found that there are two types of high susceptible subjects. One type has been "characterized by moderate alterations in consciousness and experience, a great deal of vivid imagery, moderate positive affect, but only mild-to-moderate losses in rationality and memory" (Pekala & Kumar, 2000, p. 116), whereas the second type has had "large alterations in state of consciousness and moderate altered experiences; a loss of volitional control, self-awareness, rationality, and memory; and little vivid imagery" (Pekala & Kumar, 2000, p. 116). These appear to be the differences between fantasizers and dissociaters consistent with Theodore Barber's tripartite theory. However, the PCI has also revealed complexities that do not fit a simplistic version of the theory. For instance, low but not midrange scores on hypnotic susceptibility accompanied by a subjective experience of being hypnotized have been associated with a high degree of dissociation (Pekala & Kumar, 2000). That suggests that some individuals may enter a trance but dissociate to such an extent that they cannot generate the necessary behavior to be measured on the hypnotic susceptibility scales or that they have become altogether disconnected from the hypnotic relationship with no predilection to comply with a hypnotist's suggestions.

Clearly, much remains to be done to understand hypnosis. Nonetheless, the tripartite theory helps us to make sense of the variety of hypnotic phenomena that we have considered. It allows us to see that in many cases responses to suggestions could result primarily from the engagement of cognitive processes in response to the context in which hypnosis takes place. But for a small number of individuals, there may be a discrete shift into a trance whose features vary depending on whether there is a tendency toward fantasy or dissociation. Indeed, in some cases, hypnotic responsiveness may result from the disengagement of psychological processes that function outside of what appears to be our volitional range. And is it possible, in some cases, that trance may turn out to be more interesting than we think? Could it be that trance is a gateway to a range of phenomena that normally are not accessible to us? We will take up that train of thought in chapter 6.

APPLICATIONS OF HYPNOSIS

Let us turn away from the theoretical to the practical aspects of hypnosis for the remainder of this chapter by considering the use of hypnosis for memory enhancement, the clinical applications of hypnosis, and problems that could arise from hypnosis.

Hypnotically Recalled Memories

We have seen that some excellent hypnotic subjects are amnesia-prone. But it is the opposite, *hypermnesia*, the enhanced recall of previous events, that is perhaps one of the most controversial phenomena associated with hypnosis, one that turns out to have wide-ranging practical consequences. One of the items that is found on some hypnotic susceptibility scales is that of age regression. A hypnotic subject would be asked to write her name on a pad of paper. Then it would be suggested to her that she is getting younger until she is back in a fifth-grade class. She would again be asked to write her name on the paper. Then it would be suggested that she is back in a second-grade class, and again she would be asked to write her name. A subject would be said to pass the item if the handwriting changes for either of the regressed ages (Weitzenhoffer & Hilgard, 1962).

In some cases of hypnotic age regression, individuals can apparently recall traumatic childhood events of which they were unaware in the ordinary waking state, such as the example of a medical student who recalled, as a child, seriously injuring another boy with a pitchfork, for which he was subsequently severely punished (Erickson, 1979). But are these real childhood memories or are they imagined? Are these delusional or veridical experiences? During a criminal investigation, a police officer may hypnotize witnesses or victims to try to gain additional information about a crime (Hibler, 1995). Although there have been some dramatic successes, such as, in one case, the hypnotic recall of all but one digit of a license plate number (Giannelli, 1995), there have also been "cases in which the hypnotically recalled information was clearly incorrect, despite vows of confidence from those who had been hypnotized" (Hibler, 1995, p. 320). Perhaps the most problematic are "cases in which adults undergoing psychotherapy claim to have recovered long-repressed memories of sexual abuse at the hands of parents or other family members" (Schacter, 1995, p. 2). In such cases, we have childhood memories with criminal implications. Clearly, if independent corroboration of hypnotically retrieved memories is possible, then a determination of the accuracy of such memories does not need to depend on factors intrinsic to the process of remembering itself. But what if it is not possible to find any independent evidence? How is one to assess the remembered experiences?

In general, so-called "hypnotically refreshed" (Giannelli, 1995, p. 212) memories are not reliable. The evidence concerning hypnotic hypermnesia indicates that hypnotic subjects tend to recall more information when hypnotized but that much of the additionally recalled information is incorrect (Frankel & Covino, 1997), as illustrated in the following study. Fifty-four participants were presented with "60 slides of simple black-and-white line drawings of common objects" (Dywan & Bowers, 1983, p. 184). They were then required to do a forced-recall task by being asked "to write the name of a line drawing in each of the 60 blank spaces provided for [that] purpose" (Dywan & Bowers, 1983, p. 184) on a sheet of paper, indicating which of the names "represented memories and which were just guesses" (Dywan & Bowers, 1983, p. 184). This task was repeated twice after 3-minute rest periods and then once each day for the following six days. The average number of items recalled rose from an average of 30 on the first trial to 38 by the ninth trial, but so did the number of errors "from an average of less than one error on the first trial to an average of four errors by the ninth" (Dywan & Bowers, 1983, p. 184).

Participants in the hypnosis hypermnesia study were then divided into experimental and control groups, with participants in the experimental group being hypnotized and those in the control group not being hypnotized. Participants in both groups "were told to relax and focus all their attention on the slides they had seen the week before" (Dywan & Bowers, 1983, p. 184). Participants in the hypnosis group reported an average of about five additional remembered items, whereas those in the nonhypnosis group only reported an average of about two additional remembered items. However, most of the additionally recalled items were incorrect, with an average of less than one in every five additional items being correct for either group. The most additional items that any of the participants could recall correctly was five, whereas many could not produce any correct new information at all. Perhaps not surprisingly, the increased output for the hypnotized group resulted almost entirely from the efforts of those who were high in hypnotic susceptibility. However, the hypnotized high-susceptible participants also made almost three times as many errors as were made by the hypnotized low-susceptible participants and those in the control group (Dywan & Bowers, 1983).

Considerable research has shown that personal memory is usually reconstructive in nature. Memory recall does not involve the replaying of a tape of events as they actually occurred but rather the reconstruction of experiences colored by general knowledge, subsequent events, and environmental factors at the time of retrieval. "Retrospective bias appears to be most pronounced when people attempt to remember specific episodes and least pronounced when they reflect on the general features of their autobiography" (Schacter, 1995, p. 17). The construction of erroneous memories is known as *confabulation* and the erroneous memories themselves are called *false memories* (cf. Schacter, 1995). The production of false memories can be demonstrated by reading a list of associated words to a person and then asking her if an associated word that had not been read to her had been on the list. Studies with variations on this sort of protocol have shown that people will acknowledge recognition of associated material that has never been presented to them. A problem with hypnotically refreshed memories is that hypnotic subjects tend to think that erroneous information is correct (Schacter, 1995). This appears to be particularly true when subjects can imagine information vividly or when it is accompanied by strong emotional attachment. "Emotional intensity, rather than a real experience, . . . invites confidence in the truth of what is remembered" (Frankel & Covino, 1997, p. 356). We have to be careful, not just in the case of memory recall, but also for phenomena associated with consciousness more generally, to determine as much as possible the criteria that a person uses for making judgments that something is actually true.

However, there are those who have argued that traumatic memories, precisely because of the emotional intensity that is associated with them, are not susceptible to the kinds of memory distortions that occur with ordinary biographical memories. The idea is that traumatic events, at the time that they occur, are actively repressed in the unconscious or dissociated from consciousness to protect a person against the distress that they cause. Although repression and dissociation do not refer to the same purported psychological processes, their effects are the same—namely, to isolate traumatic experiences from consciousness (MacMartin & Yarmey, 1999). Thus, it is thought that memories of traumatic events can remain unchanged (Schacter, 1995) somewhere in a person's psyche until they are reawakened in psychotherapy, perhaps with the assistance of hypnosis (Frankel & Covino, 1997). Although there is growing evidence that "emotional arousal typically enhances the accuracy of memory for the central aspects of an [emotionally arousing] event and impairs memory for more peripheral details" (Schacter, 1995, p. 18), there is no good evidence that "people can forget and then recover years of repeated, horrific abuse" (Schacter, 1995, p. 28). On the other hand, there is also "no hard scientific evidence" (Schacter, 1995, p. 28) that "people can falsely create an entire history of traumatic sexual abuse when none occurred" (Schacter, 1995, p. 28). What is needed is research that can extend the determination of the conditions under which events are likely to be remembered and the conditions under which they are likely to be distorted so that better judgments can be made about the possible accuracy of reported memories. We will return to this discussion in chapter 6 in the context of the types of trauma that have been associated with dissociation.

The Extent of Hypnotic Regression

There is another question concerning hypermnesia: How far back into childhood can a hypnotic subject be regressed and correctly remember actual events? The problem is that the further back into childhood we go, the less mature is the brain and the more questionable it is that there is any memory of events at all (Chamberlain, 1990). Few people can remember anything from before the age of 3, and it has been assumed that *infantile amnesia* exists for events that occurred before the age of 24 months. This has not stopped adults from reporting infantile memories under some conditions. Participants in a study in which they were encouraged to visualize earlier and earlier events in their lives ended up with an average age of 1.6 years for their earliest memory, with one third reporting "a memory from at or before 12 months of age" (Malinoski & Lynn, 1999, p. 336). It was assumed by the investigators that any memories reported from before the age of 24 months were unlikely to be correct (Malinoski & Lynn, 1999). This assumption has been questioned, however, on the basis of research with infants. In one study, for example, infants from 2 to 18 months of age were shown to be able to recognize familiar mobiles and trains, leading the investigators to conclude that "infants' memory processing does not fundamentally differ from that of older children and adults" (Rovee-Collier, 1999, p. 80) and that "even very young infants can remember an event over the entire infantile-amnesia period if they are periodically reminded" (Rovee-Collier, 1999, p. 80).

What about birth? Can anyone remember being born? Memories of birth have surfaced repeatedly, but is there any evidence that they are anything other than fantasy? An effort was made to answer that question in a study of 10 mother-and-child pairs in which both mother and child participants were susceptible to hypnotic hypermnesia, the child had no conscious memories of birth, and the mother assured the researcher that she "had never discussed details of the child's birth with the child" (Chamberlain, 1988, p. 105). Each of the participants was independently hypnotized and asked to recall the birth experience. The resulting interviews were recorded, transcribed, and compared.

According to the researcher, analysis of the transcribed interviews in the birth memories study indicated that there were far greater consistencies among the details of the birth memories than there were contradictions. As an example of similarity, the mother of one mother–child pair said that she had picked up the child, smelled her, looked at the child's toes, thought that the toes were deformed, and had been reassured by the nurse that they were all right, whereas the child remembered the mother smelling her, then asking the nurse why her "toes were so funny" (Chamberlain, 1988, p. 108), and being told "that they weren't deformed" (Chamberlain, 1988, p. 108). Contradictions included a child saying that her father had participated in the birth and her mother saying that the father was schizophrenic and had not been present, a discrepancy that the researchers attributed to the possibility that the child had been trying to "hide or heal" (Chamberlain, 1988, p. 110) the painful fact of her father's mental illness. After considering alternative explanations, such as the possibility of the mother having told the child details of the birth, the researcher concluded that the "birth memories appear to be genuine recollections of experience" (Chamberlain, 1988, p. 120).

The investigator has admitted that there could have been methodological improvements in the birth memories study. For example, although he indicated that interrogation during hypnosis "was conservative, avoiding leading questions and allowing subjects to speak freely" (Chamberlain, 1988, p. 105), it is possible that the hypnotist influenced the participants' reports in a biased manner. Separate hypnotists for mothers and children as well as having independent judges match mothers' and children's accounts, analogous to the procedure in the Maimonides precognitive dream experiments discussed in chapter 4, would have helped to eliminate some possible confounds. The possibility of mothers having inadvertently informed their children about their births is a more serious problem and more difficult to circumvent but could be done by using mother-and-child pairs separated since birth (cf. Chamberlain, 1986).

Mention of the Maimonides dream experiments may cue the reader as to where this discussion is heading. If we can remember birth, how about experiences before birth? Indeed, "in hypnotherapy, womb memories are nearly as common as birth memories" (Chamberlain, 1990, p. 14). Such memories occur spontaneously and sometimes appear to have been correct. Perhaps most notable are purportedly remembered unsuccessful attempts at abortion that appear to influence a person during her life. There have also been purported memories of conception, at which point we are seriously "running out of physical material for memory [storage]" (Chamberlain, 1990, p. 17), let alone sensory faculties or sufficient cognitive resources with which to have the remembered experiences in the first place. And then there are accounts of age regressing a person in hypnosis only to find that she has gone back too far and has found herself in a past lifetime. But that is a story for chapter 9. The question, of course, is whether there is anything meaningful about such accounts and, if so, whether they are what they appear to be. In isolation such questions seem absurd, but in the context of the ganzfeld and Maimonides studies, the possibility presents itself that consciousness could function outside the usual physiological constraints assumed in a materialist interpretation of reality. But these are empirical questions that need to be answered with additional research.

Clinical Applications of Hypnosis

We have already seen some clinical applications of hypnosis, such as its use to induce analgesia during surgery. Hypnotic analgesia has been shown to be effective not just for the elimination of acute pain but also for the reduction of recurrent pain in chronic conditions (e.g., Dinges et al., 1997). It has been found that hypnotic suggestions relieved pain for three quarters of participants over a number of studies and different types of pain (Lynn, Kirsch, Barabasz, Cardeña, & Patterson, 2000). Hypnosis has been used not just in forensic settings to find information about a crime and in clinical settings to recover purported traumatic memories but also in clinical settings as an adjunct to psychotherapy in general (e.g., H. Spiegel & Spiegel, 1978). Hypnosis has also been shown to be more effective than no intervention for smoking cessation (Lynn et al., 2000). In fact, "the use of hypnosis is becoming increasingly common in clinical practice" (Walling & Baker, 1996), although clinicians tend to disregard whether or not their clients can be hypnotized. In one study, for example, it was found that "although virtually all the academics regarded hypnotic susceptibility as being relevant to therapeutic outcome, only half of the clinicians did so and few measured it in clients" (West, Fellows, & Easton, 1995, p. 143). In many cases, this may be less important than it seems. For example, the effectiveness of hypnotic suggestions for pain relief is about the same for both medium and high susceptible individuals (Lynn et al., 2000).

Although there may be other treatments that are as effective as hypnosis, hypnotic procedures are relatively inexpensive and hence are sometimes used as a first effort in intervention. In chapter 2 we already considered the use of hypnosis in conjunction with REST in some instances. In general, the use of hypnosis in addition to more traditional cognitive–behavioral treatments for a number of disorders such as "obesity, insomnia, anxiety, pain, and hypertension" (Lynn et al., 2000, p. 244) has been shown to be more effective than the use of the cognitive–behavioral treatments alone. "Indeed, hypnosis may be one of the most thoroughly researched forms of psychotherapeutic intervention, with more than 7,000 publications since 1966, in more than 150 different general medicine, psychological, and interdisciplinary journals" (Nash, 2000, p. 108).

In chapter 2 we saw that the neutrophils of the immune system could be affected by imagining their activity. If such effects are possible using guided imagery, it would not be surprising to find them also with the use of hypnosis, particularly given that some excellent hypnotic subjects are particularly prone to suggested physiological effects. In one study, 45 participants were assigned to one of three groups in an effort to determine if cognitive self-regulation strategies could be used to enhance the adherence of neutrophils. Those in the control group came in for two rest sessions spaced one week apart. Blood samples were taken before and after the rest sessions to look for changes in neutrophil adherence. Participants in one experimental group also came in for two sessions but engaged in "a self-regulation exercise with imagery focused on increasing neutrophil adherence" (Olness & Kohen, 1996, p. 140). Participants in a second experimental group came in for two sessions and received the same instructions as did those in the first experimental group but received in addition "four training sessions prior to their attempts to increase neutrophil adherence" (Olness & Kohen, 1996, p. 340) that included being "led through a relaxation procedure similar to a hypnosis induction" (H. R. Hall, Minnes, Tosi, & Olness, 1992, p. 290).

The researchers in the imagery study found that only the participants in the second experimental group had a "statistically significant increase in neutrophil adherence" (Olness & Kohen, 1996, p. 340) and only "for the second session" (Olness & Kohen, 1996, p. 340). Consistent with the intentions of the participants, changes to the neutrophils were confined to adherence and did not include other characteristics. Furthermore, whereas participants in the control group demonstrated physiological evidence of relaxation, this was not the case for the successful participants in the second experimental group, implying that intentional modification of neutrophil adherence required some cognitive effort (H. Hall, Minnes, & Olness, 1993). The failure to find increased neutrophil adherence for the first experimental group may have been a result of the omission of training sessions for participants in that group rather than the presence of additional hypnosis-like features to the procedure for the second experimental group. It has been found that other cells of the immune system can also be modified using hypnosis (e.g., Ruzyla-Smith, Barabasz, Barabasz, & Warner, 1995).

There are applications of hypnosis outside forensic and clinical settings. Dissociation has been used by captured military personnel, for example, as a way of preparing to be tortured. With the potential for assisting captives with "effective dissociation, ego enhancing, stress coping, and anxiety and pain reduction" (Wood & Sexton, 1997, p. 208), instruction in self-hypnosis has been advocated as part of military training programs. In a somewhat different venue, students for whom it was suggested during hypnosis that they would "be relaxed and have excellent concentration and complete recall for their coursework" (Schreiber, 1997, p. 637) performed better on the final examination than students who were given "motivational talks" (Schreiber, 1997, p. 637). From these examples, it can be seen that there could be a broad range of applications of hypnosis for helping a person to solve problems with living (e.g., Kelly & Kelly, 1995).

Problems With Hypnosis

Let us end this chapter with a word of caution. The claim has been made by some hypnotists that hypnotic subjects cannot be harmed because they are protected by unconscious mechanisms from harmful suggestions (J. Barber, 1998b). However, in one study, one third of practitioners using hypnosis reported having experienced "unexpected complications" (West et al., 1995, p. 146) in the course of their work. One clinician, for instance, has given examples of inappropriate emotional arousal, unexpected hostility, amnesia, obedience, disorientation, paralysis, and memory contamination as problematical effects of hypnosis during psychotherapy (J. Barber, 1998b). Another problem is that in some cases hypnotic subjects fail to awaken from hypnosis at the end of a session (Gravitz, 1995). Although rare, failure to dehypnotize is not surprising given the results of the study we considered previously in which cancellation suggestions appeared to be less effective than they have normally been assumed to be. Sometimes there are problems with *stage hypnosis*. In one case, a young man experienced a psychotic breakdown after performing as a volunteer for a stage hypnotist (Allen, 1995), and in another case a healthy young woman who was frightened of electricity died following her participation in a stage hypnosis performance in which it was suggested to her that she would experience an electrical shock of 10,000 volts. Indeed, there have been complaints from people participating, or even just sitting in the audience, of adverse effects from stage hypnosis shows (Heap, 1995). Thus we see that although its applications appear to be largely benign, sometimes hypnosis can cause problems.

In the end, then, what are we to make of hypnosis? What is it? Is it mundane or extraordinary? In this chapter we considered the definition of hypnosis as a domain of phenomena to which the term "hypnosis" has been applied and then identified what those phenomena are. This information was supplemented by considering individual differences in hypnotic susceptibility and some of the academic research concerning hypnosis. According to a sociocognitive theory, hypnosis is mundane, in that what we call hypnosis is simply normal cognitive behavior that is evoked in a social situation identified as hypnosis. But there are indications that there is more to hypnosis than deliberate enactment of appropriate behavior—that hypnosis may, indeed, be better conceptualized as a special state of trance. These indications include changes in neural processing evidenced during hypnosis by those who are highly hypnotizable; behaviors in natural settings, such as pain relief during surgery, in which there appear to be actual psychological or physiological changes associated with those behaviors; and the fantasy proneness and dissociative tendencies of hypnotic virtuosos. These characteristics of hypnotic behavior suggest that something extraordinary may be going on at least some of the time during hypnosis. The tripartite theory consisting of positively set, fantasy-prone, and amnesia-prone dimensions fits the evidence but needs to be further tested empirically. In fact, considerable research is required to clarify not only the characteristics of phenomena associated with hypnosis but also the details of the psychological and physiological mechanisms through which these phenomena occur. Whether it is considered to be mundane or extraordinary, hypnosis has been widely used for practical effects such as memory enhancement and therapy. Indeed, controversies surrounding some of these practical applications will surface again in some of the following chapters.

6

TRANCE

We have considered a number of alterations of consciousness—such as daydreaming, sensory restriction, dreaming, hypnosis, fantasy-proneness, and dissociation—in which we are removed from our everyday ways of thinking about the world. And here and there, such as the ganzfeld studies, sensed presences, the Maimonides studies, and purported birth memories, we have come across intimations that alterations of consciousness may be a gateway that allows us to encounter other aspects of reality. Is that true? Materialists believe that mental events are necessarily skull-bound, whereas transcendentalists believe that they are not. But what does the evidence tell us? Is the psyche open or closed? Here and there, in dreams and hypnosis, we have come across alterations of self-identity. Who are we? Are we single or multiple entities? Are we always ourselves or are we sometimes somebody else? Combining these two lines of questioning, we can ask whether there are entities in alternate aspects of reality that can intrude into our psyches so as to change our self-identity. And if we believe that we have had strange encounters of some sort, are we crazy? And even if we are suffering from some form of psychopathology, is what is happening nonetheless real? Are experiences of intrusion delusional or veridical? Are such alterations of consciousness dangerous? All of our thematic threads surface in this chapter as we consider shamanism, possession, dissociative identity disorder, and alien abduction experiences. We may not be able to answer our questions by the end of this chapter, but perhaps we will understand them better.

In chapter 5 we defined trance as the juxtaposition of apparent awareness without actual self-determination. That definition applies sometimes to the alterations of consciousness that we are considering in this chapter, but at other times there are fundamental questions about what awareness a person may be experiencing and to what degree self-determination may or may not be present. In that sense the title "trance" fits only loosely the subject areas discussed in this chapter.

SHAMANISM

We briefly considered shamanism in chapter 1 in the context of noting the tendency to pathologize alterations of consciousness. We return to a discussion of shamanism first by describing its characteristics, then by examining the degree to which shamanism and schizophrenia are alike, and finally by stating the shamanic world view and comparing it to some of the explanatory principles of contemporary physics.

Characteristics of Shamanism

There is a variety of practices in indigenous cultures that have been classified as shamanism by investigators (e.g., Ripinsky-Naxon, 1993; Winkelman, 2000). Let us define *shamanism* as a practice in which a person deliberately alters her consciousness for the purpose of interacting with spirits in order to serve the community in which she finds herself (cf. Ripinsky-Naxon, 1993). Of course, these are ostensible spirits about which we are talking. This definition leaves out various practitioners of religion or magic who do not alter their consciousness (Cardeña, 1996) and confines the term largely to indigenous societies. Interacting with spirits can take predominantly one of two forms: *soul journeying*, whereby a shaman travels in otherworldly realms in which spirits are encountered, and *possession*, whereby spirits work through the shaman's body. More specifically, in soul journeying, a shaman may experience herself flying or falling though an opening in the earth, arriving at another level of reality that is experienced as being as real as ordinary reality, having imaginal adventures and encountering various spiritual entities in that realm, and then, on returning, being able to remember the events that transpired. In possession experiences, there is not much imagery, "but rather a sense of dizziness, alterations in body image and a not infrequent experience of weight or pressure on the shoulders or neck, frequently explained as being 'mounted' by a spirit" (Cardeña, 1996, p. 92). With possession, often there is loss of self-awareness and an inability to recall the events that occurred during the time of spirit incorporation (Cardeña, 1996).

It seems reasonable to include both soul journeying and possession in the use of the term "shamanism." Given that soul journeying appears to involve fantasy whereas possession is characterized by dissociation, we thereby set up a parallel with the distinction for good hypnotic subjects between fantasizers and dissociaters (Cardeña, 1996). Some researchers have restricted the term "shamanism" to soul journeying (e.g., Walsh, 1989). However, in practice, the two have often been associated as in the case of shamanism among the Tungus of Siberia (M. Brown, 1997) and the Tamang of Nepal (Peters, 1981). Indeed, in a study of 42 societies, shamans in 10 societies engaged in journeying, those in 18 societies used "spirit incorpora-tion" (Krippner, 1999, p. 158), 11 societies had both, and 3 had some other "different altered state" (Krippner, 1999, p. 158). The various forms of shamanism seem to have arisen in different cultures directly from the experi-ences of their people (Ripinsky-Naxon, 1993).

Shamans may, although not always (Krippner & Combs, 2002), become who they are through a process of *initiation* in response to a call (Ripinsky-Naxon, 1993). The Tamang shaman Bhirendra's calling was described by him as a "frightening encounter with fiendish ghosts in a cemetery who picked at him with spears and pulled flesh from his body until he was 'saved by a white light' that appeared once he had surrendered to his impending death" (Peters, 1989, pp. 123–124). Initiation is marked by ordeals of death and rebirth, whereby neophytes are often isolated from society, subjected to deprivation, and experience exhaustion, suffering, and symbolic death, resulting apparently in access to another realm of existence. The neophyte is reconstituted, sometimes with a change of identity, including sexual identity, and sometimes with purportedly changed body parts such as having intestines made of quartz. Psychedelic drugs are often used to induce experi-ences of the other world, including soul journeys. A second stage of the learning process consists of the shaman receiving instructions from a mentor concerning such matters as the preparation of herbal medicines and the "oral traditions and myths" (Ripinsky-Naxon, 1993, p. 87) of her people. The ordeals of initiation can be dramatically visceral as in Bhirendra's case or "barren and uneventful" (Ripinsky-Naxon, 1993, p. 89) in other cases that appear to be largely symbolic.

Shamanism and Schizophrenia

In chapter 1 we noted that altered states of consciousness have often been considered to be pathological and gave as an example a comparison of shamanism with schizophrenia. *Schizophrenia* is a psychological condition usually characterized by disorganized speech and behavior as well as the presence of psychotic symptoms such as hallucinations and delusions. Delu-sions are beliefs that are contrary to reality, such as the belief that one is being tormented; that one's internal organs have been replaced with those of another person; or that one's body, thoughts, or actions are being con-trolled by an outside force. Sometimes, rather than "an excess or distortion of normal functions" (American Psychiatric Association, 2000, p. 299) known as *positive symptoms*, there may be "a diminution or loss of normal functions" (American Psychiatric Association, 2000, p. 299) known as *nega-tive symptoms*, such as loss of emotional expression, thinking, speech, or "initiation of goal-directed behavior" (American Psychiatric Association, 2000, p. 299). To diagnose a person with schizophrenia, at least some of these symptoms need to be present to such a degree that they impair self-care or social or occupational functioning (American Psychiatric Association, 2000).

The shamanic initiation resembles schizophrenia to the extent that initiatic crises involve perceived dismemberment, disintegration of self-identity, the presence of visions, and the adoption of a world view in which the initiate believes that she is interacting with spirits. However, although there may be such similarities between the experiences of a person with schizophrenia and a neophyte shaman, the shaman's disintegration makes possible her reconstruction as a healer and her social reintegration, whereas a person with schizophrenia often remains disorganized and becomes a social outcast (Halifax, 1990). A shaman learns to gain control and to use productively the altered states of consciousness in which she finds herself at the time of her initiation (Peters, 1981). And perhaps, in some cases of schizophrenia, a similar process of reintegration can take place, leading a person to exceptional states of well-being (Halifax, 1990; Lukoff, 1985; Lukoff & Everest, 1985; Shaffer, 1978).

Whereas shamanic initiation can resemble schizophrenia, this is not true of a shaman's experiences in general. Roger Walsh (1995) has proposed a method of *phenomenological mapping*, whereby experiences in different states of consciousness can be compared along a number of dimensions. The following are some of the differences between soul journeying and schizophrenic states, which have been found using phenomenological mapping. To begin with, shamans have good *control* over entering and leaving an altered state and some control over the contents of that state, whereas there is a "dramatic reduction of control" (Walsh, 1995, p. 42) for those with schizophrenia. Whereas *concentration* is increased during soul journeying, with the shaman's attention moving "freely from object to object" (Walsh, 1995, p. 35), it has been argued that the primary characteristic of schizophrenia is the disorganization of thought as demonstrated by disorganized speech that can include jumping from one loosely associated topic to another (American Psychiatric Association, 2000). A shaman's *sense of self* is that of a spirit or soul that has been "freed from the body" (Walsh, 1995, p. 36) in what resembles an *out-of-body experience*, whereas a person with schizophrenia can have a disintegrated sense of self and rarely have out-of-body experiences (Walsh, 1995), although the prevalence of out-of-body experiences is higher among those with schizophrenia than in the general population (Alvarado, 2000). Whereas a shaman can experience positive or negative *affect* during soul journeying, the emotional expression of a person with schizophrenia is often negative, inappropriate, or absent. The *content* of experience for the shaman is coherent and determined by the cultural cosmology and purpose of the journey, whereas for a person with schizophrenia the content is "often disorganized and fragmented" (Walsh, 1995, p. 42).

There are similarities between shamanism and schizophrenia along some of Walsh's dimensions. In the case of both shamanism and schizophrenia, *arousal* can be high, *awareness of the environment* low, and there may be limited *ability to communicate* with surrounding people. However, overall, phenomenological mapping reveals that soul journeying is not the same as schizophrenia (Walsh, 1995).

Shamanism and Hypnosis

Direct comparisons have been made between hypnosis and shamanism. In one study, Etzel Cardeña requested 12 hypnotic virtuosos "to go into as deep a state of hypnosis as they could" (Cardeña, 1996, p. 92) and then asked them approximately every 5 minutes what they were experiencing. Cardeña found significant differences compared to a condition of no hypnosis. During light levels of hypnosis, there were alterations in body image followed by imaginal experiences. There was frequent "mention of floating or flying sensations . . . sinking, falling down . . . or going through tunnels" (Cardeña, 1996, p. 92), separation of the self from the physical body, and journeys to unusual worlds such as "being in a dark world [or] encountering a limitless sea" (Cardeña, 1996, p. 93). During deeper levels of hypnosis, participants heard music, saw colors and "reported synesthesia" (Cardeña, 1996, p. 93), which is the experience of a stimulus in sensory modalities other than the one in which it is received. All of the participants saw a "very bright light" (Cardeña, 1996, p. 93) "in some cases becoming one with it" (Cardeña, 1996, p. 93), some had "transcendent experiences such as being in a timeless/spaceless realm" (Cardeña, 1996, p. 93), and "intense positive emotions" (Cardeña, 1996, p. 93) were associated with these various events. "At follow-ups immediately after completing the project and at four months, every experient reported positive effects from the experiment, from mild ones such as better concentration, to a sense of profound contact with the self" (Cardeña, 1996, p. 93). To use the terminology of one of our thematic threads, it is interesting to note not only the lateral meaningfulness but also an indication of vertical meaningfulness in some of the participants' accounts.

Even without phenomenological mapping, it is not difficult to see that the experiences of the hypnotic virtuosos in Cardeña's study share many similarities with the experiences of shamans. There were also differences such as the absence among Cardeña's participants of plant and animal imagery typically found in shamanic adventures, as well as their lack of the shaman's cosmology. Nonetheless, according to Cardeña, what these data suggest is that "the alterations in consciousness found in shamanism and deep hypnosis are likely the product of innate biological/cognitive dispositions rather than the mere byproduct of a particular culture" (Cardeña, 1996, p. 94).

Shamanic World View

The Tamang shaman's cosmology is an animistic one in which good and evil events result from the influences of spirits that live, for example, in "rocks, trees, waterfalls, [and] at crossroads" (Peters, 1981, p. 4). If something goes wrong, then "a spirit agent is identified and a ritual prescription carried out in order to dispel it" (Peters, 1981, p. 4). A shaman's purpose in entering altered states of consciousness is to retrieve a stolen soul or to exorcize a person from a possessing spirit. From a materialistic point of view there are no such things as spirits, and yet some anthropologists who have lived for years among indigenous people have found that a world of spirits has "insisted it was really there" (Turner, 1992a, p. 28). This insistence has occurred in numerous ways including, for example, seeing "a large gray blob about six inches across" (Turner, 1992b, p. 149) emerge from a sick woman's back during an African Ndembu healing ritual (Turner, 1992a). However, one has to be careful when interpreting accounts of such visual impressions as evidence of spirits because some shamans have regularly used props such as ashes to create the appearance of removing spirits from a person's body (Peters, 1981). The question is, are there really spirits?

It is interesting that we have so much difficulty with the unseen explanatory principles of indigenous people yet take for granted the unseen explanatory principles of contemporary physics. Quantum mechanics, a theory about the composition of matter, is a myth that we have invented to talk about an unseen level of reality that gives rise to the world of appearances. In the mythology of quantum mechanics, at the subatomic level, physical reality exists only as a continuum of possibilities with varying probabilities until such time as an observation is made and a single physical reality becomes evident. There has been some speculation that conscious or nonconscious intent determines which possibility is brought into manifestation (Barušs, 1986; Walker, 1970, 1977, 2000). The physicist Fred Alan Wolf (1991), who has participated in shamanic rituals, has maintained "that the shamanic and quantum worlds are virtually the same" (Leviton, 1992, p. 51). Wolf has emphasized the importance of intent for the shamanic world view so that it is intent that "moves synchronicity [and] that weaves events into a tapestry of coherence" (Leviton, 1992, p. 52). Intent, for Wolf as physicist and Wolf as shaman, literally creates the world that we experience. In this sense, the unseen realms of the shaman may be the unseen realms of contemporary physics (Leviton, 1992), although one has to be careful not to overextend the similarities between the two world views (cf. Restivo, 1978, 1982). In other words, spirits may be as real as the stuff of which matter is made.

POSSESSION

We have briefly considered the soul journeying aspect of shamanism, but what about possession? Let us briefly examine possession and then channeling, a phenomenon that may or may not include possession.

Characteristics of Possession

Possession can be defined as a "condition in which a person has been taken over by an external entity" (Barušs, 1996, p. 158). Well, we need to be a little bit careful with this definition. A person can be said to have been possessed, in the sense of having been invaded by a spirit, without exhibiting any unusual alterations of consciousness, such as in cases of illness attributed to evil spirits. To be more precise, the term *possession trance* can be used for possession in which alterations of consciousness are evident (Bourguignon, 1979). Varieties of possession experiences can also include "voluntary and involuntary possession" (Krippner, 1997, p. 344), possession that proceeds in distinct phases, differences in reactions to being possessed by different entities (Krippner, 1997), and the malevolence or benevolence of possessing entities (cf. Krippner, 1994).

As part of a field study, the anthropologist Larry Peters undertook to become a shaman under the tutelage of the Tamang shaman Bhirendra. Peters was invited to a "purification ritual" (Peters, 1981, p. 10) to "see whether or not the gods would come to possess [him]" (Peters, 1981, p. 10), handed a drum, and told "to play along" (Peters, 1981, p. 10). Drumming is thought to induce alterations of consciousness. However, nothing happened to Peters "while Bhirendra and his disciples shook furiously" (Peters, 1981, p. 10). Finally, Peters "started to shake consciously" (Peters, 1981, p. 10), gradually letting go so that "the shaking in [his] legs became more automatic" (Peters, 1981, p. 10) and he "began to shake" (Peters, 1981, p. 10) and bounce "all over the room" (Peters, 1981, p. 10). When they saw Peters start shaking, Bhirendra and his other disciples became certain that Peters "had been chosen by a god to become a shaman" (Peters, 1981, p. 11). However, in spite of losing control of his movements and becoming frightened, Peters did not feel the presence of an "alien power" (Peters, 1981, p. 11).

During a subsequent ritual, again while drumming, Peters felt his "mind split off from [his] body" (Peters, 1981, p. 14), so that he was watching his "body shaking and jumping into the air as if [his] consciousness was separated from it" (Peters, 1981, p. 14). Then suddenly, he found himself "flying over a quiet valley towards a green glow" (Peters, 1981, p. 14) as though he were dreaming. There was light before him and "the upper torso of a green figure" (Peters, 1981, p. 14) visible through the open windows of the top floor of a three-story house. It was from what appeared to be an eye in the figure that the green light was emanating. Peters realized that he was dreaming as he "felt water being poured on [his] head" (Peters, 1981, p. 14) by Bhirendra. Here we have various elements that we have already encountered such as automaticity associated with actions during hypnosis, dissociation, and what appears to have been hypnagogic imagery, but no possession, even though that had been the intention of the rituals.

There is certainly no shortage of accounts of people believed to have been possessed (Coons, 1993). During Peters's purification ritual, another of Bhirendra's disciples "shook furiously" (Peters, 1981, p. 10) and "became possessed by his grandfather" (Peters, 1981, p. 10). Bhirendra himself would become possessed, sometimes by a "tiger spirit" (Peters, 1981, p. 8), at which time he would run around "on all fours, growling and pounding on windows and doors" (Peters, 1981, p. 8). There have been cases of possession in religious contexts. For example, in some Christian movements such as Pentacostalism the practice of *glossolalia*, "speaking in tongues" (Hood, Spilka, Hunsberger, & Gorsuch, 1996, p. 201), has been encouraged (Coons, 1993). There have been cases of apparent possession outside the context of shamanism and religion. Sumitra, a woman who lived in India, after seemingly having died and been revived, believed that she was Shiva, a woman who had died violently about two months previously in a village about 100 kilometers away. Sumitra recognized 23 people known to Shiva and "showed in several respects new behavior that accorded with Shiva's personality and attainments" (Stevenson, Pasricha, & McClean-Rice, 1989, p. 81). For example, Sumitra insisted on being called Shiva, changed her style of dress so that it was more in the manner of Shiva's, and showed increased fluency and interest in reading and writing. There appeared to have been no normal means whereby Sumitra could have obtained "knowledge of the people and events in Shiva's life" (Stevenson et al., 1989, p. 81). The investigators concluded that possession or reincarnation was the most plausible explanation (Stevenson et al., 1989).

Channeling

There has been the flourishing of a new form of spirituality toward the end of the 20th century, as we shall note in chapter 8, with channeling as one of its "most controversial expressions" (M. Brown, 1997, p. viii). *Channeling* can be defined as the communication of information or energy from apparently nonphysical sources such as spirits (cf. Barušs, 1996; M. Brown, 1997; Hastings, 1988, 1991; Klimo, 1987). There are various degrees to which a person can presumably be taken over by an entity during channeling (Barušs, 1996), from *trance channeling*, in which possession occurs, to *conscious channeling*, in which it does not. There has been a range of entities channeled, with some, such as biblical figures or beings identified by late-19th-century Theosophists, having reached "the status of public-domain spirits" (M. Brown, 1997, p. 156). Perhaps the most popular entity to be channeled has been Jesus (Barušs, 1996). Jane Roberts, known for having channeled an entity called Seth (M. Brown, 1997), has also channeled William James. The James channeled by Roberts has purportedly communicated his ideas regarding his view from the balcony of life, world developments since his time, and the nature of life after death, and has expressed regret that, during his lifetime, while he had "evidence of the soul's existence" (J. Roberts, 1978, p. 138) from his own experience, he had "dismissed this as beside the point since in no way could [he] produce the scientific proof that . . . could demonstrate to others the actuality of such a hypothesis" (J. Roberts, 1978, p. 138). It is difficult to know how many people are involved with channeling, although it is known that some purportedly channeled books have sales of a half-million copies or more (M. Brown, 1997).

The following is an example of contemporary North American channeling that was brought to my attention:

> Basically what happened is that a strong, cold wind moved into the centre of my body, and information began to pour through my brain and mouth that was not my own—though I was clearly aware of what I was saying and often made or added my own comments to the information I heard and spoke. I spoke to each person in the circle about her role in the spiritual work she had undertaken, basically clarifying issues or addressing hidden questions she had. I seemed to know their thoughts and spoke to them directly. I saw things (the questions in the minds of the participants and the answers to their queries) in images and words. As this process unfolded, the "entity" when asked, named itself. There was a point after the channelling started when others could feel a cold wind moving through the room, circling, settling, and moving around. The whole thing lasted perhaps one hour or so, and at the end of it I was quite tired. In fact, over the next two days I felt feverish, alternately cold and very hot and had to rest. I felt very energized during the experience but extremely done in afterwards, including the exhaustion lasting several days.

In this report we can see dissociation, the occurrence of events perceived to be paranormal, identification of an external entity, and some subsequent somatic effects. There was a spiritual context in which an apparently meaningful interchange occurred between the channeled entity and those present. What happened?

The quality of the information produced during channeling varies from the banal to the profound (Baruss, 1996; Hastings, 1991). Does any of it originate outside of a person herself? And, irrespective of source, is any of it worth hearing or reading? Judging from its popularity and the respect that it has garnered in some quarters (Hastings, 1988), the answer to the second question is yes, whereas the answer to the first question is difficult to determine. Of course, for a materialist, there are no nonphysical domains from which to obtain information, nor can there be actual soul journeys or possession by external entities. Shamanism, possession, and channeling are products of fantasy and dissociation. In the Western culture, the notion of demonic possession, in particular, has been replaced with a mental disorder known as dissociative identity disorder (Ross, 1996). Let us have a brief look at this disorder.

DISSOCIATIVE IDENTITY DISORDER

In this section we will describe and give some examples of the characteristics of this disorder, note the presence of trauma as an etiological factor, and compare this disorder to possession.

Characteristics of Dissociative Identity Disorder

Dissociative identity disorder (DID) is a condition whose primary characteristic is the presence of "distinct personality states that take turns being in executive control of the body and are separated by varying degrees of amnesia" (Ross, 1996, p. 14). About three to nine times as many women as men have been diagnosed with DID (American Psychiatric Association, 2000). Rather than coming to the attention of mental health professionals, men with DID may end up in prison, given that "a high incidence of dissociative disorders [has been found] among convicted sex offenders" (Kluft, 1996, p. 351). The overall prevalence of DID is difficult to determine, with incidence figures of 3% to 5% of undiagnosed DID for psychiatric admissions to hospitals and an incidence of about 1% for the general population (Kluft, 1996).

We need to be careful not to confuse dissociative identity disorder with schizophrenia. In schizophrenia, there is a breakdown of thinking, emotions, and behavior at the microscopic level, so to speak, so that an individual's sentences, succession of emotional states, and motor behavior are demonstrably impaired. The breakdown in DID is more macroscopic, in that the basic functions of the psyche continue to be operative, but there is a fragmentation of self-identity (cf. Kluft, 1996). DID has, however, been confused with other mental disorders in clinical settings so that those eventually diagnosed with DID spend an average of seven years in the mental health system before being given a diagnosis of DID. One of the frequent previous diagnoses is that of schizophrenia, with 41% of 236 people with DID having been labeled as being schizophrenic according to one study (Ross, Norton, & Wozney, 1989). The use of diagnostic categories other than DID could be due, in part, to the fact that some psychiatrists simply do not believe that DID exists. This appears to be particularly the case in Canada, where a survey of psychiatrists' attitudes toward DID in three comparable Canadian cities found levels of disbelief peaking at 41% in London (Mai, 1995). The problem is that DID "does not undergo spontaneous remission and rarely resolves in a treatment that fails to address it directly" (Kluft, 1996, p. 348), as found in a longitudinal study of 210 people with DID. Given that successful treatments for DID have been developed, an early and proper diagnosis could circumvent years of suffering for those for whom it occurs (Ross et al., 1989).

Description of Alternate Personalities

In dissociative identity disorder each alternate personality "may be experienced as if it has a distinct personal history, self-image, and identity, including a separate name" (American Psychiatric Association, 2000, p. 526). It is important to note that what occurs is the appearance of the presence of separate personalities. Indeed, as we shall see in the following example, the manifested personalities could perhaps more appropriately be characterized as caricatures of personalities, which, in many cases, are clearly inconsistent with a person's physical features. It is also possible that, at least in some cases, the appearance of such personalities results from a person's interaction with her therapist. We will keep these qualifications in mind as we consider a typical description of someone with dissociative identity disorder.

The following are among the "more than 29 personalities" (Reich, 1989b, p. A6) experienced by a woman named Brenda. Christina, age 34, "wears glasses, has short, curly, auburn hair and greenish eyes" (Reich, 1989b, p. A7). She "talks in a low voice" (Reich, 1989b, p. A7), is "very serious" (Reich, 1989b, p. A7), and does not smile. Her purpose in Brenda's psychological makeup is to deal "with anger by expressing feelings verbally" (Reich, 1989b, p. A7). She is "the disciplinarian for Brenda's son" (Reich, 1989b, p. A7). Janice, age 16, has "shoulder-length auburn hair, green eyes, slim build" (Reich, 1989b, p. A7), and "dresses casually" (Reich, 1989b, p. A7). She "speaks with a strong foreign accent from the years

Brenda lived overseas and laughs about the destruction she causes" (Reich, 1989b, p. A7). She is an alcoholic with an attraction for bars and casual sex. Her purpose is to express "anger by misbehaving and emotionally hurting others" (Reich, 1989b, p. A7). Cindy is 19, attractive, thin, with "shoulder-length brown hair" (Reich, 1989b, p. A7). She is "quiet, somewhat shy" (Reich, 1989b, p. A7), and "talks in a near whisper" (Reich, 1989b, p. A7). She is "still coming to grips with being a teenager" (Reich, 1989b, p. A7) because she has recently grown from 11 to 19 "with the help of a therapist" (Reich, 1989b, p. A7). Her purpose is to deal with sexual problems.

Brenda also has childlike personalities. Liza, 3½, is short and heavy with freckles and long pigtails. She "speaks in a child-like voice, slurring her words, talking slowly" (Reich, 1989b, p. A7). Her purpose is to "act like a normal child" (Reich, 1989b, p. A7) so that "the therapist would be fooled into thinking nothing was wrong" (Reich, 1989b, p. A7). Penny, age 6, has long, blond, curly hair. She has the "facial expressions and gestures . . . of a shy six-year-old" (Reich, 1989b, p. A7). She also "has dyslexia, which causes her to print backwards" (Reich, 1989b, p. A7) in the form of "mirror-writing" (Reich, 1989b, p. A7). Her purpose is to bear the pain when Brenda is being harmed. Helen is 11 years old, tall, thin, with buck teeth, and messy hair and clothes. She is frightened and shy, and responsible for "a specific sexual practice she doesn't want revealed" (Reich, 1989b, p. A7).

Usually a person with DID will have at least one alter who she identifies as being of the sex opposite to her biological sex, with one study finding this to be true in 63% of 236 cases (Ross et al., 1989). Brenda, for example, has a male alter named Ronald (Reich, 1989b).

Different alternate personalities can hold down different jobs until they start interfering with one another. In Brenda's case, "Marion was working as a home renovator" (Reich, 1989b, pp. A6–A7) when Ronald emerged one day and put a hole through the drywall with a hammer. In addition to Marion having been a home renovator, Gillian had been "a gourmet chef in a hotel" (Reich, 1989b, p. A6), Christina had been a commercial artist, and Margaret and Mary had real estate licenses and had been successful real estate agents. The income from these jobs had been "deposited in bank accounts in the name of the personality who held the job" (Reich, 1989b, p. A7) so that "Brenda did not know she had saved this money or where to find it" (Reich, 1989b, p. A7).

"The process by which control of the body passes from one personality to another is called *switching*" (Hurley, 1985c, p. 3) and usually occurs in one or two seconds. Switching can be voluntary or involuntary and can occur in response to a person's physiological or psychological condition or environmental situation (Hurley, 1985c). Switching can also occur in dreams, "usually nightmares" (Barrett, 1996a, p. 71). Some examples of Brenda's switching were given previously. Another example is the emergence of Penny to play with Brenda's son, "silently so as not to give herself away" (Reich, 1989b, p. A6). As we have seen, switching can sometimes happen at inopportune times. Brenda has found herself "in a strange place with a strange man" (Reich, 1989b, p. A6) after Janice had picked him up. In another case, "during surgery in a London hospital, a frightened personality emerged wide awake on the operating room table while the host was under anesthesia" (Reich, 1989a, p. A6). Apparently this "caused no end of grief" (Reich, 1989a, p. A6) for the surprised surgeons.

Physiological changes can accompany switching between personalities with apparent insensitivity to anesthesia being among the most dramatic. There can be "differences in visual acuity, pain tolerance, symptoms of asthma, sensitivity to allergens, and response of blood glucose to insulin" (American Psychiatric Association, 2000, p. 527). For example, allergies to animals such as cats can disappear with a change to a personality that is apparently not allergic to them (Hurley, 1985d, p. 20). In one study, more than one third of clinicians reported having seen changes of handedness, half of their clients "were reported to have alternate personalities who responded differently to the same medications" (Putnam, 1984, p. 32), three quarters of the clients "had alternate personalities with different physical symptoms, and one quarter had alternate-personality specific allergies" (Putnam, 1984, p. 32). Sometimes there are dermatological reactions that are specific to alternate personalities. For example, a woman who had had lighted cigarettes put out on her skin would manifest burn marks that would last for 6 to 10 hours when "the personality that received burns took over during therapy sessions" (Hurley, 1985d, p. 20). Given the rapid changes in physiology that sometimes accompany changes of personality, it is not surprising that people with DID sometimes apparently "heal more quickly than other people" (Hurley, 1985d, p. 20). Just as in chapter 2 we saw that changes to the immune system can sometimes correspond to imagined changes, with DID we see that physiological changes follow on changes of self-identity. It would be instructive to learn how such changes are brought about, both to understand the role of personality factors in disease (cf. Putnam, 1984) and to seek to duplicate beneficial effects in people who do not have DID (Hurley, 1985d).

Trauma as an Etiological Factor

People with DID who come to the attention of mental health practitioners have often been severely traumatized during childhood, usually through sexual or physical abuse, neglect, or witnessing a violent death. Examples of trauma have ostensibly included sexual exploitation by care-givers and relatives, torture, being buried alive, and being given inappropriate adult medication to try to treat abuse (Hurley, 1985a). Across a number of studies the rates of reported abuse have ranged from 89% to 98%, with at least some corroboration of abuse having been found for 73% to 95% of people with DID (Kluft, 1996).

Whereas the memories of traumatic events may be essentially correct, caution is needed with regard to the interpretation of the "precise details" (Kluft, 1996, p. 353) of abuse given by adults. In chapter 5, we considered the argument that memory for traumatic events is encoded differently from memory for everyday events. Indeed, there is evidence "that traumatic experiences are processed by the brain differently from normal experiences" (D. Brown, Scheflin, & Hammond, 1998) so that "traumatic experiences are initially imprinted as sensations or feeling states" (van der Kolk, 1996, p. 296) rather than being integrated into a personal narrative as part of autobiographical memory. At some later point in time these sensations and emotions may resurface as flashbacks (Krystal, Bennett, Bremner, Southwick, & Charney, 1996) "with the same vividness as if the subject were having the experience all over again . . . frequently leaving victims in a state of speechless terror, in which they may be unable to articulate precisely what they are feeling and thinking" (McFarlane & van der Kolk, 1996, p. 565). Once these images and emotions have resurfaced, the person for whom they have occurred seeks to make some sense of them (van der Kolk, 1996) through "inferential narrative smoothing" (Nadel & Jacobs, 1998, p. 156) by knitting together fragments of memories into a "plausible autobiographical episode" (Nadel & Jacobs, 1998, p. 156). Thus, confabulation enters the process at the point of creating an autobiographical narrative.

Richard Kluft has proposed a *four-factor theory* of dissociative identity disorder. The first factor is a *biological potential for dissociation*. This is probably related to the dissociation dimension of hypnotizability, in that "DID pa-tients, when stable and cooperative enough for such testing, are highly hypnotizable on standard instruments" (Kluft, 1996, p. 356). The second factor is the presence of *overwhelming experiences* such as those mentioned previously. The third factor is that of *shaping influences*, both intrapsychic and environmental, that lead to the particular alter personalities that de-velop. For example, alters can develop that are based on television characters. The fourth factor is *absence of restorative experiences* following traumatization (Kluft, 1996), so that there are no opportunities for healing (Hurley, 1985a). What appears to happen is that children who are unremittingly traumatized and have the capacity for dissociation will enlist intrapsychic and environ-mental resources to create alternate identities as a way of coping with the trauma.

Dynamics of Alternate Personalities

"At the time of diagnosis . . . approximately two to four personalities are in evidence" (Kluft, 1996, p. 344), with more manifesting in the course of treatment. Less elaborated alters, known as *fragments* may also be present. About 15% to 25% of people with DID are complex cases with at least 26 alters (Kluft, 1996), as in the case of Brenda or another case, Cassandra, with purportedly "180 personalities or fragments" (Hurley, 1985c, p. 4). With an apparently unlimited possibility of splitting, the alters can better be thought of as reconfigurations of the organization of the mind rather than as segments of a unit (Kluft, 1996). The purpose of the splitting is to "create alternative self-structures and psychological realities within which or by virtue of which emotional survival is facilitated" (Kluft, 1996, p. 344). One way to appreciate the extent of fragmentation of self-identity that can occur in DID is to note that, in one study, 26% of 23 psychotherapy clients treated for DID "had had personalities experience the same dream from different perspectives" (Barrett, 1996a, p. 74) so that "two or more personalities reported dreaming at the same time and experiencing each other as characters" (Barrett, 1996a, p. 75) in their dreams.

The *host personality* is "the personality who is in control of the body for the greatest percentage of time during a given period" (Hurley, 1985b, p. 22) and is usually "depressed, anxious, . . . compulsively good, . . . conscience-stricken, . . . and suffers both psychophysiological symptoms and time loss and/or time distortion" (Kluft, 1996, p. 345). But then there is a variety of alters as we have seen in the case of Brenda. There can be *childlike personalities* who can recall the traumas, *anesthetic personalities* whose purpose is to block out pain, *guardians of memories and secrets*, *expressers of forbidden pleasurable or antisocial impulses*, *inner persecutors* that are "often based on identification with the aggressor" (Kluft, 1996, p. 345), and *inner self-helpers* whose purpose is to try to reintegrate the personality (Damgaard, 1987).

Alters seek to affect one another so that whoever has control of the body may be subjected to the influences of other alters. In one study, 82% of 28 participants with DID experienced "recurrent command hallucinations" (Kluft, 1996, p. 347), and 100% experienced strong emotions "that were associated with alters that were not ostensibly in control . . . at the time, but which were . . . flooding the alter that was 'out' with their subjective experiences" (Kluft, 1996, p. 347). In the same study of dreams in DID already cited, it was found that 26% of 23 people with DID "had at least one personality able to design dreams to be experienced by other personalities" (Barrett, 1996a, p. 77). Inner persecutors in particular try to make an impact on whichever personality is present in the body without emerging by "urging it toward self-harm or suicide" (Kluft, 1996, p. 347) or by seizing motor control, for example, to fling the body "down the stairs" (Kluft, 1996, p. 347) or "steer an automobile toward an embankment" (Kluft, 1996, p. 347), much to the horror of the personality that is out. In one study it was found that 72% of 236 people with DID had attempted suicide and that 2% had succeeded (Ross et al., 1989).

Amnesia for important personal information is one of the defining symptoms of dissociative identity disorder (American Psychiatric Association, 2000). However, amnesia need not always be present, and when it is it can be selective, so that there can be awareness by one personality of the "thoughts, feelings or actions of other alters" (Hurley, 1985c, p. 5). Such awareness is known as *coconsciousness*. In general, there will be a complex constellation of relationships among alters that often recapitulates the alleged abuse relationships between the person with DID and her abusers. The greater the degree of coconsciousness and cooperation among alters the less likely it is that switching would be noticed (cf. Kluft, 1996). In fact, "many alter systems are organized in such a way as to keep themselves secret and may become very skilled in covering over their DID phenomena" (Kluft, 1996, p. 348).

Treatment consists of trying to establish coconsciousness between alters, soliciting the assistance of self-helpers, and integrating the alter personalities (cf. Wilbur & Kluft, 1989). It is interesting, in light of the possibility of symbolic portrayal of one's situation in dreams, that Barrett found that 83% of 23 people with DID had had their multiplicity depicted in dreams, for example, by seeing themselves in a photo booth ending up with pictures of other people rather than themselves. This does not mean, of course, that all dreams of changes in identity are symptomatic of DID. With regard to treatment, in rare cases, "lasting integration of two personalities" (Barrett, 1996a, p. 79) seems to have taken place in a dream, suggesting that integration in dreams could be developed into a therapeutic method (Barrett, 1996a).

Dissociative Identity Disorder and Possession

Are channeling and possession just instances of dissociative identity disorder? Is the mind closed? In one study, "ten trance channels" (Hughes, 1992, p. 182) were interviewed "to determine the degree of overlap between the complex of symptoms that characterizes [DID], and the phenomenological experience of the trance channels" (Hughes, 1992, p. 182). Although "three of the ten channels" (Hughes, 1992, p. 187) could have met diagnostic criteria for what is now called DID, none of them had the relevant secondary features, such as "handwriting changes,

... periods of missing time, ... flashbacks, ... auditory hallucinations, [or] speaking of oneself in the plural tense" (Hughes, 1992, p. 186). There were numerous other differences, not the least of which was the fact that DID usually has a traumatic origin, whereas trance channeling is often a learned behavior acquired by using visualization techniques in a meditative context (Hughes, 1992). Channeling is not DID, but that does not mean that the mind is not closed.

A better case could be made that possession trance is just dissociative identity disorder. In one study it was found that 29% of 236 people with DID had a personality that was "identified as a demon" (Ross et al., 1989, p. 415) and 21% had a "personality identified as a dead relative" (Ross et al., 1989, p. 415). In some cases possession appears to have been a coping mechanism used "in reaction to severe emotional stress or conflict" (Ward, 1989, p. 132), for which exorcism appears to have served a psychotherapeutic function. Recent studies have shown, however, "that interventions of an exorcistic nature can have deleterious effects in DID patients" (Kluft, 1996, p. 353), suggesting that possession is not just DID. There are other differences between possession and DID (Coons, 1993; Ferracuti, Sacco, & Lazzari, 1996), so that "it seems overly facile to equate [DID] with involuntary possession" (Krippner, 1994, p. 352).

Rather than dissociative identity disorder serving as an explanation for possession, could it be the other way around? Could part of the explanation for DID be possession? Are the demon and dead relative alter personalities really demons and dead relatives? Is the mind open? Perhaps severe childhood trauma functions as an initiatic crisis, breaking down the boundaries of the psyche so that the intrusion of spirits becomes possible. Krippner has observed that in Brazil some healers who have been aware of DID have given dual diagnoses of DID and "involuntary spirit possession" (Krippner, 1994, p. 354). Perhaps both DID and possession can coincide with the need to determine the composition of the mixture in the case of each separate psyche.

But maybe the answers to these questions are much simpler. The apparent ease of fragmentation, multiplicity of alters, and unrealistic features of self-identity in DID make us question the extent to which alters are separate and real aspects of a psyche. Could it be that people with DID are simply responding strategically to different social situations by exhibiting various personas analogous to the flexibility of positively set hypnotic subjects in responding to suggestions? That may be true, at least in part. However, we need to be careful not to ignore the complexity of phenomena that occur with DID. These problems of reality, self-identity, and pathology are brought into even sharper focus when considering people who believe that they have been abducted by aliens.

ALIEN ABDUCTION EXPERIENCES

Among the most enigmatic contemporary phenomena are alien abduc-tion experiences, which are characterized by the belief that one has been taken "against one's will by apparently non-human entities, usually to a location interpreted as an alien spacecraft" (Appelle, Lynn, & Newman, 2000, p. 254) where one has been subjected to various "physical and psycho-logical procedures" (Appelle et al., 2000, p. 254). It seems ridiculous to think that these experiences could be what they appear to be, nor is there evidence acceptable to skeptics that aliens are actually abducting people (Mack, 1999), yet neither are there currently any other compelling explana-tions for the abduction phenomenon (Appelle, 1996). The subject matter itself is often treated with derision by scientists (e.g., Park, 2000), and those who try to study abduction experiences have sometimes been viciously attacked for doing so (Mack, 1999). The incidence of abduction experiences has been difficult to determine, but estimates have ranged from about .04% to 2% of the population. When one physician queried 266 colleagues and patients, 43 of them said that they had seen a UFO, and 4 of those were considered to be probable abduction cases, resulting in an incidence figure of 1.5% (J. G. Miller, 1994a). In a survey of 1,564 adults in the United States in the year 2000, 43% believed that UFOs were real, whereas 42% believed that UFOs were imaginary, with 15% volunteering the response that they were not sure. Furthermore, 1% maintained that they had "had an encounter with beings from another planet" (Fox, 2000, p. 56), which translates into 2,700,000 Americans. In other words, alleged encounters with aliens appear to be not insignificant occurrences and hence, if for no other reason, merit serious scrutiny, whatever the explanation for them may eventually turn out to be.

Let us start by describing the characteristics of alien abduction experi-ences and giving an example. Then we will consider some explanations for them as well as some of the critical features of alien abduction experiences that make them enigmatic. We will conclude this section by comparing alien abduction experiences with shamanism, and noting the transformative effects that they can have on those who experience them.

Characteristics of Alien Abduction Experiences

In general, abduction experiences begin with an initial contact that may occur while a person is in her home or driving an automobile. There may be unexplained lights or buzzing sounds and perception of the presence of humanoid beings or a strange craft. "After the initial contact, the abductee is commonly 'floated' (the word most commonly used) down the hall, through the wall or windows of the house, or through the roof of the car" (Mack,

1994a, pp. 18–19) and into a spacecraft of some sort. An experiencer may realize that she has been paralyzed by one of the beings and feel terrorized by her strange circumstances and sense of helplessness. During the time of her abduction, family members may claim that the experiencer was missing. She may find herself in a brightly lit room with curved, white walls and ceilings in which there are "body-conforming chairs and tables" (Mack, 1994a, p. 22) and computer-like equipment. The most commonly described alien beings are the " 'grays,' humanoid beings three to four feet in height" (Mack, 1994a, p. 22) with large heads, "long arms with three or four long fingers" (Mack, 1994a, p. 22), thin torsos, spindly legs, and large, black, compelling eyes. An experiencer may be subjected to various procedures in which "instruments are used to penetrate virtually every part" (Mack, 1994a, p. 23) of her body including the head and, most commonly, reproductive system. Male experiencers have reported having sperm samples taken and females have reported having been impregnated and the subsequent possibly human–alien fetuses removed and placed "into containers on the ships" (Mack, 1994a, p. 24). An experiencer may be shown images of the destruc-tion of the earth through nuclear holocaust, pollution, or natural disasters, and informed of human responsibility for the fate of the planet. An experi-encer is returned, usually to the place from which she was abducted, and generally feels tired afterward, as though she had "been through some sort of stressful experience" (Mack, 1994a, p. 26; see also D. M. Jacobs, 1998).

A person who has apparently been abducted will often have periods of missing time for which she cannot remember what happened, and it is during this time that the abduction ostensibly occurred. For example, Carol was staying at a state park in the United States when she found herself walking alone down a hill to her log cabin with no idea what time it was. She realized that it was getting dark and wondered what she had done all day. She had some hot dogs, baked beans, and coffee for dinner and then threw up. The next morning "she was surprised to see her car in the middle of the road" (Bryan, 1995, p. 311). As soon as she touched the door handle of the car she remembered the events of the previous day.

Carol remembered that she had been sitting on the porch of her cabin when she had noticed fog drifting "slowly down the hill toward her" (Bryan, 1995, p. 298). She was alarmed by the fog and panicked when she saw "two thin, short gray legs" (Bryan, 1995, p. 298) at the bottom of it. She ran into the cabin, realized that she could not lock out the beings, grabbed her car keys, and ran toward her car. Three small, gray beings were "floating down the hill . . . like skiers . . . [with their] knees and ankles locked" (Bryan, 1995, p. 299). Carol slid into the car and started the motor. The three small grays were now only a few feet in front of her. She put the car in reverse and backed out onto the road. One of the grays "had raised his arm and was pointing at the front end of Carol's car" (Bryan, 1995, p. 299).

The car went out of gear. Carol tried to put the car back in reverse but the "shift lever slid through the gears as if through butter" (Bryan, 1995, p. 299). At that point she said out loud that she would go with the beings because she did not want them to further damage her car. She found herself floating up the hill and "then, suddenly, she was inside their ship" (Bryan, 1995, p. 299). The room in which she found herself had a "white, curved interior wall [that] was rounded and seamless" (Bryan, 1995, p. 299). She was floated to a reclining chair that "molded itself to her form" (Bryan, 1995, p. 300).

The three small grays who had brought her had moved out of Carol's line of sight but eventually three tall grays appeared. Carol heard in her head one of the tall beings telling her that she would be changed and that the things that were being done to her were important. Carol asked why they were important and was told that she did not need to know, leading her to feel that the grays were arrogant and using her as they would use a tool. The grays then proceeded to inject her with various colored fluids and draw blood from her arm. When Carol tried to find out why her blood was being taken, the tall gray said that she had to be tested "to see if everything's okay" (Bryan, 1995, p. 304; emphasis removed) and reiterated again that she would be changed. Then the gray told her that she must "only eat cow things" (Bryan, 1995, p. 304; emphasis removed). Carol protested, saying that "human beings cannot eat just cow" (Bryan, 1995, p. 304; emphasis removed), to which the being replied that she could because she was changed. She asked about horses with pads in place of hooves, which she had seen previously in a dream and was shown pictures of horses milling about on a screen whose feet she could not see. When she protested that she could not see the horses' feet, the screen with the horses was replaced with one with cows that had tubes sticking out from their sides. She was told that "Cows are changed. Horses are changed. People are changed" (Bryan, 1995, p. 307; emphasis removed). And she was also told not to act crazy. Then she was allowed to get dressed, was led down a corridor, told to look at one of a number of "square boxes aligned along the corridor's left-hand wall" (Bryan, 1995, p. 309), and found herself walking down the hill toward the log cabin in the state park.

A week later Carol awoke "in pain with two more fresh punctures just below her belly button" (Bryan, 1995, p. 311), which was one of the sites on her body where she had previously received injections. "A clear fluid was leaking from the holes" (Bryan, 1995, p. 311). A week after that she had blood on her arm and blood coming from the same holes in her stomach. "Furthermore, every time she accidentally ate something that was not a beef or dairy product, she broke out in a rash and suffered severe stomach cramps" (Bryan, 1995, p. 311).

Explanations of Alien Abduction Experiences

What are we to make of abduction experiences such as this? Perhaps the first thing that comes to mind is that those who report such accounts are afflicted with a mental disorder. However, despite efforts to find it, there is little evidence of psychopathology among experiencers (Appelle et al., 2000; Newman & Baumeister, 1996). This is not to say that there are no psychological disturbances among experiencers who appear to be suffering from stress consistent with that induced by trauma (Appelle et al., 2000) and "accompanying psychiatric conditions" (Mack, 1994b, p. 373). However, any emotional disorders that are present are insufficient to account for the alleged abduction experiences (Mack, 1994b).

It has been suggested that alien abduction experiences are somehow related to dissociation (Bryan, 1995). The idea is that some sort of trauma occurs that leads to dissociation and false memories about alien abduction. The obvious candidate is childhood sexual abuse, although fewer than one quarter of experiencers have reported sexual abuse (McLeod, Corbisier, & Mack, 1996). Nonetheless, given that there is a correlation between reported childhood abuse and reported alien abduction experiences, it has been suggested that the alien abduction scenarios are screen memories of actual sexual abuse. The idea is that remembering the actual sexual abuse is too traumatic, so an abduction scenario is made up in its stead (Appelle et al., 2000). However, when asked to rate how upset they were at the time of abduction on a scale from 0 to 10 with 10 being "as upset as they could possibly imagine" (McLeod et al., 1996, p. 164), "experiencers rated their distress 10 to 100" (McLeod et al., 1996, p. 164). In fact, one of the characteristic features of the abduction phenomenon is the degree to which experiencers feel abject terror in association with their experiences (Bryan, 1995). In one case, in a direct comparison, abduction experiences were perceived to be much more painful and fearful than being raped (Mack, 1999). It is not clear why a traumatic event would be covered up with an apparently even more traumatic one. It is also not clear how reports of sexual abuse could become reports of alien abductions (Appelle, 1996) or, indeed, how a highly articulated narrative could be produced that has nothing to do with "any of the actual experiences that led to the dissociation" (Mack, quoted in Bryan, 1995, p. 268).

In a similar vein, it has been suggested that some of the experiencers may have created false memories regarding surgical procedures to which they have been exposed in the past (J. Wilson, 1992). However, a comparison of alien and human medical procedures reveals notable differences. Alien doctors seem to be unconcerned with the chest and upper abdomen, both of which are often a target of attention for human doctors. On the other hand, although the cranium is "a great focal point of the aliens' exam . . . their techniques are strange" (J. G. Miller, 1994b, p. 59). Aliens tend to stare at experiencers. In Carol's case, one of the aliens pushed his face so close to hers that, if he had had one, his nose would have bumped into hers. She found herself looking directly "into his huge, oval, nonreflective black eyes" (Bryan, 1995, p. 308) from which she could not get away. By the time the alien had finished staring "she was left with a headache" (Bryan, 1995, p. 308). Aliens have also been reported to have completely removed an experiencer's eye and then replaced it, something that human doctors do not do (J. G. Miller, 1994b). As with purported childhood sexual abuse, it is not clear how misremembered medical procedures could end up with the distortions found in alien abduction accounts.

Nonetheless, it could be argued that these experiences must somehow be delusions (Banaji & Kihlstrom, 1996), false memories (Newman, 1997), or fantasies (Appelle et al., 2000). In that regard, it is noteworthy that hypnosis has been used in 71% to 90% of cases to recover these purported memories (Newman & Baumeister, 1996), and in chapter 5 we saw already the unreliability of hypnotic hypermnesia. However, some abduction researchers have argued that in some sense, experiencers' memories are switched off during their experiences and that hypnosis "seems uniquely capable of undoing the amnesia that occurs in the abductions" (Mack, quoted in Bryan, 1995, p. 318). Although this may seem to be an overly facile rationale for the use of hypnosis, from a practical point of view, whether or not hypnosis has been used seems to make little difference because "hypnotically recovered material does not differ in basic structure from material reported by individuals with a clear waking memory of abduction events" (McLeod et al., 1996, p. 166). Certainly Carol's consciously recalled experiences are as lurid as many of the accounts in the abduction literature that have been obtained with the use of hypnosis. Arguing against confabulation theories is the fact that experiencers do not score higher than the general population on measures of hypnotic susceptibility and fantasy-proneness (Appelle et al., 2000).

Critical Features of Alien Abduction Experiences

According to John Mack, who has been approached by more than 3,000 individuals concerning their abduction experiences (McLeod et al., 1996), there are a number of features of the abduction phenomenon that must be taken into account in any explanation for it. The first is the *sincerity* of the people who report such experiences. Based on his background in forensic psychiatry, Mack cannot find any reason to suppose that experiencers are motivated "to distort their experience or to lie or to self-aggrandize" (Mack, quoted in Bryan, 1995, p. 258). Nor is it "uncommon for an experiencer to prefer to be diagnosed with a mental illness rather than believe that the experience happened in a physical sense" (McLeod et al., 1996, p. 159). The second feature is the *intensity of emotion*, particularly fear, displayed by experiencers when they recall abduction experiences. Something has traumatized these people (Bryan, 1995).

The third feature of abduction experiences that needs to be explained is the *narrative consistency* (Bryan, 1995) of the accounts of abduction experiences (Mack, 1994b). Critics, however, have pointed out the similarities between alien abduction accounts and the fictional portrayal of aliens in the media, so that the consistency of fantasized accounts could be a result of the prevalence of stories about aliens in our culture (Appelle, 1996). On the other hand, some of the investigators who have documented these narratives have argued that there is consistency among abduction reports with regard to details that have never been published. For example, there are apparently strong resemblances between notational systems attributed to aliens that have been recalled by experiencers (Hopkins, 2000). The fourth feature, which we have already mentioned, is the *absence of any mental illness* that could account for the behavior of experiencers (Bryan, 1995; Mack, 1994b). The fifth feature is the presence of *corroborative physical evidence* (Bryan, 1995) that is enough "to win over those who are prepared to believe in the phenomenon but not enough to convince the skeptic" (Mack, 1999, p. 10). Corroborative physical evidence has included UFO sightings, missing people, body lesions, and apparent implants (Mack, 1999). For example, Carol's oozing and bleeding puncture wounds following purported abductions could be considered as corroborative physical evidence. The sixth feature is the association of abduction experiences with UFO sightings by other witnesses (Bryan, 1995).

The seventh feature of abduction experiences that needs to be explained, according to Mack, is their *presence in children*. Children as young as 2 years of age have talked about being taken up into the sky or having things stuck into them. Finding abduction accounts in young children argues to some extent against the contention that these accounts reflect the influence of the media considering that such an influence would be expected to be somewhat less in young children (Bryan, 1995; Mack, 1994b). Not only have children apparently been involved, but some of the phenomena associated with abduction experiences also appear to be transgenerational. Carol's father had experienced missing time twice in the 1930s and could not be found by others looking for him during those periods of missing time. Her grandfather had gotten up in the middle of dinner one day in a daze, walked out of the house, and was never seen again. There could, of course, be mundane explanations for both of these cases. Carol's 4-year-old granddaughter had drawn a picture of a flying machine and a gray being who, she had said, sometimes took her up in the flying machine. Her granddaughter also played with an imaginary ball that she said had been given to her by the gray being's friends and that she acknowledged was "sort of" (Bryan, 1995, p. 296) invisible.

But there are also problems with the ET *hypothesis* (Appelle, 1996). Just as there have been cases in which people appear to have been missing during abduction experiences, there have been others in which they clearly were not missing. For example, an Australian woman lapsed into unconsciousness in the presence of two UFO investigators and described to them being abducted into a round room in which she observed the presence of an entity (Basterfield, 1994). Even if abduction experiences have actually been associated with UFOs, and one third of investigated UFOs do not have prosaic explanations (Appelle, 1996), that does not mean that experiencers are being taken aboard spacecraft being flown by extraterrestrials (Vallee, 1990). It is also interesting to note "that the piloters of UFOs have been taking on aspects of our own most disturbing behavior" (Grossinger, 1989, p. 46) by "treating sentient beings with precisely the kind of scientific contempt we now exhibit epidemically, carrying out clandestine operations complete with cover stories" (Grossinger, 1989, pp. 46–47). There have been suggestions that some abduction experiences are clandestine government experiments (e.g., Vallee, 1991). Alternatively, we could be somehow projecting our own disturbing behavior in a way that becomes objectively visible (Grossinger, 1989).

Alien Abduction Experiences and Shamanism

In some respects at least, alien abduction accounts resemble shamanic initiations. To begin with, the experiencer appears to be "somehow entranced" (Ring, 1989, p. 17) during the time of the abduction and goes on a journey to another level of being where she is terrorized and has to face the possibility of her own death. She meets with spirits in the form of alien beings and is dismembered to varying degrees in a round chamber symbolic of "a womb or a place of new beginnings" (Ring, 1989, p. 17). She telepathically receives some sort of important information and then is mysteriously returned to the ordinary world within which she may end up taking on a new role as a healer. Indeed, many experiencers move past the stage of terror and come to view their abduction experiences as an awakening that can include the awakening of "powerful psychic gifts" (Mack, 1999, p. 253). They may come to develop meaningful connections to the alien beings, including feelings "of love so profound as to be felt to be incompatible with earthly love" (Mack, 1999, p. 19). They may also become aware of the precarious plight of the earth and seek to do what they can to help. In other words, alien abduction experiences can trigger a process of self-transformation much as shamanic initiatic crises can. The question is whether such transformation "derives simply from a kind of stretching of the psychic sinews that can occur with any sort of trauma and recovery process" (Mack, 1999, p. 229) or whether there is something about the abduction phenomenon itself that promotes this.

Some shamans themselves have claimed to have encountered aliens, including grays, as part of the panoply of spirits with whom they purportedly interact and, in some cases, have had the same degrading experiences as other experiencers. The alien entities encountered by shamans are characterized by the shaman's inability to manage them using her skills, by the intense energies that may be transmitted to the shaman, by a "transtribal universalism that they represent" (Mack, 1999, p. 165), and by a direct link to "divine intelligence" (Mack, 1999, p. 165) that these beings seem to possess. Alien entities are more progressive and have more to do with the future than other beings the shaman may encounter who have more to do with the traditions of the past (Mack, 1999). But now we are back to the question of whether the psyche is open or closed. If spirits are real for the shaman at another level of reality, is it possible that aliens are also real but nonphysical?

According to Mack, the transformation that occurs for experiencers is not just generic transformation resulting from an effort to heal trauma but also depends, in part, on the *ontological shock* (Mack, 1999, p. 55) that occurs when the boundaries between the normal physical world and the world of the aliens are shattered (Mack, 1999). McKenna has argued that "science has begun to threaten the existence of the human species as well as the ecosystem of the planet" (McKenna, 1989, p. 24), so that "a shock is necessary for the culture" (McKenna, 1989, p. 24). A shock that is sufficient to stop the "materialist juggernaut" (Mack, 1999, p. 296) by producing a "radical change in consciousness" (Mack, 1999, p. 296) or, as one experiencer has said, the abduction phenomenon is one part of "a spiritual emergence" (Mack, 1999, p. 256) of humanity.

So where does this leave us? What are we to think of alterations of consciousness such as shamanic journeying, possession, dissociative identity disorder, and alien abduction experiences? To begin with, we have come across surprisingly little psychopathology. Even dissociative identity disorder, which is regarded as a mental disorder, can be viewed as a healthy way of dealing with an unhealthy situation—namely trauma. These alterations of consciousness certainly raise questions about our identity. What does it mean to be someone other than who we ordinarily think we are? Or to believe that we are spirits, freed from our bodies, able to interact with other spirits in a nonphysical realm? In fact, is there a nonphysical realm in which spirits and aliens can be encountered? Are these experiences delusional or real? Is the psyche open or closed? I will leave it to the reader to make up her own mind.

7

PSYCHEDELICS

We started out in this book examining the ordinary waking state and then considered some naturally occurring and behaviorally evoked alterations of consciousness. As we have proceeded, the alterations have become increasingly dramatic, some with sinister aspects. In this chapter we will consider chemically induced alterations. Chemicals that have psychological effects are known as *psychoactive drugs*, and those that are illegal are called *illicit drugs* (Levinthal, 1996). We will not try to survey all psychoactive drugs but will confine ourselves to a discussion of the psychedelics, whose prototype is *d-lysergic acid diethylamide* (Grinspoon & Bakalar, 1979), which we will abbreviate as *LSD*, and to two drugs often considered in the same context as the psychedelics, *3,4-methylenedioxymethamphetamine (MDMA)* and *marijuana* (Naranjo, 1986). All of these can loosely be regarded as psychedelics, with the LSD-like drugs sometimes referred to as *major psychedelics* and marijuana as a *minor psychedelic* (Tart, 1972a). The possession and use of most of these drugs are illegal in North America (Grinspoon & Bakalar, 1979).

I want to make it clear that, whatever I say about them in this chapter, in no way am I advocating the use of illicit drugs. In addition to the moral imperative not to engage in illegal activities is the undesirability of supporting criminal organizations that produce and distribute illicit drugs and the danger of ingesting substances whose composition is unknown. With regard to the last of these dangers, in some studies in the past, it was found that "drugs advertised as mescaline, psilocybin, or THC . . . practically never have these drugs in them" (Tart, 1972a, p. 386). For example, ordinary mushrooms from a supermarket have been laced with various drugs and sold as magic mushrooms "at high prices to unsuspecting customers" (Weil & Rosen, 1993, p. 99). The drugs "PCP and ketamine [have been] frequently misrepresented and sold as mescaline, LSD, marijuana, amphetamine, or cocaine" (Levinthal, 1996, p. 197). And, in the past, the drug 4-methoxyamphetamine has often been "passed off as the love drug MDA, though it is ten times more powerful and has killed many of its users" (Lavigne, 1999, p. 373). More recently, of 28 pills sent to a laboratory for testing that were supposed to be MDMA, popularly known as *ecstasy*, 15 of the pills contained MDMA or related drugs, "three contained no drugs at all" (Sferios, 1999, p. 47), and 10 contained unrelated drugs. Of the 10 pills containing unrelated drugs, eight of them contained *dextromethorphan*, a cough suppressant. Users of pills containing dextromethorphan have reported "nausea, [delirium], itchy skin, loss of motor control, and audio and visual hallucinations" (Sferios, 1999, p. 47) with effects sometimes lasting for "36 hours or longer" (Sferios, 1999, p. 47). In some cases, emergency medical attention has been required (Sferios, 1999). The use of illicit drugs is not only illegal but also dangerous.

Let us start with the modern beginnings of psychedelic drug use by considering the invention of LSD and the proliferation of psychedelics in the 1960s. After that we will examine the effects of some specific psychoactive drugs, then their adverse and therapeutic effects, and finally end with a discussion of an experiment to induce mystical experiences using psychedelics. Two of our thematic threads in particular run through this chapter. Do psychedelic drugs create a pathological condition, or do they enhance well-being? Are psychedelic drugs dangerous or beneficial? Other threads are also present, often just below the surface, but at other times brought explicitly into the discussion.

MODERN BEGINNINGS

As a doctoral student I took a graduate course in consciousness with a professor who was fond of reminding me again and again that we would not be discussing consciousness were it not for the effects of the widespread use of psychedelics in the 1960s (cf. Blewett, 1969). What happened during that era? What was it that was so profound? Before looking at the psychedelic sixties, let us go back to the invention of LSD some decades previously.

The Invention of LSD

In 1938 Albert Hofmann was looking for new medicines at the Sandoz company in Basel, Switzerland, when he produced a new chemical, the 25th in a series of lysergic acid compounds that he designated as "LSD-25" (Hofmann, 1979/1980, p. 12). Testing with animals proved uninteresting and so it was discontinued. However, Hofmann had "a peculiar presentiment" (Hofmann, 1979/1980, p. 14) that LSD "could possess properties other than those established in the first investigations" (Hofmann, 1979/ 1980, p. 14), and so he produced some once again. On April 16, 1943, during the last stage of the synthesis, he was interrupted in his work by feelings of restlessness and slight dizziness, forcing him to go home. At home he lay down and closed his eyes. He found that his imagination was so stimulated that for 2 hours he "perceived an uninterrupted stream of fantastic pictures, extraordinary shapes with intense, kaleidoscopic play of colors" (Hofmann, 1979/1980, p. 15). Hofmann reasoned that some of the LSD must have been absorbed through his fingertips during the crystallization process.

Three days after his first experience, Hofmann took what he assumed to be a conservative dose of 250 micrograms of LSD, unaware of the potency of the drug that he had created. Again he had to go home. "The dizziness and sensation of fainting" (Hofmann, 1979/1980, p. 17) were so pronounced that he could no longer stand and was forced to lie down. "Everything in the room spun around, and the familiar objects and pieces of furniture assumed grotesque, threatening forms" (Hofmann, 1979/1980, p. 17). The worlds outside and inside him disintegrated, and he felt as though a demon had invaded him against which his will was impotent. He was "seized by the dreadful fear of going insane" (Hofmann, 1979/1980, p. 18), believed himself to be outside his body, and wondered if he were dying. Gradually his terror subsided, and Hofmann began to enjoy the "fantastic images" (Hofmann, 1979/1980, p. 19) that "surged" (Hofmann, 1979/1980, p. 19) toward him, "alternating, variegated, opening and then closing themselves in circles and spirals" (Hofmann, 1979/1980, p. 19). Sounds became changing, vivid images, each "with its own consistent form and color" (Hofmann, 1979/1980, p. 19). The following morning, he felt refreshed and found sensory experiences to be extraordinarily pleasurable.

Hofmann believed that the new compound could be particularly useful in psychiatry so that, after other employees at Sandoz had confirmed the effects of LSD, samples of the drug were sent to various research institutions. By 1960, more than 500 papers about LSD had been published (Grinspoon & Bakalar, 1979).

John Lilly "obtained some LSD-25 from the Sandoz Company" (Lilly, 1978, p. 123) and injected himself with 100 micrograms before climbing into an isolation tank. He was terrified, having received warnings that it was dangerous to take LSD without supervision. But then he reasoned with himself that he could control his brain circuits and neutralize the fear. He relaxed as the LSD effects began with sensations of electrical excitation coursing through his body. "The darkness, the silence, the wetness, and the warmth disappeared. The external reality of the tank disappeared" (Lilly, 1978, p. 127). His awareness of his body and his brain disappeared. All that was left was "a small point of consciousness in a vast domain" (Lilly, 1978, p. 128). He felt that light was being formed into atoms and atoms into light directed by "a vast consciousness" (Lilly, 1978, p. 128). Time had ceased to exist, so that he was in "an eternal place, with eternal processes generated by beings far greater than [himself]" (Lilly, 1978, p. 128). Eventually he reentered his body, got out of the tank, and wrote up his notes (Lilly, 1978).

A number of names have been proposed for the classification of drugs such as lysergic acid diethylamide to appropriately characterize them. In the first article concerning LSD in 1947, it was called a *phantasticum* (Grinspoon & Bakalar, 1979). Particularly in the context of drug laws and medical research (Grinspoon & Bakalar, 1979), psychedelics have often been classified as *hallucinogens*, drugs that produce hallucinations (Levinthal, 1996). However, that is not an altogether accurate term, given that it is rare during intoxication with psychedelics to mistake imaginary events as being physically real (Grinspoon & Bakalar, 1979), if that is to be taken as the meaning of "hallucination" (cf. Aggernæs, 1972). Rather, what occur are distortions of ordinary perceptions of the environment, so that the word *illusionogenic* has been proposed as an alternative to hallucinogenic (Levinthal, 1996).

Psychedelics are *psychotropic* in the sense of being mind-altering (Grob & Harman, 1995). The question is whether the alterations are detrimental or beneficial. One of the terms with pejorative connotations is *psycholytic*, meaning mind-dissolving (Levinthal, 1996), although psycholytic has also been used to mean just mind-freeing or mind-loosening, referring to the release of "emotional and cognitive inhibitions" (Grob & Harman, 1995, p. 8). These drugs have also been called *psychodysleptic*, meaning mind-disrupting (Levinthal, 1996) and *psychotomimetic*, meaning "mimicking or inducing psychosis" (Grob & Harman, 1995, p. 8). The last of these meanings in particular has been contested, for example, by pointing out that it was not surprising that participants in early studies acted in a psychotic manner given that they were carried out in sterile hospital settings by psychiatrists in white coats (Tart, 1972a). The term *psychotropic* also refers to moving a person "closer to a normal state of mind" (Levinthal, 1996, p. 377) and can thereby be used to indicate beneficial effects. Our preferred term *psychedelic*, meaning mind manifesting or soul revealing (Grob & Harman, 1995), was coined in 1956 by the Canadian psychiatrist Humphry Osmond, who was researching the psychotherapeutic benefits of such drugs (Mangini, 1998). And finally, because they sometimes appear to "awaken or generate mystical experiences" (Forte, 1997a, p. 1), psychedelics have also been referred to as *entheogens*.

.The Psychedelic Sixties

Psychedelic drug use received a substantial impetus during the 1960s from Timothy Leary, an academic psychologist at Harvard University (Grinspoon & Bakalar, 1979), whose "advice to people in America" (Leary, 1965/

1970, p. 287) was to "turn on, tune in, and drop out" (Leary, 1965/1970, p. 287). On taking psychedelic drugs for the first time, Leary had "the deepest religious experience of [his] life" (Leary, 1965/1970, p. 13), convincing him that he "had awakened from a long ontological sleep" (Leary, 1965/1970, p. 13), a process that he characterized as "turning on." This is the same ontological awakening that sometimes occurs for those who have had alien abduction experiences, as we noted in chapter 6, and that is typical of those tending toward the extraordinarily transcendent position of the material-transcendent dimension of beliefs about consciousness and reality. "Tuning in" referred to harnessing one's "internal revelations to the external world" (Leary, 1965/1970, p. 287), as, for example, in the form of artistic expression (Leary, 1965/1970). And "dropping out" meant to "gracefully detach [one-self] from the social commitments to which [one was] addicted" (Leary, 1965/1970, p. 291), so as to be able to pursue an authentic spiritual quest (Leary, 1965/1970).

After hundreds of psychedelic drug trips, Leary maintained that he and his colleague Richard Alpert had moved beyond the usual concerns of academic psychologists. They came to believe that careful scientific evaluation of psychedelics was pointless and instead held group sessions that resembled "a cross between religious convocations and wild parties" (Grinspoon & Bakalar, 1979, p. 65). In terms of our thematic threads, it is possible that this change of strategy represented an attempted vertical shift in meaningfulness. Leary and Alpert gained considerable media attention as a result of their connection with Harvard University, from which they ended up being dismissed in 1963. Leary believed that people's lives consisted of playing games of which they were unconscious but from which they could be liberated by the psychedelics. He was the most charismatic proponent of a mixture of social commentary, hedonism, and Eastern religions that "became, mostly in diffuse and vulgarized versions, the founding philosophy of the hippie movement" (Grinspoon & Bakalar, 1979, p. 65).

By the late 1960s, psychedelic drugs had spawned a counterculture with characteristic lifestyles, leaders, "status distinctions and internal rivalries" (Grinspoon & Bakalar, 1979, p. 68), which could be found in enclaves in cities around the world. Some of the participants had a sense of being present in the midst of significant events that were somehow right. They believed that the energy of the counterculture would prevail against the established medical and legal norms of society. Those who used LSD were charged by the authorities with being "sick and dangerous" (Grinspoon & Bakalar, 1979, p. 68), to which drug advocates replied "that it was they, the established powers, who were sick and dangerous" (Grinspoon & Bakalar, 1979, p. 68) because they were afraid to see the emptiness of their own lives and desperately tried to prevent others from becoming liberated from repressive social control. Medical personnel and lawmakers were accused of approving enslaving drugs such as alcohol and nicotine and prohibiting the liberating psychedelics. LSD had apparently become the sacrament that provided anyone who wanted them with visionary experiences that had previously "been the property of solitary mystics" (Grinspoon & Bakalar, 1979, p. 71) and esoteric collectives. This direct experience was at the heart of what appeared to be "a transformation in consciousness that would sweep the world" (Grinspoon & Bakalar, 1979, p. 68).

In the United States, psychedelic drugs such as LSD were freely available to physicians until 1963, at which time restrictions were placed on their availability. In 1966 laws against the manufacture and sale of psychedelics came into effect and, in some states, laws against possession were enacted. In 1968 possession became illegal throughout the United States. Then, in "the Comprehensive Drug Abuse Prevention and Control Act of 1970" (Grinspoon & Bakalar, 1979, p. 310), many psychedelic drugs "became Schedule I Controlled Drugs, a designation that indicates lack of safety even in medically supervised use, high abuse potential, and no current accepted medical use" (Mangini, 1998, p. 396). The rest of the world followed the lead of the United States, and legitimate research using psychedelic drugs virtually ground to a halt (Grinspoon & Bakalar, 1979).

Although the psychedelic movement did not survive, nor create a promised revolution, "many of the several million people who used LSD never abandoned the idea that in some sense they had achieved expanded awareness" (Grinspoon & Bakalar, 1979, p. 86). One psychiatrist who studied psychedelics during the 1950s and 1960s has said subsequently that "not a single person believes that LSD represents a folly of our youth" (quoted in Rayl, 1989, p. 30). People's LSD experiences prompted interest in spiritual practices, particularly those of the East, as a way of exploring consciousness without the use of drugs (Grinspoon & Bakalar, 1979). For example, after leaving Harvard University, Alpert traveled to India in 1967, where he settled down to study with a guru, Neem Karoli Baba (Dass, 1979), who, Alpert has claimed, showed no effects of intoxication after having swallowed 915 micrograms of LSD (Dass, 1971). In a 1990 questionnaire survey of Tibetan Buddhist practitioners, Tart found that 77% of 64 respondents "reported previous experience with major psychedelics" (Tart, 1991, p. 148) and 32% claimed that major psychedelics had contributed at least somewhat to attracting them to Tibetan Buddhism.

A quarter-century after being banned, some government-sanctioned research with psychedelics quietly resumed "in the early 1990s" (Grob & Harman, 1995, p. 7). Previously, the emphasis on the unique ability to powerfully alter "experience, perception, understanding, and belief in the nature of reality" (Grob & Harman, 1995, p. 7) had backfired precisely because these drugs undermined the "conventional structures of authority"

(Grob & Harman, 1995, p. 7). In the 1990s, however, the strategy was to consider these drugs as any other drugs to be investigated not for their phenomenological but "for their physiological and neurological . . . effects" (Grob & Harman, 1995, p. 7), with possible eventual uses, for example, in the treatment of severe substance abuse and "pain and depression" (Grob & Harman, 1995, p. 6) associated with terminal illnesses.

• VARIETIES OF PSYCHEDELICS

Let us survey the effects of some specific psychedelics, including a subsection in which we briefly consider the possible brain mechanisms through which they act, and then look at the effects of the related drugs MDMA and marijuana.

LSD

"LSD is one of the most potent drugs known" (Weil & Rosen, 1993, p. 95), with doses as small as 10 micrograms producing "some mild euphoria, loosening of inhibitions, and empathic feeling" (Grinspoon & Bakalar, 1979, p. 11). Psychedelic effects begin at around 50 to 100 micrograms and "increase up to about 400 or 500 micrograms" (Grinspoon & Bakalar, 1979, p. 11). A typical dose is 50 to 150 micrograms, with effects beginning within 45 to 60 minutes and ending 5 to 12 hours after ingestion (Levinthal, 1996). The physiological effects of LSD are variable and appear to follow from the psychological effects, although "increased heart rate, blood pressure, and body temperature" (Grinspoon & Bakalar, 1979, p. 11), dilated pupils, and "mild dizziness" (Grinspoon & Bakalar, 1979, p. 11) are common. The psychological effects of psychoactive drugs in general (Weil & Rosen, 1993), and LSD in particular (Levinthal, 1996), depend, to some extent, on set and setting. The term *set* refers to the expectations that a person has at the time of taking a drug. We have already seen the importance of expectations in other alterations of consciousness such as sensory restriction and hypnosis. *Setting* refers to the "physical, social, and cultural" (Weil & Rosen, 1993, p. 226) environment in which a drug is taken. In general, as we saw in the examples given previously, LSD produces an "intensification of mental processes" (Grinspoon & Bakalar, 1979, p. 12) with vivid perceptions, magnified feelings, and profound introspective thoughts. Perceptual changes can include the intensification and distortion of sensory impressions, synesthesia, and, with eyes closed, the presence of geometric patterns, fantastic landscapes, and symbols (Grinspoon & Bakalar, 1979; see also R. K. Siegel, 1977; R. K. Siegel & Jarvik, 1975). There can be dramatic mood swings from happiness to sadness and back again (Levinthal, 1996), as well as the simultaneous presence of disparate emotions (Grinspoon & Bakalar, 1979). A person may visualize herself as a participant in an imaginary drama, believe herself to be encountering mythical beings, or experience a "boundless, timeless, and ineffable" (Grinspoon & Bakalar, 1979, p. 13) domain that transcends everyday life.

An anthropologist with an interest in "animal metamorphosis rites" (Masters & Houston, 1966, p. 75) took about 500 micrograms of LSD with an expectation that a metamorphosis would take place. He abandoned himself to some "appropriate ritual music" (Masters & Houston, 1966, p. 76) and found himself yielding to "a wild, animalistic sensuality and emotional outpouring" (Masters & Houston, 1966, p. 76). After some period of time, he found himself on his hands and knees in front of a "full-length mirror . . . confronted by a huge, magnificent specimen of a tiger" (Masters & Houston, 1966, p. 76). He felt himself having a tiger's body in a way that he had never felt his own body (Masters & Houston, 1966). Reacting to the image in the mirror, "partly anyhow" (Masters & Houston, 1966, p. 77), as if it were another tiger that he had unexpectedly encountered, the anthropologist made "spitting and snarling noises" (Masters & Houston, 1966, p. 77) and prepared for combat. Eventually he turned away from the mirror and "padded restlessly around the apartment, still making those sounds that somehow indicated to [him] bafflement and rage" (Masters & Houston, 1966, p. 77). He returned to "human consciousness . . . by gradations" (Masters & Houston, 1966, p. 77), realizing that he had not been "very happy as a tiger" (Masters & Houston, 1966, p. 77) yet feeling "that the tiger represented some valid and essential aspect of what or who [he was]" (Masters & Houston, 1966, p. 77). This account raises the question of whether the Tamang shaman Bhirendra, whom we discussed in chapter 6, experienced himself in a manner that was similar to that of the anthropologist under the influence of LSD.

Psilocybin

McKenna was walking across a meadow in Colombia with some friends when one of them "pointed out a single large specimen" (McKenna, 1993, p. 2) of the mushroom *Stropharia cubensis*. McKenna ate the whole thing and kept walking. A while later, he "paused and stretched" (McKenna, 1993, p. 2), sat "heavily on the ground" (McKenna, 1993, p. 2), and felt a "silent thunder . . . shake the air" (McKenna, 1993, p. 2). For McKenna, "things stood out with a new presence and significance" (McKenna, 1993, p. 2). *Stropharia cubensis* is one of about 90 mushroom species that contain *psilocybin* or *psilocin* (Grinspoon & Bakalar, 1979), which were identified and named by Hofmann in 1958 after examining *Psilocybe mexicana* mushrooms (Hofmann, 1979/1980). Psilocybin, the more stable of the two compounds

(Hofmann, 1979/1980), gets converted to psilocin when ingested, with 15 milligrams or more of psilocybin resulting in a trip that "generally lasts from two to five hours" (Levinthal, 1996, p. 189). The physiological effects of psilocybin are "like LSD but gentler" (Grinspoon & Bakalar, 1979, p. 17), and the psychological effects are similar to those of LSD except that they tend to be more "visual, less intense" (Grinspoon & Bakalar, 1979, p. 17), and less dysphoric (see also Schultes & Winkelman, 1996). We shall see other examples of psilocybin experiences toward the end of this chapter.

Mescaline

The *peyote cactus*, containing more than 30 psychoactive substances, including *mescaline*, is one of a number of cacti with psychedelic effects that has been used by native people from northern Mexico and the southwestern United States from at least as early as 100 BCE (Grinspoon & Bakalar, 1979). One way of ingesting peyote is to cut and dry the tops of the cactus to form *buttons* that can then be eaten. The buttons have a bitter taste and "can cause vomiting, headaches, and . . . nausea" (Levinthal, 1996, p. 191). An effective dose of mescaline is about 200 milligrams or about three to five buttons, with effects lasting from 8 to 12 hours. The drug is said to produce more intense physiological arousal and to result in a more sensual, perceptual, and stable trip than LSD (Grinspoon & Bakalar, 1979). In general, however, LSD, psilocybin, and mescaline produce similar effects (Hollister & Sjoberg, 1964).

Huston Smith, on taking mescaline, was struck by the apparent fact that the drug "acted as a psychological prism" (H. Smith, 2000, p. 10) revealing multiple layers of the mind from among which he could move at will by shifting his attention. Although these layers were all real, they ranged in importance from "the clear, unbroken Light of the Void" (H. Smith, 2000, p. 11) to levels with "multiple forms" (H. Smith, 2000, p. 11) and lower intensities, leading him to conclude that descriptions of the "brain as a reducing valve" (H. Smith, 2000, p. 11) were accurate. Furthermore, seeing the structure of these layers of reality had the "force of the sun" (H. Smith, 2000, p. 11) against which "everyday experience reveals only flickering shadows in the dim cavern" (H. Smith, 2000, p. 11). For Smith, ideas about the nature of reality that had previously been merely conceptual were now verified through direct perception.

DMT

The chemical compound *N,N-dimethyltryptamine (DMT)* has been found throughout the living natural world, including the human brain, but has also been synthesized (Strassman, 2001). When 50 milligrams or more of DMT are smoked or injected, effects similar to those of LSD—except of greater intensity—begin almost immediately and end after about a half hour (Grinspoon & Bakalar, 1979). In one case, a young woman was told that she would see God and was injected with DMT. Everything happened much too quickly. Where there had previously been "doors and cabinets" (Masters & Houston, 1966, p. 162) now there were "parallel lines falling away into absurdities" (Masters & Houston, 1966, p. 162). She had been promised that she would see God so she closed her eyes. There was something there, all right. It started as a pinpoint and grew into a formless shape until it became a "cosmic diamond cat" (Masters & Houston, 1966, p. 163) that filled all of space. It was all that existed. The cat "moved in rhythmic spasms" (Masters & Houston, 1966, p. 163) accompanied by a shrill voice telling her that she was "a wretched, pulpy, flaccid thing; a squishy-squashy worm" (Masters & Houston, 1966, p. 163), and she knew that "this was the only reality [she] had ever known" (Masters & Houston, 1966, p. 163).

The use of high doses of DMT has sometimes led to reports of experiences that are similar to alien abduction experiences. "Contact with 'aliens,' being experimented on in highly technological settings, implantation of devices, and transmission of information" (Strassman, 1997, p. 158) have all been found with DMT intoxication (Strassman, 1997). Indeed, those with a penchant for conspiracy theories can speculate that alien abduction experiences result from covert government mind control projects using psychedelics on unsuspecting citizens (cf. Lammer & Lammer, 1999), analogous to apparent covert experimentation with LSD by the Central Intelligence Agency on unsuspecting citizens in the 1950s (Marks, 1979). When examined more closely, however, there are differences between alien contacts under the influence of DMT and spontaneous alien abduction experiences. For example, in a series of studies by Rick Strassman, in which volunteers were injected with DMT, "clowns, reptiles, mantises, bees, spiders, cacti, and stick figures" (Strassman, 2001, p. 185) were encountered but, apparently, no grays. Nonetheless, it would be interesting to determine whether experiencers have heightened levels of DMT during apparent spontaneous abduction experiences.

Ayahuasca

In the region of the upper Amazon in South America, native people, including many shamans (Shanon, 2001), drink a psychedelic cocktail called *ayahuasca* or *yagé* (Schultes, 1982). It is made by pounding and cooking in water the woody (Weil & Rosen, 1993) *Banisteriopsis* vines (Schultes, 1982), such as *Banisteriopsis caapi*, and usually adding other plants to "lengthen and heighten the intoxication" (Schultes & Winkelman, 1996, p. 218), such as *Psychotria viridis* (Schultes, 1982). *Banisteriopsis* itself contains a number of psychoactive ingredients such as the *beta-carbolines*, including "harmine, harmaline and tetrahydroharmine" (Schultes, 1982, p. 212). There are differing accounts of the effective doses of the beta-carbolines, with probably about 200 milligrams of harmine or harmaline being needed for a 4- to 8-hour trip (Grinspoon & Bakalar, 1979). The inclusion of *Psychotria viridis* adds DMT to ayahuasca. Normally DMT is broken down in the stomach by monoamine oxydase (Weil & Rosen, 1993). However, the beta-carbolines inhibit the action of monoamine oxydase so that DMT remains active (Schultes & Winkelman, 1996). The addition of DMT to ayahuasca is said to make for "better and brighter visions" (Weil & Rosen, 1993, p. 105).

Ayahuasca is known as a purgative in part because it induces vomiting and severe diarrhea (Schultes & Winkelman, 1996). Other physiological effects include "increases in blood pressure and cardiac rate, profuse sweating, tremors, pricking feeling in the skin, and a buzzing sound in the ears" (Schultes & Winkelman, 1996, p. 219). Psychologically there can be "a sense of flying" (Schultes & Winkelman, 1996, p. 218); images of "coloured lights" (Schultes & Winkelman, 1996, p. 218), "geometric patterns" (Schultes & Winkelman, 1996, p. 218), and animals such as "jaguars, birds, and reptiles" (Grinspoon & Bakalar, 1979, p. 15); and "visions of spirit helpers, demons, deities, and distant events" (Schultes & Winkelman, 1996, p. 15). "The dreamlike sequences are sometimes said to be longer, more vivid, and more realistic than those produced by mescaline or LSD" (Schultes & Winkelman, 1996, p. 15). Some native people have attributed a number of purportedly paranormal abilities to the ingestion of ayahuasca, such as "acquiring protective spirits" (Schultes & Winkelman, 1996, p. 220), determining "the causes and cures of diseases" (Schultes & Winkelman, 1996, p. 220), prophesying the future, "contacting distant relatives" (Schultes & Winkelman, 1996, p. 220), and "gaining direction and guidance throughout life" (Schultes & Winkelman, 1996, p. 220). Indeed, at one time the psychoactive ingredients of *Banisteriopsis* were named *telepathines* (Schultes, 1982), presumably to reflect the alleged extrasensory empowerment that they provided (Grinspoon & Bakalar, 1979).

Benny Shanon has studied the phenomenology of ayahuasca during more than 2 years in South America by interviewing "almost 200 individuals" (Shanon, 2001, p. 39) and "partaking of the brew" (Shanon, 2001, p. 39) himself about 130 times. Nonordinary experiences of time can occur with psychedelics, and Shanon has noted such experiences with the use of ayahuasca. In an ordinary waking state of consciousness, time appears to flow for each person at a uniform rate, ordering events temporally from the past to the future at measured distances from the present. Under the influence of ayahuasca, the experienced rate of flow of time may change, usually so that more time appears to have passed "than actually has" (Shanon, 2001, p. 42). The ordering of events with regard to which came before, which afterward, which belong to the past, and which to the future, sometimes, but rarely, become confused. More frequently, distinctions between temporal relations are deemed to be irrelevant. Temporal indeterminacy is intertwined with uncertainty as to which cognitive events are memories, which are perceptions, and which are thoughts about the future. In some cases the perceived temporal distance between events can change, usually in the direction of making them appear to be closer in time to the present than they actually are, so that scenes from ancient history may seem quite recent.

In more extreme cases of altered temporality, the ayahuasca drinker may experience herself as displaced from the present, observing a sequence of events during some other time period as though "two distinct points in time" (Shanon, 2001, p. 44) had intersected, "that of the observer and that of the scene being viewed" (Shanon, 2001, p. 44). The experience is not one of remembering events from one's own perspective but of actually observing them from the point of view of an independent observer as though one were looking "through a small and distant hole" (Shanon, 2001, p. 44). If ayahuasca drinkers are sufficiently inebriated, they may experience themselves to be "outside of time" (Shanon, 2001, p. 45) altogether. A "divine or cosmic" (Shanon, 2001, p. 45) dance with rhythmical patterns of movement may be considered not to take place in time but "in a realm totally different from the ordinary one" (Shanon, 2001, p. 45). Numerous times "ayahuasca drinkers [have reported] that under the intoxication they have experienced eternity" (Shanon, 2001, p. 47), with associated "feelings of well-being and bliss, grace and spiritual uplifting" (Shanon, 2001, p. 47).

The Neuropharmacology of Psychedelics

In the context of drug use, the term *tolerance* refers to the need for increased amounts of a substance in order to achieve a desired effect or "a markedly diminished effect with continued use of the same amount of the substance" (American Psychiatric Association, 2000, p. 192). Tolerance for LSD develops "within two or three days" (Grinspoon & Bakalar, 1979, p. 11) and then disappears just as quickly. The pattern of tolerance is similar for psilocybin, mescaline, and DMT. Furthermore, there is *cross-tolerance* between many of the psychedelics, including LSD, psilocybin, and mescaline (Grinspoon & Bakalar, 1979), meaning that intoxication with one of them will inhibit the effectiveness of a second one if taken shortly after the first. Cross-tolerance suggests that these drugs may have common effects in the brain.

Because the LSD molecule is structurally similar to the neurotransmitter serotonin, as indeed are also psilocybin, DMT, and the beta-carbolines (cf. Grinspoon & Bakalar, 1979), investigators reasoned that psychedelic effects result from the mediation of serotonergic neural pathways in the brain (B. L. Jacobs, 1987). In fact, it has been demonstrated that many psychedelic drugs, such as LSD, DMT, and psilocybin, increase activity in serotonergic pathways by stimulating the $5\text{-}HT_2$ subtype of serotonergic receptors (Sadzot et al., 1989; Strassman, 1996; Vollenweider et al., 1997). It would be convenient to say that psychedelic effects always result from stimulation of $5\text{-}HT_2$ receptors particularly because, for many psychedelics, there is a strong correlation between psychedelic potency in humans and the ability to bind to $5\text{-}HT_2$ receptors in animal studies (Glennon, Titeler, & McKenney, 1984). However, psychedelics appear to have other molecular actions whereby serotonergic activity is potentiated (cf. Fiorella, Helsley, Lorrain, Rabin, & Winter, 1995; Krebs & Geyer, 1994; Grinspoon & Bakalar, 1979/1997; Strassman, 1996; Vollenweider et al., 1997), and it is not clear that mescaline, whose molecular structure does not resemble the serotonin molecule, binds to $5\text{-}HT_2$ receptors at all (Glennon et al., 1984; Sadzot et al., 1989), although it may activate them indirectly (Appel & Callahan, 1989).

MDMA

The synthetic compound (Levinthal, 1996) MDMA is somewhat removed from the other psychedelics in that its perceptual and emotional effects are less dramatic than those "associated with LSD or mescaline" (Grinspoon & Bakalar, 1979/1997, p. xix). Because the drug characteristically engenders a sense of closeness to other people, it has been called an *entactogen*. It is usually taken orally in doses of 75 to 175 milligrams (Grinspoon & Bakalar, 1979/1997), with effects lasting from 4 to 6 hours (Weil & Rosen, 1993). Tolerance usually develops with high doses and repeated use. Physiological reactions include increased "heart rate and blood pressure, dry mouth, loss of appetite, jaw clenching or teeth grinding, and sometimes a mild hangover with fatigue for a day afterward" (Grinspoon & Bakalar, 1979/1997, p. xix). Psychological effects include improved mood, emotional responsiveness, "enhanced susceptibility to emotional and sensory stimuli" (Vollenweider, Gamma, Liechti, & Huber, 1998, p. 247), loosened self-identification, "intensification of sensory perception" (Vollenweider, Gamma, et al., 1998, p. 248), and moderate thought disorder such as "accelerated thinking, thought blocking, and impaired decision making" (Vollenweider, Gamma, et al., 1998, p. 249).

There is considerable controversy concerning the possibility of chronic brain damage associated with the use of MDMA (cf. Baggott, 2000, p. 3). MDMA causes an increase in serotonin activity and, to a lesser extent, dopamine (Vollenweider, Gamma et al., 1998), with its effects on $5\text{-}HT_2$ receptors being unclear (cf. Liechti, Baumann, Gamma, & Vollenweider, 2000; Sadzot et al., 1989). In some animal studies, administration of MDMA in doses somewhat higher than the effective dose levels in humans "has been found to lead to serotonin depletion and long-term axon terminal damage" (Vollenweider, Gamma, et al., 1998, p. 242). Damage to serotonergic nerve cells has also been seen in rats given high doses of MDMA and in rats given high doses of fluoxetine (Kalia, O'Callaghan, Miller, & Kramer, 2000). It has also been found that neonatal rats given MDMA show impaired performance on learning and memory tasks with implications for possible toxic effects of MDMA during the third trimester in humans (Broening, Morford, Inman-Wood, Fukumura, & Vorhees, 2001). Although these results from animal studies do not necessarily imply neurotoxicity at effective doses in humans, they do speak to the need for caution regarding human research with MDMA.

Marijuana

Marijuana and other drugs derived from the hemp plant, *Cannabis sativa* (Weil & Rosen, 1993), when used in high doses, can have effects similar to those of LSD and psilocybin (Grinspoon & Bakalar, 1979). Whereas tolerance does develop to marijuana (Ameri, 1999; Jones, 1971; Jones & Benowitz, 1976), there is no cross-tolerance with LSD, psilocybin, and mescaline (Grinspoon & Bakalar, 1979). The main psychoactive ingredient of marijuana, Δ^9-*tetrahydrocannabinol* (Emrich, Leweke, & Schneider, 1997), which we will abbreviate simply as THC, has been found to stimulate neurotransmitter receptors that have come to be known as *cannabinoid receptors* (Emrich et al., 1997). If receptors for THC exist, then that means that the body must make chemicals to fit those receptors. And, indeed, *endogenous cannabinoids*, such as *anandamide*, have been found to be naturally occurring in the brain (Ameri, 1999). The pattern of cannabinoid receptors suggests that the "cannabinoid/anandamide system may be involved in higher cognitive and emotional functions" (Emrich et al., 1997, p. 804), with THC known also to stimulate the reward systems of the brain (Gardner & Lowinson, 1991).

Marijuana is usually smoked as a hand-rolled cigarette with noticeable effects lasting from 2 to 4 hours and low levels of THC remaining stored in fatty tissue for several days. In fact, the breakdown products of THC can be detected in the urine days and sometimes weeks after exposure to marijuana has occurred and sometimes when exposure has been confined to "passive inhalation of marijuana smoke-filled air" (Levinthal, 1996, p. 209). Physiological effects include increased heart rate, "dilation of blood vessels on the cornea resulting in bloodshot eyes" (Levinthal, 1996, p. 209), and "drying of the mouth" (Levinthal, 1996, p. 209). Other physiological effects such as hunger or enhanced sexual responsiveness are inconsistent and may partially result from differences in expectations of the drug users. Psychological and behavioral effects include feeling good, being more aware of surroundings, laughing at innocuous events, finding profundity in mundane ideas, and slowing of time (Levinthal, 1996). Various forms of double consciousness can occur, including awareness of one's intoxicated condition without the ability or desire to change it and the impression that one is watching oneself. Apparently freed from the constraints of rational thinking, there is an increased richness of imagination and occurrence of insights about the nature of reality, giving the marijuana user a sense of enhanced creativity (Grinspoon, 1971). Distracting thoughts typically intrude during intoxication, impairing performance on attention and memory tasks and resulting in disjointed speech, with drug users often forgetting the subject matter of a conversation (Levinthal, 1996). As can be imagined, the operation of motor vehicles is impaired, including impaired "coordination, tracking, perception, vigilance and performance" (Ameri, 1999, p. 318), not just during the time of intoxication but also for up to 24 hours afterward.

The subjective experience of intoxication with marijuana appears to be, at least partially, a learned response. Novice marijuana smokers may not report the same degree of intoxication as experienced users, even though their decrements in cognitive performance are the same (Carlin, Post, Bakker, & Halpern, 1974). On the other hand, it is known that experienced smokers can report the psychological effects of marijuana without having ingested any of the drug. In one study, 100 participants were each given two marijuana cigarettes to smoke separated by a time span of at least 2 days. One cigarette contained 9 milligrams of THC, whereas the other had had all of its THC removed. Participants had to rate the subjective level of intoxication on a scale from 0 to 100, with 100 being "maximally intoxicated" (Jones, 1971, p. 158). Not surprisingly, the average rating for the marijuana cigarette, at 61, was higher than the average rating for the placebo, which was 34. However, when the 25 most frequent marijuana users were considered alone, the average ratings of 52 and 48 were not significantly different. In other words, experienced marijuana users were unable to distinguish between a real marijuana cigarette and an impotent one, suggesting that, at least in part, the subjective experiences associated with marijuana intoxication are learned.

LONG-TERM EFFECTS OF PSYCHEDELICS

We have seen in the previous examples some of the dramatic changes of perception, emotions, and thoughts that can occur during intoxication with psychedelics, including the presence of acute anxiety. The worst situation is one in which there is a "fixed intense emotion or distorted thought" (Grinspoon & Bakalar, 1979, p. 158) such as "remorse, suspicion, delusions of persecution or of being irreversibly insane" (Grinspoon & Bakalar, 1979,

p. 158). An extension of this situation is the "metaphysical bad trip" (Grinspoon & Bakalar, 1979, p. 158) in which "the drug taker's . . . wretched feelings are seen as revelations of the ultimate nature of the universe" (Grinspoon & Bakalar, 1979, p. 158) such as the woman's encounter with a cosmic cat given previously. In general, however, "painful or frightening feelings" (Grinspoon & Bakalar, 1979, p. 158) are an expected part of psychedelic experiences and may prove to be valuable sources of information about oneself.

Sometimes the disorganization of the mind induced by psychedelics does not end with the end of a drug trip but persists for months (Grinspoon & Bakalar, 1979) or years (Abraham & Aldridge, 1993) after the termination of psychedelic drug use. For example, there can be an increase in hypnagogic imagery, and dreams may "take on the vividness, intensity, and perceptual peculiarities of drug trips" (Grinspoon & Bakalar, 1979, p. 160).

Let us briefly consider two long-term adverse consequences of psychodelic drug use—namely, perceptual and psychotic effects—as well as some of the potentially beneficial therapeutic uses of psychedelics.

Perceptual Effects of Psychedelics

Perhaps the most common adverse effect of psychedelics is the occurrence of *flashbacks*, "the transitory recurrence of emotions and perceptions originally experienced while under the influence of a psychedelic drug" (Grinspoon & Bakalar, 1979, p. 159) that can last for "seconds or hours" (Grinspoon & Bakalar, 1979, p. 159) and can include any of the features of the drug experience itself. Usually they are only somewhat disturbing, although occasionally they can "turn into repeated frightening images or thoughts" (Grinspoon & Bakalar, 1979, p. 159). Flashbacks can sometimes be triggered by intoxication with drugs such as marijuana and selective serotonin reuptake inhibitors (Grinspoon & Bakalar, 1979/1997). Indeed, there is a "psychopharmacological resemblance" (Grinspoon & Bakalar, 1979/1997, p. xviii) between psychedelics and SSRIs, with not only reports of SSRIs triggering flashbacks but also an apparent heightening of SSRI activity by psychedelics (Grinspoon & Bakalar, 1979/1997; cf. Picker, Lerman, & Hajal, 1992).

With the accumulation of more research, the perceptual aspects of flashbacks have been subsumed in a broad category of postpsychedelic perceptual disturbances called *hallucinogen persisting perception disorder* (American Psychiatric Association, 2000). These long-term alterations of perception "lasting from fractions of a second to 5 years in duration" (Abraham & Aldridge, 1993, p. 1331) can include, among other distortions, intensification of color, changes in size, images of geometric forms, images in the peripheral visual fields, afterimages, and stationary images of moving objects

(American Psychiatric Association, 2000). This disorder has been considered to possibly arise from as little as a single dose of LSD and to be "slowly reversible or irreversible" (Abraham & Aldridge, 1993, p. 1331). The brain appears to function in a manner that maintains *synaptic homeostasis*, so that flooding of receptor sites with chemical agents that can activate them leads to a compensatory attenuated response. In one study, "repeated administration of LSD to rats was found to decrease the availability of the 5-HT$_2$ receptor subtype" (B. L. Jacobs, 1987, p. 389). In another study, "chronic administration of LSD over a period of seven days was found to result in alterations in behavior of rats that were detectable more than thirty days after the drug treatment" (King & Ellison, 1989, p. 72). Some investigators have thought it possible that hallucinogen persisting perception disorder may result from long-term changes to the structure of serotonergic neurons (Abraham & Aldridge, 1993), whereas others have considered it to be "chiefly a post-traumatic reaction, or the effect of a lower threshold for the involuntary production of imagery and fantasy" (Grinspoon & Bakalar, 1979/1997, p. xviii).

Psychotic Effects of Psychedelics

To what extent do psychedelic drugs cause psychosis? There has been a great deal of confusion with regard to this question. Given that changes to serotonin receptor binding have been noted in those with schizophrenia, that some medication used in the treatment of schizophrenia blocks 5-HT$_2$ receptors, and that some psychedelics "can elicit schizophrenia-like symptoms in humans" (Vollenweider, Vollenweider-Scherpenhuyzen, Bäbler, Vogel, & Hell, 1998, p. 3897), it has been hypothesized "that excessive [5-HT$_2$] receptor activation . . . may be a critical factor in psychotic symptom formation and cognitive deficits in schizophrenia" (Vollenweider, Vollenweider-Scherpenhuyzen, et al., 1998, p. 3902), at least in some cases. If that is true, then psychedelics could precipitate schizophrenia. Others have argued that the similarities between psychedelic intoxication and schizophrenia are superficial rather than substantive (Bravo & Grob, 1996; Levinthal, 1996), in which case the question becomes that of whether psychedelics can cause some form of psychosis resembling schizophrenia that persists after the termination of a drug trip. Certainly there have been those who have experienced "mood swings, visual hallucinations, mania, grandiosity, and religiosity" (Abraham & Aldridge, 1993, p. 1329) following the use of LSD, whether or not the criteria for the diagnostic label of *hallucinogen-induced psychotic disorder* have been met (American Psychiatric Association, 2000). In older clinical and experimental studies with LSD, incidence figures for psychosis following use of psychedelics have ranged from 0.08% to 4.6% (Abraham & Aldridge, 1993).

It turns out that many of those with psychedelic psychoses have had "prior histories of psychosis" (Abraham & Aldridge, 1993, p. 1330). For example, in a summary of three studies it was found that 37% to 49% of those hospitalized for LSD psychosis had received "previous psychiatric treatment" (Abraham & Aldridge, 1993, p. 1330). In a direct comparison of schizophrenics with and without previous drug use and a control group of people without schizophrenia, it was found that those using drugs had had better psychological adjustment before the onset of schizophrenia than those not using drugs but worse psychological adjustment than the non-schizophrenic controls (Breakey, Goodell, Lorenz, & McHugh, 1974). This raises the question of whether the drugs precipitated a psychosis or instead had an ameliorative effect on a disorder that would have manifested anyway. A problem with this particular study was the conflation of the effects of psychedelics with those of other drugs, given that hallucinogens were not the only drugs previously used by the participants (Breakey et al., 1974). In fact, among those with schizophrenia who had used drugs, multiple drug use was common, making it difficult to implicate any single drug "as a causative agent for chronic psychosis" (Boutros & Bowers, 1996, p. 268) not only because of the confounding effects of the other drugs but also because "the psychotomimetic effect of different drugs of abuse can be additive" (Boutros & Bowers, 1996, p. 266). Nonetheless, differences have been found between acute psychoses that developed 2 to 7 days after using LSD and psychoses in which no drugs had been used, suggesting that some people may be vulnerable to psychoses induced by psychedelics (Abraham & Aldridge, 1993).

Therapeutic Effects of Psychedelics

Given the apparent sensitivity of psychedelic experiences to the expectations of the drug taker and to the environment in which she finds herself, it is perhaps not surprising that early studies with LSD found it to be psychotomimetic (Tart, 1972a), even if persistent psychoses were rare. However, these early pessimistic evaluations of psychedelics gave way to more optimistic ones in which psychedelics were seen to have potential therapeutic value (Hoffer, 2000).

Therapeutic use of psychedelics has been conceptualized as being either psycholytic or psychedelic. The point of *psycholytic psychotherapy* has been to use repeated small doses of psychedelics as an adjunct to psychotherapy in order to assist in bringing unconscious material into awareness (Bravo & Grob, 1996). When used in this manner, "the beneficial effects of LSD" (Mogar, 1972, p. 402) have been associated with "reduced defensiveness, the reliving of early childhood experiences, increased access to unconscious material, and greater emotional expression"(Mogar, 1972, p. 402). For example, LSD-assisted psychotherapy has been used with survivors of Nazi concentration camps to help them to resurrect and come to terms with their experiences, thereby alleviating years of depression, guilt, and posttraumatic stress disorder (Bravo & Grob, 1996). More dramatic in its implementation is *psychedelic psychotherapy*, in which single large doses have been used in an effort to produce a transcendent experience with an accompanying reorientation of a person's beliefs and self-image (Mogar, 1972). Claims were made that when psychedelics were used in this manner, then "intractable disorders" (Bravo & Grob, 1996, p. 337) such as "chronic alcoholism, antisocial behavior" (Bravo & Grob, 1996, p. 337), and autism could be successfully treated and "the pain and anguish of those suffering from terminal illness" (Bravo & Grob, 1996, p. 337) could be alleviated. How valid were these assertions?

Let us consider the use of psychedelic psychotherapy in the treatment of alcoholism, for which impressive claims had initially been made. The idea was that LSD could prompt an overwhelming transcendent experience in alcoholics similar to a "profound religious conversion" (Ludwig, Levine, & Stark, 1970, p. 5), resulting in a "new lease on life" (Ludwig et al., 1970, p. 5) and a healthier "perspective on themselves and others" (Ludwig et al., 1970, p. 5). Arnold Ludwig and his colleagues decided to test these claims. They randomly assigned 176 alcoholic hospital inpatients into four groups of 44 each. All of the patients received milieu therapy (Ludwig et al., 1970), a form of humane institutionalized care (Carson, Butcher, & Mineka, 1996). Patients in one group received only the milieu therapy; those in a second group received, in addition, a single LSD session; those in a third group received psychotherapy as well as LSD; and those in a fourth group received LSD, psychotherapy, and hypnosis. The researchers' rationale for the last of these combinations was that the use of hypnosis would allow the LSD sessions to be more structured and hence of greater therapeutic benefit. Participants in this group would receive a high dose of LSD and then be hypnotized while the LSD took effect. Once the drug effects began, participants would be led in discussions of their major problems and then "given posthypnotic suggestions to continue working on [their] problems and to make a greater effort in accepting responsibility and leading a more productive life" (Ludwig et al., 1970, p. 48). Then hypnotized participants were awakened from trance and all participants in LSD sessions were left alone in a room with paper and a pencil in case they desired to write about their experiences (Ludwig et al., 1970, p. 48).

In Ludwig's study, despite the fact that the "dramatic accounts" (Ludwig et al., 1970, p. 127) written by patients in the latter part of their sessions "were all that could have been hoped for" (Ludwig et al., 1970, p. 241), there was no evidence that any of the LSD sessions made a difference in therapeutic outcome at follow-up intervals of up to one year. Furthermore, there was no measurable relationship between the "degree of alteration in consciousness" (Ludwig et al., 1970, p. 183) that had been achieved during the LSD sessions and "therapeutic or personality change" (Ludwig et al., 1970, p. 183). The results of this study were consistent with the results of a number of other studies done around the same time in which there were either no differences in outcome with the use of LSD or the differences disappeared by the time of 6-month follow-ups (Ludwig et al., 1970). Although there have been some criticisms of Ludwig's study, it has been acknowledged to be "the most methodologically elaborate and rigorously constructed study of LSD therapy for treatment of alcoholism" (Mangini, 1998, p. 401).

Stanislav Grof has done extensive research concerning the administration of psychedelic drugs to those who were dying of cancer (Grof, 1987). The purpose of the psychedelic therapy was "not treatment of cancer, but relief from emotional and physical pain and change of the attitude toward death through deep mystical experiences induced by psychedelics" (Grof, 1987, p. 136). Indeed, among the benefits of psychedelics has been relief from pain, "on occasion even in individuals who did not respond to high dosages of powerful narcotics" (Grof & Halifax, 1978, p. 118). Moreover, the analgesic effects of psychedelics have sometimes persisted for weeks after their acute effects have worn off (Nichols, 1999). In some cases pain has been attenuated or has simply disappeared entirely. In other cases, pain has still been present but has no longer monopolized a person's attention and emotional resources. Psychedelics have also changed people's attitudes toward death. Those who had transcendent experiences during their psychedelic sessions "developed a deep belief in the ultimate unity of all creation" (Grof & Halifax, 1978, p. 127), so that death appeared to be but "a transition into a different type of existence" (Grof & Halifax, 1978, p. 127). We keep coming across the purported transcendental effects of psychedelic drugs, so perhaps we should have a closer look at those.

TRANSCENDENTAL EFFECTS OF PSYCHEDELICS

The transcendental effects of psychedelics were the focus of attention in the most controversial study in the psychology of religion, the Good Friday experiment (Hood et al., 1996), in which divinity students were given psilocybin before participating in a Good Friday service on April 20, 1962 (Malmgren, 1994). Let us consider this experiment, including the details of the characterization of transcendence that was used.

The Good Friday Experiment

Walter Pahnke, a doctoral student in Religion and Society at Harvard University (Pahnke, 1963), conducted the Good Friday experiment "with Timothy Leary as his principal academic advisor" (Doblin, 1991, p. 1) to determine the extent to which "experiences described by mystics" (Pahnke, 1963, p. 2) were similar to those induced by psychedelics. Because of their importance in psychedelic experiences, "the effects of set and setting were planned to maximize the possibility that mystical phenomena would occur" (Pahnke, 1963, p. 87).

The 20 primary participants in the Good Friday experiment, mostly theological students (Pahnke, 1963; H. Smith, 2000), were prepared for the experiment in a manner that was "meant to maximize positive expectation, trust, confidence, and reduction of fear" (Pahnke, 1963, p. 87). Participants were divided into five groups of four with, in addition, two leaders familiar with the effects of psilocybin, assigned to each group. "The chief purpose of these leaders was to aid in creating a friendly and trust-filled set and setting" (Pahnke, 1963, p. 94). On the basis of random assignment, two of the student participants in each group received 30 milligrams of psilocybin, and one leader received 15 milligrams of psilocybin, while the other two students and the other leader each received 200 milligrams of nicotinic acid. The effects of nicotinic acid are to cause relaxation and flushing of the skin. The purpose of giving nicotinic acid to the students in the control group was to encourage the suggestion that it was they who had received the psilocybin because all of the students "knew that psilocybin produced various somatic effects, but none of [them] had ever had psilocybin or any related substance before the experiment" (Pahnke, 1963, p. 89). The point was that this was to have been a double blind study, so that those in the experimental and control groups could not identify who was in which group.

Eighty minutes after swallowing their capsules, the participants in the Good Friday experiment moved into a "small prayer chapel" (Pahnke, 1963, p. 98) in Marsh Chapel in Boston into which was piped a live Good Friday service led by Rev. Howard Thurman, the chaplain of Boston University (Malmgren, 1994). Disorder ensued as the half of the participants who had received the psilocybin "were in a condition where social decorum meant nothing, and the other half were more interested in the spectacle that was unfolding before them than in the service proper" (H. Smith, 2000, p. 101). After the 2½ hour service the participants remained in the chapel and nearby rooms until the effects of the drug had worn off, at which time they left. Data concerning their experiences were collected from student participants immediately following the service, within days, and at six months (Pahnke, 1963). In addition, Rick Doblin (1991) did a long-term follow-up 24 to 27 years later with nine of the participants from the control group and seven from the experimental group.

Examples of Psychedelic Experiences

Mike Young was one of the student participants in the Good Friday experiment who happened to get psilocybin. His psychedelic experience began very gently with the intensification of colors, etching of geometric figures around objects, and the presence of after-images trailing people who moved. On closing his eyes, Young was greeted with "an incredible kaleidoscope of visual wonderment" (Malmgren, 1994, p. 1F). Subsequently he had difficulty keeping track of what was happening inside and what was happening outside his head. Eventually swirling bands of color resolved themselves into a "radial design, like a mandala" (Malmgren, 1994, p. 1F) with different colors leading out from the center, each representing a different path in life that he could take. Young felt that he himself was at the center of the circle, immobilized "for what felt like an eternity" (Malmgren, 1994, p. 1F) by agonizing indecision. He has said that then he died, and, in dying, realized the freedom of becoming who he could be. Years later Young understood this vision to be about "his struggle to make a career choice" (Malmgren, 1994, p. 1F). The visions went on intermittently for another three hours, but they were pleasant, and then the drug trip "tapered off" (Malmgren, 1994, p. 1F), and "he started to notice what was going on around him" (Malmgren, 1994, p. 1F). Young has said of his experiences that "religious ideas that [had been] interesting intellectually before . . . now . . . were connected to something much deeper than belief and theory" (Malmgren, 1994, p. 1F).

Psychedelic experiences, no matter the preparation, are not necessarily uniformly pleasant. In that regard, they can be likened to the experiences that can occur during shamanic initiation. While immobilized with indecision in the center of his mandala, Young had the "incredibly painful" (Malmgren, 1994, p. 1F) sensation that his "insides [were] being clawed out" (Malmgren, 1994, p. 1F). Of the seven psilocybin participants interviewed by Doblin, only two reported having had Good Friday experiences that were "completely positive without significant psychic struggles" (Doblin, 1991, p. 21). The remainder of the participants had experienced difficult moments that had been "resolved during the course of the Good Friday service and according to the subjects contributed to their learning and growth" (Doblin, 1991, p. 21).

Although Pahnke did not mention the incident in his thesis, one of the students who had received psilocybin had had a particularly unpleasant experience. Huston Smith, one of the group leaders, has recalled that that participant had gone to the front of the chapel where he had given "an

incoherent homily, blessed the congregation with the sign of the cross"
(H. Smith, 2000, p. 102), left the chapel, found an open door, left the
building, and taken off down the street. Smith had pursued the man and
tried to convince him to come back into the church. Unable to do so,
Smith had run back to get help and eventually, with the assistance of
Pahnke and another helper, the three men had been able to walk the
participant back into the church where he had been injected with the
antipsychotic drug thorazine. It appeared that the man had believed that
"God . . . had chosen him to announce to the world the dawning of the
Messianic Age, a millennium of universal peace" (H. Smith, 2000, p. 103)
and was suiting his actions to his new beliefs. Needless to say, this participant's evaluation of his experiences has been "heavily negative" (H. Smith,
2000, p. 104), and he has refused to participate in Doblin's follow-up
study.

Psychedelics and Mysticism

In preparation for the experiment, Pahnke had analyzed the literature
concerning *mystical experiences* and identified nine core characteristics that
appeared to be independent of cultural interpretations. The first characteristic is that of *unity*, which can be either *internal*, if the subject–object
dichotomy is transcended within a person, or *external*, if transcendence
occurs "between the usual self and the external world of sense impressions"
(Pahnke & Richards, 1972, p. 411). Internal unity occurs when "normal
sense impressions" (Pahnke & Richards, 1972, p. 411) and "the usual sense
of individuality" (Pahnke & Richards, 1972, p. 411) fall away so that one
is left with "pure consciousness" (Pahnke & Richards, 1972, p. 411), whereas
external unity involves increased awareness of particular sense impressions
until one's identity merges with the sensory world in the recognition of an
underlying oneness.

The second characteristic identified by Pahnke is that of *noetic quality*
whereby one has direct insight into the nature of being that is accompanied
by the certainty that such knowledge is truly real and not a "subjective
delusion" (Pahnke & Richards, 1972, p. 412). Third is the *transcendence
of space and time*, although spatial transcendence may be only partial in
external unity (Pahnke, 1963). Fourth is a *sense of sacredness* "defined as a
nonrational, intuitive, hushed, palpitant response in the presence of inspiring
realities" (Pahnke & Richards, 1972, p. 414). Fifth is a *deeply felt positive
mood* that can include "feelings of joy, love, blessedness, and peace" (Pahnke
& Richards, 1972, p. 414). Sixth is *paradoxicality*, the characteristic that
"significant aspects of mystical consciousness are felt by the experiencer to
be true in spite of" (Pahnke & Richards, 1972, p. 415) violating normal
logical principles. An example of paradoxicality would be the claim that

one has "experienced an empty unity that at the same time contains all reality" (Pahnke & Richards, 1972, p. 415). Seventh is the alleged *ineffability* of mystical experiences, the inability to adequately express transcendent events in words. Eighth is *transiency*, the transient nature of mystical experiences relative to the permanence of everyday consciousness. The ninth characteristic of mystical experiences is the *positive change in attitude or behavior* that they can engender, at least insofar as self-reports of such changes are accurate (Pahnke & Richards, 1972).

On the basis of written descriptions and responses to a 147-item questionnaire designed to assess the presence of the characteristics of mystical consciousness, participants "who received psilocybin experienced phenomena that were apparently indistinguishable from, if not identical with, certain categories defined by the typology of mystical consciousness" (Pahnke & Richards, 1972, p. 426). Numerical analyses revealed statistically significant differences in scores between the experimental and control groups on all of the characteristics of mystical experiences except sacredness (Pahnke & Richards, 1972). These differences were still present at the time of the long-term follow-up (Doblin, 1991). The following are some of the comments made by participants who received psilocybin. One said that he "lapsed into a period of complete lostness of self" (Pahnke, 1963, p. 131), and another said that "the more [he] let go, the greater sense of oneness [he] received" (Pahnke, 1963, p. 131), illustrating aspects of internal unity. A participant commented that he "was living in the most beautiful reality [he] had ever known, and it was eternal" (Pahnke, 1963, p. 144), indicating transcendence of time. Deeply felt positive mood was found in the comment of a participant who said that he "had a brief but violently intense feeling of joy" (Pahnke, 1963, p. 150). And alleged ineffability is found in the comment by a participant who said that he "cannot describe the sense of the Divine" (Pahnke, 1963, p. 184). In general, Pahnke's research supported the notion that, with the right set and setting, the use of psychedelic drugs can lead to experiences with characteristics that are similar to mystical experiences.

Where does this leave us? What have we learned about psychedelics? What is most salient, perhaps, is the degree to which psychedelics can force alterations of consciousness and the frequently disruptive manner in which that can happen. There is potential for disorganization but also potential for reorganization and an opportunity to think about reality in a different way from that of the ordinary waking state of consciousness. Most impressive, perhaps, are the transcendent insights that can ensue during intoxication, although their noetic value cannot be verified by observers in the ordinary waking state. But the disruptions associated with psychedelics, in some cases, can be long-lasting, such as perceptual distortions and psychoses that can persist after the period of actual intoxication. On balance, then, do psychedelics bring about pathology or well-being? Are they dangerous or beneficial? Political situations can vary both geographically and temporally with regard to the sanctioned use of psychedelics, so that their possible potential uses cannot always be explored and exploited. But the transcendent aspects of psychedelic experiences in which deepening of meaning appears to take place are similar to characteristics of mystical experiences. What, then, about the occurrence of such experiences without a little help from external chemical agents? Let us turn next to a more general discussion of transcendence.

8

TRANSCENDENCE

In the last chapter we considered Pahnke's Good Friday experiment in which participants given the psychedelic psilocybin ostensibly had mystical experiences. Mystical experiences are a type of *transcendence* (Maslow, 1971/1976) in that one is in a state of being that is in some sense superior to ordinary existence. But that calls forth a number of fundamental questions associated with our thematic threads. Is there any sense in which transcendence is other than imaginary? In other words, is a materialist account of transcendent experiences adequate? Are transcendent events meaningless or meaningful? Are they mundane or extraordinary? Are the insights that arise in transcendent states delusions, or are they true? Are the meanings of such insights lateral or vertical? Our discussion will lead us to consideration of exceptional well-being, spontaneous transcendent experiences, meditation, spiritual aspiration, and some explanations for transcendent states.

VARIETY OF TRANSCENDENT EXPERIENCES

Perhaps we can start by asking what makes a person happy. Well, we have to be a little bit careful because what we really want to talk about is human well-being, which is more variegated than simple hedonic pleasure (Ryff, 1995). Indeed, some of the greatest achievements of transcendence have occurred in the context of human suffering (e.g., Frankl, 1946/1984, 1948/1997, 1995/1997). However, even entering the discussion on the felicitous side of well-being, there is a variety of ways in which exceptional human functioning has been characterized. Let us consider three of those characterizations: flow, peak experiences, and mystical experiences.

Flow

Contrary to what we may naively suppose, Mihaly Csikszentmihalyi (1988) has found that one of the things that can improve the quality of a person's experience is to be faced with challenges that are more demanding than everyday living. When a person's skills match the difficulties of the challenges, a state of consciousness that Csikszentmihalyi has called *flow* can occur in which there is joyous and creative "total involvement with life" (Csikszentmihalyi, 1990, p. xi). I often enter such a state of consciousness when I am teaching. I become absorbed in drawing on my knowledge of the subject matter and organizing it into a narrative structure. The usual concerns of everyday life disappear into the background, and I lose track of time. Although it requires considerable effort, paradoxically this creative activity proceeds spontaneously and is accompanied by a sense of enjoyment.

Csikszentmihalyi found eight components of the experience of flow, at least one of which was mentioned when participants were asked "to describe how it felt when their lives were at their fullest, when what they did was most enjoyable" (Csikszentmihalyi, 1990, p. 48). The first of these components has already been mentioned—namely, *engagement in a challenge for which we have the requisite skills*. The second is *absorption in the challenging activity so that one's awareness merges with one's actions*. However, even though one's actions may flow spontaneously in an absorbed state, they are not effortless because they require the full engagement of one's physical or psychological skills. The third and fourth components of flow are the *setting of clear goals* and the *presence of feedback that the goals are being reached*. In many situations, the goals are unambiguous, and feedback is immediate. Other situations pose amorphous challenges that need to be structured by introducing goals and feedback. Writing this book, for example, had to be structured into more manageable tasks such as gathering the necessary resources, writing each draft, and writing each chapter within each draft.

The fifth component of flow found by Csikszentmihalyi (1990) is the *attenuation of one's usual concerns* while one is absorbed in a challenging task. The sixth is the *opportunity to exercise control* in a situation, such as with mountain climbing, or at least to have the perception that one is in control, such as with gambling at games of chance. The seventh component of flow is related to the second and fifth in that it is the *loss of self-awareness*. Loss of awareness of the self can be accompanied by *identification with one's environment* or with other participants with whom one is engaged in the activity. For example, even though it was many years ago, I still remember the few moments one evening when I felt a magical sense of connectedness to other choristers while singing on stage during a concert. It was not just that we were creating music together as a group but I also felt as though the boundaries between us had been erased and we were one organism with a single voice. The eighth component of flow is *freedom from the uniform ordering of time* as normally measured by a clock.

Peak Experiences

Using a strategy similar to Csikszentmihalyi's, Abraham Maslow asked people to list and describe the most wonderful experiences of their lives. On the basis of their responses, Maslow characterized the changes to cognition and self-identity that can occur during these *peak experiences*. He found, for example, that sometimes peak experiences were felt to be perfect, complete, self-sufficient, self-validating, intrinsically valuable, and a source of justification for one's life. As such, they have been experienced as being "good and desirable" (Maslow, 1968, p. 81; emphasis removed) and never as "evil or undesirable" (Maslow, 1968, p. 81; emphasis removed), with the word "sacred" sometimes used to characterize them. Loss of self-awareness and temporary fusion with that which is not oneself can occur in peak experiences to the point of complete absorption in the object of one's attention, so that it appears "as if it were all there was in the universe, as if it were all of Being, synonymous with the universe" (Maslow, 1968, p. 74). In other peak experiences, particularly those identified as mystical, religious, or philosophical, "the whole of the world is seen as unity, as a single rich live entity" (Maslow, 1968, p. 88; emphasis removed). Related to absorption, there can also be "disorientation in time and space" (Maslow, 1968, p. 80; emphasis removed) so that, for example, time may simultaneously seem to be both moving rapidly and standing still. Affect can change, with there being a loss of fear and hesitation, and an expression of greater love, compassion, and acceptance of the world. Many of the features of peak experiences described by Maslow mirror those found by Csikszentmihalyi, including flow itself, which Maslow has characterized as effortless, graceful, and decisive functioning.

Mystical Experiences

In some cases, peak experiences could be mystical experiences according to the characteristics used by Pahnke, which we introduced in chapter 7. Peak experiences are certainly not all mystical experiences because not everyone asked to describe their most wonderful experiences has had an experience meeting Pahnke's criteria. Efforts have been made to determine the frequency of mystical experiences in the general population by conducting surveys in which questions have been asked about having had such experiences. The content of these questions has differed widely, as have the number of affirmative responses, resulting in a range of about 20% to 74% of the population claiming to have had some sort of significant mystical experience. A prudent approach to these figures has suggested that about

"35% of persons sampled affirm some intense spiritual experience" (Hood et al., 1996, p. 247). In the consciousness survey of academics and professionals conducted by Robert Moore and myself in 1986, we found that 47% of respondents claimed to "have had an experience [that] could best be described as a transcendent or mystical experience" (Baruss, 1990, p. 169). However, in one study in which 34% of 305 participants agreed that they had been "close to a powerful spiritual force that seemed to lift [them] outside of [themselves]" (Thomas & Cooper, 1980, p. 78), analysis of the participants' more detailed reports indicated that only 1% actually met the criteria for having had mystical experiences.

When people are asked about transcending the normal human condition, at least along the dimension of having enjoyable and wonderful experiences, reports of flow, peak experiences, and mystical experiences have been obtained. These types of experiences have sometimes been conceptualized as lying on a continuum of consciousness, with those tending toward the mystical being properly regarded as transcendent (Waldron, 1998). Although it is overly facile to align transcendent experiences in this way (cf. Maxwell & Tschudin, 1990; Privette, 1983), we shall focus on those psychological events that meet at least some of the criteria for mystical experiences. Let us begin with some examples.

EXAMPLES OF SPONTANEOUS TRANSCENDENCE

I have chosen some fairly well-known examples of transcendent experiences that occurred under quite different circumstances: from observing the earth from space, to observing the sun from the earth; and from being of apparently sound mind, to being poisoned and coming close to death. We will consider a fourth example, that of Franklin Merrell-Wolff, later in the chapter.

Edgar Mitchell

On his way back from the moon, with the spacecraft functioning perfectly and not requiring his attention, Apollo 14 astronaut Edgar Mitchell had a chance to reflect on his journey. He fell into a quiet reverie as he looked out the window at the earth and the heavens from the vantage point of space. Despite its peaceful appearance, he knew that the earth was torn by discord and war. Yet, as he looked beyond the earth to the larger universe, he experienced a profound shift in his understanding of reality. He felt a sense of harmony and "interconnectedness with the celestial bodies surrounding [the] spacecraft" (Mitchell, 1996, p. 58). He has rejected the efforts of others to cast his experience as a religious one, although he was shaken "to the very core" (Mitchell, 1996, p. 58) by the silent authority of his feeling of connectedness to an intelligent "natural process" (Mitchell, 1996, p. 58). Even though he has found ways of characterizing it, Mitchell has been convinced that what he felt "always will be an ineffable experience" (Mitchell, 1996, p. 59). On returning to earth Mitchell changed the course of his career and "became a full-time student of . . . the totality of consciousness" (Mitchell, 1996, p. 71), founding the Institute of Noetic Sciences for its multidisciplinary study. For all that he has resisted such categorization, the characteristics of external unity, noetic quality, alleged ineffability, transiency, and positive changes in behavior, which we noted in chapter 7, indicate the similarity to mystical experiences of Mitchell's epiphany during his moon voyage.

Allan Smith

Allan Smith was sitting alone one evening watching a sunset when he "noticed that the level of light in the room as well as that of the sky outside seemed to be increasing slowly" (A. Smith & Tart, 1998, p. 100). It was not that the sun had gotten brighter, for "the light seemed to be coming from everywhere" (A. Smith & Tart, 1998, p. 100). As the intensity of light increased, Smith's mood improved, and time seemed to slow down. After a while, "the sense of time passing stopped entirely" (A. Smith & Tart, 1998, p. 100), so that "only the present moment existed" (A. Smith & Tart, 1998, p. 100), and he found himself in an ecstatic state in an "intense . . . light field" (A. Smith & Tart, 1998, p. 100). At that point, Smith "merged with the light and everything, including [himself], became one unified whole" (A. Smith & Tart, 1998, p. 100). Distinctions between subject and object disappeared in a "timeless, unitary state of being" (A. Smith & Tart, 1998, p. 100). For Smith, perhaps the most significant aspect of his experience was his knowledge, beyond words, that the universe worked as a harmonious whole and that God, with which he had become united, was the loving and benign "ground of being" (A. Smith & Tart, 1998, p. 101). Or at least, that is the best description that he could give of an experience that was indescribable. Judged afterward, the mystical experience, or cosmic consciousness, appeared to have lasted for about 20 minutes before fading. Subsequently, Smith lost interest in the scientific research that he had been doing as an academic and instead turned to those subject areas that would allow him to "explore spirituality" (A. Smith & Tart, 1998, p. 101), eventually receiving graduate degrees in consciousness studies and in theology.

John Wren-Lewis

John Wren-Lewis, when he was 60 years of age in 1983, was traveling by bus with his wife in Thailand when he was poisoned after eating candy, apparently laced with morphine, that had been given to him by a thief. He had unknowingly ingested a potentially fatal dose as judged by the subsequent coma. It was some hours after awakening in a hospital room and orienting himself to all that had occurred that Wren-Lewis began to wonder why it was that the "rather shoddy hospital room seemed transcendentally beautiful" (Wren-Lewis, 1988, p. 110). At first he wondered whether his changed perception was the result of the morphine with which he had been told that he had probably been poisoned but then thought that the drug effects should have worn off. Then he wondered if he had had a near-death experience of the sort that we shall describe in chapter 9, so he relaxed and tried to take himself back in his imagination to a point in time just before he had awakened from the coma (Wren-Lewis, 1988). What came to mind was that he had emerged from "a deep but dazzling darkness" (Wren-Lewis, 1994, p. 109) that was still there behind his ordinary consciousness.

Once recognized, the darkness that Wren-Lewis experienced was not a vague impression but was so palpable that he kept checking the back of his skull as it seemed to have been sawn off, exposing his "brain to the dark infinity of space" (Wren-Lewis, 1994, p. 109). Wren-Lewis felt as though he were looking through the wrong end of a telescope, "perceiving everything very sharply from an immense distance—yet at the same time [he] had the uncanny sense that [he] actually *was* each thing perceiving itself" (Wren-Lewis, 1994, p. 110). In fact he was the "timeless, spaceless void which in some indescribable way was total aliveness" (Wren-Lewis, 1991, p. 5) and which "budded out into manifestation" (Wren-Lewis, 1991, p. 5) as "Everything-that-is, experiencing itself through the bodymind called John" (Wren-Lewis, 1991, p. 5). Unlike his "personal consciousness" (Wren-Lewis, 1994, p. 110), the darkness was an "impersonal consciousness" (Wren-Lewis, 1994, p. 110) that "*seemed to know everything from the inside*" (Wren-Lewis, 1994, p. 110) and from which everything around him arose anew at each moment. The presence of the darkness was accompanied by a sense of "surprised satisfaction" (Wren-Lewis, 1994, p. 110), peace (Wren-Lewis, 1988), love (Wren-Lewis, 1994), bliss, and "joy beyond joy" (Wren-Lewis, 1988, p. 113). Again, we see the characteristics of a mystical experience, in this case one of internal unity.

One of the differences between mystical experiences as defined by Pahnke in chapter 7 and that of Wren-Lewis is that Wren-Lewis's mystical state of consciousness persisted indefinitely. However, once in a while, every day, Wren-Lewis would find that he would slip out of the mystical state "for minutes or even hours at a stretch *without even noticing*" (Wren-Lewis, 1994, p. 110). Eventually he would realize that something was wrong, whereupon the shining dark would come "flooding back" (Wren-Lewis, 1988, p. 117) as if its presence in his consciousness had become his "baseline" (Wren-Lewis, 1994, p. 110). Wren-Lewis has argued that it would be a "complete misnomer" (Wren-Lewis, 1991, p. 6) to regard his endarkened state as an "*altered* state of consciousness" (Wren-Lewis, 1991, p. 6) because his state of being was not a "high from which [he] can come down" (Wren-Lewis, 1991, p. 5) but rather a normal state in which things are truly just what they are. His previous state of ordinary consciousness, however, was a "real alteration" (Wren-Lewis, 1991, p. 6) in that it was an "artificially blinkered or clouded condition wherein the bodymind has the absurd illusion that it is somehow a separate individual entity over against everything else" (Wren-Lewis, 1991, p. 6). Whose conception of reality is correct—our interpretation that Wren-Lewis's endarkenment is an altered state of consciousness or his realization that our ordinary constricted condition is an altered state of consciousness? Just as our ordinary consciousness seems self-evidently real to us, so his ordinary consciousness seems self-evidently real to him.

What is it that allows a person to have an ongoing sense of exceptional well-being such as that enjoyed by Wren-Lewis? Huston Smith (2000) was disappointed that 20 years of meditation failed to provide him with the mystical experiences that occurred, as we saw in chapter 7, the first time that he took mescaline. Wren-Lewis has also been pessimistic about the effectiveness of strategies typically used to try to attain transcendent states (Wren-Lewis, 1994) but has realized that, much as he would like to do so, he has no advice to give regarding the attainment of mystical states because he "could scarcely recommend taking a potentially fatal dose of poison" (Wren-Lewis, 1991, p. 7). Wren-Lewis has proposed the hypothesis that transcendent consciousness is blocked by hyperactivity of a psychological survival mechanism within each of us. A person gets so locked into trying to secure the future of her "individual consciousness" (Wren-Lewis, 1994, p. 113) that she shuts out the "underlying universal consciousness, with its every-present-moment happiness, peace and wonder" (Wren-Lewis, 1994, p. 113). Coming close to death breaks the "spell *because the survival-mechanism gives up at this point*" (Wren-Lewis, 1994, p. 113), sometimes giving a person access to knowledge of "what consciousness really is" (Wren-Lewis, 1994, p. 113). The result is that, on coming back from the brink of death, sometimes the functioning of the survival mechanism gets restored without the previous hyperactivity.

Comparison of Transcendent and Psychedelic Experiences

Experiences such as those of participants in the Good Friday Experiment, discussed in chapter 7, raise the question of whether mystical experiences induced by psychedelic drugs are the same as spontaneous mystical experiences. As we have seen, the description by Young of his experiences confirms the spiritual value that psychedelic experiences can have. However, Young has indicated to me that he did not say at the time that his had been a mystical experience and that he has "never been sure that what [he] had constituted a mystical experience." It is interesting to note some of the comments made by those who have had both psychedelic and profound mystical experiences. Wren-Lewis, for example, had been a participant in "a long series of high-dosage psychedelic experiments in England in the late 1960s" (Wren-Lewis, 1994, p. 110). Although he had had "some remarkable experiences" (Wren-Lewis, 1994, p. 110) with psychedelics, "none was even remotely like [the] state of quintessential equanimity and stability" (Wren-Lewis, 1994, p. 110) of his endarkenment. In particular, his psychedelic experiences were ecstatic states in which he got "high" (Wren-Lewis, 1994, p. 110), whereas the transcendent consciousness that he experienced subsequent to his narcotic coma had "the sense of being completely ordinary and obvious" (Wren-Lewis, 1994, p. 110). Alpert, 30 years after his dismissal from Harvard University, has suggested that experiences induced by psychedelics are analogues of mystical states or, at best, transient genuine transcendent events. According to Alpert, although it may be possible to use psychedelics to attain the more subtle states described in Eastern spiritual practices, no one seems to know how to use them for that purpose (Kinney & Smoley, 1993).

It may be that psychedelics not only do not provide a person with the full measure of transcendent states but are also antithetical to their proper expression. In Buddhism there has been a prohibition against the use of "intoxicants to the point of heedlessness, loss of mindfulness, or loss of awareness" (Forte, 1997b, p. 120). It has been argued that LSD experiences are imitative, can be misleading, and could possibly prevent a person from "being able to realize the real thing" (Rosch, 1999, p. 223). Similarly, Douglas Baker (1975) has expressed concern that, although both alcohol and psychedelics can induce transcendent experiences, they damage subtle aspects of a person's physiology that may not heal within her lifetime. He has cautioned, furthermore, that spiritual practices should not be undertaken until a person has recovered from the drug effects. Such claims are difficult to evaluate because there is no direct evidence for them, and they have simply been dismissed by some psychedelic researchers (e.g., Stolaroff, 1993). Nonetheless, such concerns raise questions about the value of psychedelics as entheogens.

MEDITATION

Meditation refers to mental strategies whose purpose is to effect transcendent states of consciousness (cf. Baruš, 1996; Gifford-May & Thompson, 1994), although the term is usually restricted to those strategies that have been practiced in Asia and to their reformulations in Western culture (Taylor, 1997). Well, even such a broad definition gives perhaps undue coherence to the variety of practices with different aims and methods that have been subsumed under the rubric of meditation. We should note as well that the process of appropriation by the West has changed the context of meditation. Whereas the intention of meditation in Asia has been the cultivation of radical transformations of consciousness with soteriological consequences, it has been used in the West largely to enhance physical and psychological well-being, with particular emphasis on the reduction of blood pressure and stress. In accordance with that, the scientific approach to meditation has largely consisted of measuring the physiological and cognitive aspects of meditation practice in order to establish its clinical benefits, often without taking into account differences in effects brought about by different styles of meditation (Andresen, 2000). Some of our thematic threads surface. Are physiological and cognitive approaches to meditation adequate for understanding its experiential features? Is meditation mundane or extraordinary? Is there any increase in meaningfulness in meditation? Is meditation dangerous or beneficial? Let us look first at the empirical investigation of meditation before turning to a discussion of its more transcendent features.

Transcendental Meditation

The greatest volume of published studies has been concerned with *transcendental meditation* (TM; Taylor, 1997), a type of meditation that was introduced by Maharishi Mahesh Yogi on his arrival in North America in 1959 after having "spent almost his entire life in India" (Mason, 1994, p. 4). The basic technique, as I understand it, consists of repeating a word that appears to have no meaning over and over again silently to oneself while sitting with eyes closed for about 20 minutes. Whenever one finds oneself thinking about anything other than that word, one redirects attention to it and resumes its repetition. The word, called a *mantra*, is one of a number of words derived from "standard Sanskrit sources" (Goleman, 1977/1988, p. 67) that have been assigned in the past to a person by transcendental meditation instructors on the basis of her age group (Morris, 1984; Persinger, 1980; Scott, 1978).

Tart has reported his "personal experience of doing TM for one year" (Tart, 1971, p. 135). He found that he became a more relaxed person with an increased ability to still his mind. He found initially that both recent and remote memories of unprocessed psychological material would occur during meditation, tapering off and giving way to "current-events material" (Tart, 1971, p. 137) over the course of the year. Contrary to claims of its benefits by members of the TM organization, Tart did not experience "a joyful, oceanic feeling" (Tart, 1971, p. 136) and loss of "all sense of self" (Tart, 1971, p. 136). There were some apparent physiological changes in that he found that, while meditating, he had increased resistance to cold, and his enjoyment of alcohol decreased, in part because he began to get headaches after drinking more than small amounts of alcohol (Tart, 1971). Individuals' experiences in meditation can be quite different from one another, and it is not clear from case studies to what extent any changes are the result of meditation, the result of nonspecific factors associated with meditation such as motivation to meditate, or independent of meditation altogether. I practiced TM conscientiously as best I could for two years but could not identify any benefits from it. What has more systematic research revealed?

Physiology of Meditation

In the early 1970s Herbert Benson and his colleagues began to report the results of physiological studies of TM practitioners. What they found was a pattern of decreased physiological arousal during the time of meditation that Benson called the *relaxation response* (Benson, 1975). Furthermore, investigators found that the relaxation response could be induced in various ways other than TM, including a technique devised by Benson in which the word "one" played a role similar to that of the mantra in TM. However it has been induced, the relaxation response has been associated with lowered heart rates (Benson, 1983), reduced blood pressure (Andresen, 2000), lowered respiratory rates, and decreased oxygen consumption (Benson, 1983). The relaxation response and some forms of meditation have been beneficial in the treatment of hypertension, cardiovascular diseases, headaches, pain, premenstrual syndrome, insomnia, infertility, anxiety, depression, hostility, and stress. Because of the demonstrated effectiveness of meditation for alleviating these various disorders, it has become part of the therapeutic repertoire of many health professionals (Andresen, 2000). More recently, Benson has turned to the study of the role of beliefs and expectations in healing (Taylor, 1997), contributing to a general trend toward the recognition of cognitive factors in health.

A question arises of whether the state of rest known as the relaxation response is a unique altered state of consciousness or one that we have already encountered, namely sleep. Some investigators have claimed that the therapeutic benefits of TM, in particular, may be a result of time spent asleep during meditation. In one study, five TM meditators, each of whom had had at least two and a half years of experience with TM, were monitored after being required either to meditate or nap for 40 minutes. Physiological measures using electroencephalographs, electro-oculographs, and electromyographs were taken, and participants were asked to indicate afterward whether they had felt drowsy or had fallen asleep. Each meditator participated in five meditation sessions and five nap sessions, although only the last four of each type of session were included in data analyses to compensate for initial adjustment to the laboratory. The investigators found that 40% of meditation time was spent in sleep stages 2, 3, and 4, with those sleep stages appearing for "more than a quarter of the meditation time" (Pagano, Rose, Stivers, & Warrenburg, 1976, p. 308) in 13 of the 20 meditation sessions. For 12 of those 13 sessions, participants indicated afterward that they had fallen asleep. Furthermore, 7 of those 13 sessions were rated as typical by the meditator. There were no significant overall differences between the meditation and nap sessions with regard to time spent in stages 2, 3, or 4 of sleep, although differences were found for one of the five meditators individually. It is hard not to draw the conclusion that meditators doing TM, four of whom in this study were instructors of TM, often fall asleep during meditation (Pagano et al., 1976). Similar results have been found by some other investigators (e.g., Younger, Adriance, & Berger, 1975).

Considerable effort has been expended taking physiological measures, including electroencephalographs, during various types of meditation. In the interests of extracting some of the features of the physiological effects of meditation for the following comments, I have, perhaps unfairly, blurred the distinctions between different meditation practices. In general, meditation has been associated with increases first in alpha activity, then theta activity, followed in some cases of deep meditation by beta activity around 20 cps. Given that slow, rolling eye movements characteristic of stage 1 sleep have been found during meditation, the suggestion has been made that meditation may consist of the ability to sustain the hypnagogic state. Or, as we have seen in the previous paragraph, meditation may consist of periodically falling asleep. Or perhaps, given that the beta activity of deep meditation for some meditators is accompanied by loss of chin muscle tone, reduced responsiveness to sensory stimuli, and the ability to signal investigators (Andresen, 2000), meditation may have something to do with lucid dreaming. Maybe all of these possibilities occur in different types of meditation.

Some investigators have argued that careful examination of electrophysiological records indicates differences between meditation and sleep (e.g., Benson, 1975; Jevning & O'Halloran, 1984). In particular, during some types of meditation there can be uniformity of electroencephalographic waveforms across the surface of the brain, known as *coherence*, sometimes lasting for more than 40 seconds, which is something that does not occur when a person just falls asleep. Furthermore, the presence of alpha coherence has been correlated with clarity of experience and cessation of breathing. Studies with experienced meditators using more sophisticated brain imaging techniques such as positron emission tomography have also verified that at least some types of meditation are different from just resting and light sleep (Andresen, 2000).

Relaxation, shown often to be associated with meditation in physiological studies, is not always present. As we have mentioned already, some meditators may show beta wave activity during meditation. Furthermore, meditation used for the purposes of relaxation can sometimes result in increased levels of stress for some individuals, in some cases because meditation appears to facilitate recall of traumatic childhood memories (J. J. Miller, 1993). Nor is relaxation itself a homogeneous state but rather a diverse array of mental states and behaviors associated in various ways with the relaxation response (cf. J. C. Smith, Amutio, Anderson, & Aria, 1996). If not relaxation, what then, is the defining feature of meditation?

Styles of Meditation

It has been a unique interest of Western investigators to try to extract the essence of meditation from the myriad of techniques available for their scrutiny (Taylor, 1997). Perhaps we can do so by conceptualizing meditation as a way of working on our minds through directed attention, introspection, and volition. We recall from chapter 2 that our naive ability to introspect is problematic and that about one third of our thoughts are predominantly spontaneous. In various studies, some types of meditation have been found to improve attention, increase intentional involvement, and decrease the intrusion of irrelevant thoughts. In fact, because those are cognitive qualities that are necessary for scholarly work, it is not surprising that studies of TM, in particular, have shown improved intelligence, academic performance, and memory recall for meditators (Murphy & Donovan, 1997). There are three main patterns of attention, introspection, and volition that can be identified, which we will call *styles of meditation*.

In *concentrative meditation*, one seeks to confine attention to a single object of thought (Baruss, 1996). There is a great variety of ways in which that is done even within specific traditions. As we have seen already, in TM meditation, purportedly derived from Hindu sources (Mason, 1994), a meditator focuses on the repetition of a word. Buddhist meditators may seek to imagine a visual representation of the Buddha (Wallace, 1998). Western forms of concentrative meditation can include keeping one's mind on a particular theme such as love for one's fellow human beings (Ferrucci, 1982). What often happens, not surprisingly given what we know about thinking, is that spontaneous thoughts arise that are unrelated to the chosen topic. When that happens, as done in TM, one can simply return one's attention to the object of meditation. However, controlling one's thoughts means that one needs to introspect so as to monitor their contents and to exercise one's will in order to redirect the stream of consciousness back to the object of meditation as well as to persist in one's task (cf. Wallace, 1998). Clearly there are also significant differences among meditation practices that would fall within our definition of concentrative meditation. Paying attention to one's breath, for example, would be quite different from intellectually exploring an idea. And *discursive meditation*, in which a single topic of meditation is replaced with a sequence of topics along a theme (cf. Wallace, 1998), would likely be different from attention to a static object.

One of the claimed consequences of concentrative meditation in which there is an effort to deepen one's understanding of the object of meditation is that a person's proficiency in keeping her mind on a particular object leads to exhaustion of what she ordinarily knows about it, relinquishing of control by the rational faculty, and intrusion of latent transcendent aspects of the mind, revealing hidden meanings of the object (Barušs, 1996). However, it is not clear what psychological processes are involved in such revelations or even if the same psychological processes play a role in the different types of concentrative meditation.

The question also arises of how concentrative and, in particular, discursive meditation differs from the cognitive activity of a scholar or a scientist when she concentrates on understanding a particular topic of interest to her. Just as insights regarding the contents of one's thoughts can occur for a meditator, they can also occur for a scholar or a scientist, irrespective of whether or not we conceptualize such insights as incursions from a transcendent realm of being (Barušs, 1996). Realizing that meditation developed at least as far back as a couple of millennia ago within largely preliterate cultures, it seems to me that the purpose of meditation may have been, in part, to provide practitioners with some of the cognitive skills that are taken for granted in our Western civilization as a result of extensive public and postsecondary education. Nonetheless, although we have often been able to use our minds to build complex intellectual edifices, we have rarely learned to know our minds themselves. We will next consider another style of meditation, sometimes called *witnessing meditation*, whose purpose is specifically to provide the practitioner with knowledge about the nature of the mind.

When I lived for a while in the Canadian Atlantic province of Nova Scotia, sometimes on Sunday mornings I made my way to a drafty farmhouse hidden away from the main roads in the highlands along the province's northwestern shore. A small group of us, sometimes just two or three, would gather to practice witnessing meditation led by an elderly Buddhist meditation practitioner. A fire would often be burning in a fireplace in the meditation room as we sat on cushions on the floor facing a low altar furnished with burning candles and other religious paraphernalia. In the witnessing meditation that we practiced, the idea was to sit with open eyes and a straight back and to pay attention to whatever sensations, feelings, and thoughts occurred for us. As mental events took place, we were to label and dismiss them without judgment. If judgments occurred, they were to be regarded as just more mental events and perfunctorily labeled and dismissed. If our minds wandered, on realizing that they had wandered, we were to label and dismiss that realization as well. The point was to witness what transpired in the mind rather than to try to suppress or change it. The process of attending to, labeling, and dismissing mental events is known as *mindfulness*. Sustained mindfulness is said to eventually develop into *insight*, "whereby realizations about the nature of mind emerge" (Baruss, 1996, p. 67).

Not used to sitting on a cushion with my legs tucked underneath me, within minutes of the beginning of witnessing meditation, I would find that my legs would begin to ache. As time went by, the aching in my legs would become so painful that I could barely contain myself. Thus my meditation practice consisted of noticing and labeling the pain in my legs. After a half hour or so we would stop the sitting meditation and practice walking meditation for a while. In walking meditation, the idea was to pay particular attention to the kinesthetic sensations that were present as we walked. In fact, restricting the locus of attention constitutes one of the variations of witnessing meditation (Tart, 1988). As another example, during sitting meditation, one could pay attention only to sensations in the left half of the body. Another variation is not to label mental events but just to register them (Baruss, 1996). After walking, we would practice more sitting meditation. As another change of pace, someone would read aloud for a while from a Buddhist text. Then we would go back to sitting meditation practice.

In a structural sense, in witnessing meditation, attention is directed to the objects of consciousness—that is to say, to the thoughts themselves. In my case, I was thinking about my aching legs. However, the focus of the meditation is really on the introspective process whereby one recognizes which thoughts one is having, with the will being used to sustain that mindfulness. From an information processing point of view, the question then arises of whether the mind is serial or parallel. Are the introspective observations interjections into a single experiential stream, or do they belong to a parallel process (cf. Flanagan, 1992)? Can the insight of witnessing meditation itself distinguish between the alternatives? Can meditation determine whether the mind is constrained by the brain? If there is little agreement about the physiological effects of meditation, there is even less clarity about its cognitive effects and ontological implications.

In concentrative meditation, the point is to attend to a chosen object of consciousness. In witnessing meditation, the focus is on monitoring the contents of the experiential stream. In contrast to both concentrative and witnessing meditation, when practicing *reflexive meditation*, attention is placed on the subject of consciousness, the one who does the monitoring and willing and for whom there are objects of consciousness (Barušs, 1996). As pointed out in chapter 2, from a cognitive point of view, there is no self other than the biological organism for whom information processing occurs and a representation of the information processing system within the system itself. From that perspective, looking for the subject of consciousness would trivially involve attending to the representation of the self as simply another object in the experiential stream. But to try to regard the subject as an object is to err in this type of meditation. The whole point is to find the subject as subject—not as object. Or, to use the terminology of chapter 1, the point of reflexive meditation is to isolate consciousness₃, the sense of existence of the subject of mental acts. This was the style of meditation used by Franklin Merrell-Wolff, who has tried to describe, as clearly as possible, the events that occurred for him and the conclusions that he derived from them.

Merrell-Wolff's Transcendental Philosophy

While studying philosophy as a graduate student, after having completed an undergraduate degree in mathematics (Barušs, 1996), Merrell-Wolff "became convinced of the probable existence of a transcendent mode of consciousness that could not be comprehended within the limits of our ordinary forms of knowledge" (Merrell-Wolff, 1994, pp. 251–252). According to Merrell-Wolff, our ordinary forms of knowledge consist of sensory impressions and rational thinking, which do not allow us to know anything other than the "appearance of things" (Merrell-Wolff, 1995a, p. 32). In 1936, after 24 years of effort (Barušs, 1996), Merrell-Wolff realized that he did not need to silence his thinking as he had been attempting to do in meditation but simply to isolate "the subjective pole of consciousness" (Merrell-Wolff, 1994, p. 263). He conceptualized consciousness metaphorically as primarily streaming from the subject to the object, thereby creating the phenomenal world of one's experience. What Merrell-Wolff has claimed to have been able to do has been to create "a separation in the flow of consciousness" (Merrell-Wolff, 1995b, p. 147) and to redirect part of the stream back toward the subject. When that has happened, the objects of consciousness have become dimmed and have lost much of their relevance while "the reverse flow toward the subject [has been] like a Light highly intensified" (Merrell-Wolff, 1995b, p. 147). Merrell-Wolff has likened the resultant intensification of consciousness "to the rising of another Sun so bright as to dull forever thereafter the light of the physical sun" (Merrell-Wolff, 1995b, p. 147). For Merrell-Wolff, reflexive meditation led to a transcendent state of consciousness in which the subject–object duality characteristic of ordinary thinking was replaced by *consciousness-without-an-object* and later, spontaneously, by *consciousness-without-an-object-and-without-a-subject* (Merrell-Wolff, 1994). *Appearance* in the ordinary waking state of consciousness had given way to *reality* in the transcendent state (Merrell-Wolff, 1995a).

Just as Allan Smith's mystical experience developed smoothly out of his ordinary experience, so Merrell-Wolff has conceptualized a continuous relationship between the everyday and mystical states. In particular, for Merrell-Wolff, "Reality is inversely proportional to Appearance" (Merrell-Wolff, 1995a, p. 61), so that the more that something can be conceptually grasped, the less it is real, whereas the more something is tenuous, the closer it is to reality. The turning of the light of consciousness on itself revealed that which is real using a third way of knowing, which Merrell-Wolff named *introception*, whereby knowledge results from identity with that which is known (Merrell-Wolff, 1995b). This is reminiscent of Wren-Lewis's sense of knowing from the inside. From the outside, which is to say, from the perspective of everyday consciousness, such knowledge is so abstract and universal that it is "barely discernible as being of noetic character" (Merrell-Wolff, 1994, p. 265). Such is the noetic quality of introception.

In a like manner, by examining the events that occurred for him, Merrell-Wolff has elaborated on some of the other characteristics of mystical experiences that we enumerated in chapter 7. For example, Merrell-Wolff has discussed both the nature of unity as well as the sense in which it was permanent. He has said that transcendence brought with it a change of self-identity so that he felt as though "the roots of [his] consciousness" (Merrell-Wolff, 1994, p. 264) had been "forcibly removed" (Merrell-Wolff, 1994, p. 264) from the domain of everyday existence and "instantaneously transplanted into a supernal region" (Merrell-Wolff, 1994, p. 264) in which he was identified with "THAT which supports this universe" (Merrell-Wolff, 1995a, p. 51). Just as in the case of Wren-Lewis, Merrell-Wolff has maintained that the change of self-identity has not only been permanent but has also seemed to be "a much more normal state of emplacement than ever the old rooting had been" (Merrell-Wolff, 1994, p. 264). However, he did not continuously remain in a transcendent state of consciousness but moved in and out of it, noting each time a discontinuity so that "one consciousness blacks out and immediately another consciousness takes over" (Merrell-Wolff, 1995a, p. 51). In fact, Merrell-Wolff has said that he has "deliberately passed up and down, trying to maintain continuity of consciousness" (Merrell-Wolff, 1995a, p. 51) during the transition but that "it could not be done" (Merrell-Wolff, 1995a, p. 51). He has used the term *escalating self* to refer to the identity of the self that can move between the two states of consciousness (Merrell-Wolff, 1995a).

Merrell-Wolff has tried to characterize the positive valence of the transcendent events that occurred for him. For example, he has compared the feelings during transcendent events to inebriation "with that other wine of which the Persian mystics sing" (Merrell-Wolff, 1995a, p. 23). However, even drug metaphors fell short. "The mystics will write in terms that seem like impossible exaggeration, but the fact is that there is no language whatsoever that is not an understatement in the expressing of the value" (Merrell-Wolff, 1995a, p. 50). In fact, "to suggest the Value of this transcendental state of consciousness requires concepts of the most intensive possible connotation and the modes of expression that indicate the most superlative value art can devise" (Merrell-Wolff, 1994, p. 263).

According to Merrell-Wolff, the strength of Western culture has been the development of theoretical thinking, which can be used in the effort to attain transcendent states of consciousness. Following on ideas suggested by Northrop (1946/1966), Merrell-Wolff has maintained that there is a theoretic continuum ranging from a determinate pole, represented by science and mathematics, to an indeterminate pole, the "transcendent ground of knowledge" (Baruš, 1996, p. 155). Concepts that are concerned with physical objects can be said to be *perceptually thick* but *introceptually thin*. Such concepts belong toward the determinate pole of the theoretic continuum. On the other hand, abstract concepts, such as mathematical constructions, lie closer to the indeterminate pole and can be said to be *perceptually thin* but *introceptually thick*. That is to say, concepts lying toward the indeterminate pole have something of the nature of transcendent knowledge about them (Merrell-Wolff, 1995b). At the borderline of the relative and transcendent lie concepts that are determinate–indeterminate. "Insofar as they are determinate, they can be used for communication" (Baruš, 1996, p. 90), whereas their indeterminate aspect means that they are metaphorically "filled with something from above" (Merrell-Wolff, 1995a, p. 36). In fact, for Merrell-Wolff, determinate–indeterminate concepts are not important in themselves. Rather, their value lies in their use as vessels for the transcendent.

Because mathematical constructions are perhaps the most abstract concepts in Western culture, mathematics is the most faithful representation of introceptual knowledge and thus becomes the route by which we can approach transcendent states of consciousness "most directly, most freely" (Merrell-Wolff, 1995a, p. 27). According to Merrell-Wolff, there are three aspects to *mathematical yoga*, the use of mathematics as an approach to transcendent states of consciousness. The first is engagement with mathematics so that one's thinking tends toward determinate–indeterminate concepts. The second is the cultivation of meaning so that mathematical constructions are not regarded as vacuous arrays of symbols but embraced within one's meaningful understanding of reality. And because movement toward the indeterminate pole of the theoretic continuum appears to the personality as movement toward nothingness, resulting in self-annihilation, the third aspect of a mathematical approach to transcendent consciousness is complete emptying of oneself (Barušs, 2000c).

SPIRITUAL ASPIRATION

As we can see from the effort and philosophy of Merrell-Wolff, meditation is seldom practiced in isolation from other activities whose combined purpose is to effect a transformation of consciousness. Such activities have been labeled as *spiritual* or *religious*. The notion of religion, however, which previously had a broader scope, has taken on a negative valence, perhaps unfairly, with its meaning having become restricted to institutional forms of religious observance that often inhibit a person's self-expression. Spirituality, on the other hand, has a positive valence and "is said to be a search for meaning, for unity, for connectedness, for transcendence, for the highest of human potential" (Pargament, 1999, p. 6) without implying adherence to any particular doctrines (Remen, 1998). Furthermore, whereas there has been a decline in participation in institutionalized religion in North America (Bibby, 1987; Wuthnow, 1998), spirituality has flourished in a visionary "shadow culture" (Taylor, 1999, p. 9) made up of those who have disengaged from the normative values of mainstream culture to become spiritual seekers. Best-selling books proclaiming that "there is, in fact, a spiritual world" (Taylor, 1999, p. 11) target the "largely white, middle class, and slightly overeducated" (Taylor, 1999, p. 11) spiritual pilgrims who are "searching for universal truth, largely according to the dictates of the Western rationalist tradition" (Taylor, 1999, p. 11). The activities in which aspirants may engage include meditation (Kornfield, 1990), channeling (M. Brown, 1997), ritual, the practice of moral integrity, service for the benefit of humanity (cf. Wuthnow, 1999), and various psychological techniques aimed at self-transformation (Barušs, 1996; Ferrucci, 1982). Thus meditation could form part of a spiritual lifestyle in either a traditional religious context (e.g., Wallace, 1998) or contemporary North American spirituality.

Dimensions of Spirituality

Douglas MacDonald found five *dimensions of spirituality* when he used statistical analyses to evaluate the results of a spectrum of paper-and-pencil measures of spirituality given to a total of 1472 undergraduate students in two studies. One dimension, Cognitive Orientation Towards Spirituality, pertains to a person's ideas about spirituality and its personal relevance. Although this dimension does not explicitly involve "the expression of beliefs through religious means" (MacDonald, 2000, p. 187), it was highly correlated with a second dimension, Religiousness, that reflects Judeo–Christian beliefs and behaviors. A third dimension is the Experiential/Phenomenological Dimension of Spirituality concerned with the "experiential expressions of spirituality" (MacDonald, 2000, p. 187), including religious, mystical, and peak experiences. Existential Well-Being is a dimension that involves the "sense of meaning and purpose for existence" (MacDonald, 2000, p. 187) and one's competence in dealing with life's difficulties. A fifth dimension is that of Paranormal Beliefs (MacDonald, 2000), including beliefs in extrasensory perception, precognition, and apparitions. In the course of his study, MacDonald (1997) found that the dimensions of spirituality were largely independent of personality traits and also of psychopathology. In other words, spirituality is not just an aspect of personality, as personality has ordinarily been conceptualized, nor is it related to a known mental disorder. In fact, claiming to have had transcendent experiences is "consistent with psychological well-being" (Baruš, 1996, p. 73).

It is interesting to note that paranormal beliefs surface as an aspect of spirituality in MacDonald's studies, and, indeed, the survey results of others have indicated that people who report having had mystical experiences also frequently report having had paranormal experiences. Such correlations may simply be reflecting participants' "assertion of experiencing a reality different from that postulated by mainstream science" (Hood et al., 1996, p. 248). That hypothesis is consistent with results found by Robert Moore and myself in our 1986 consciousness survey in which we found that beliefs in extrasensory perception and in reincarnation were correlated with claims of having had transcendent or mystical experiences, out-of-body experiences, and experiences that "science would have difficulty explaining" (Baruš, 1990, p. 123). On the other hand, our results are equally consistent with a transliminality hypothesis, whereby some people may be more attuned to aspects of reality in which both mystical and anomalous experiences are more likely to occur. Efforts to separate out the paranormal from the mystical in survey research have not always been successful (Hood et al., 1996).

Separation of the paranormal from at least some of the other dimensions of spirituality appears to be more evident for those who are in late adulthood. One of my students did a study in which she gave MacDonald's Expressions of Spirituality Inventory (MacDonald, 2000) for the measurement of the five dimensions of spirituality to 30 participants with an average age of 73 years. In comparing the scores that she found for each of the five dimensions with those of the 938 participants in MacDonald's second study, whose average age was 21 years, the average scores on the Cognitive Orientation Towards Spirituality dimension and Religiousness dimension were both significantly higher for her participants than MacDonald's. This was consistent with other research, indicating that people tend to become more spiritual in late adulthood. However, the scores for the Paranormal Beliefs dimension dropped significantly from an average of 27 ($SD = 11$) for MacDonald's participants to 20 ($SD = 9$) for her participants, suggesting either that spirituality in late adulthood loses its paranormal aspects or, what is more likely, that paranormal beliefs are not part of spirituality for an older generation (Heintz & Baruss, 2001).

EXPLANATIONS OF TRANSCENDENCE

How are we to understand what is happening to a person in the course of having a transcendent experience? What kinds of explanations could account for them? Are transcendent experiences what they appear to be? In particular, do they really have the noetic features attributed to them, for example, by Merrell-Wolff? Are transcendent states delusions or signs of psychopathology? Are they dangerous or beneficial? Here we return to our thematic threads, in particular our perspectives concerning consciousness, beliefs about consciousness and reality, and the distinction between lateral and vertical meaningfulness.

Reductionist Theories

Perhaps transcendent states of consciousness are caused by irregularities of brain function. Michael Persinger has advanced a theory that experiences of God result from "temporal lobe transients" (Persinger, 1987, p. 16; emphasis removed), periods of transient electrical instability in the temporal lobes, areas of the cortex located toward the sides of the brain. He has based his theory, in part, on the observation that temporal lobe epilepsy, in which there is periodic, intense, uncontrolled neural activity in the temporal lobes, has been associated with some of the features of experiences of God. For example, during a seizure, a person may perceive landscapes or alien beings that could be described as "little men, glowing forms, or bright, shining sources" (Persinger, 1987, p. 17). There may be a "sense of familiarity (déjà vu) with events that have never been experienced" (Persinger, 1987, p. 18), "altered meaning" (Persinger, 1987, p. 18), and conviction concerning the reality of whatever experiences have been triggered by the neural storms. Persinger has been careful to point out that transcendent experiences are not epileptic seizures but rather a "more organized pattern of temporal lobe activity" (Persinger, 1987, p. 19; emphasis removed) "precipitated by subtle psychological factors such as personal stress, loss of a loved one, and the dilemma of anticipated death" (Persinger, 1987, p. 19).

Together with a colleague, Persinger has also found that application of weak magnetic fields to the brains of participants has resulted in the elicitation of feelings of sensed presence, suggesting a neurological basis for "reports of visitations by spirits, gods and extraterrestrial entities" (Cook & Persinger, 1997, p. 683). Furthermore, in some cases the presence moved when participants focused on its location, suggesting that this may be the reason for attributing cognizance to the sensed presence (Cook & Persinger, 1997). Perhaps most persuasively, Persinger has measured "inconspicuous" (Persinger, 1987, p. 16) electrical seizures associated with "reports of cosmic bliss" (Persinger, 1987, p. 16) during meditation and prayer. "With a single burst in the temporal lobe, people find structure and meaning in seconds" (Persinger, 1987, p. 17). There have also been more elaborate physiological theories based on known brain functioning that have been proposed to account for transcendent experiences (e.g., Mandell, 1980).

Suppose for a moment that eventually the patterns of brain activity associated with transcendence were to have been correctly identified. Would their identification suffice as an explanation of transcendent states of consciousness? The answer to that question would probably depend on one's beliefs about the nature of consciousness and reality. If reality is thought to be physical, in a naive sense, and consciousness is assumed to be a byproduct of brain activity, then identification of the brain processes that produce specific alterations of consciousness would be all that one could hope to achieve by way of an explanation. However, if one were to have transcendentalist leanings, whereby consciousness would be considered to exist apart from the brain, then knowledge of brain activity during transcendence would not be an explanation but just the identification of neurological correlates of events occurring in transcendent states of consciousness. The analogy of a television program can be used to illustrate the difference. All I can see when I watch a hockey game on television are images moving across a screen. If I did not know any better, I would be misled into believing that the hockey game was taking place inside the television set. I could erroneously prove to myself that the television was the source of the hockey game by playing a digital video disk of another hockey game and seeing the same sorts of images on the screen (cf. Baruss, 1996). Analogously, the fact that mystical experiences can be induced by psychedelic drugs, epileptic seizures, or magnetic fields does not mean that there cannot also be transcendent phenomenological events that have similar corresponding patterns of neurological activity (cf. d'Aquili & Newberg, 1999, 2000a, 2000b; Rosch, 1999; Saver & Rabin, 1997).

Inherent in efforts to reduce mystical experiences to underlying physiological activity is the assumption that religious attributions by those having the experiences are actually misattributions, in that spurious neurophysiological activity gets misinterpreted in noetic terms. There are many variations on the explanation of mysticism as *erroneous attribution*. Freud, for example, postulated that feelings of unity are recollections from one's infancy of unity, perhaps with one's mother, to which religious beliefs get attached. According to this view, two errors are involved in mystical experiences: "an erroneous belief in the existence of a God, and the erroneous interpretation of regressive experiences as evidence of union with God" (Hood et al., 1996, p. 229). Other psychoanalysts have gone even further by "declaring mystical experience to be a sign of severe regression and a loss of reality orientation" (Wulff, 2000, p. 419). Certainly if mystical experiences are conceptualized as misattributions, then those who have them risk being labeled as deluded or mentally ill (Hood et al., 1996).

One of the observations often made regarding mystical experiences is that they have common characteristics, be they physiological or phenomenological, that are independent of one's interpretation of them. We have been using a list derived from Pahnke, although there are others (e.g., Stace, 1960; A. Smith & Tart, 1998). However, those who advocate a *contextual* (Wulff, 2000) or *constructivist* explanation maintain that the contents of mystical experiences, as for all experiences, "are a product of one's culture" (Baruss, 1996, p. 75), which would explain why there are cultural differences in religious experiences. For example, "the Jewish mystic rarely, if ever" (Katz, 1978, p. 34), experiences "loss of self in unity with God" (Katz, 1978, p. 34). Rather, the Jewish mystics' experiences are ones of "loving intimacy" (Katz, 1978, p. 35) with a God that remains other than oneself. It has been argued, furthermore that reports of such experiences are not just the result of cultural overlays on what are inherently unitive experiences (Katz, 1978).

Transcendence as Exceptional Functioning

One of the problems with a contextual approach to mystical experiences is that some such experiences appear to have had unexpected features that had not been predicted within the experiencer's frame of reference. Such has been the case, for example, with the Christian contemplative Bernadette Roberts, who has said that she "had fallen outside [her] own, as well as the traditional frame of reference, when [she] came upon a path that seemed to begin where the writers on the contemplative life had left off" (B. Roberts, 1993, pp. 10–11). In the 1986 consciousness survey by Robert Moore and myself, the claim that one's "ideas about life have changed dramatically in the past" (Baruss, 1990, p. 123) was correlated with claims of having had transcendent or mystical experiences. Although such a correlation does not establish causality, it is consistent with the reports of epiphanies in transcendent states of consciousness. The antithesis of the contextual position is that of the *perennial philosophy* (Huxley, 1945), whereby mystical experiences are conceptualized as transcultural events interpreted according to the "categories, beliefs, and language that are brought to them" (Baruš, 1996, p. 75).

Sometimes transcendent experiences are explained as a further stage in the evolution of consciousness (Hood et al., 1996). That mysticism is a form of *evolved consciousness* (Hood et al., 1996) was the position taken by Richard Maurice Bucke, who said that "Cosmic Consciousness . . . is a higher form of consciousness than that possessed by the ordinary man" (Bucke, 1901/1991, p. 1). Bucke has spent considerable effort describing the purported historical development of the capacity to discriminate colors as an analogy for the evolutionary development of cosmic consciousness. According to Bucke, although the capacity for seeing in color has become widespread, the relative frequency of color-blindness attests to its evolutionary recency. Analogously, cosmic consciousness, Bucke believed, was a relatively new faculty that had been seen in only a handful of the "best specimens of the race" (Bucke, 1901/1991, p. 65). Other investigators, however, who have conceptualized transcendent events in naturalistic terms have "assumed that mystical states are common" (Hood et al., 1996, p. 231) and have solicited and classified reports of their occurrence (Hood et al., 1996; see also Maxwell & Tschudin, 1990).

Perhaps, consistent with the perennial philosophy and evolutionary theory, transcendent states of consciousness are what they appear to be, a form of *heightened awareness* (Hood et al., 1996) in which a person encounters the ground of being, however such an encounter is conceptualized. The key to this explanation is the recurrence of a noetic quality in reports of mystical experiences. But how are we to know that the knowledge conveyed during heightened awareness is not a delusion? When I asked this question of Allan Smith, he said that the difference between ordinary consciousness and cosmic consciousness was like the difference between seeing in black and white and seeing in color. A person who sees in color sees the same things as the person who sees in black and white except that what she sees has an added dimension to it. In the same way, knowledge during cosmic consciousness consists of adding to one's knowledge rather than replacing that knowledge with something else. Furthermore, just as it is impossible to convince someone who is color-blind of the existence of color, so it is not possible to prove to those who have never experienced it that transcendent knowledge is true. Another way in which Allan Smith has conceptualized knowledge resulting from cosmic consciousness has been to liken it to seeing a new color while in a nonordinary state of consciousness and subsequently being able to visualize the new color at will in an ordinary state of consciousness. Whether or not the new color is a hallucination or delusion is beside the point because its existence through whatever means becomes a fact about the real world. Allan Smith has said that "what one learns about the nature of reality from cosmic consciousness is self validating in the same way."

A noetic quality was present also in a spontaneous transcendent state of consciousness that occurred for me at one time. Everything that I ordinarily knew, including all the things that I did not like about my life, were all still there. However, I seemed to have some sort of extraordinary insight, into which the things I ordinarily knew fit perfectly in a harmonious whole (Baruš, 1996). Since that time, in the course of my scientific studies, I have learned to thoroughly question the legitimacy of such transcendent knowledge. However, I think that it would be a mistake to dismiss out of hand the possibility of there being real noetic value associated with mystical experiences given that the synthetic aspect of transcendent knowledge lends credibility to it for those for whom it has occurred.

Once again, in this chapter, alterations of consciousness have pushed the boundaries of our ordinary understanding of reality, this time, by looking at transcendent experiences. Unlike the phenomena of chapter 6, the question of psychopathology barely arises with regard to transcendent states. On the contrary, we seek to cultivate flow and to meditate for the sake of physical and psychological health. But meditation and spiritual strategies more generally are aimed at more than well-being. We can try to free ourselves from the constraints of our everyday ways of thinking about the world and seek states of consciousness in which the ground of being is revealed. Suppose we succeed—unexpectedly, as in the case of Wren-Lewis, or as the culmination of years of effort, as in the case of Merrell-Wolff? What do such mystical experiences mean? What do they tell us? In what ways do they expand our understanding of reality? I leave it to the reader to answer these questions.

There is one last class of alterations of consciousness left to consider, perhaps the most controversial of all: that associated with death. Let us see if we can push the boundaries of our knowledge even further. Let us turn to the final topic.

9

DEATH

What happens when we die? Does consciousness get extinguished or does it survive in some form? Is the altered state of death a state of oblivion, or is it one of seemingly normal or perhaps even enhanced functioning? On the one hand, within scientism, these are questions that are not supposed to be asked. We are supposed to believe that consciousness is a byproduct of the brain so that when the brain ceases to function, then so does consciousness. Popular opinion, on the other hand, holds that life does continue after death. In a 1982 Gallup poll, 67% of respondents from the general population claimed that they believed in life after death, whereas the figures were only 32% for doctors and 16% for scientists (Fenwick & Fenwick, 1995). Moore and I found that 26% of our 1986 sample of 334 academics and professionals (Barušs, 1990) and 27% of our 1996 sample of 212 consciousness researchers agreed that "Personal consciousness continues after physical death" (Barušs & Moore, 1998, p. 487). Within authentic science, questions about life after death are not a matter of belief but a matter of examining whatever relevant evidence bears on them. What, then, does the evidence reveal? Let us leave that question for the end of this chapter. In the meantime, there are alterations of consciousness associated with death that are intrinsically interesting.

It is important to note that in the following discussion we are describing people's experiences. We will also posit theories as to what these experiences may mean, but the occurrence of the experiences themselves is not an issue (cf. Irwin, 1994). What is an issue are the meanings that these experiences often have for those for whom they occur. Not surprisingly, in dealing with fundamental questions concerning our existence, all of our thematic threads arise in this chapter, although some of them are more dominant than others. Is materialism the correct explanation of reality? Are experiences associated with death delusional or veridical? Are they mundane or extraordinary? And, of course, is the psyche open or closed?

OUT-OF-BODY EXPERIENCES

We have already encountered out-of-body experiences throughout this book, when discussing sensory restriction, dreaming, hypnosis, trance, drug-induced states, and transcendent states. Let us now directly consider their characteristics, their possibly veridical nature, and a cognitive theory to account for them.

Characteristics of Out-of-Body Experiences

An *out-of-body experience* (OBE) is an experience in which a person has a "somaesthetic sense of being located outside" (Alvarado, 2000, p. 184) of her physical body (cf. Irwin, 1994), even though sometimes she may otherwise feel as though she were in her "ordinary state of consciousness" (Tart, 1998, p. 77). The prevalence of OBEs is about 10% in the general population, 25% among college students, 42% for people with schizophrenia, 44% among marijuana users, 48% for those belonging to parapsychology groups, and 88% among fantasy-prone individuals (Alvarado, 2000). Moore and I found figures of 23% and 31% in our 1986 and 1996 surveys (Barušs, 1990; Barušs & Moore, 1998). Furthermore, there is a tendency for those reporting having had OBEs to report having had more than one (Alvarado, 2000).

The following example is a report of an out-of-body experience that was written by one of my students.

> There have been a few incidents in the past in which I have awoken in the middle of the night and been unable to move. It is as though my mind is wide awake, perhaps more so than usual, and yet my body is in a coma. This can be very scary and yet exhilarating at the same time. One time in particular stands out. One I will never forget.
>
> I awoke in this state one night, only I wasn't in my bedroom. I was looking down at my sleeping boyfriend in his apartment. I could see everything clearly and knew without a doubt that I was not dreaming. I saw his dog in the corner and the pile of clothes next to the bed. I knew I was there and yet my body was asleep at my house.
>
> I awoke moments later and called my boyfriend. I immediately began to describe his bedroom in detail—the red shirt I had bought him crumpled next to his pillow, the position of the dog, the half drunk glass of water on the night stand—details that I never would have known had I not been there. And they were all true. We were both terrified and yet had never felt closer. I had had an out-of-body experience, where my mind journeyed to its own destination and my body was left behind.

If it is possible that we really can leave our bodies while we are alive, then it is plausible that that may also be what happens when we die. That is the relevance of research concerning OBEs to the *survival hypothesis,* which is the hypothesis "that a disembodied consciousness or some such discarnate element of human personality might survive bodily death at least for a time" (Irwin, 1994, p. 183).

Perceptions During Out-of-Body Experiences

Perhaps the most obvious question that comes to mind is whether perceptions during OBEs are delusional or veridical. In considering that question, we need to note that only some OBEs pertain to the physical world. For example, Robert Monroe, who had numerous OBEs following some spontaneous occurrences, maintained that OBEs are a way of exploring nonphysical aspects of the universe in which he has encountered intelligent beings, most of whom were not human (Monroe, 1994). Validation of such explorations would require some means of access to events in nonphysical domains. In part, this could be done through the perceptions of others who claim to have similar abilities, a research strategy that could easily be undertaken. Usually the question of validity is confined to OBEs taking place in environments corresponding to the physical world. Based on aggregated data from a number of studies, an average of 19% of experiencers have claimed to have made observations during their OBEs that were verified, although there is reason to distrust that prevalence figure (Alvarado, 2000). Did they really see what was happening? In some cases, such as the example given previously, experiencers can satisfy themselves regarding the accuracy of their perceptions. The overall results of formal investigations, however, have been ambiguous.

The obvious type of experiment to test the idea that veridical perceptions can occur during OBEs would be to have a participant induce an OBE and then identify targets set out by the experimenter. Tart has conducted a number of such studies. In one case he had encountered a woman who claimed that, since childhood, occasionally when she was asleep, she felt that she had awakened mentally and "was floating near the ceiling, looking down on her physical body" (Tart, 1998, pp. 78–79). Tart suggested to her that she make up 10 slips of paper numbered from 1 through 10 to keep in a box beside her bed. On retiring for the night she was to randomly choose one to place facing upward on a bedside table without looking at it. If she found herself outside her body during the night she was to observe the number on the piece of paper and check in the morning to see if she had got it right. Subsequently "she reported that she had tried the experiment seven times" (Tart, 1998, p. 79) and had been right about the number each time.

After her successful OBE self-experiment, Tart was able to have the woman spend four nights in his sleep laboratory. Once the participant was lying in bed and the polysomnograph was running smoothly, Tart would go to his office, randomly select a five digit number from a table of random numbers, write the number on a piece of paper, carry the paper in an "opaque folder" (Tart, 1998, p. 80) back into the participant's room, and, without exposing the number to the participant, place the paper on a shelf with the number facing upward so that it could only be seen by someone at least 6½ feet above the floor. Although she said that she had occasionally been "out" (Tart, 1998, p. 81) on the first three nights, the participant "had not been able to control her experiences enough to be in position to see the target number" (Tart, 1998, p. 81). However, on the fourth night she awakened at one point and gave the number as 25132 which was, indeed, the correct number. The participant had also thought that the target piece of paper was to have been propped up against the wall but "correctly reported that it was lying flat" (Tart, 1998, p. 81). This is probably the best known of the studies getting positive results (Alvarado, 2000).

There have been studies other than Tart's in which participants with induced OBEs "have been able to identify remote targets to a statistically significant degree" (Irwin, 1994, p. 232) but still others in which no statistically significant effect was found (Alvarado, 2000). In another study conducted by Tart, hypnotized participants who fell in the "upper 10% of hypnotic susceptibility" (Tart, 1998, p. 91) were given the suggestion that they would have an OBE during which they were to go to another room across the hall and view some target materials that had been placed on a table. "All the participants reported vivid OBEs that seemed like real experiences to them" (Tart, 1998, p. 91), but none of them could identify the target materials.

It may well be that not all out-of-body experiences are alike. In particular, the experience of someone who has had spontaneous OBEs on an ongoing basis since childhood is likely to be different from the experience of someone who has been given a hypnotic suggestion to have an OBE. However, we should not be surprised that in some cases targets have been correctly identified by participants, considering that there is good evidence for extrasensory perception in some situations such as in the ganzfeld studies reviewed in chapter 1. The question is, are participants actually outside of their physical bodies in cases of correct identification in OBE studies, or is some other mechanism at work? Given the difficulty in trying to establish the veridicality of out-of-body perceptions, it is not surprising that studies concerning the mechanism by which they take place are even less conclusive (cf. Irwin, 1994). However, as we shall see shortly, sometimes there are features of OBEs in the context of near-death experiences that provide interesting material for speculation.

A Cognitive Theory of Out-of-Body Experiences

Susan Blackmore, who herself has had out-of-body experiences, has advanced a cognitive theory to explain them. The idea is that we are always creating a cognitive model of the world with ourselves in it based on sensory information from the environment surrounding us and from our own bodies. Most of the time, because we engage in various physical activities, we imagine ourselves to be inside of our bodies. However, sometimes our images of the world and of ourselves break down. Without sensory input, for example, we are forced to rely on our memory and imagination to supply us with "a body image and a world" (Blackmore, 1993, p. 177). When that happens, rather than imaging ourselves located within our bodies, we may tend to adopt a "bird's-eye view" (Blackmore, 1993, p. 177) that then appears to us to be real. Hence we think that we are outside of our bodies looking at them. Support for this theory comes from examining the characteristics of those who have frequent OBEs. For example, "people who dream in bird's-eye view or see themselves in their dreams are more likely to have OBEs" (Blackmore, 1993, p. 180). In fact, in some studies but not others various dream variables such as the presence of vivid dreams, lucid dreams, and flying dreams have been correlated with the incidence of OBEs. In general, researchers have found that the best predictors of someone having OBEs are absorption in imaginal activity, fantasy-proneness, high hypnotizability, and dissociative tendencies (Alvarado, 2000). In other words, those with apparently the most flexible models of the world are those most likely to report having had OBEs. However, it should be noted that, because these are correlational studies, they do not prove that OBEs are just the product of memory and the imagination. It may be just that those with greater imaginative skills are also those more likely to actually find themselves outside of their bodies if there is any sense in which that could actually occur.

NEAR-DEATH EXPERIENCES

A *near-death experience (NDE)* is an experience that a person reports having had around the time that she was close to death (cf. Greyson, 2000), with about 9% to 18% of those who have been demonstrably close to death having had an NDE (Greyson, 1998; see also Parnia, Waller, Yeates, & Fenwick, 2001). Let us examine the characteristics of NDEs, reductionist explanations for them, and some cross-cultural and logical considerations. In the course of our discussion, we will introduce some unusual examples: an NDE that occurred during a specialized surgical procedure, NDEs of those who are blind, and distressing NDEs.

Characteristics of Near-Death Experiences

It was Raymond Moody in his book *Life After Life* who gave what is probably the best known identification and characterization of NDEs on the basis of interviews with people who had come close to physical death in the course of injury or illness and people who had been resuscitated after they had been thought to be dead (Moody, 1975). The following have been among the features that Moody has found. After a period of intense pain, a person may feel a "very real sense of peace and painlessness" (Moody, 1988, p. 7). She may have an out-of-body experience in which she sees her own body. She may be "propelled into darkness" (Moody, 1988, p. 9) either by entering a tunnel, going through a door, or ascending a staircase, only to find that it is a "passageway toward an intense light" (Moody, 1988, p. 9) that does not hurt her eyes. She may meet friends and relatives who have died as well as, perhaps, a being of light who may be identified as a spiritual figure consistent with her religious tradition. There may be a life review in which the events of her life are replayed, usually from a third-person perspective and in such a way that she can feel the effects that her actions have had on those she has influenced. Then at some point she would end up back in her body (Moody, 1988).

Despite the usually gratifying nature of an NDE, a person who has had one tends to value life (Morse, 1992). As a consequence of the life review, she may come to believe that the most important things in life are love and knowledge, because these are two qualities of a person that survive death, and hence be motivated to improve the quality of her relationships with others and pursue knowledge that "contributes to the wholeness of the person" (Moody, 1988, p. 35).

Do NDEs have anything to do with actual death? After all, experiences similar to NDEs have been reported from people who were nowhere near physical death (Moody, 1977; see also Ring, 1992; van Quekelberghe, Göbel, & Hertweck, 1995). However, one of the most striking aftereffects of NDEs is that many of those who have had them have a dramatically reduced fear of death (Greyson, 1994; see also van Lommel, van Wees, Meyers, & Elfferich, 2001). Although this reduced fear of death can occur without belief in an afterlife, in one study 48% of 350 experiencers reported having become convinced of the survival of life after death. For example, sometimes experiencers have characterized their NDEs as previews of death (Fenwick & Fenwick, 1995). But do these experiences address what death is really like? Just how close to death have people been who have given these types of accounts? Death, at the time at which it occurs, is not a fixed state but a biological process (Brody, 1999; see also Bernat, 1999). A person may no longer be breathing and there may be no heartbeat, but the brain may still be functioning. People do not have automobile collisions or even heart attacks in hospital wards with electrodes pasted to their skulls. However, there have been some surgical procedures in which brain activity has been measured, as in the following example.

An Example of a Near-Death Experience

Michael Sabom studied the case of Pam Reynolds, a woman in the United States who underwent a "surgical procedure known as hypothermic cardiac arrest" (Sabom, 1998, p. 37) to excise an aneurysm in her brain. Among other things, after she was anaesthetized, her eyes were taped shut, small, molded speakers were placed in her ears, and EEG electrodes were attached to her head to record her brain activity. The speakers were used to expose Pam to 100-decibel clicks that would ordinarily show up on the EEG as auditory-evoked potentials, which are indicative of the brain's capacity to respond to sensory stimulation. A bone saw was used to cut out "a large section of Pam's skull" (Sabom, 1998, p. 41). The blood from her body was routed through a machine used to circulate and cool it. Her heart was stopped, her brain waves flattened, and her body temperature was lowered to 60°F. There was no response to the auditory clicks. Then "the head of the operating table was tilted up" (Sabom, 1998, p. 43) and the bypass machine was switched off so that all of the blood drained from Pam's body. The aneurysm was excised and then the process was reversed with the bypass machine turned on, the blood warmed, and the heart restarted. The EEG signals gradually returned, indicating the resumption of brain activity. Seven hours after being brought into it, with about four of those occupied with the surgery itself, Pam was taken from the operating room (Sabom, 1998). Although it can be argued about how little brain activity there must be to consider a person dead (Brody, 1999), it is fairly clear in this case that, at least for a period of time, Pam's physical condition was such that she could reasonably have been considered dead were it not for the surgical environment in which she found herself.

According to Pam, she remembers being brought into the operating room and then experiencing "a loss of time" (Sabom, 1998, p. 38). Eventually she became aware of a sound that felt as though it were pulling her out of the top of her head. She could apparently see what was happening in the operating room with vision that was "brighter and more focused and clearer than normal vision" (Sabom, 1998, p. 41). She realized that the sound was coming from the bone saw that the surgeon was using. And although she did not see the saw being used on her head, she did give what turned out to be a somewhat accurate description of the saw and the container that held its blades. She also apparently heard a conversation about her veins and arteries being small, and indeed, the small size of her veins and arteries did become a matter of concern during the surgery. Then at one point, she felt that she was being pulled into a "tunnel vortex" (Sabom, 1998, p. 44) and found herself ascending rapidly. While she was in the vortex, she heard her grandmother calling her, so she continued moving through a dark shaft, at the end of which was a "very little tiny pinpoint of light that kept getting bigger and bigger and bigger" (Sabom, 1998, p. 44). It became so bright that she put her hands up in front of her face. However, she could not see her hands even though she knew that they were there. There were different figures in the light that resolved themselves into people, many of whom were deceased relatives whom she recognized, such as her grandmother, uncle, cousin, and grandfather (Sabom, 1998).

During the encounter with her relatives, it was made clear to Pam that she could not go further into the light as then she would be unable to go back into her body. Her relatives fed her with "something sparkly" (Sabom, 1998, p. 45), making her feel strong. Eventually her uncle took her back through the tunnel. When she got to the end of the tunnel, she saw that her body looked "like a train wreck" (Sabom, 1998, p. 46), and she did not want to get back into it. Her uncle communicated to her "that it was like jumping into a swimming pool" (Sabom, 1998, p. 46) and pushed her. She found herself back in her body with rock music playing in the background as the chief surgeon's assistants closed her surgical wounds.

Reductionist Explanations of Near-Death Experiences

There have been various explanations of near-death experiences in terms of physiological changes occurring in the brain at the time of death. Blackmore, for example, has proposed a number of neurophysiological factors that could collectively create such experiences. Clearly, at some point in the process of dying, the brain runs out of oxygen. Blackmore has hypothesized that depletion of oxygen to the brain could trigger NDEs, although whether or not that happens would depend both on the rate of depletion and the manner in which it occurs. According to Blackmore, moderate rates of oxygen loss could trigger NDEs, whereas, for example, intoxication with drugs such as barbiturates would cause mental confusion rather than clarity and would be "implicated in damping down NDEs near death rather than causing them" (Blackmore, 1993, p. 55). Linked to the loss of oxygen is a buildup of carbon dioxide, which has been associated in previous studies with the perception of bright lights, OBEs, and memories of the past. Also, given that endorphins are released during times of stress, they are likely released when someone is close to death and could explain the painlessness, peace, and joy that have become associated with the occurrence of NDEs. Furthermore, the presence of endorphins could set off seizures in the temporal lobe, thereby triggering memories that are experienced as a life review. According to Blackmore, "there is no soul, spirit, astral body or anything at all that leaves the body during NDEs and survives after death" (Blackmore, 1993, p. 114). These are all illusions that can be explained by neurophysiological changes and disrupted cognitive processing for example, as explained previously with regard to out-of-body experiences. Apparently correct perceptions during NDEs are the result of "prior knowledge, fantasy and lucky guesses and the remaining operating senses of hearing and touch" (Blackmore, 1993, p. 115). These have been some of the elements of Blackmore's theory.

How well does Blackmore's theory account for Pam's NDE? Pam certainly ran out of oxygen. What is not clear is the time at which Pam's NDE occurred, although the implication is that the NDE continued from the time that the bone saw was used right through the hypothermic cardiac arrest until the rock music was being played at the end of the procedure. What is known is that Pam had been given "massive amounts" (Sabom, 1998, p. 184) of barbiturates and that no seizure activity had been detected by the EEG so that, according to Blackmore's own theory, an NDE would have been unlikely to have occurred. Furthermore, Pam had not only been anaesthetized during the time that she purportedly witnessed events in the operating room, but her eyes had also been taped shut and molded speakers had been placed in her ears, eliminating the possibility of physical sight or hearing. More generally, physiological theories have been criticized on the grounds that the types of disruptions to the brain that occur in the course of death would normally lead to a disorganization of thought rather than to vivid and coherent experiences. Thus, a lack of oxygen to the brain results in confusion, disorientation, fragmentation of perceptions, and loss of consciousness, rather than "clear, coherent visions" (Fenwick & Fenwick, 1995, p. 214). Furthermore, if NDEs occur as oxygen is being lost, how would they ever be remembered, considering it takes a period of time for experiences to be consolidated in memory, during which time there could well not be any oxygen available to the brain (Fenwick & Fenwick, 1995)? We would expect problems of memory consolidation that would be at least as severe as those encountered on falling asleep, which we noted in chapter 3.

There are other problems with Blackmore's theory as well. It is unlikely that NDEs could be attributed to heightened levels of carbon dioxide because not only would such heightened levels coincide with a lack of oxygen but they can also produce possibly violent "convulsive muscle movements" (Fenwick & Fenwick, 1995, p. 216) that have never been reported with NDEs. Endorphins are likely to be present but their role in NDEs could be quite circumscribed. It turns out that grand mal seizures during epilepsy are accompanied by high levels of endorphins that continue to be high subsequent to the seizure, but that a person feels exhausted afterward, rather than ecstatic (Fenwick & Fenwick, 1995). Nor are life reviews or any of the other features of near-death experiences frequent occurrences among long-distance runners whose levels of endorphins would be expected to be elevated

(Kellehear, 1996). Furthermore, it has been suggested that endorphins could be effective in treating epilepsy considering that, in some animal studies, endorphins have appeared to attenuate seizure activity rather than to augment it (Ramabadran & Bansinath, 1990). In Pam's case, in which proper data could be gathered, there was no evidence of epileptic seizures anyway.

But there are also problems with Pam's experience as anomalous. The account of her experience was not documented until more than three years after its occurrence, during which time she may have learned details of the events that occurred from those who were familiar with them (Hyman, 2001). There is more credibility in accounts collected within days of a person's having had an NDE (e.g., van Lommel et al., 2001). Furthermore, of the events actually remembered by Pam, as mentioned previously, there is no way of knowing when they occurred. It may well be that there was no awareness, in the sense of subjective consciousness$_2$, during the time of the operation. Certainly there was no consciousness$_1$ or behavioral consciousness$_2$ during at least part of the procedure. The NDE may have occurred well before or after the hypothermic cardiac arrest, when the brain was functioning properly. Some version of a reductionist explanation may yet turn out to be correct.

Near-Death Experiences of the Blind

There is a group of near-death experiences that is interesting to consider—namely the near-death experiences of the blind. Kenneth Ring collaborated in a retrospective study of near-death and out-of-body experiences of 31 blind participants, 14 of whom had been blind since birth (Ring & Cooper, 1997; Ring & Valarino, 1998). The near-death experiences of the 21 participants who had had them turned out to be "indistinguishable from those of sighted persons" (Ring & Cooper, 1997, p. 108) with regard to the typical features of NDEs such as feelings of peace, OBEs, "traveling through a tunnel" (Ring & Cooper, 1997, p. 108), encountering a light, and experiencing a life review. In particular, with regard to visual elements, 15 of the 21 participants "claimed to have had some kind of sight" (Ring & Cooper, 1997, p. 115), with all but one of the remaining 6 having been blind from birth. It is possible that some of the congenitally blind who did not report having had sight may nonetheless have experienced some kind of seeing without having recognized it for what it was. For example, one of the participants said that he did not know how to explain the perceptions that he had had because he did not know what was meant by "seeing" (Ring & Cooper, 1997, p. 115).

Sight that occurs during an NDE can be particularly clear and detailed, as attested to by both those who had been able to see and then had lost their sight, thereby allowing them to have a basis for comparison, as well as by those who were congenitally blind. For example, one of the participants who had been blind from birth maintained that he could clearly see billions of books in a library during a "transcendental phase of his NDE" (Ring & Cooper, 1997, p. 116), even though he reminded himself at the time that he could not see. The visual impressions of those blind from birth are particularly striking because their brains have never had the opportunity to be properly developed for visual processing (cf. Hirsch & Spinelli, 1971). Thus, for example, those blind from birth or who lost their sight before 5 years of age generally do not report having any "visual imagery in their dreams" (Kerr, 2000, p. 488), although their dreams are otherwise indistinguishable from those of sighted people. Indeed, some of the congenitally blind participants who had had NDEs said that their NDEs were radically different from their dreams precisely because of the presence of visual imagery (Ring & Cooper, 1997).

Closer analysis of the reports of vision during the NDEs of the blind participants revealed that the visual aspects of NDEs may not have much to do with seeing as sighted individuals ordinarily do with the eyes, but may be some form of direct knowing that the investigators have called *transcendental awareness*. "In this type of awareness, it is not of course that the eyes see anything; it is rather that the mind itself sees, but more in the sense of 'understanding' or 'taking in' than of visual perception as such" (Ring & Cooper, 1997, p. 140). In a separate study of near-death experiences, a sighted woman reported that during her NDE she could simultaneously see everything in detail all at once, including the tiles on the ceiling, the tiles on the floor, and "every single hair and the follicle out of which it grew on the head of the nurse standing beside the stretcher" (Ring & Cooper, 1997, p. 139). Transcendental awareness is not confined to those who are blind but in fact may be a manner of perception that occurs more generally during NDEs, OBEs, transcendent states, and apparent perinatal experiences.

Most near-death experiences that have been reported have been characterized by "profound feelings of peace or bliss, joy, and a sense of cosmic unity" (Greyson & Bush, 1992, p. 95). Indeed, Ring has maintained that "in their essence, *NDEs have nothing inherently to do with death at all*, much less with life after death" (Ring, 1987, p. 174) but that they are, instead, instances of cosmic consciousness during which a person can become aware of her expanded eternal nature. However, there have also been reports of distressing near-death experiences.

Distressing Near-Death Experiences

Bruce Greyson, with one of his colleagues, analyzed a sample of 50 accounts of distressing near-death experiences and classified them into three types. The first type is a prototypical NDE that is interpreted as being terrifying. For example, a man said that he had screamed that he was not ready and asked God to help him after having been drawn through a funnel at the end of which was a blinding light and flashing crystal into which it appeared that he would fall. In some cases the terror has been replaced with peace partway through an NDE apparently as the experiencer "stops fighting the experience and accepts it" (Greyson & Bush, 1992, p. 100). The second type of distressing NDE is one in which a person has a "paradoxical sensation of ceasing to exist entirely, or of being condemned to a featureless void for eternity" (Greyson & Bush, 1992, p. 101). One woman, for example, during the delivery of her child, found herself "rocketing through space" (Greyson & Bush, 1992, p. 102) until she encountered a group of black and white circles that "made a clicking sound as they snapped black to white, white to black" (Greyson & Bush, 1992, p. 102) whose message was that she had never existed, that she had been "allowed to make it up" (Greyson & Bush, 1992, p. 102), that "it was all a joke" (Greyson & Bush, 1992, p. 102), and that that was all that there was to reality. Her experience had been "more than real: absolute reality" (Greyson & Bush, 1992, p. 102), and she was absolutely convinced that she "had seen what the other side was" (Greyson & Bush, 1992, p. 102). This experience is reminiscent of the perturbing experience of the woman who encountered the cosmic diamond cat during DMT intoxication, as recounted in chapter 7.

A third type of distressing NDE is one involving explicitly hellish imagery. For example, one man who hanged himself from a utility shed in an attempt to commit suicide believed that he was surrounded by demons chattering "like blackbirds" (Greyson & Bush, 1992, p. 105), waiting to drag him to hell to torment him. He decided he needed help, so, in his out-of-body state, he ran into the house to alert his wife. When she could not hear him, he "went right into her body" (Greyson & Bush, 1992, p. 105) until he "made contact" (Greyson & Bush, 1992, p. 105), and "she grabbed a knife from the kitchen" (Greyson & Bush, 1992, p. 105) and ran outdoors to cut him down. Although there have been various theories to explain distressing near-death experiences, including some from Christian perspectives (e.g., Rawlings, 1978), none of them has been particularly convincing (cf. Greyson & Bush, 1992), nor, for that matter, as we have seen, have the theories for pleasant near-death experiences been compelling.

Cross-Cultural Studies

Cross-cultural studies of societies such as those of China, India, and the native people of North America, Australia, and the south Pacific have revealed similarities but also differences in the content of near-death experiences. For example, encountering "deceased or supernatural beings" (Kellehear, 1996, p. 32) in a socially and physically pleasant world of the dead is a feature common to many cultures. Out-of-body experiences, although known to occur in the "majority of cultures" (Kellehear, 1996, p. 33), may not necessarily occur, or may occur inconsistently during NDEs in some non-Western cultures. A life review of some form occurs in some non-Western cultures such as the Chinese and the Indian but is largely missing from aboriginal accounts. The tunnel, however, does not appear to occur in most non-Western near-death experiences (Kellehear, 1996).

Although they may be a byproduct of insufficient non-Western data, as they stand, these cultural differences strengthen the argument that NDEs cannot simply be experiential byproducts of the physiological changes taking place in a dying brain. Because people in some cultures have never reported seeing a tunnel, although they may have experienced a period of darkness, it would appear that tunnel imagery during NDEs may not be the result of physiological events but of psychological development in a modern technological culture. Similarly, life reviews have occurred in societies admonishing personal responsibility through Hindu, Buddhist, or Christian religions but not in traditional native societies, suggesting a role for cultural factors in NDEs (Kellehear, 1993), whether that be to shape an escapist reaction to imminent death (cf. Ehrenwald, 1974; Noyes & Kletti, 1976, 1977) or to embody a universal experience of an immortal consciousness (cf. Baruss, 1996).

Logical Considerations

There are a couple of logical points that it is necessary to keep in mind with regard to near-death experiences. The first has to do with assertions by some experiencers that their NDEs were as real as or more real than ordinary reality. What we have in such cases are comparisons being made regarding the degree of reality of subjective states. Some of the most robust results in psychological research, such as Weber's law concerning perceived differences in stimulus intensities (Gescheider, 1985), are based on participants' judgments of changes in their subjective states. If we are to afford the same credibility to introspective comparisons of felt reality as we do to introspective comparisons of stimulus intensity, then, in some sense, either NDEs are as real as everyday reality or everyday reality is as illusory as NDEs. Of course, our sense of what is real may not be a good indicator of what is actually real. After all, as we have seen, not only have some who have experienced transcendent states become convinced of an underlying felicitous harmony to the universe, but others during near-death experiences have become convinced that life is meaningless. By the same argument, however, the feeling of reality cannot be used as justification for the ontological primacy of everyday experiences (Baruss, 1996).

The second logical point has to do with the manner in which truth is assigned to statements about the nature of reality. It is difficult to prove a universal contention such as the materialist assertion that all phenomena are the result of physiological processes because one has to show that it applies to all possible cases. On the other hand, to disprove such a contention, only a single counterexample is necessary—not two, three, or a preponderance of counterexamples, but only one. That means that if only one of the claims of veridical anomalous perception during an out-of-body experience turns out to be correct, then not all perception is mediated by the physical senses. If only one near-death experience actually occurred during the time that a person's brain was incapable of coherent cognitive functioning, then the brain is not the cause of all experience. And if only one experiencer's consciousness really did persist while her physical body was functionally dead, then consciousness does not end with death. Of course, many of those who have had an NDE believe that their experience is the needed counterexample to a materialist interpretation of reality (Baruš, 1996).

PAST-LIFE EXPERIENCES

Past-life experiences are a person's impressions of herself as a particular person in a previous lifetime (cf. Mills & Lynn, 2000). These impressions can occur spontaneously or through alterations of consciousness whose purpose is to regress a person into the past. Let us first consider the spontaneous past-life experiences of children and then the past-life experiences of adults.

Children's Past-Life Experiences

Sometimes children, from the time that they first learn to speak until about 7 years of age, spontaneously report having lived previous lives. Ian Stevenson, who has collected more than 2,500 such cases, has noted that apparent recall of a previous life can be accompanied by statements made by a child about the previous personality's life that are consistent with an actual deceased person's life but have no referents "in the current life" (Mills & Lynn, 2000, p. 289), by behavioral traits such as phobias "that are uncharacteristic of the person's current life but are meaningful in the context of a past-life identity" (Mills & Lynn, 2000, p. 289), by the presence of skills identified with the previous personality that are not related to a child's current life, and by birthmarks or birth defects that the child or others have attributed to physical conditions or markings of the deceased person (Mills & Lynn, 2000). Some of these features are illustrated in the following case.

An Example of a Past-Life Experience

While she was pregnant with him, Süleyman Çapar's mother had a dream in which a man, whom she claims she did not know at the time, had approached her on horseback and told her that he had been killed by a blow from a shovel and that he wanted to stay with her. When Süleyman was born in 1966 in the village of Madenli, Turkey, the back of his head "was depressed and soft" (Stevenson, 1997a, p. 1438). The "bone of the skull" (Stevenson, 1997a, p. 1439) in that area was still "noticeably depressed" (Stevenson, 1997a, p. 1439) in 1973, with the surface of the skin being uneven and having "the appearance of a healed scar" (Stevenson, 1997a, p. 1439). Shortly after he began to speak, Süleyman "pointed away from his house and said that he wanted to go to 'the stream' " (Stevenson, 1997a, p. 1429). He began to allude to a previous lifetime in which he had been a miller who had been killed by a customer during a quarrel. His mother allowed him to lead her to the village of Ekber, which is about 5 or 6 kilometers by road, where he pointed out a house in which he said that he had lived in a previous life. On a separate trip when he was about 2½ years old, Süleyman's father took him to Ekber at which time he identified "the mother of the man whose life he seemed to be remembering" (Stevenson, 1997a, p. 1429).

It became clear to Süleyman's parents that the man whose life Süleyman was apparently remembering was that of a miller in Ekber, named Mehmet Bekler, who had been killed in 1965 during a quarrel by a blow to the back of the head with a flour shovel wielded by Mehmet Bayrakdar. Although the details of the quarrel are unclear, a hospital postmortem report included the information that "a portion of the skull of the approximate size of the palm of the hand was fractured and depressed about a centimeter" (Stevenson, 1997a, p. 1432) and that death had occurred as a result of trauma to the head. Süleyman appeared to have identified with Mehmet Bekler given that Süleyman used the present tense to refer to the people from his previous life, that after his initial visits he liked to visit with members of Mehmet Bekler's family, exhibiting a "somewhat possessive attitude toward their property" (Stevenson, 1997a, p. 1433), and that "when Süleyman saw Mehmet Bayrakdar once in Madenli, he pointed to him and said angrily: 'He killed me" (Stevenson, 1997a, p. 1438). By 1977, Süleyman was "gradually forgetting" (Stevenson, 1997a, p. 1442) the details of his previous life and, although he still liked to visit with surviving members of Mehmet Bekler's family in Ekber, his father discouraged him from doing so.

Was Süleyman Çapar the reincarnation of Mehmet Bekler? Although Stevenson has stated that "reincarnation is at least a plausible interpretation" (Stevenson, 1997a, p. 2066) for cases such as this one, he has never encountered the perfect case, nor has he been able to eliminate all other explanations (Stevenson, 1997b). One of the flaws with this case is that Stevenson did not find and investigate it until 1973, at which time Süleyman was about 7 years old and had met with the previous personality's family. Of 18 statements about the previous personality attributed to Süleyman by his father, 14 were verified to be true. Ideally, investigators would arrive at the time that a child begins to make statements about a previous personality before there has been any contact with the previous personality's family, rather than having to rely on retrospective attributions at the time of a later investigation. Another flaw in the case is that it is likely that Süleyman's father had known of the murder of Mehmet Bekler at the time that it occurred, and his mother had identified the man in her dream as Mehmet Bekler six months after its occurrence, so we could speculate that his parents may have influenced Süleyman to identify himself with Mehmet Bekler. In part, the argument for reincarnation in this case rests on the apparent association between the manner of Mehmet Bekler's death and Süleyman's birth defect. Given that "the best overall estimate of the incidence of birth defects is about 2% of births" (Stevenson, 1997b, p. 115), such an association would be a statistically rare event.

In Süleyman Çapar's case, even if normal means of information transfer could be ruled out and the birth defect persuasively tied to the manner of death of the previous personality, we would still not have evidence for reincarnation, just the contention that aspects of Mehmet Bekler's personality and condition at the time of death had somehow become impressed on young Süleyman's psyche and physiology. Although children with past-life experiences rarely develop dissociative identity disorder in adulthood (Mills & Lynn, 2000), nonetheless we have seen in chapter 6 that a person's identity is not always fixed, so that the cause of past-life experiences could be more complex than a simple transmigration of souls.

Past-Life Regression

In chapter 5 we saw that people have been hypnotically regressed back to childhood, infancy, birth, and gestation, although there have been serious questions about how many, if any, of the conjured experiences had actually occurred. Brian Weiss had regressed a woman back to her childhood during psychotherapy using hypnosis, but her symptoms did not improve as much as he had expected. Perhaps a traumatic incident lay even earlier in her childhood than the ones that had already been uncovered. To explore this possibility, Weiss gave the woman the suggestion that she would "go back to the time from which [her] symptoms [arose]" (Weiss, 1992, p. 19). But instead of going back once again to her early childhood, the woman ended up going back 4,000 years into a previous lifetime. Weiss was "shocked and skeptical" (Weiss, 1992, p. 19). This had never happened to him before. But the woman's condition improved dramatically with continued regression to past lives, so that "within a few months she was totally cured, without the use of any medicines" (Weiss, 1992, p. 20). Not surprisingly, "anyone who is a good hypnotic subject can be almost guaranteed to produce at least one past life, and often a string of them, when given a past-life regression" (Fenwick & Fenwick, 1999, p. 27).

Past-life experiences can occur in contexts other than those that are labeled as hypnosis. Various guided imagery techniques have been used in which a person is led through a process of relaxation and then told to imagine herself symbolically being transported to a previous life, for example, by going down a stairway, being taken back in time by a spaceship, or finding herself at the bottom of a clear pool (Lucas, 1993; see also Harman, 1994). The *christos technique* is one such guided imagery procedure. It begins by having a person lie with eyes closed on the floor while her forehead and ankles are rubbed vigorously. Next she is asked to visualize herself progressively expanding beyond the confines of her physical body. Then she is asked to imagine and describe the outside of the front door of her house, then to describe her surroundings from the roof of the house, and then to describe what she sees from increasingly greater heights above the roof. Finally, the person is told to land feet first, to describe her feet on landing, and then to describe the details of her appearance and the appearance of the environment in which she finds herself. After that the person can be asked questions about events in that lifetime and told to move forward or backward in time as necessary (Glaskin, 1976). I have used this technique a number of times and have yet to encounter anyone who would not naturally find herself apparently experiencing a previous lifetime.

The question, of course, is whether these past-life experiences refer to real events in real past lives. The answer is, probably not. Or at least, not most of them. Most are probably just fantasies (cf. Schumaker, 1995; Stevenson, 1994; Venn, 1986). It has been argued that past-life regression phenomena result from suggestions on the part of hypnotists, expectations of participants, and the demands of the social situation within which hypnosis takes place (R. A. Baker, 1982), with participants in one study developing identities that reflected the expectations of the hypnotist (Spanos, Menary, Gabora, DuBreuil, & Dewhirst, 1991). However, as we have seen, not all past-life regression involves hypnosis. Also, in addition to the work of Stevenson and his colleagues, there have been other cases in which the details of purported previous lifetimes that the experiencers could not reasonably have known have apparently matched the descriptions of their past-life experiences (e.g., Bowman, 2001; Cockell, 1993; Glaskin, 1974, 1979; Goldberg, 1997; Grof, 1987).

Perhaps the most striking case of a past-life experience by an adult is that of an American woman who, in the 1970s, apparently recalled, through hypnosis, dreams, flashbacks, and self-hypnosis, a previous lifetime as a woman named Antonia who lived in 16th-century Spain. Not only did she recall having had such a lifetime but she also gave hundreds of specific details of the circumstances of Antonia's life at that time. Linda Tarazi, who spent three years investigating the validity of these statements, was struck by their accuracy. For example, the woman referred to the presence of a college in Cuenca whose faculty and students, she insisted, had "met regularly at Antonia's inn" (Tarazi, 1990, p. 321). Tarazi could find no such college listed in encyclopedias, history books, or travel books. During a visit to Cuenca, "the archivist at the Municipal Archives . . . said he had never heard of one" (Tarazi, 1990, p. 321). It was only after inquiries at a couple of universities that she found an "old seven-volume work in Spanish" (Tarazi, 1990, p. 321), in which "the founding of a college in Cuenca in the mid-16th century" (Tarazi, 1990, p. 321) was mentioned. The woman also correctly provided details such as the "date of the first publication of the Edict of Faith on the Island of Hispaniola" (Tarazi, 1990, p. 316) and the "dates and contents of the Spanish indexes of prohibited books and how they differed from the Roman Index" (Tarazi, 1990, p. 317). In fact, Tarazi has said that, although no record of Antonia herself could be found, she could not find any errors in the woman's account of the circumstances in which Antonia's life could have been lived, nor did it appear that the woman had acquired that information through normal means during her current lifetime. Though it is not the only explanation, the possibility that in some sense the woman had actually been Antonia cannot be ruled out.

Past-Life Therapy

One of our thematic threads is concerned with whether or not phenomena in alterations of consciousness are delusional or veridical. Another is concerned with their dangers and benefits. Irrespective of whether or not past lives are fictional or actual, regression to past lives may serve a therapeutic purpose, perhaps through projecting a person's psychological conflicts onto a historical pastiche. When used as a therapeutic strategy, *past-life therapy* has been said to be useful primarily "with clients who are ready to assume greater responsibility for their lives and who are open to exploring how repressed emotional response patterns are related to current difficulties" (Jue, 1996, p. 378). Conditions that are thought to respond to past-life therapy "include unexplained phobias, psychosomatic problems lacking any known cause, and anomalous experiences" (Jue, 1996, p. 378; see also Knight, 1995; Lucas, 1993). The woman who was treated by Weiss got better. Tarazi's client, on the other hand, appeared to become obsessed with the life of

Antonia, and therapeutic strategies were needed to reorient her to her actual life (Tarazi, 1990). The problem is that there have been almost no outcome studies of past-life therapy (e.g., Freedman, 1997), so that its effectiveness as a therapeutic strategy is unknown (cf. Stevenson, 1994).

Let us consider one last question about past-life experiences: Could unexplained phobias be traced to events in previous lives? In his study of children's spontaneous past-life experiences, Stevenson has found a correspondence between the presence of phobias in a current life and the manner of death of the purported previous personality. Thus, for example, "a child who claims to remember a life that ended in drowning may have a phobia of being immersed in water [and] one who claims to remember a life that ended in stabbing may have a fear of bladed weapons" (Stevenson, 1990, p. 247). Phobias have been present more often when violent deaths were recalled than natural deaths. "In a series of 240 cases in India phobias occurred in 53 (39%) of the 135 cases with violent death, but in only 3 (3%) of the 105 cases having a natural death" (Stevenson, 1990, p. 247). Sometimes fears have generalized to stimuli similar to those at the time of the purported previous personality's death, and sometimes they have been isolated to specific stimuli that were present at death, both of which would be expected in phobias following traumatic events. For example, a Turkish boy who claimed to have remembered a previous life in which he had been killed when a van in which he had been riding had "crashed against the abutment of a narrow bridge" (Stevenson, 1990, p. 247) had both a generalized fear of automobiles and a specific fear of "the bridge where the accident had occurred" (Stevenson, 1990, p. 247). As with the benefits of past-life therapy in general, it is not clear that finding past-life associations to phobias has any therapeutic value.

THE QUESTION OF LIFE AFTER DEATH

Let us return now to the question of life after death by first mentioning some of the phenomena associated with mediumship and then considering the question of survival.

Mediumship

In chapter 6 we considered the possibility that there are alterations of consciousness, such as channeling, in which a person may appear to have contact with beings external to her own psyche. In addition to many of the other terms used to refer to such contact has been that of *mediumship* with *mental mediums*, apparently having the ability to "communicate with deceased personalities" (Irwin, 1994, p. 20), among other skills, and *physical mediums,* in addition, apparently having "the power to influence the physical state of objects" (Irwin, 1994, p. 20), such as producing rapping noises or displacing furniture. In some empirical studies, information about the dead given by mediums has turned out to be correct without any evidence of any normal means by which that data could have been obtained (Irwin, 1994; G. Schwartz, 2002).

Let us briefly consider a case of physical mediumship. In Scole, England, researchers attended 32 meetings from October 1995 to August 1997 of a group of four people who met twice a week in the basement of a house for the purpose of contacting spirits. Two of the group were mediums who would enter and remain in a "trance state" (Keen, Ellison, & Fontana, 1999, p. 180) for the 2- to 2½-hour duration of a session. Ten different spirits apparently spoke through the two mediums, sometimes in a manner that was uncharacteristic of the mediums. The sessions included conversations between the spirits and those present as well as the manifestation of various anomalous physical phenomena. Among the physical phenomena were markings on 15 rolls of film that had usually been left unopened in their cases during the sessions but nonetheless were often found afterward to contain a variety of phrases written in English, German, French, Latin, and Greek, as well as various drawings including Chinese ideograms (Keen et al., 1999).

During the final session attended by the regular investigators, an audio-tape recorder with the microphone removed was connected to a "primitive semi-conductor (germanium) apparatus" (Keen et al., 1999, p. 297) that one of the investigators had built to the specification of the purported spirits. The investigators had brought their own packet of audio cassette tapes, removed one at random, marked the surface of the cassette on four locations, and inserted it into the microphone-less tape recorder, which was turned on record and kept under the control of one of the investigators throughout the session. During the session, music with an overriding voice message could be heard coming from the microphone-less cassette recorder. The music was Rachmaninoff's Second Piano Concerto, which, according to the spirits, was being played by the composer himself. After the session, the tape was inspected and found to have the four identifying marks. When the tape was played, it was found to contain the piano concerto with the overriding voice along with a great deal of white noise but none of the background sounds that had been present in the room at the time, as evidenced by a normal tape recording that had also been made during the session. "In the course of over 20 sittings the investigators were unable to detect any direct indication of fraud or deception" (Keen et al., 1999, p. 157) and concluded that the evidence favored the hypothesis that "intelligent forces, whether originating in the human psyche or from discarnate sources" (Keen et al., 1999, p. 157) were responsible for the anomalous Scole phenomena.

There is overlap between physical mediumship and *poltergeist experiences* in which sounds occur and objects are moved around without apparent human agency (Irwin, 1994). The apparent tampering by spirits with electronic devices, such as the music and voice on tape in the Scole experiment, has become a field of investigation of its own that started with *electronic voice phenomenon*, consisting of apparently anomalous voices on tape, and has diversified to *instrumental transcommunication*, which, in addition to voices on tape, has included apparently anomalous telephone, television, and computer messages. Much of this investigation, however, has been done outside mainstream scientific and academic institutions and has been difficult to evaluate (Barušs, 2001a).

The Evidence for Survival

We have been considering alterations of consciousness associated with death, which are interesting in their own right, as well as mediumship, which has been directly implicated in research concerning life after death. But what about death itself? Does consciousness survive death in any meaningful way? Materialists would say no, whereas transcendentalists would say yes. In keeping with a scientific approach, what does the evidence reveal? Lines of investigation concerning survival have included the study of out-of-body experiences, near-death experiences, past-life experiences, apparent contact with discarnate entities by mediums, poltergeist experiences, electronic voice phenomenon, and instrumental transcommunication. There has been disagreement with regard to the interpretation of this body of evidence. Clearly, additional research in all of these areas is required to clarify the nature of the phenomena in question.

There has sometimes been a tendency on the part of critics to dismiss evidence for survival because it does not fit a mechanistic world view (Grof, 1987), whereas those less critical have compared the tendency to ignore evidence for survival with "standing at the foot of Mount Everest and insisting that [one] cannot see a mountain" (C. Wilson, 1990, p. 16). Clearly, the evidence for survival needs to be examined on its own merits, irrespective of one's opinions about the nature of reality. A second tendency on the part of critics has been to insist on ruling out any possibility of fraud on the part of the participants in studies concerning survival before accepting the results. The possibility of fraud is clearly a legitimate concern given that cases of fraud have been documented in the past (Almeder, 1992). However, just because one can imagine a way in which participants or the scientists studying them could have perpetrated a hoax does not mean that fraud is always the most plausible explanation. In many cases, such as the Scole experiment, the complexity of events would have necessitated a hoax of elaborate proportions with nothing apparently to be gained by the participants (Keen, 2001), so that explanations other than fraud must be seriously considered.

Are experiences associated with death meaningless or meaningful? Are they what they appear to be? Are they delusional or veridical? Are they mundane or extraordinary? Can materialist theories adequately account for them? Are they beneficial? What do they tell us about our self-identity? Is the psyche closed or open? Is there life after death? Again, I will leave the reader to answer these questions herself.

10

CONCLUSION

We have surveyed the spectrum of alterations of consciousness, from the ordinary waking state, through sensory restriction, sleep, dreams, hypnosis, trance, drug-induced states, transcendence, and experiences associated with death. What is striking about the ground that we have covered is the amount of polarization in this area of investigation: the mind is a by-product of the brain versus the brain is a vehicle for the mind; dreams are meaningless versus dreams are messages; hypnosis is just ordinary behavior in a social situation labeled as hypnosis versus hypnosis is a special state of trance; shamanism is just schizophrenia versus shamanism is a means of communicating with spirits; dissociative identity disorder (DID) does not exist versus multiple personalities are present in DID; people who believe they have been abducted by aliens are crazy versus people really are being abducted by aliens; psychedelics are dangerous versus psychedelics are divine sacraments; mystical experiences are nothing but aberrant brain activity versus enlightenment is conferred in mystical experiences; death is oblivion versus personal consciousness continues after death. Perhaps the best way to tie together some of the material in this book would be to use our thematic threads as the basis for a summary discussion. In the process of doing so, let me take the opportunity to make some comments about directions for further research.

RECAPITULATION OF THEMATIC THREADS

In chapter 1, the following 10 thematic threads, associated with fundamental questions about the nature of reality, were introduced, with the idea that they would help us to discuss alterations of consciousness.

Physiological, Cognitive, and Experiential Perspectives

Our first thread was that of the three perspectives taken when approaching consciousness. Although all three were used throughout the book, the physiological perspective underlay our discussions of sleep and psychedelic states, the cognitive perspective was most evident in cognitive theories such as those for dreaming and OBEs, and the experiential perspective became particularly significant for unusual phenomena such as transcendence and near-death experiences. All three perspectives need to be considered as much as possible in any further research, and the interactions between these perspectives need to be established more fully. For example, what physiological changes accompany the perceptual changes associated with hypnotic suggestions of analgesia? Is it possible in any way to determine if near-death experiences occur during the actual time that someone is near death, and, if so, what are the physiological correlates, if any, that correspond to them? What is the nature of the knowledge associated with the noetic quality of transcendent states of consciousness? The effort to make these links is perhaps most evident in psychoneuroimmunology when trying to understand how psychological events can affect physiological ones.

Material Versus Transcendent Beliefs

It is hard to overemphasize the importance of the material-transcendent dimension of beliefs about consciousness and reality for the understanding of alterations of consciousness. The ways in which phenomena are conceptualized, the kinds of research programs that are carried out, and the interpretation of the results of research depend on the beliefs of investigators. For example, if the world is conceptualized as a physical place in a naive sense and consciousness as just an emergent property of processes in the brain, then there is no point in research aimed at looking for life after death. It is important for scientists to examine their own beliefs, to learn to rely on the data rather than their predilections, and to go wherever the evidence leads them.

Delusional Versus Veridical Experiences

Remaining open to transcendental interpretations of reality involves taking into greater account phenomenological data. But that raises the question of whether the events occurring in people's experiences are what they appear to be. Do we really know what is in our minds? Are there really presences that can be sensed? Do some dreams really foretell the future? Did hypnotically recalled perinatal events happen? Are people really being abducted by aliens? Does time really change during intoxication with ayahuasca? Are insights that occur during transcendent states really true? Can people really see what is happening in the environment around them during OBEs? Is an NDE really a preview of death? Are there previous lives to be remembered? Or are these all delusions? Or are some of them delusions and some of them veridical? If some of them are veridical, which ones? Our beliefs about consciousness and reality will likely determine our answers to these questions. We need to follow the empirical evidence as far as it will take us. But we also need to learn more about introspection to determine if there are ways of discriminating between that which is imaginary and that which is real. Maybe some of what we think is imaginary will turn out to be real, and some of what we think is real may turn out to be imaginary. Is the ordinary, everyday world actually real, or is it imaginary?

Mundane Versus Extraordinary Phenomena

Directly related to the question of the veridical nature of experiences is that of whether the phenomena occurring in alterations of consciousness are mundane or extraordinary. Are the correspondences between precognitive dreams and subsequent events incidental or actual? Is hypnosis just more ordinary cognition triggered by a particular social situation, or is it a special state? Are the phenomena associated with physical mediumship the result of hoaxes, or is there some other explanation? Sometimes it seems to me that there is an attitude within scientism that the world is a boring place and that anything interesting that appears to be happening can be explained in mundane terms. That may often be true but should not be used as a judgmental heuristic for evaluating individual events.

Meaningless Versus Meaningful Events

Maybe something is not happening in the real world, and maybe there is a mundane explanation for it, but is it nonetheless meaningful? Are fantasies during daydreaming meaningful? Are dreams meaningful? Are NDEs meaningful? Given that hypnagogic imagery appears to be autosymbolic, are there nonrational sources of information about ourselves? Are hypnopompic images answers to questions? What about intuition? Can we account for the presence of intuition in mundane terms as a heuristic used in reasoning, or is there something extraordinary about it? Does it stem from the superconscious? Do we have a superconscious? What is transcendental awareness such as that found among near-death experiencers? Research is needed to understand any ways in which nonrational meaningfulness and knowledge can occur. Such research is necessary to understand the potentially symbolic interpretation of events in alterations of consciousness.

Lateral Versus Vertical Meaningfulness

Not only could we extend the periphery of what is meaningful laterally through consideration of the use of ways of knowing other than the rational, but in some cases there could also be an apparent vertical extension through the deepening of meaning such as with Merrell-Wolff's introception. Existential questions have purportedly been resolved in some transcendent states of consciousness precisely because of the noetic quality of such states. But in what sense is such enlightenment really knowledge? We can recall the cases of DMT intoxication and distressing NDE in which there was absolute conviction that the world is a terrible place. What are the cognitive and physiological correlates of the deepening of meaning? Is it possible to develop meditation techniques that could be used by scientists to facilitate the occurrence of transcendent experiences for themselves as an investigative method? Perhaps something along the lines of mathematical yoga? Given the significance of the deepening of meaning for those for whom it occurs, it is important to know more about it.

Psychopathology Versus Well-Being

We have considered actual psychopathology in this book such as schizophrenia, sleep disorders, DID, and impairments associated with drug use. There has been a tendency in the past to regard some altered states as pathological, such as shamanic soul journeying and transcendence, even though they are quite different in character from psychological disorders. And some alterations of consciousness that look as though they should be some kind of psychopathology, such as alien abduction experiences, cannot be accounted for in terms of known mental disorders. It is important in trying to understand alterations of consciousness not to instinctively label as pathological that which we do not understand but rather to leave the question open as to whether or not some form of mental disease is present until more is known about it.

We have also considered alterations that are characterized by exceptional well-being. Most notable among these are transcendent states such as flow, peak experiences, and mystical experiences. In many cases, it is not the type of alteration but the nature of an individual's experience in an alteration of consciousness that determines whether that experience will be felicitous or not. We have seen that occur with daydreams, sensory deprivation, hypnagogia, dreams, trance, drug-induced states, and near-death experiences.

Dangerous Versus Beneficial Alterations

Related to questions of psychopathology and well-being are those concerned with the dangers and benefits of phenomena in alterations of consciousness. Are psychoactive drugs such as fluoxetine and LSD dangerous or beneficial? Under what conditions does sensory restriction cease to be therapeutic and begin to be dangerous? Are alien abduction experiences dangerous and, if so, what can be done to stop them?

But many of the alterations of consciousness lend themselves to therapeutic efforts. Guided imagery has been utilized to try to improve physical and psychological functioning. Dreams have been interpreted for the sake of self-understanding and, in the form of lucid dreams, harnessed for self-development. Hypnosis has been used in a wide range of situations, such as analgesia during surgery. DID may in and of itself be a healthy response to an unhealthy situation. Psychedelics have been given to addicts to treat their addictions and have also been given to the dying to help them with intractable pain. Meditation has been used to counteract stress. And past-life regression has been part of some psychotherapists' repertoires of therapeutic strategies. The volume of research concerning the effectiveness of these efforts is varied, with numerous studies for some of them, such as hypnosis, and almost none for others, such as past-life regression. It would make sense to carefully examine the therapeutic potential of all of the procedures that could be developed in any of these alterations of consciousness.

The Nature of the Self

The question of the nature of the self has certainly been opened up in this book. Is the self a thought that appropriates to itself previously aggregated ideas about what it is like? Is it just a representation of the biological organism within its own information-processing system? How is it that self-identity can change so readily for hypnotic virtuosos? What gets disconnected during dissociation? Does the self leave the body during soul journeying and out-of-body experiences? Who is the self for a person with DID? What is happening during the double consciousness of marijuana intoxication? Is the self eternal as it appears to be during transcendent states of consciousness? Have we lived previous lives? Does the self survive death? I think that there needs to be research aimed at better understanding the nature of the self in light of the changes of self-identity in alterations of consciousness.

Closed Versus Open Psyche

At the root of much of the disparity concerning consciousness is the question of whether the psyche is open or closed. Is consciousness bound by the skull, or does it extend spatially and temporally? The answers to these questions depend on the answers to questions about the extent to which phenomena associated with alterations of consciousness are what they appear to be. Are we being deluded, or are some of the events occurring in some of these alterations veridical? Are the results of the ganzfeld studies valid? Are sensed presences objective in some sense? Do precognitive dreams foretell future events? Can perinatal events be known through hypnotic regression? Do shamans encounter spirits? Does intoxication with ayahuasca lead to liberation from the constraints of time? Are NDEs a preview of death? Do mediums give voice to the dead? In other words, is consciousness a product of the brain, or is the brain a vehicle of expression for consciousness?

ALTERNATIVE EXPLANATIONS OF REALITY

Where does consideration of the thematic threads leave us? We are used to thinking that the only objective reality that exists is the reality that we encounter through our sensory modalities. Of course, we know that there is more to physical reality than what we can perceive, because our physical senses are attuned to only a narrow range of physical events. Visible light, for instance, is only a fraction of the spectrum of electromagnetic radiation. Perhaps objective reality, whether we call it physical or not, is more extensive than we ordinarily think. And, as our consciousness is altered away from attending to sensory impressions in an ordinary way, perceptual abilities may emerge that allow us to glimpse aspects of reality that we cannot apprehend with our physical senses. Such perceptual possibilities are suggested by the transcendent awareness that appears to occur during the out-of-body component of near-death experiences. Although it is possible that it could give us knowledge that would ordinarily be acquired through physical sight, it may be that transcendent awareness is more oriented to the perception of aspects of reality that are not available to the physical senses. It may also be that, just as we have a perspective from which we perceive the physical world with our physical senses, so we may have a perspective, our interpretation of reality, from which we perceive other aspects of reality so that their appearance conforms, in part, to our expectations.

It may also be that in addition to directly perceiving aspects of an extended objective reality, events that occur in such a reality could intrude into our ordinary world. Such a possibility is suggested by physiological changes accompanying shifts among alters in DID, physiological correlates of alien abduction experiences, birth defects of children who remember previous lives, and phenomena associated with physical mediumship. I want to stress that I am speculating in making these suggestions. Our brains may be devices that give us access to a range of phenomena that result in our having ordinary waking experiences, but, simultaneously, constrict our consciousness unless we can put our brains out of commission or modify them so as to act as transducers between different aspects of reality.

I think that studying alterations of consciousness forces us to examine our beliefs about reality. Maybe there is more to it than we ordinarily think.

Perhaps transcendent states really do reveal something about the nature of reality. Maybe alterations of consciousness are a doorway to nonordinary aspects of reality. The richness of phenomena associated with alterations of consciousness provides us with an interesting spectrum of human experiences. It is my hope that this overview of alterations of consciousness has helped to expand the reader's understanding of the human psyche, raised some questions about the nature of consciousness and reality, and inspired a deeper appreciation of the mystery of life.

REFERENCES

Aanstoos, C. M. (1987). The psychology of computer models and the question of the imagination. In E. L. Murray (Ed.), *Imagination and phenomenological psychology* (pp. 48–77). Pittsburgh, PA: Duquesne University Press.

Abraham, H. D., & Aldridge, A. M. (1993). Adverse consequences of lysergic acid diethylamide. *Addiction, 88*, 1327–1334.

Ader, R., & Cohen, N. (1975). Behaviorally conditioned immunosuppression. *Psychosomatic Medicine, 37*(4), 333–340.

Ader, R., & Cohen, N. (1982). Behaviorally conditioned immunosuppression and murine systemic lupus erythematosus. *Science, 215*(4539), 1534–1536.

Ader, R., & Cohen, N. (1993). Psychoneuroimmunology: Conditioning and stress. *Annual Review of Psychology, 44*, 53–85.

Adler, N., & Matthews, K. (1994). Health psychology: Why do some people get sick and some stay well? *Annual Review of Psychology, 45*, 229–259.

Aggernæs, A. (1972). The difference between the experienced reality of hallucinations in young drug abusers and schizophrenic patients. *Acta Psychiatrica Scandinavica, 48*(4), 287–299.

Ahsen, A. (1988). Hypnagogic and hypnopompic imagery transformations. *Journal of Mental Imagery, 12*(2), 1–50.

Alarcón, A., Capafons, A., Bayot, A., & Cardeña, E. (1999). Preference between two methods of active-alert hypnosis: Not all techniques are created equal. *American Journal of Clinical Hypnosis, 41*(3), 269–276.

Aldrich, M. S. (1999). *Sleep medicine.* New York: Oxford University Press.

Allen, D. S. (1995). Schizophreniform psychosis after stage hypnosis. *The British Journal of Psychiatry, 166*, 680.

Almeder, R. (1992). *Death and personal survival: The evidence for life after death.* Lanham, MD: Rowman & Littlefield.

Alvarado, C. S. (2000). Out-of-body experiences. In E. Cardeña, S. J. Lynn, & S. Krippner (Eds.), *Varieties of anomalous experience: Examining the scientific evidence* (pp. 183–218). Washington, DC: American Psychological Association.

Ameri, A. (1999). The effects of cannabinoids on the brain. *Progress in Neurobiology, 58*, 315–348.

American Psychiatric Association. (2000). *Diagnostic and statistical manual of mental disorders* (4th ed., text revision). Washington, DC: Author.

Andresen, J. (2000). Meditation meets behavioural medicine: The story of experimental research on meditation. *Journal of Consciousness Studies, 7*(11–12), 17–73.

Antrobus, J. (2000). Theories of dreaming. In M. H. Kryger, T. Roth, & W. C. Dement (Eds.), *Principles and practice of sleep medicine* (3rd ed., pp. 472–481). Philadelphia: W. B. Saunders.

Appel, J. B., & Callahan, P. M. (1989). Involvement of 5-HT receptor subtypes in the discriminative stimulus properties of mescaline. *European Journal of Pharmacology, 159*, 41–46.

Appelle, S. (1996). The abduction experience: A critical evaluation of theory and evidence. *Journal of UFO Studies, 6*, 29–78.

Appelle, S., Lynn, S. J., & Newman, L. (2000). Alien abduction experiences. In E. Cardeña, S. J. Lynn, & S. Krippner (Eds.), *Varieties of anomalous experience: Examining the scientific evidence* (pp. 253–282). Washington, DC: American Psychological Association.

Armitage, R., Emslie, G., & Rintelmann, J. (1997). The effect of fluoxetine on sleep EEG in childhood depression: A preliminary report. *Neuropsychopharmacology, 17*(4), 241–245.

Armitage, R., Trivedi, M., & Rush, A. J. (1995). Fluoxetine and oculomotor activity during sleep in depressed patients. *Neuropsychopharmacology, 12*(2), 159–165.

Aserinsky, A., & Kleitman, N. (1953). Regularly occurring periods of eye motility, and concomitant phenomena, during sleep. *Science, 118*, 273–274.

Aserinsky, E. (1996). Memories of famous neuropsychologists: The discovery of REM sleep. *Journal of the History of the Neurosciences, 5*(3), 213–227.

Assagioli, R. (1965). *Psychosynthesis: A manual of principles and techniques.* New York: Penguin.

Baggott, M. (2000). An exchange of views about MDMA neurotoxicity and MDMA research. *MAPS: Bulletin of the Multidisciplinary Association for Psychedelic Studies, 10*(1), 3–4.

Baker, D. (1975). *Meditation (the theory and practice).* Essendon, UK: Author.

Baker, D. (1977). *The spiritual diary.* Potters Bar, UK: College of Spiritual Enlightenment and Esoteric Knowledge.

Baker, D., & Hansen, C. (1977). *In the steps of the master.* Essendon, UK: Douglas Baker.

Baker, R. A. (1982). The effect of suggestion on past-lives regression. *American Journal of Clinical Hypnosis, 25*(1), 71–76.

Banaji, M. R., & Kihlstrom, J. F. (1996). The ordinary nature of alien abduction memories. *Psychological Inquiry, 7*(2), 132–135.

Barabasz, A. (2000). EEG markers of alert hypnosis: The induction makes a difference. *Sleep and Hypnosis, 2*(4), 164–169.

Barabasz, A. F., Baer, L., Sheehan, D. V., & Barabasz, M. (1986). A three-year follow-up of hypnosis and restricted environmental stimulation therapy for smoking. *International Journal of Clinical and Experimental Hypnosis, 34*(3), 169–181.

Barabasz, A., Barabasz, M., & Bauman, J. (1993). Restricted environmental stimulation technique improves human performance: Rifle marksmanship. *Perceptual and Motor Skills, 76*, 867–873.

Barabasz, A., Barabasz, M., Jensen, S., Calvin, S., Trevisan, M., et al. (1999). Cortical event-related potentials show the structure of hypnotic suggestions is crucial. *International Journal of Clinical and Experimental Hypnosis, 47*(1), 5–22.

Barabasz, M., Barabasz, A., & Dyer, R. (1993). Chamber REST reduces alcohol consumption: 3, 6, 12, and 24 hour sessions. In A. F. Barabasz & M. Barabasz (Eds.), *Clinical and experimental restricted environmental stimulation: New developments and perspectives* (pp. 163–173). New York: Springer-Verlag.

Barabasz, M., Barabasz, A., & O'Neill, M. (1991). Effects of experimental context, demand characteristics, and situational cues: New data. *Perceptual and Motor Skills, 73*, 83–92.

Barber, J. (1998a). The mysterious persistence of hypnotic analgesia. *International Journal of Clinical and Experimental Hypnosis, 46*(1), 28–43.

Barber, J. (1998b). When hypnosis causes trouble. *International Journal of Clinical and Experimental Hypnosis, 46*(2), 157–170.

Barber, T. X. (1999). A comprehensive three-dimensional theory of hypnosis. In I. Kirsch, A. Capafons, E. Cardeña-Buelna, & S. Amigó (Eds.), *Clinical hypnosis and self-regulation: Cognitive–behavioral perspectives* (pp. 21–48). Washington, DC: American Psychological Association.

Baron, P. H. (1989). Fighting cancer with images. In H. Wadeson, J. Durkin, & D. Perach (Eds.), *Advances in art therapy* (pp. 148–168). New York: John Wiley & Sons.

Barrett, D. (1996a). Dreams in multiple personality disorder. In D. Barrett (Ed.), *Trauma and dreams* (pp. 68–81). Cambridge, MA: Harvard University Press.

Barrett, D. (1996b). Fantasizers and dissociaters: Two types of high hypnotizables, two different imagery styles. In R. G. Kunzendorf, N. P. Spanos, & B. Wallace (Eds.), *Hypnosis and imagination* (pp. 123–135). Amityville, NY: Baywood.

Barrett, D. (1996c). Introduction. In D. Barrett (Ed.), *Trauma and dreams* (pp. 1–6). Cambridge, MA: Harvard University Press.

Barušs, I. (1986). Quantum mechanics and human consciousness. *Physics in Canada, 42*(1), 3–5.

Baruŝs, I. (1987). Metaanalysis of definitions of consciousness. *Imagination, Cognition and Personality, 6*(4), 321–329.

Baruŝs, I. (1990). *The personal nature of notions of consciousness: A theoretical and empirical examination of the role of the personal in the understanding of consciousness.* Lanham, MD: University Press of America.

Baruŝs, I. (1993). Can we consider matter as ultimate reality? Some fundamental problems with a materialist interpretation of reality. *Ultimate Reality and Meaning: Interdisciplinary Studies in the Philosophy of Understanding, 16*(3–4), 245–254.

Baruŝs, I. (1996). *Authentic knowing: The convergence of science and spiritual aspiration.* West Lafayette, IN: Purdue University Press.

Baruŝs, I. (2000a). Overview of consciousness research. *Informatica: An International Journal of Computing and Informatics, 24*(2), 269–273.

Baruŝs, I. (2000b). Psychopathology of altered states of consciousness. *Journal of Baltic Psychology, 1*(1), 12–26.

Baruŝs, I. (2000c). Transition to transcendence: Franklin Merrell-Wolff's mathematical yoga. *Integralis: Journal of Integral Consciousness, Culture, and Science, 1*(0). Retrieved Sept. 14, 2000, from http://rocky.unca.edu/combs/IntegralAge/Wolff.htm

Baruŝs, I. (2001a). Failure to replicate electronic voice phenomenon. *Journal of Scientific Exploration, 15*(3), 355–367.

Baruŝs, I. (2001b). The art of science: Science of the future in light of alterations of consciousness. *Journal of Scientific Exploration, 15*(1), 57–68.

Baruŝs, I., & Moore, R. J. (1989). Notions of consciousness and reality. In J. E. Shorr, P. Robin, J. A. Connella, & M. Wolpin (Eds.), *Imagery: Current perspectives* (pp. 87–92). New York: Plenum Press.

Baruŝs, I., & Moore, R. J. (1992). Measurement of beliefs about consciousness and reality. *Psychological Reports, 71,* 59–64.

Baruŝs, I., & Moore, R. J. (1997, Spring). Beliefs about consciousness and reality: Highlights of Tucson II consciousness survey. *Consciousness Bulletin,* 5–6.

Baruŝs, I., & Moore, R. J. (1998). Beliefs about consciousness and reality of participants at 'Tucson II.' *Journal of Consciousness Studies, 5*(4), 483–496.

Barwise, J. (1986). Information and circumstance. *Notre Dame Journal of Formal Logic, 27*(3), 324–338.

Basterfield, K. (1994). Abductions: The Australian experience. In A. Pritchard, D. E. Pritchard, J. E. Mack, P. Kasey, & C. Yapp (Eds.), *Alien discussions: Proceedings of the abduction study conference held at MIT, Cambridge, MA* (pp. 178–186). Cambridge, MA: North Cambridge.

Bauer, H. H. (1992). *Scientific literacy and the myth of the scientific method.* Urbana: University of Illinois Press.

Bem, D. J. (1994). Response to Hyman. *Psychological Bulletin, 115*(1), 25–27.

Bem, D. J., & Honorton, C. (1994). Does psi exist? Replicable evidence for an anomalous process of information transfer. *Psychological Bulletin, 115*(1), 4–18.

Bengston, W. F., & Krinsley, D. (2000). The effect of the "laying on of hands" on transplanted breast cancer in mice. *Journal of Scientific Exploration, 14*(3), 353–364.

Benington, J. H. (2000). Sleep homeostasis and the function of sleep. *Sleep, 23*(7), 959–966.

Benson, H. (1975). *The relaxation response.* New York: William Morrow.

Benson, H. (1983). The relaxation response: Its subjective and objective historical precedents and physiology. *Trends in Neurosciences, 6,* 281–284.

Bentall, R. P. (2000). Hallucinatory experiences. In E. Cardeña, S. J. Lynn, & S. Krippner (Eds.), *Varieties of anomalous experience: Examining the scientific evidence* (pp. 85–120). Washington, DC: American Psychological Association.

Bernat, J. L. (1999). Refinements in the definition and criterion of death. In S. J. Youngner, R. M. Arnold, & R. Schapiro (Eds.), *The definition of death: Contemporary controversies* (pp. 83–92). Baltimore: Johns Hopkins University Press.

Bibby, R. W. (1987). *Fragmented Gods: The poverty and potential of religion in Canada.* Toronto, Canada: Irwin.

Blackmore, S. (1993). *Dying to live: Near-death-experiences.* Buffalo, NY: Prometheus.

Blewett, D. B. (1969). *The frontiers of being.* New York: Award.

Bliwise, D. L. (1996). Historical change in the report of daytime fatigue. *Sleep, 19*(6), 462–464.

Bonnet, M. H. (2000). Sleep deprivation. In M. H. Kryger, T. Roth, & W. C. Dement (Eds.), *Principles and practice of sleep medicine* (3rd ed., pp. 53–71). Philadelphia: W. B. Saunders.

Borbély, A. A., & Achermann, P. (2000). Sleep homeostasis and models of sleep regulation. In M. H. Kryger, T. Roth, & W. C. Dement (Eds.), *Principles and practice of sleep medicine* (3rd ed., pp. 377–390). Philadelphia: W. B. Saunders.

Bosnak, R. (1996). Integration and ambivalence in transplants. In D. Barrett (Ed.), *Trauma and dreams* (pp. 217–230). Cambridge, MA: Harvard University Press.

Botta, S. A. (1999). Self-hypnosis as anesthesia for liposuction surgery. *American Journal of Clinical Hypnosis, 41*(4), 299–301.

Bourguignon, E. (1979). *Psychological anthropology: An introduction to human nature and cultural differences.* New York: Holt, Rinehart and Winston.

Boutros, N. N., & Bowers, Jr., M. B. (1996). Chronic substance-induced psychotic disorders: State of the literature. *Journal of Neuropsychiatry and Clinical Neurosciences, 8*(3), 262–269.

Bowers, K. S. (1976). *Hypnosis for the seriously curious.* New York: W. W. Norton.

Bowers, K. S. (1992). Imagination and dissociation in hypnotic responding. *International Journal of Clinical and Experimental Hypnosis, 40*(4), 253–275.

Bowers, K. S., & Woody, E. Z. (1996). Hypnotic amnesia and the paradox of intentional forgetting. *Journal of Abnormal Psychology, 105*(3), 381–390.

Bowman, C. (2001). *Return from heaven: Beloved relatives reincarnated within your family*. New York: HarperCollins.

Braid, J. (1960). *Braid on hypnotism: The beginnings of modern hypnosis* (A. E. Waite, Ed., Rev. ed.). New York: Julian. (Original work published 1842 to 1883)

Braun, A. R., Balkin, T. J., Wesensten, N. J., Gwadry, F., Carson, R. E., et al. (1998). Dissociated pattern of activity in visual cortices and their projections during human rapid eye movement sleep. *Science, 279*, 91–95.

Bravo, G., & Grob, C. (1996). Psychedelic psychotherapy. In B. W. Scotton, A. B. Chinen, & J. R. Battista (Eds.), *Textbook of transpersonal psychiatry and psychology* (pp. 335–343). New York: BasicBooks.

Breakey, W. R., Goodell, H., Lorenz, P. C., & McHugh, P. R. (1974). Hallucinogenic drugs as precipitants of schizophrenia. *Psychological Medicine, 4*(3), 255–261.

Brentano, F. (1960). The distinction between mental and physical phenomena. (D. B. Terrell, Trans.). In R. M. Chisholm (Ed.), *Realism and the background of phenomenology* (pp. 39–61). Glencoe, IL: Free Press. (Reprinted from *Psychologie vom empirischen standpunkt*, 1874, Vol. I, Book II, Chap. i)

Brody, B. A. (1999). How much of the brain must be dead? In S. J. Youngner, R. M. Arnold, & R. Schapiro (Eds.), *The definition of death: Contemporary controversies* (pp. 71–82). Baltimore: Johns Hopkins University Press.

Broening, H. W., Morford, L. L., Inman-Wood, S. L., Fukumura, M., & Vorhees, C. V. (2001). 3,4-Methylenedioxymethamphetamine (ecstasy)-induced learning and memory impairments depend on the age of exposure during early development. *The Journal of Neuroscience, 21*(9), 3228–3235.

Broughton, R. (1986). Human consciousness and sleep/waking rhythms. In B. B. Wolman & M. Ullman (Eds.), *Handbook of states of consciousness* (pp. 461–484). New York: Van Nostrand Reinhold.

Broughton, R. J. (2000). NREM arousal parasomnias. In M. H. Kryger, T. Roth, & W. C. Dement (Eds.), *Principles and practice of sleep medicine* (3rd ed., pp. 693–706). Philadelphia: W. B. Saunders.

Broughton, R. S. (1991). *Parapsychology: The controversial science*. New York: Ballantine.

Brown, D., Scheflin, A. W., & Hammond, D. C. (1998). *Memory, trauma treatment, and the law*. New York: W. W. Norton.

Brown, M. F. (1997). *The channeling zone: American spirituality in an anxious age*. Cambridge, MA: Harvard University Press.

Bryan, C. D. B. (1995). *Close encounters of the fourth kind: A reporter's notebook on alien abduction, UFOs, and the conference at M.I.T.* New York: Arkana.

Bucke, R. M. (1991). *Cosmic consciousness: A study in the evolution of the human mind*. New York: Arkana. (Original work published 1901)

Bulkeley, K. (1999). *Visions of the night: Dreams, religion, and psychology*. Albany: State University of New York Press.

Cardeña, E. (1996). "Just floating on the sky." A comparison of hypnotic and shamanic phenomena. In D. Eigner & R. van Quekelbherge (Eds.), *Jahrbuch für transkulturelle medizin und psychotherapie* (Yearbook of cross-cultural medicine and psychotherapy) *Vol. 1994. Trance, Besessenheit, Heilrituale und Psychotherapie* (Trance, possession, healing rituals and psychotherapy) (pp. 85–98). Berlin: Verlag für Wissenschaft und Bildung.

Cardeña, E., Lynn, S. J., & Krippner, S. (Eds.). (2000). *Varieties of anomalous experience: Examining the scientific evidence*. Washington, DC: American Psychological Association.

Carlin, A. S., Post, R. D., Bakker, C. B., & Halpern, L. M. (1974). The role of modeling and previous experience in the facilitation of marijuana intoxication. *Journal of Nervous and Mental Disease, 159*(4), 275–281.

Carlson, N. R. (1994). *Physiology of behavior* (5th ed.). Boston: Allyn and Bacon.

Carskadon, M. A., & Dement, W. C. (2000). Normal human sleep: An overview. In M. H. Kryger, T. Roth, & W. C. Dement (Eds.), *Principles and practice of sleep medicine* (3rd ed., pp. 15–25). Philadelphia: W. B. Saunders.

Carskadon, M. A., & Rechtschaffen, A. (2000). Monitoring and staging human sleep. In M. H. Kryger, T. Roth, & W. C. Dement (Eds.), *Principles and practice of sleep medicine* (3rd ed., pp. 1197–1215). Philadelphia: W. B. Saunders.

Carson, R. C., Butcher, J. N., & Mineka, S. (1996). *Abnormal psychology and modern life* (10th ed.). New York: HarperCollins.

Cavallero, C., Cicogna, P., Natale, V., Occhionero, M., & Zito, A. (1992). Slow wave sleep dreaming. *Sleep, 15*(6), 562–566.

Chalmers, D. J. (1995). Facing up to the problem of consciousness. *Journal of Consciousness Studies, 2*(3), 200–219.

Chamberlain, D. B. (1986). Reliability of birth memory: Observations from mother and child pairs in hypnosis. *Journal of the American Academy of Medical Hypnoanalysts, 1,* 89–98.

Chamberlain, D. B. (1988). *Babies remember birth: And other extraordinary scientific discoveries about the mind and personality of your newborn*. Los Angeles: Jeremy P. Tarcher.

Chamberlain, D. B. (1990). The expanding boundaries of memory. *ReVision: The Journal of Consciousness and Change, 12*(4), 11–20.

Cheyne, J. A., Newby-Clark, I. R., & Rueffer, S. D. (1999). Relations among hypnagogic and hypnopompic experiences associated with sleep paralysis. *Journal of Sleep Research, 8,* 313–317.

Cheyne, J. A., Rueffer, S. D., & Newby-Clark, I. R. (1999). Hypnagogic and hypnopompic hallucinations during sleep paralysis: Neurological and cultural construction of the night-mare. *Consciousness and Cognition, 8,* 319–337.

Child, I. L. (1985). Psychology and anomalous observations: The question of ESP in dreams. *American Psychologist, 40*(11), 1219–1230.

Cialdini, R. B. (1988). *Influence: Science and practice* (2nd ed.). New York: HarperCollins.

Cockell, J. (1993). *Across time and death: A mother's search for her past life children*. New York: Fireside.

Cook, C. M., & Persinger, M. A. (1997). Experimental induction of the "sensed presence" in normal subjects and an exceptional subject. *Perceptual and Motor Skills, 85,* 683–693.

Coons, P. M. (1993). The differential diagnosis of possession states. *Dissociation,* 6(4), 213–221.

Council, J. R., Chambers, D., Jundt, T. A., & Good, M. D. (1991). Are the mental images of fantasy-prone persons really more "real"? *Imagination, Cognition and Personality, 10*(4), 319–327.

Csikszentmihalyi, M. (1988). The flow experience and its significance for human psychology. In M. Csikszentmihalyi & I. S. Csikszentmihalyi (Eds.), *Optimal experience: Psychological studies of flow in consciousness* (pp. 15–35). Cambridge: Cambridge University Press.

Csikszentmihalyi, M. (1990). *Flow: The psychology of optimal experience.* New York: HarperPerennial.

Csikszentmihalyi, M., & Csikszentmihalyi, I. (1988). Introduction to Part IV. In M. Csikszentmihalyi & I. S. Csikszentmihalyi (Eds.), *Optimal experience: Psychological studies of flow in consciousness* (pp. 251–265). Cambridge: Cambridge University Press.

Damgaard, J. A. (1987). The inner self helper: Transcendent life within life? *Noetic Sciences Review, 5,* 24–28.

d'Aquili, E. G., & Newberg, A. B. (1999). *The mystical mind: Probing the biology of religious experience.* Minneapolis, MN: Fortress.

d'Aquili, E. G., & Newberg, A. B. (2000a). The neuropsychology of aesthetic, spiritual, and mystical states. *Zygon, 35*(1), 39–51.

d'Aquili, E., & Newberg, A. (2000b, May/June). Wired for ultimate reality: The neuropsychology of religious experience. *Science & Spirit Magazine, 11*(2), 12–13.

Dass, B. R. (1971). *Be here now.* San Cristobal, NM: Lama Foundation.

Dass, R. (1979). *Miracle of love: Stories about Neem Karoli Baba.* New York: E. P. Dutton.

De Koninck, J. (2000). Waking experiences and dreaming. In M. H. Kryger, T. Roth, & W. C. Dement (Eds.), *Principles and practice of sleep medicine* (3rd ed., pp. 502–509). Philadelphia: W. B. Saunders.

De Pascalis, V. (1999). Psychophysiological correlates of hypnosis and hypnotic susceptibility. *International Journal of Clinical and Experimental Hypnosis, 47*(2), 117–143.

Dement, W. C. (2000). History of sleep physiology and medicine. In M. H. Kryger, T. Roth, & W. C. Dement (Eds.), *Principles and practice of sleep medicine* (3rd ed., pp. 1–14). Philadelphia: W. B. Saunders.

Dennett, D. C. (1978). *Brainstorms: Philosophical essays on mind and psychology.* Montgomery, VT: Bradford.

Digman, J. M. (1990). Personality structure: Emergence of the five-factor model. *Annual Review of Psychology, 41,* 417–440.

Dinges, D. F., Whitehouse, W. G., Orne, E. C., Bloom, P. B., Carlin, M. M., et al. (1997). Self-hypnosis training as an adjunctive treatment in the management of pain associated with sickle cell disease. *International Journal of Clinical and Experimental Hypnosis, 45*(4), 417–432.

Doblin, R. (1991). Pahnke's "Good Friday experiment": A long-term follow-up and methodological critique. *Journal of Transpersonal Psychology, 23*(1), 1–28.

Domhoff, G. W. (2000). Methods and measures for the study of dream content. In M. H. Kryger, T. Roth, & W. C. Dement (Eds.), *Principles and practice of sleep medicine* (3rd ed., pp. 463–471). Philadelphia: W. B. Saunders.

Dorsey, C. M., & Bootzin, R. R. (1997). Subjective and psychophysiologic insomnia: An examination of sleep tendency and personality. *Biological Psychiatry: A Journal of Psychiatric Research, 41*(1), 209–216.

Dorsey, C. M., Lukas, S. E., & Cunningham, S. L. (1996). Fluoxetine-induced sleep disturbance in depressed patients. *Neuropsychopharmacology, 14*(6), 437–442.

Dossey, L. (1992). Era III medicine: The next frontier. *ReVision: A Journal of Consciousness and Transformation, 14*(3), 128–139.

Dywan, J., & Bowers, K. (1983). The use of hypnosis to enhance recall. *Science, 222*(4620), 184–185.

Eccles, J. C. (Ed.). (1966). *Brain and conscious experience: Study week September 28 to October 4, 1964, of the Pontificia Academia Scientiarum.* New York: Springer-Verlag.

Ehrenwald, J. (1974). Out-of-the-body experiences and the denial of death. *Journal of Nervous and Mental Disease, 159*(4), 227–233.

Emrich, H. M., Leweke, F. M., & Schneider, U. (1997). Towards a cannabinoid hypothesis of schizophrenia: Cognitive impairments due to dysregulation of the endogenous cannabinoid system. *Pharmacology Biochemistry and Behavior, 56*(4), 803–807.

Erickson, M. H. (1979). Self-exploration in the hypnotic state. In D. Goleman & R. J. Davidson (Eds.), *Consciousness: Brain, states of awareness, and mysticism* (pp. 155–158). New York: Harper & Row.

Everson, C. A. (1997). Clinical manifestations of prolonged sleep deprivation. In M. Fisher (Series Ed.) & W. J. Schwartz (Vol. Ed.), *Monographs in clinical neuroscience: Vol. 15. Sleep science: Integrating basic research and clinical practice* (pp. 34–59). Basel, Switzerland: Karger.

Ewin, D. M., Levitan, A. A., & Lynch, D. F., Jr. (1999). Comment on "Self-hypnosis as anesthesia for liposuction surgery." *American Journal of Clinical Hypnosis, 41*(4), 302.

Farthing, G. W. (1992). *The psychology of consciousness.* Englewood Cliffs, NJ: Prentice Hall.

Feinberg-Moss, B. B., & Oatley, K. (1990). Guided imagery in brief psychodynamic therapy: Outcome and process. *British Journal of Medical Psychology, 63,* 117–129.

Fenwick, P., & Fenwick, E. (1995). *The truth in the light: An investigation of over 300 near-death experiences*. New York: Berkeley.

Fenwick, P., & Fenwick, E. (1999). *Past lives: An investigation into reincarnation memories*. London: Headline.

Ferracuti, S., Sacco, R., & Lazzari, R. (1996). Dissociative trance disorder: Clinical and Rorschach findings in ten persons reporting demon possession and treated by exorcism. *Journal of Personality Assessment, 66*(3), 525–539.

Ferrucci, P. (1982). *What we may be: Techniques for psychological and spiritual growth through psychosynthesis*. Los Angeles: Jeremy P. Tarcher.

Fiorella, D., Helsley, S., Lorrain, D. S., Rabin, R. A., & Winter, J. C. (1995). The role of the 5-HT$_{2A}$ and 5-HT$_{2C}$ receptors in the stimulus effects of hallucinogenic drugs III: The mechanistic basis for supersensitivity to the LSD stimulus following serotonin depletion. *Psychopharmacology, 121*, 364–372.

Flanagan, O. (1992). *Consciousness reconsidered*. Cambridge, MA: MIT Press.

Forte, R. (1997a). Introduction. In R. Forte (Ed.), *Entheogens and the future of religion* (pp. 1–5). San Francisco: Council on Spiritual Practices.

Forte, R. (1997b). Psychedelic experience and spiritual practice: A Buddhist perspective: An interview with Jack Kornfield. In R. Forte (Ed.), *Entheogens and the future of religion* (pp. 119–135). San Francisco: Council on Spiritual Practices.

Foulkes, D. (1966). *The psychology of sleep*. New York: Charles Scribner's Sons.

Foulkes, D. (1985). *Dreaming: A cognitive-psychological analysis*. Hillsdale, NJ: Erlbaum.

Foulkes, D. (1990). Dreaming and consciousness. *European Journal of Cognitive Psychology, 2*(1), 39–55.

Foulkes, D. (1996). Dream research: 1953–1993. *Sleep, 19*(8), 609–624.

Fox, C. (2000, March). The search for extraterrestrial life. *Life*, 46–51, 54, 56.

Frank, N. C., Spirito, A., Stark, L., & Owens-Stively, J. (1997). The use of scheduled awakenings to eliminate childhood sleepwalking. *Journal of Pediatric Psychology, 22*(3), 345–353.

Frankel, F. H., & Covino, N. A. (1997). Hypnosis and hypnotherapy. In P. S. Appelbaum, L. A. Uyehara, & M. R. Elin (Eds.), *Trauma and memory: Clinical and legal controversies* (pp. 344–359). New York: Oxford University Press.

Frankl, V. E. (1984). *Man's search for meaning* (Rev. ed.). New York: Washington Square. (Original work published 1946)

Frankl, V. E. (1997). *Man's search for ultimate meaning*. New York: Insight. (Original work published 1948)

Frankl, V. E. (1997). *Victor Frankl—Recollections: An autobiography* (J. Fabry & J. Fabry, Trans.). New York: Insight. (Original work published 1995)

Freedman, T. B. (1997). Past life and interlife reports of phobic people: Patterns and outcome. *The Journal of Regression Therapy, 11*(1), 91–94.

Freud, S. (1950). *The interpretation of dreams* (A. A. Brill, Trans.). New York: Random House. (Original work published 1900)

Gardner, E. L., & Lowinson, J. H. (1991). Marijuana's interaction with brain reward systems: Update 1991. *Pharmacology Biochemistry & Behavior, 40*(3), 571–580.

Gescheider, G. A. (1985). *Psychophysics: Method, theory, and application* (2nd ed.). Hillsdale, NJ: Erlbaum.

Giannelli, P. C. (1995). The admissibility of hypnotic evidence in U.S. courts. *International Journal of Clinical and Experimental Hypnosis, 43*(2), 212–233.

Gifford-May, D., & Thompson, N. L. (1994). "Deep states" of meditation: Phenomenological reports of experience. *Journal of Transpersonal Psychology, 26*(2), 117–138.

Gillin, J. C., & Drummond, S. P. A. (2000). Medication and substance abuse. In M. H. Kryger, T. Roth, & W. C. Dement (Eds.), *Principles and practice of sleep medicine* (3rd ed., pp. 1176–1195). Philadelphia: W. B. Saunders.

Giorgi, A. (1987). Phenomenology and the research tradition in the psychology of the imagination. In E. L. Murray (Ed.), *Imagination and phenomenological psychology* (pp. 1–47). Pittsburgh, PA: Duquesne University Press.

Glaskin, G. M. (1974). *Windows of the mind: Discovering your past and future lives through massage and mental exercise.* New York: Delacorte.

Glaskin, G. M. (1976). *Worlds within: Probing the Christos experience.* London: Wildwood House.

Glaskin, G. M. (1979). *A door to eternity: Proving the Christos experience.* London: Wildwood House.

Glennon, R. A., Titeler, M., & McKenney, J. D. (1984). Evidence for 5-HT$_2$ involvement in the mechanism of action of hallucinogenic agents. *Life Sciences, 35,* 2505–2511.

Glickson, J. (1989). The structure of subjective experience: Interdependencies along the sleep–wakefulness continuum. *Journal of Mental Imagery, 13*(2), 99–106.

Goldberg, B. (1997). *The search for Grace.* St. Paul, MN: Llewellyn.

Goldblatt, R. (1979). *Topoi: The categorial analysis of logic.* Amsterdam: North-Holland.

Goldstein, M. S., & Sipprelle, C. N. (1970). Hypnotically induced amnesia versus ablation of memory. *International Journal of Clinical and Experimental Hypnosis, 18*(3), 211–216.

Goleman, D. (1988). *The meditative mind: The varieties of meditative experience.* Los Angeles: Jeremy P. Tarcher. (Original work published 1977)

Gorassini, D. R., & Spanos, N. P. (1986). A social–cognitive skills approach to the successful modification of hypnotic susceptibility. *Journal of Personality and Social Psychology, 50*(5), 1004–1012.

Graffin, N. F., Ray, W. J., & Lundy, R. (1995). EEG concomitants of hypnosis and hypnotic susceptibility. *Journal of Abnormal Psychology, 104*(1), 123–131.

Graham, K. R. (1986). Explaining "virtuoso" hypnotic performance: Social psychology or experiential skill? *Behavioral and Brain Sciences, 9*(3), 473–474.

Gravitz, M. A. (1995). Inability to dehypnotize—Implications for management: A brief communication. *International Journal of Clinical and Experimental Hypnosis*, 43(4), 369–374.

Greyson, B. (1994). Reduced death threat in near-death experiencers. In R. A. Neimeyer (Ed.), *Death anxiety handbook: Research, instrumentation, and application* (pp. 169–179). Washington, DC: Taylor & Francis.

Greyson, B. (1996). Distance healing of patients with major depression. *Journal of Scientific Exploration*, 10(4), 447–465.

Greyson, B. (1998). The incidence of near-death experiences. *Medicine & Psychiatry*, 1, 92–99.

Greyson, B. (2000). Near-death experiences. In E. Cardeña, S. J. Lynn, & S. Krippner (Eds.), *Varieties of anomalous experience: Examining the scientific evidence* (pp. 315–352). Washington, DC: American Psychological Association.

Greyson, B., & Bush, N. E. (1992). Distressing near-death experiences. *Psychiatry: Interpersonal and Biological Processes*, 55(1), 95–110.

Grinspoon, L. (1971). *Marihuana reconsidered*. Cambridge, MA: Harvard University Press.

Grinspoon, L., & Bakalar, J. B. (1979). *Psychedelic drugs reconsidered*. New York: Basic.

Grinspoon, L., & Bakalar, J. B. (1997). *Psychedelic drugs reconsidered*. New York: Lindesmith Center. (Original work published 1979)

Grob, C., & Harman, W. (1995). Making sense of the psychedelic issue. *Noetic Sciences Review*, 35, 4–9, 37–41.

Grof, S. (1987). Survival of consciousness after death: Myth and science. In J. S. Spong (Ed.), *Consciousness and survival: An interdisciplinary inquiry into the possibility of life beyond biological death* (pp. 135–164). Sausalito, CA: Institute of Noetic Sciences.

Grof, S., & Halifax, J. (1978). *The human encounter with death*. New York: E. P. Dutton.

Grond, M., Pawlik, G., Walter, H., Lesch, O. M., & Heiss, W.-D. (1995). Hypnotic catalepsy-induced changes of regional cerebral glucose metabolism. *Psychiatry Research: Neuroimaging*, 61(3), 173–179.

Grossinger, R. (1989). Giving them a name. *ReVision: The Journal of Consciousness and Change*, 11(4), 43–48.

Grunstein, R., & Sullivan, C. (2000). Continuous positive airway pressure for sleep breathing disorders. In M. H. Kryger, T. Roth, & W. C. Dement (Eds.), *Principles and practice of sleep medicine* (3rd ed., pp. 894–912). Philadelphia: W. B. Saunders.

Guilleminault, C., & Anagnos, A. (2000). Narcolepsy. In M. H. Kryger, T. Roth, & W. C. Dement (Eds.), *Principles and practice of sleep medicine* (3rd ed., pp. 676–686). Philadelphia: W. B. Saunders.

Halifax, J. (1990). The shaman's initiation. *ReVision: The Journal of Consciousness and Change, 13*(2), 53–58.

Hall, H., Minnes, L., & Olness, K. (1993). The psychophysiology of voluntary immunomodulation. *International Journal of Neuroscience, 69,* 221–234.

Hall, H. R., Minnes, L., Tosi, M., & Olness, K. (1992). Voluntary modulation of neutrophil adhesiveness using a cyberphysiologic strategy. *International Journal of Neuroscience, 63,* 287–297.

Hall, J. A. (1977). *Clinical uses of dreams: Jungian interpretations and enactments.* New York: Grune & Stratton.

Hanson, S. J., & Burr, D. J. (1990). What connectionist models learn: Learning and representation in connectionist networks. *Behavioral and Brain Sciences, 13*(3), 471–489.

Hardy, J. (1987). *A psychology with a soul: Psychosynthesis in evolutionary context.* London: Arkana.

Harman, W. (1994). Past lives put to present use. *Noetic Sciences Review, 29,* 20–22.

Harman, W., & Rheingold, H. (1984). *Higher creativity: Liberating the unconscious for breakthrough insights.* Los Angeles: Jeremy P. Tarcher.

Harrison, J. R., & Barabasz, A. F. (1991). Effects of restricted environmental stimulation therapy on the behavior of children with autism. *Child Study Journal, 21*(3), 153–166.

Haskell, R. E. (1986). Cognitive psychology and dream research: Historical, conceptual, and epistemological considerations. *Journal of Mind and Behavior, 7*(2 & 3), 131–159.

Hastings, A. (1988). Exceptional abilities in channeling. *Noetic Sciences Review, 6,* 27–29.

Hastings, A. (1991). *With the tongues of men and angels: A study of channeling.* Fort Worth, TX: Holt, Rinehart and Winston.

Hauri, P. J. (2000). Primary insomnia. In M. H. Kryger, T. Roth, & W. C. Dement (Eds.), *Principles and practice of sleep medicine* (3rd ed., pp. 633–639). Philadelphia: W. B. Saunders.

Heap, M. (1995). A case of death following stage hypnosis: Analysis and implications. *Contemporary Hypnosis, 12*(2), 99–110.

Heintz, L. M., & Baruss, I. (2001). Spirituality in late adulthood. *Psychological Reports, 88,* 651–654.

Heron, W. (1957). The pathology of boredom. *Scientific American, 196*(1), 52–56.

Hibler, N. S. (1995). Using hypnosis for investigative purposes. In M. I. Kurke & E. M. Scrivner (Eds.), *Police psychology into the 21st century* (pp. 319–336). Hillsdale, NJ: Erlbaum.

Hilgard, E. R. (1973a). The domain of hypnosis: With some comments on alternative paradigms. *American Psychologist, 28*(11), 972–982.

Hilgard, E. R. (1973b). A neodissociation interpretation of pain reduction in hypnosis. *Psychological Review, 80*(5), 396–411.

Hilgard, E. R. (1979). The hypnotic state. In D. Goleman & R. J. Davidson (Eds.), *Consciousness: Brain, states of awareness, and mysticism* (pp. 147–150). New York: Harper & Row.

Hilgard, E. R. (1980). Consciousness in contemporary psychology. *Annual Review of Psychology, 31,* 1–26.

Hilgard, E. R. (1987). *Psychology in America: A historical survey.* San Diego, CA: Harcourt Brace Jovanovich.

Hill, C. E. (1996). Dreams and therapy. *Psychotherapy Research, 6*(1), 1–15.

Hill, C. E., & Rochlen, A. B. (1999). A cognitive–experiential model for working with dreams in psychotherapy. In L. Vandecreek & T. L. Jackson (Eds.), *Innovations in clinical practice: A source book* (pp. 467–480). Sarasota, FL: Professional Resource Press.

Hill, O. W., Jr. (1987). Intuition: Inferential heuristic or epistemic mode? *Imagination, Cognition and Personality, 7*(2), 137–154.

Hirsch, H. V. B., & Spinelli, D. N. (1971). Modification of the distribution of receptive field orientation in cats by selective visual exposure during development. *Experimental Brain Research, 12,* 509–527.

Hirshkowitz, M., & Moore, C. A. (2000). Computers in sleep medicine. In M. H. Kryger, T. Roth, & W. C. Dement (Eds.), *Principles and practice of sleep medicine* (3rd ed., pp. 1302–1307). Philadelphia: W. B. Saunders.

Hirshkowitz, M., Moore, C. A., & Minhoto, G. (1997). The basics of sleep. In M. R. Pressman & W. C. Orr (Eds.), *Understanding sleep: The evaluation and treatment of sleep disorders* (pp. 11–34). Washington, DC: American Psychological Association.

Hobson, J. A. (1988). *The dreaming brain.* New York: Basic.

Hobson, J. A. (1990). Dreams and the brain. In S. Krippner (Ed.), *Dreamtime and dreamwork: Decoding the language of the night* (pp. 215–223). Los Angeles: Jeremy P. Tarcher.

Hobson, J. A. (1997). Consciousness as a state-dependent phenomenon. In J. D. Cohen & J. W. Schooler (Eds.), *Scientific approaches to consciousness* (pp. 379–396). Mahwah, NJ: Erlbaum.

Hobson, J. A., & McCarley, R. W. (1977). The brain as a dream state generator: An activation-synthesis hypothesis of the dream process. *American Journal of Psychiatry, 134*(12), 1335–1348.

Hobson, J. A., Pace-Schott, E. F., & Stickgold, R. (2000). Consciousness: Its vicissitudes in waking and sleep. In M. S. Gazzaniga (Ed. in chief), *The new cognitive neurosciences* (2nd ed. pp. 1341–1354). Cambridge, MA: MIT Press.

Hock, R. R. (1999). *Forty studies that changed psychology: Explorations into the history of psychological research* (3rd ed.). Upper Saddle River, NJ: Prentice Hall.

Hoffer, A. (2000). Treating mental illness with psychedelics. *MAPS: Bulletin of the Multidisciplinary Association for Psychedelic Studies, 10*(3), 20.

Hofmann, A. (1980). *LSD: My problem child* (J. Ott, Trans.). New York: McGraw-Hill. (Original work published 1979)

Hofstadter, D. R. (1979). *Gödel, Escher, Bach: An eternal golden braid*. New York: Basic.

Hollister, L. E., & Sjoberg, B. M. (1964). Clinical syndromes and biochemical alterations following mescaline, lysergic acid diethylamide, psilocybin and a combination of the three psychotomimetic drugs. *Comprehensive Psychiatry, 5*(3), 170–178.

Holyoak, K. J., & Spellman, B. A. (1993). Thinking. *Annual Review of Psychology, 44*, 265–315.

Honorton, C. (1974). Tracing ESP through altered states of consciousness. In J. White (Ed.), *Frontiers of consciousness: The meeting ground between inner and outer reality* (pp. 159–168). New York: Julian.

Hood, R. W., Jr., Spilka, B., Hunsberger, B., & Gorsuch, R. (1996). *The psychology of religion: An empirical approach* (2nd ed.). New York: Guilford Press.

Hopkins, B. (2000). Hypnosis and the investigation of UFO abduction accounts. In D. M. Jacobs (Ed.), *UFOs and abductions: Challenging the borders of knowledge* (pp. 215–240). Lawrence: University Press of Kansas.

Horne, J. (1988). *Why we sleep: The functions of sleep in humans and other mammals*. Oxford: Oxford University Press.

Horstmann, S., Hess, C. W., Bassetti, C., Gugger, M., & Mathis, J. (2000). Sleepiness-related accidents in sleep apnea patients. *Sleep, 23*(3), 383–389.

Houran, J., & Lange, R. (1998). Modeling precognitive dreams as meaningful coincidences. *Psychological Reports, 83*, 1411–1414.

Howe, R. B. K. (1991a). Introspection: A reassessment. *New Ideas in Psychology, 9*(1), 25–44.

Howe, R. B. K. (1991b). Reassessing introspection: A reply to Natsoulas, Lyons, and Ericsson and Crutcher. *New Ideas in Psychology, 9*(3), 383–394.

Hughes, D. J. (1992). Differences between trance channeling and multiple personality disorder on structured interview. *Journal of Transpersonal Psychology, 24*(2), 181–192.

Hunt, H. T. (1986). Some relations between the cognitive psychology of dreams and dream phenomenology. *Journal of Mind and Behavior, 7*(2&3), 213–228.

Hurley, T. J., III. (1985a). Etiology of multiple personality: From abuse to alter personalities. *Institute of Noetic Sciences: Investigations: A Research Bulletin, 1*(3/4), 11–13.

Hurley, T. J., III. (1985b). Glossary of key concepts. *Institute of Noetic Sciences: Investigations: A Research Bulletin, 1*(3/4), 22.

Hurley, T. J., III. (1985c). Inner faces of multiplicity: Contemporary look at a classic mystery. *Institute of Noetic Sciences: Investigations: A Research Bulletin, 1*(3/4), 3–6.

Hurley, T. J., III. (1985d). Multiplicity & the mind–body problem: New windows to natural plasticity. *Institute of Noetic Sciences: Investigations: A Research Bulletin, 1*(3/4), 19–21.

Hurley, T. J., III. (1985e). Possession, dynamic psychiatry & science: The historical fortunes of MPD. *Institute of Noetic Sciences: Investigations: A Research Bulletin, 1*(3/4), 19–21.

Huxley, A. (1945). *The perennial philosophy*. New York: Harper & Brothers.

Hyman, R. (1994). Anomaly or artifact? Comments on Bem and Honorton. *Psychological Bulletin, 115*(1), 19–24.

Hyman, R. (2001). Anomalous experiences in a mundane world. *Contemporary Psychology, 46*(5), 453–456.

Irwin, H. J. (1994). *An introduction to parapsychology* (2nd ed.). Jefferson, NC: McFarland.

Jackendoff, R. (1987). *Consciousness and the computational mind*. Cambridge, MA: MIT Press.

Jacobs, B. L. (1987). How hallucinogenic drugs work. *American Scientist, 75*(4), 386–392.

Jacobs, D. M. (1998). *The threat*. New York: Simon & Schuster.

Jahn, R. G. (2001). 20th and 21st century science: Reflections and projections. *Journal of Scientific Exploration, 15*(1), 21–31.

Jahn, R. G., & Dunne, B. J. (1987). *Margins of reality: The role of consciousness in the physical world*. San Diego, CA: Harcourt Brace Jovanovich.

James, E. (2001). *Personality correlates of beliefs about consciousness and reality*. Unpublished bachelor's thesis, University of Regina, Regina, Saskatchewan, Canada.

James, W. (1983). *The principles of psychology*. Cambridge, MA: Harvard University Press. (Original work published 1890)

Japp, F. R. (1898). Kekulé memorial lecture. *Journal of the Chemical Society: Transactions, 73*, 97–138.

Jeans, J. (1937). *The mysterious universe* (New rev. ed.). New York: MacMillan.

Jevning, R. A., & O'Halloran, J. P. (1984). Metabolic effects of transcendental meditation: Toward a new paradigm of neurobiology. In D. H. Shapiro, Jr., & R. N. Walsh (Eds.), *Meditation: Classic and contemporary perspectives* (pp. 465–472). Hawthorne, NY: Aldine.

Jewkes, S., & Baruš, I. (2000). Personality correlates of beliefs about consciousness and reality. *Advanced Development: A Journal on Adult Giftedness, 9*, 91–103.

Johnson, C. P. L., & Persinger, M. A. (1994). The sensed presence may be facilitated by interhemispheric intercalation: Relative efficacy of The Mind's Eye, Hemi-Sync Tape, and bilateral temporal magnetic field stimulation. *Perceptual & Motor Skills, 79*, 351–354.

Jones, R. T. (1971). Tetrahydrocannabinol and the marijuana-induced social "high," or the effects of the mind on marijuana. In A. J. Singer (Vol. Ed.), *Annals of the New York Academy of Sciences: Vol. 191. Marijuana: Chemistry, pharmacology, and patterns of social use* (pp. 155–165). New York: New York Academy of Sciences.

Jones, R. T., & Benowitz, N. (1976). The 30-day trip—Clinical studies of cannabis tolerance and dependence. In M. C. Braude & S. Szara (Eds.), *A monograph* of the *National Institute on drug abuse: Vol. 2. Pharmacology of marihuana* (pp. 627–642). New York: Raven.

Jouvet, M. (1999). *The paradox of sleep: The story of dreaming* (L. Garey, Trans.). Cambridge, MA: Bradford. (Original work published 1993)

Jue, R. W. (1996). Past-life therapy. In B. W. Scotton, A. B. Chinen, & J. R. Battista (Eds.), *Textbook of transpersonal psychiatry and psychology* (pp. 377–387). New York: BasicBooks.

Jung, C. G. (1965). *Memories, dreams, reflections* (Rev. ed.). (A. Jaffé, Recorder & Ed.; R. Winston & C. Winston, Trans.). New York: Vintage.

Jung, C. G. (1969). *The structure and dynamics of the psyche* (2nd ed.). In W. McGuire (Executive Ed.), H. Read, M. Fordham, & G. Adler (Eds.), & R. F. C. Hull (Trans.), *The collected works of C. G. Jung: Vol. 8*. Princeton, NJ: Princeton University Press. (Original work written 1916 to 1965)

Jung, C. G. (1971). *Psychological types*. In W. McGuire (Executive Ed.), H. Read, M. Fordham, & G. Adler (Eds.), H. G. Baynes (Trans.), & R. F. C. Hull (Revisor of English trans.), *The collected works of C. G. Jung: Vol. 6*. Princeton, NJ: Princeton University Press. (Original work without appendix published 1921)

Kahn, D., Krippner, S., & Combs, A. (2000). Dreaming and the self-organizing brain. *Journal of Consciousness Studies, 7*(7), 4–11.

Kales, A., & Kales, J. D. (1984). *Evaluation and treatment of insomnia*. New York: Oxford University Press.

Kalia, M., O'Callaghan, J. P., Miller, D. B., & Kramer, M. (2000). Comparative study of fluoxetine, sibutramine, sertraline and dexfenfluramine on the morphology of serotonergic nerve terminals using serotonin immunohistochemistry. *Brain Research, 858*, 92–105.

Katz, S. T. (1978). Language, epistemology, and mysticism. In S. T. Katz (Ed.), *Mysticism and philosophical analysis* (pp. 22–74). New York: Oxford University Press.

Keen, M. (2001). The Scole investigation: A study in critical analysis of paranormal physical phenomena. *Journal of Scientific Exploration, 15*(2), 167–182.

Keen, M., Ellison, A., & Fontana, D. (1999). The Scole report: An account of an investigation into the genuineness of a range of physical phenomena associated with a mediumistic group in Norfolk, England. *Proceedings of the Society for Psychical Research, 58* (Pt. 220), 149–392.

Kellehear, A. (1993). Culture, biology, and the near-death experience: A reappraisal. *Journal of Nervous and Mental Disease, 181*(3), 148–156.

Kellehear, A. (1996). *Experiences near death: Beyond medicine and religion*. New York: Oxford University Press.

Kelly, S. F., & Kelly, R. J. (1995). *Imagine yourself well: Better health through self-hypnosis*. New York: Plenum Press.

Kerr, N. H. (2000). Dreaming, imagery, and perception. In M. H. Kryger, T. Roth, & W. C. Dement (Eds.), *Principles and practice of sleep medicine* (3rd ed., pp. 482–490). Philadelphia: W. B. Saunders.

Kihlstrom, J. F. (1985). Hypnosis. *Annual Review of Psychology, 36,* 385–418.

King, W., Jr., & Ellison, G. (1989). Long-lasting alterations in behavior and brain neurochemistry following continuous low-level LSD administration. *Pharmacology Biochemistry & Behavior, 33,* 69–73.

Kinney, J., & Smoley, R. (1993). The Gnosis interview: Ram Dass. *Gnosis: A Journal of the Western Inner Traditions, 26,* 42–50.

Kirsch, I., & Lynn, S. J. (1995). The altered state of hypnosis: Changes in the theoretical landscape. *American Psychologist, 50*(10), 846–858.

Klimo, J. (1987). *Channeling: Investigations on receiving information from paranormal sources.* Los Angeles: Jeremy P. Tarcher.

Klinger, E. (1971). *Structure and functions of fantasy.* New York: Wiley-Interscience.

Klinger, E. (1978). Modes of normal conscious flow. In K. S. Pope & J. L. Singer (Eds.), *The stream of consciousness: Scientific investigations into the flow of human experience* (225–258). New York: Plenum Press.

Klinger, E. (1990). *Daydreaming: Using waking fantasy and imagery for self-knowledge and creativity.* Los Angeles: Jeremy P. Tarcher.

Klinger, E. (1999). Thought flow: Properties and mechanisms underlying shifts in content. In J. A. Singer & P. Salovey (Eds.), *At play in the fields of consciousness: Essays in honor of Jerome L. Singer* (pp. 29–50). Mahwah, NJ: Erlbaum.

Klinger, E. (2000). Daydreams. In A. E. Kazdin (Ed. in Chief) *Encyclopedia of psychology: Vol. 2.* Washington, DC, and New York: American Psychological Association and Oxford University Press.

Klinger E., & Cox, W. M. (1987). Dimensions of thought flow in everyday life. *Imagination, Cognition and Personality, 7*(2), 105–128.

Klinger, E., & Kroll-Mensing, D. (1995). Idiothetic assessment experience sampling and motivational analysis. In J. N. Butcher (Ed.), *Clinical personality assessment: Practical approaches,* (pp. 267–277). New York: Oxford University Press.

Kluft, R. P. (1996). Dissociative Identity Disorder. In L. K. Michelson & W. J. Ray (Eds.), *Handbook of dissociation: Theoretical, empirical, and clinical perspectives* (pp. 337–366). New York: Plenum Press.

Knight, Z. (1995). The healing power of the unconscious: How can we understand past life experiences in psychotherapy? *South African Journal of Psychology, 25*(2), 90–98.

Knox, V. J., Morgan, A. H., & Hilgard, E. R. (1974). Pain and suffering in ischemia: The paradox of hypnotically suggested anesthesia as contradicted by reports from the "hidden observer." *Archives of General Psychiatry, 30,* 840–847.

Koriat, A. (2000). The feeling of knowing: Some metatheoretical implications for consciousness and control. *Consciousness and Cognition, 9,* 149–171.

Kornfield, J. (1990). On meditation and the Western mind. *Noetic Sciences Review, 17,* 11–17.

Krebs, K. M., & Geyer, M. A. (1994). Cross-tolerance studies of serotonin receptors involved in behavioral effects of LSD in rats. *Psychopharmacology, 113*, 429–437.

Krippner, S. (1981). Access to hidden reserves of the unconscious through dreams in creative problem solving. *Journal of Creative Behavior, 15*(1), 11–22.

Krippner, S. (1993). The Maimonides esp-dream studies. *Journal of Parapsychology, 57*, 39–54.

Krippner, S. (1994). Cross-cultural treatment perspectives on dissociative disorders. In S. J. Lynn & J. W. Rhue (Eds.), *Dissociation: Clinical and theoretical perspectives* (pp. 338–361). New York: Guilford Press.

Krippner, S. (1997). The varieties of dissociative experience. In S. Krippner & S. M. Powers (Eds.), *Broken images, broken selves: Dissociative narratives in clinical practice* (pp. 336–361). Bristol, PA: Brunner/Mazel.

Krippner, S. (1999). The varieties of hypnotic experience. *Contemporary Hypnosis, 16*(3), 157–159.

Krippner, S., & Achterberg, J. (2000). Anomalous healing experiences. *Varieties of anomalous experience: Examining the scientific evidence* (pp. 353–395). Washington, DC: American Psychological Association.

Krippner, S., & Combs, A. (2002). The neurophenomenology of shamanism: An essay review. *Journal of Consciousness Studies, 9*(3), 77–82.

Krippner, S., & Dillard, J. (1988). *Dreamworking: How to use your dreams for creative problem-solving.* Buffalo, NY: Bearly.

Krippner, S., & George, L. (1986). Psi phenomena as related to altered states of consciousness. In B. B. Wolman & M. Ullman (Eds.), *Handbook of states of consciousness* (pp. 332–364). New York: Van Nostrand Reinhold.

Kryger, M. H. (2000). Monitoring respiratory and cardiac function. In M. H. Kryger, T. Roth, & W. C. Dement (Eds.), *Principles and practice of sleep medicine* (3rd ed., pp. 1217–1230). Philadelphia: W. B. Saunders.

Krystal, J. H., Bennett, A., Bremner, J. D., Southwick, S. M., & Charney, D. S. (1996). Recent developments in the neurobiology of dissociation: Implications for posttraumatic stress disorder. In L. K. Michelson & W. J. Ray (Eds.), *Handbook of dissociation: Theoretical, empirical, and clinical perspectives* (pp. 163–190). New York: Plenum Press.

Kurtz, P. (Ed.). (1985). *A skeptic's handbook of parapsychology.* Buffalo, NY: Prometheus.

LaBerge, S. (1990a). Lucid dreaming: Psychophysiological studies of consciousness during REM sleep. In R. R. Bootzin, J. F. Kihlstrom, & D. L. Schacter (Eds.), *Sleep and cognition* (pp. 109–126). Washington, DC: American Psychological Association.

LaBerge, S. (1990b, Winter). Naps: The best time for lucid dreaming? *NightLight: The Lucidity Institute Newsletter, 2*(1), 5–8.

LaBerge, S., & Gackenbach, J. (1986). Lucid dreaming. In B. B. Wolman & M. Ullman (Eds.), *Handbook of states of consciousness* (pp. 159–198). New York: Van Nostrand Reinhold.

LaBerge, S., & Gackenbach, J. (2000). Lucid dreaming. In E. Cardeña, S. J. Lynn, & S. Krippner (Eds.), *Varieties of anomalous experience: Examining the scientific evidence* (pp. 151–182). Washington, DC: American Psychological Association.

LaBerge, S., & Rheingold, H. (1990). *Exploring the world of lucid dreaming*. New York: Ballantine.

Lambert, S. A. (1996). The effects of hypnosis/guided imagery on the postoperative course of children. *Journal of Developmental and Behavioral Pediatrics, 17*(5), 307–310.

Lambie, J. A., & Marcel, A. J. (2002). Consciousness and the varieties of emotion experience: A theoretical framework. *Psychological Review, 109*(2), 219–259.

Lammer, H., & Lammer, M. (1999). *MILABS: Military mind control & alien abduction*. Lilburn, GA: IllumiNet.

Lavigne, Y. (1999). *Death dealers: Cocaine from Colombia, heroin from Asia, crack cocaine from the kid next door: The true story of how drugs hit the streets and who pays the price*. Toronto: HarperCollins.

Leary, T. (1970). *The politics of ecstasy*. St. Albans, UK: Paladin. (Original work published 1965)

Lester, D. S., Felder, C. C., & Lewis, E. N. (Eds.). (1997). *Annals of the New York Academy of Sciences, Vol. 820. Imaging brain structure and function: Emerging technologies in the neurosciences*. New York: New York Academy of Sciences.

Levinthal, C. F. (1996). *Drugs, behavior, and modern society*. Boston: Allyn and Bacon.

Levitan, L., & LaBerge, S. (1990, Fall). Beyond nightmares: Lucid resourcefulness vs helpless depression. *NightLight: The Lucidity Institute Newsletter, 2*(4), 1–3, 9–11.

Leviton, R. (1992, July/Aug.). Through the shaman's doorway: Dreaming the universe with Fred Alan Wolf. *Yoga Journal*, 48–55, 102.

Libet, B., Freeman, A., & Sutherland, K. (1999). Editors' introduction: The volitional brain: Towards a neuroscience of free will. *Journal of Consciousness Studies, 6*(8–9), ix–xxii.

Liechti, M. E., Baumann, C., Gamma, A., & Vollenweider, F. X. (2000). Acute psychological effects of 3, 4-methylenedioxymethamphetamine (MDMA, "ecstasy") are attenuated by the serotonin uptake inhibitor citalopram. *Neuropsychopharmacology, 22*(5), 513–521.

Lilly, J. C. (1978). *The scientist: A novel autobiography*. Philadelphia: J. B. Lippincott.

Lindbergh, C. A. (1953). *The Spirit of St. Louis*. New York: Charles Scribner's Sons.

Lipson, M. (1987). Objective experience. *Noûs, 21*, 319–343.

Lockwood, M. (1989). *Mind, brain & the quantum: The compound 'I.'* Oxford: Blackwell.

Lucas, W. B. (1993). *Regression therapy: A handbook for professionals. Vol. 1: Past-life therapy.* Crest Park, CA: Deep Forest.

Ludwig, A. M. (1966). Altered states of consciousness. *Archives of General Psychiatry, 15,* 225–234.

Ludwig, A. M., Levine, J., & Stark, L. H. (1970). *LSD and alcoholism: A clinical study of treatment efficacy.* Springfield, IL: Charles C. Thomas.

Lukoff, D. (1985). The diagnosis of mystical experiences with psychotic features. *Journal of Transpersonal Psychology, 17*(2), 155–181.

Lukoff, D., & Everest, H. C. (1985). The myths in mental illness. *Journal of Transpersonal Psychology, 17*(2), 123–153.

Lycan, W. G. (1987). *Consciousness.* Cambridge, MA: MIT Press.

Lynn, S. J., Kirsch, I., Barabasz, A., Cardeña, E., & Patterson, D. (2000). Hypnosis as an empirically supported clinical intervention: The state of the evidence and a look to the future. *International Journal of Clinical and Experimental Hypnosis, 48*(2), 239–259.

Lynn, S. J., Pintar, J., & Rhue, J. W. (1997). Fantasy proneness, dissociation, and narrative construction. In S. Krippner & S. M. Powers (Eds.), *Broken images, broken selves: Dissociative narratives in clinical practice* (pp. 274–302). Bristol, PA: Brunner/Mazel.

Lynn, S. J., & Rhue, J. W. (1988). Fantasy proneness: Hypnosis, developmental antecedents, and psychopathology. *American Psychologist, 43*(1), 35–44.

Lyons, W. (1986). *The disappearance of introspection.* Cambridge, MA: MIT Press.

Mac Lane, S., & Moerdijk, I. (1992). *Sheaves in geometry and logic: A first introduction to topos theory.* New York: Springer-Verlag.

MacDonald, D. A. (1997). *The development of a comprehensive factor analytically derived measure of spirituality and its relationship to psychological functioning.* Unpublished doctoral dissertation, University of Windsor, Windsor, Ontario, Canada.

MacDonald, D. A. (2000). Spirituality: Description, measurement, and relation to the five factor model of personality. *Journal of Personality, 68*(1), 153–197.

Mack, J. E. (1994a). *Abduction: Human encounters with aliens* (Rev. ed.). New York: Ballantine.

Mack, J. E. (1994b). Why the abduction phenomenon cannot be explained psychiatrically. In A. Pritchard, D. E. Pritchard, J. E. Mack, P. Kasey, & C. Yapp (Eds.), *Alien discussions: Proceedings of the abduction study conference held at MIT, Cambridge, MA* (pp. 372–374). Cambridge, MA: North Cambridge.

Mack, J. E. (1999). *Passport to the cosmos: Human transformation and alien encounters.* New York: Three Rivers.

MacMartin, C., & Yarmey, A. D. (1999). Rhetoric and the recovered memory debate. *Canadian Psychology/Psychologie Canadienne, 40*(4), 343–358.

Madsen, P. L., Holm, S., Vorstrup, S., Friberg, L., Lassen, N. A., et al. (1991). Human regional cerebral blood flow during rapid-eye-movement sleep. *Journal of Cerebral Blood Flow and Metabolism, 11,* 502–507.

Mai, F. M. (1995). Psychiatrists' attitudes to multiple personality disorder: A questionnaire study. *Canadian Journal of Psychiatry, 40,* 154–157.

Malamud, J. R. (1986). Becoming lucid in dreams and waking life. In B. B. Wolman & M. Ullman (Eds.), *Handbook of states of consciousness* (pp. 590–612). New York: Van Nostrand Reinhold.

Malinoski, P. T., & Lynn, S. J. (1999). The plasticity of early memory reports: Social pressure, hypnotizability, compliance, and interrogative suggestibility. *International Journal of Clinical and Experimental Hypnosis, 47*(4), 320–345.

Malmgren, J. (1994, Nov. 27). Tune in, turn on, get well? *St. Petersburg Times,* p. 1F.

Mandell, A. J. (1980). Toward a psychobiology of transcendence: God in the brain. In J. M. Davidson & R. J. Davidson (Eds.), *The psychobiology of consciousness* (pp. 379–464) New York: Plenum Press.

Mandler, G. (1985). *Cognitive psychology: An essay in cognitive science.* Hillsdale, NJ: Erlbaum.

Mangini, M. (1998). Treatment of alcoholism using psychedelic drugs: A review of the program of research. *Journal of Psychoactive Drugs, 30*(4), 381–418.

Markman, A. B., & Gentner, D. (2001). Thinking. *Annual Review of Psychology, 52,* 223–247.

Marks, J. (1979). *The search for the "Manchurian candidate": The CIA and mind control.* New York: Times.

Maslow, A. H. (1968). *Toward a psychology of being* (2nd ed.). New York: Van Nostrand Reinhold.

Maslow. A. H. (1976). *The farther reaches of human nature.* Harmondsworth, UK: Penguin. (Original work published 1971)

Mason, P. (1994). *The Maharishi: The biography of the man who gave transcendental meditation to the world.* Shaftesbury, UK: Element.

Masters, R. E. L., & Houston, J. (1966). *The varieties of psychedelic experience.* New York: Holt, Rinehart and Winston.

Mauer, M. H., Burnett, K. F., Ouellette, E. A., Ironson, G. H., & Dandes, H. M. (1999). Medical hypnosis and orthopedic hand surgery: Pain perception, postoperative recovery, and therapeutic comfort. *International Journal of Clinical and Experimental Hypnosis, 47*(2), 144–161.

Mavromatis, A. (1987a). *Hypnagogia: The unique state of consciousness between wakefulness and sleep.* London: Routledge & Kegan Paul.

Mavromatis, A. (1987b). On shared states of consciousness and objective imagery. *Journal of Mental Imagery, 11*(2), 125–130.

Maxwell, M., & Tschudin, V. (1990). *Seeing the invisible: Modern religious and other transcendent experiences.* London: Arkana.

McAleney, P., & Barabasz, A. (1993). Effects of flotation REST and visual imagery on athletic performance: Tennis. In A. F. Barabasz & M. Barabasz (Eds.), *Clinical and experimental restricted environmental stimulation: New developments and perspectives* (pp. 79–85). New York: Springer-Verlag.

McAleney, P. J., Barabasz, A., & Barabasz, M. (1990). Effects of flotation restricted environmental stimulation on intercollegiate tennis performance. *Perceptual and Motor Skills, 71*, 1023–1028.

McCall Smith, A., & Shapiro, C. M. (1997). Sleep disorders and the criminal law. In C. Shapiro & A. McCall Smith (Eds.), *Forensic aspects of sleep* (pp. 29–64). Chichester, UK: John Wiley & Sons.

McConkey, K. M., Wende, V., & Barnier, A. J. (1999). Measuring change in the subjective experience of hypnosis. *International Journal of Clinical and Experimental Hypnosis, 47*(1), 23–39.

McFarlane, A. C., & van der Kolk, B. A. (1996). Conclusions and future directions. In B. A. van der Kolk, A. C. McFarlane, & L. Weisaeth (Eds.), *Traumatic stress: The effects of overwhelming experience on mind, body, and society* (pp. 559–575). New York: Guilford Press.

McKenna, T. (1989). A conversation over saucers. *ReVision: The Journal of Consciousness and Change, 11*(3), 23–30.

McKenna, T. (1993). *True hallucinations: Being an account of the author's extraordinary adventures in the devil's paradise.* New York: HarperSanFrancisco.

McLeod, C. C., Corbisier, B., & Mack, J. E. (1996). A more parsimonious explanation for UFO abduction. *Psychological Inquiry, 7*(2), 156–168.

Merrell-Wolff, F. (1994). *Franklin Merrell-Wolff's experience and philosophy: A personal record of transformation and a discussion of transcendental consciousness.* Albany: State University of New York Press.

Merrell-Wolff, F. (1995a). *Mathematics, philosophy & yoga: A lecture series presented at the Los Olivos Conference Room in Phoenix, Arizona, in 1966.* Phoenix, AZ: Phoenix Philosophical Press.

Merrell-Wolff, F. (1995b). *Transformations in consciousness: The metaphysics and epistemology.* Albany: State University of New York Press.

Metcalfe, J. (2000). Feelings and judgments of knowing: Is there a special noetic state? *Consciousness and Cognition, 9*, 178–186.

Metcalfe, J., & Shimamura, A. P. (Eds.). (1994). *Metacognition: Knowing about knowing.* Cambridge, MA: MIT Press.

Miller, J. G. (1994a). Envelope epidemiology. In A. Pritchard, D. E. Pritchard, J. E. Mack, P. Kasey, & C. Yapp (Eds.), *Alien discussions: Proceedings of the abduction study conference held at MIT, Cambridge, MA* (pp. 232–235). Cambridge, MA: North Cambridge.

Miller, J. G. (1994b). Medical procedural differences: Alien versus human. In A. Pritchard, D. E. Pritchard, J. E. Mack, P. Kasey, & C. Yapp (Eds.), *Alien discussions: Proceedings of the abduction study conference held at MIT, Cambridge, MA* (pp. 59–64). Cambridge, MA: North Cambridge.

Miller, J. J. (1993). The unveiling of traumatic memories and emotions through mindfulness and concentration meditation: Clinical implications and three case reports. *Journal of Transpersonal Psychology, 25*(2), 169–180.

Miller, M. F., Barabasz, A. F., & Barabasz, M. (1991). Effects of active alert and relaxation hypnotic inductions on cold pressor pain. *Journal of Abnormal Psychology, 100*(2), 223–226.

Mills, A., & Lynn, S. J. (2000). Past-life experiences. In E. Cardeña, S. J. Lynn, & S. Krippner (Eds.), *Varieties of anomalous experience: Examining the scientific evidence* (pp. 283–313). Washington, DC: American Psychological Association.

Milton, J. (1999). Should ganzfeld research continue to be crucial in the search for a replicable psi effect? Part I. Discussion paper and introduction to an electronic-mail discussion. *Journal of Parapsychology, 63,* 309–333.

Milton, J., & Wiseman, R. (1999). Does psi exist? Lack of replication of an anomalous process of information transfer. *Psychological Bulletin, 125*(4), 387–391.

Mistlberger, R. E., & Rusak, B. (2000). Circadian rhythms in mammals: Formal properties and environmental influences. In M. H. Kryger, T. Roth, & W. C. Dement (Eds.), *Principles and practice of sleep medicine* (3rd ed., pp. 321–333). Philadelphia: W. B. Saunders.

Mitchell, E. (with Williams, D.). (1996). *The way of the explorer: An Apollo astronaut's journey through the material and mystical worlds.* New York: G. P. Putnam's Sons.

Mogar, R. E. (1972). Current status and future trends in psychedelic (LSD) research. In C. T. Tart (Ed.), *Altered states of consciousness* (pp. 391–408). Garden City, NY: Anchor.

Monroe, R. A. (1994). *Ultimate journey.* New York: Doubleday.

Montgomery, G. H., DuHamel, K. N., & Redd, W. H. (2000). A meta-analysis of hypnotically induced analgesia: How effective is hypnosis? *International Journal of Clinical and Experimental Hypnosis, 48*(2), 138–153.

Montplaisir, J., Nicolas, A., Godbout, R., & Walters, A. (2000). Restless legs syndrome and periodic limb movement disorder. In M. H. Kryger, T. Roth, & W. C. Dement (Eds.), *Principles and practice of sleep medicine* (3rd ed., pp. 742–752). Philadelphia: W. B. Saunders.

Moody, R. A., Jr. (1975). *Life after life: The investigation of a phenomenon—Survival of bodily death.* Covington, GA: Bantam/Mockingbird.

Moody, R. A., Jr. (1977). *Reflections on life after life.* Covington, GA: Bantam/Mockingbird.

Moody, R. A., Jr. (1988). *The light beyond.* New York: Bantam.

Morris, S. (1984, Jan.). Games. *Omni, 6*(4), 82, 128–129.

Morse, M. (with Perry, P.). (1992). *Transformed by the light: The powerful effect of near-death experiences on people's lives.* New York: Villard.

Murphy, M., & Donovan, S. (1997). *The physical and psychological effects of meditation: A review of contemporary research with a comprehensive bibliography 1931–1996* (2nd ed.). Sausalito, CA: Institute of Noetic Sciences.

Nadel, L., & Jacobs, W. J. (1998). Traumatic memory is special. *Current Directions in Psychological Science, 7*(5), 154–157.

Naranjo, C. (1986). Drug-induced states. In B. B. Wolman & M. Ullman (Eds.), *Handbook of states of consciousness* (pp. 365–394). New York: Van Nostrand Reinhold.

Nash, M. R. (2000). The status of hypnosis as an empirically validated clinical intervention: A preamble to the special issue. *International Journal of Clinical and Experimental Hypnosis, 48*(2), 107–112.

Nashida, T., Yabe, H., Sato, Y., Hiruma, T., Sutoh, T., et al. (2000). Automatic auditory information processing in sleep. *Sleep, 23*(6), 821–828.

Natsoulas, T. (1983a). Concepts of consciousness. *Journal of Mind and Behavior, 4*(1), 13–59.

Natsoulas, T. (1983b). The experience of a conscious self. *Journal of Mind and Behavior, 4*(4), 451–478.

Natsoulas, T. (1999). A rediscovery of presence. *Journal of Mind and Behavior, 20*(1), 17–41.

Netter, F. H. (1986). *The CIBA collection of medical illustrations. Volume 1: Nervous system. Part I: Anatomy and physiology.* West Caldwell, NJ: CIBA.

Newman, L. S. (1997). Intergalactic hostages: People who report abduction by UFOs. *Journal of Social and Clinical Psychology, 16*(2), 151–177.

Newman, L. S., & Baumeister, R. F. (1996). Toward an explanation of the UFO abduction phenomenon: Hypnotic elaboration, extraterrestrial sadomasochism, and spurious memories. *Psychological Inquiry, 7*(2), 99–126.

Nichols, D. (1999). From Eleusis to PET scans: The mysteries of psychedelics. *MAPS: Bulletin of the Multidisciplinary Association for Psychedelic Studies, 9*(4), 50–55.

Nielsen, T. A. (1995). Describing and modeling hypnagogic imagery using a systematic self-observation procedure. *Dreaming, 5*(2), 75–94.

Nisbett, R. E., & Wilson, T. D. (1977). Telling more than we can know: Verbal reports on mental processes. *Psychological Review, 84*(3), 231–259.

Noble, J., & McConkey, K. M. (1995). Hypnotic sex change: Creating and challenging a delusion in the laboratory. *Journal of Abnormal Psychology, 104*(1), 69–74.

Northrop, F. S. C. (1966). *The meeting of East and West: An inquiry concerning world understanding.* New York: Collier. (Original work published 1946)

Noyes, R., Jr., & Kletti, R. (1976). Depersonalization in the face of life-threatening danger: An interpretation. *Omega, 7*(2), 103–114.

Noyes, R., Jr., & Kletti, R. (1977). Depersonalization in response to life-threatening danger. *Comprehensive Psychiatry, 18*(4), 375–384.

Olness, K., & Kohen, D. P. (1996). *Hypnosis and hypnotherapy with children* (3rd ed.). New York: Guilford Press.

Olson, J. M., & Zanna, M. P. (1993). Attitudes and attitude change. *Annual Review of Psychology, 44*, 117–154.

O'Regan, B. (1983). Psychoneuroimmunology: The birth of a new field. *Investigations: A Bulletin of the Institute of Noetic Sciences, 1*(2), 1–2.

Orloff, J. (1996). *Second sight*. New York: Warner.

Orne, M. T. (1959). The nature of hypnosis: Artifact and essence. *Journal of Abnormal and Social Psychology, 58*, 277–299.

Orne, M. T., & Scheibe, K. E. (1964). The contribution of nondeprivation factors in the production of sensory deprivation effects: The psychology of the "panic button." *Journal of Abnormal and Social Psychology, 68*(1), 3–12.

Ornstein, R. E. (1972). *The psychology of consciousness*. New York: Viking.

Oswald, I., Taylor, A. M., & Treisman, M. (1960). Discriminative responses to stimulation during human sleep. *Brain: A Journal of Neurology, 83*, 440–453.

Oxman, T. E., Rosenberg, S. D., Schnurr, P. P., Tucker, G. J., & Gala, G. (1988). The language of altered states. *Journal of Nervous and Mental Disease, 176*(7), 401–408.

Pagano, R. R., Rose, R. M., Stivers, R. M., & Warrenburg, S. (1976). Sleep during transcendental meditation. *Science, 191*(4224), 308–310.

Pahnke, W. N. (1963). *Drugs and mysticism: An analysis of the relationship between psychedelic drugs and the mystical consciousness*. Unpublished doctoral dissertation, Harvard University.

Pahnke, W. N., & Richards, W. A. (1972). Implications of LSD and experimental mysticism. In C. T. Tart (Ed.), *Altered states of consciousness* (pp. 409–439). Garden City, NY: Anchor.

Paivio, A., & te Linde, J. (1982). Imagery, memory, and the brain. *Canadian Journal of Psychology, 36*(2), 243–272.

Pargament, K. I. (1999). The psychology of religion *and* spirituality? Yes and no. *International Journal for the Psychology of Religion, 9*(1), 3–16.

Park, R. L. (2000). Welcome to planet earth. *The Sciences, 40*(3), 20–24.

Parnia, S., Waller, D. G., Yeates, R., & Fenwick, P. (2001). A qualitative and quantitative study of the incidence, features and aetiology of near death experiences in cardiac arrest survivors. *Resuscitation, 48*, 149–156.

Partinen, M., & Hublin, C. (2000). Epidemiology of sleep disorders. In M. H. Kryger, T. Roth, & W. C. Dement (Eds.), *Principles and practice of sleep medicine* (3rd ed., pp. 558–579). Philadelphia: W. B. Saunders.

Pekala, R. J. (1991). *Quantifying consciousness: An empirical approach*. New York: Plenum Press.

Pekala, R. J., & Cardeña, E. (2000). Methodological issues in the study of altered states of consciousness and anomalous experiences. In E. Cardeña, S. J. Lynn, & S. Krippner (Eds.), *Varieties of anomalous experience: Examining the scientific evidence* (pp. 47–82). Washington, DC: American Psychological Association.

Pekala, R. J., & Kumar, V. K. (2000). Operationalizing "trance" I: Rationale and research using a psychophenomenological approach. *American Journal of Clinical Hypnosis, 43*(2), 107–135.

Persinger, M. A. (with Carrey, N. J., & Suess, L. A.). (1980). *TM and cult mania*. North Quincy, MA: Christopher.

Persinger, M. A. (1987). *Neuropsychological bases of God beliefs*. New York: Praeger.

Peters, L. G. (1981). An experiential study of Nepalese shamanism. *Journal of Transpersonal Psychology, 13*(1), 1–26.

Peters, L. G. (1989). Shamanism: Phenomenology of a spiritual discipline. *Journal of Transpersonal Psychology, 21*(2), 115–137.

Petrie, K. J., Booth, R. J., & Pennebaker, J. W. (1998). The immunological effects of thought suppression. *Journal of Personality and Social Psychology, 75*(5), 1264–1272.

Picker, W., Lerman, A., & Hajal, F. (1992). Potential interaction of LSD and fluoxetine. *American Journal of Psychiatry, 149*(6), 843–844.

Privette, G. (1983). Peak experience, peak performance, and flow: A comparative analysis of positive human experiences. *Journal of Personality and Social Psychology, 45*(6), 1361–1368.

Putnam, F. W. (1984). The psychophysiologic investigation of multiple personality disorder: A review. *Psychiatric Clinics of North America, 7*(1), 31–39.

Radin, D. I. (1997). *The conscious universe: The scientific truth of psychic phenomena*. New York: HarperEdge.

Ramabadran, K., & Bansinath, M. (1990). Endogenous opioid peptides and epilepsy. *International Journal of Clinical Pharmacology, Therapy and Toxicology, 28*(2), 47–62.

Rawlings, M. (1978). *Beyond death's door*. London: Sheldon.

Rayl, A. J. S. (1989, June). Encyclopedia psychedelia. *Omni, 11*(9), 30, 96.

Rechtschaffen, A., & Kales, A. (Eds.). (1968). *A manual of standardized terminology, techniques and scoring system for sleep stages of human subjects*. Bethesda, MD: U.S. Department of Health, Education, and Welfare; Public Health Service—National Institutes of Health; National Institute of Neurological Diseases and Blindness; Neurological Information Network.

Register, P. A., & Kihlstrom, J. F. (1986). Finding the hypnotic virtuoso. *International Journal of Clinical and Experimental Hypnosis, 34*(2), 84–97.

Reich, D. (1989a, Oct. 14). Multiple personality disorder. *London Free Press*, p. A6.

Reich, D. (1989b, Oct. 14). The 29 lives of Brenda. *London Free Press*, pp. A6–A7.

Remen, R. N. (1998). On defining spirit. *Noetic Sciences Review, 47*, 64.

Restivo, S. P. (1978). Parallels and paradoxes in modern physics and Eastern mysticism: I—A critical reconnaissance. *Social Studies of Science, 8*, 143–181.

Restivo, S. (1982). Parallels and paradoxes in modern physics and Eastern mysticism: II—A sociological perspective on parallelism. *Social Studies of Science, 12*(1), 37–71.

Ring, K. (1987). Near-death experiences: Intimations of immortality? In J. S. Spong (Ed.), *Consciousness and survival: An interdisciplinary inquiry into the possibility of life beyond biological death* (pp. 165–176). Sausalito, CA: Institute of Noetic Sciences.

Ring, K. (1989). Near-death and UFO encounters as shamanic initiations: Some conceptual and evolutionary implications. *ReVision: The Journal of Consciousness and Change, 11*(3), 14–22.

Ring, K. (1992). *The omega project: Near-death experiences, UFO encounters, and mind at large.* New York: William Morrow.

Ring, K., & Cooper, S. (1997). Near-death and out-of-body experiences in the blind: A study of apparent eyeless vision. *Journal of Near-Death Studies, 16*(2), 101–147.

Ring, K., & Valarino, E. E. (1998). *Lessons from the light: What we can learn from the near-death experience.* Portsmouth, NH: Moment Point.

Ripinsky-Naxon, M. (1993). *The nature of shamanism: Substance and function of a religious metaphor.* Albany: State University of New York Press.

Roberts, B. (1993). *The experience of no-self: A contemplative journey* (Rev. ed.). Albany: State University of New York Press.

Roberts, J. (1978). *The afterdeath journal of an American philosopher: The world view of William James.* Englewood Cliffs, NJ: Prentice-Hall.

Robins, R. W., & John, O. P. (1997). The quest for self-insight: Theory and research on accuracy and bias in self-perception. In R. Hogan, J. Johnson, & S. Briggs (Eds.), *Handbook of personality psychology* (pp. 649–679). San Diego: Academic Press.

Roe, C. A. (1999). Critical thinking and belief in the paranormal: A re-evaluation. *British Journal of Psychology, 90*, 85–98.

Roehrs, T., Carskadon, M. A., Dement, W. C., & Roth, T. (2000). Daytime sleepiness and alertness. In M. H. Kryger, T. Roth, & W. C. Dement (Eds.), *Principles and practice of sleep medicine* (3rd ed., pp. 43–52). Philadelphia: W. B. Saunders.

Roehrs, T., & Roth, T. (1997). Hypnotics, alcohol, and caffeine: Relation to insomnia. In M. R. Pressman & W. C. Orr (Eds.), *Understanding sleep: The evaluation and treatment of sleep disorders* (pp. 339–355). Washington, DC: American Psychological Association.

Rosch, E. (1999). Is wisdom in the brain? *Psychological Science, 10*(3), 222–224.

Rosenthal, D. M. (2000). Consciousness, content, and metacognitive judgments. *Consciousness and Cognition, 9*, 203–214.

Ross, C. A. (1996). History, phenomenology, and epidemiology of dissociation. In L. K. Michelson & W. J. Ray (Eds.), *Handbook of dissociation: Theoretical, empirical, and clinical perspectives* (pp. 3–24). New York: Plenum Press.

Ross, C. A., & Joshi, S. (1992). Paranormal experiences in the general population. *Journal of Nervous and Mental Disease, 180*(6), 357–361.

Ross, C. A., Norton, G. R., & Wozney, K. (1989). Multiple personality disorder: An analysis of 236 cases. *Canadian Journal of Psychiatry, 34*(5), 413–418.

Rovee-Collier, C. (1999). The development of infant memory. *Current Directions in Psychological Science, 8*(3), 80–85.

Rumelhart, D. E., Hinton, G. E., & McClelland, J. L. (1986). A general framework for parallel distributed processing. In D. E. Rumelhart, J. L. McClelland, and the PDP Research Group (Eds.), *Parallel distributed processing: Explorations in the microstructure of cognition: Volume 1: Foundations* (pp. 45–76). Cambridge, MA: MIT Press.

Ruzyla-Smith, P., & Barabasz, A. (1993). Effects of flotation REST on the immune response: T-cells, B-cells, helper and suppressor cells. In A. F. Barabasz & M. Barabasz (Eds.), *Clinical and experimental restricted environmental stimulation: New developments and perspectives* (pp. 223–237). New York: Springer-Verlag.

Ruzyla-Smith, P., Barabasz, A., Barabasz, M., & Warner, D. (1995). Effects of hypnosis on the immune response: B-cells, T-cells, helper and suppressor cells. *American Journal of Clinical Hypnosis, 38*(2), 71–79.

Ryff, C. D. (1995). Psychological well-being in adult life. *Current Directions in Psychological Science, 4*(4), 99–104.

Sabom, M. (1998). *Light & death: One doctor's fascinating account of near-death experiences*. Grand Rapids, MI: Zondervan.

Sadzot, B., Baraban, J. M., Glennon, R. A., Lyon, R. A., Leonhardt, S., et al. (1989). Hallucinogenic drug interactions at human brain 5-HT$_2$ receptors: Implications for treating LSD-induced hallucinogenesis. *Psychopharmacology, 98*, 495–499.

Sanders, M. H. (2000). Medical therapy for obstructive sleep apnea-hypopnea syndrome. In M. H. Kryger, T. Roth, & W. C. Dement (Eds.), *Principles and practice of sleep medicine* (3rd ed., pp. 879–893). Philadelphia: W. B. Saunders.

Saver, J. L., & Rabin, J. (1997). The neural substrates of religious experience. *Journal of Neuropsychiatry and Clinical Neurosciences, 9*(3), 498–510.

Schacter, D. L. (1995). Memory distortion: History and current status. In D. L. Schacter (Ed.), *Memory distortion: How minds, brains, and societies reconstruct the past* (pp. 1–43). Cambridge, MA: Harvard University Press.

Schneider, J., Smith, C. W., Minning, C., Whitcher, S., & Hermanson, J. (1990). Guided imagery and immune system function in normal subjects: A summary of research findings. In R. G. Kunzendorf (Ed.), *Mental imagery* (pp. 179–191). New York: Plenum Press.

Schnyer, D. M., & Allen, J. J. (1995). Attention-related electroencephalographic and event-related potential predictors of responsiveness to suggested posthypnotic amnesia. *International Journal of Clinical and Experimental Hypnosis, 43*(3), 295–315.

Schreiber, E. H. (1997). Use of group hypnosis to improve college students' achievement. *Psychological Reports, 80*, 636–638.

Schultes, R. E. (1982). The beta-carboline hallucinogens of South America. *Journal of Psychoactive Drugs, 14*(3), 205–220.

Schultes, R. E., & Winkelman, M. (1996). The principal American hallucinogenic plants and their bioactive and therapeutic properties. In M. Winkelman & W. Andritzky (Eds.), *Jahrbuch für transkulturelle medizin und psychotherapie*

(Yearbook of cross-cultural medicine and psychotherapy) Vol. 1995. *Sakrale Heilpflanzen, Bewußtsein und Heilung: Transkulturelle und interdisziplinäre Perspektiven* (Sacred plants, consciousness and healing: Cross-cultural and interdisciplinary perspectives) (pp. 205–239). Berlin: Verlag für Wissenschaft und Bildung.

Schumaker, J. F. (1995). *The corruption of reality: A unified theory of religion, hypnosis, and psychopathology.* Amherst, NY: Prometheus.

Schwartz, G. E. (2002). (with Simon, W. L.). *The afterlife experiments: Breakthrough scientific evidence of life after death.* New York: Pocket Books.

Schwartz, W. J. (1997). Introduction: On the neurobiology of sleep and sleep disorders not yet known. In M. Fisher (Series Ed.) & W. J. Schwartz (Vol. Ed.), *Monographs in clinical neuroscience: Vol. 15. Sleep science: Integrating basic research and clinical practice* (pp. 1–8). Basel, Switzerland: Karger.

Schweitzer, P. K. (2000). Drugs that disturb sleep and wakefulness. In M. H. Kryger, T. Roth, & W. C. Dement (Eds.), *Principles and practice of sleep medicine* (3rd ed., pp. 441–461). Philadelphia: W. B. Saunders.

Scott, R. D. (1978). *Transcendental misconceptions.* San Diego, CA: Beta.

Searle, J. R. (2000). Consciousness, free action and the brain. *Journal of Consciousness Studies, 7*(10), 3–22.

Sferios, E. (1999). Report from DanceSafe: Laboratory analysis program reveals DXM tablets sold as "Ecstasy." *MAPS: Bulletin of the Multidisciplinary Association for Psychedelic Studies, 9*(4), 47–48.

Shaffer, J. B. P. (1978). *Humanistic psychology.* Englewood Cliffs, NJ: Prentice-Hall.

Shanon, B. (2001). Altered temporality. *Journal of Consciousness Studies, 8*(1), 35–58.

Shaughnessy, J. J., & Zechmeister, E. B. (1994). *Research methods in psychology* (3rd ed.). New York: McGraw-Hill.

Shear, J. (1996). The hard problem: Closing the empirical gap. *Journal of Consciousness Studies, 3*(1), 54–68.

Shor, R. E., & Orne, E. C. (1962). *Manual: Harvard Group Scale of Hypnotic Susceptibility: Form A.* Palo Alto, CA: Consulting Psychologists Press.

Siegel, J. M. (2000). Brainstem mechanisms generating REM sleep. In M. H. Kryger, T. Roth, & W. C. Dement (Eds.), *Principles and practice of sleep medicine* (3rd ed., pp. 112–133). Philadelphia: W. B. Saunders.

Siegel, R. K. (1975). Introduction. In R. K. Siegel & L. J. West (Eds.), *Hallucinations: Behavior, Experience, and Theory* (pp. 1–7). New York: John Wiley & Sons.

Siegel, R. K. (1977). Hallucinations. *Scientific American, 237*(4), 132–140.

Siegel, R. K., & Jarvik, M. E. (1975). Drug-induced hallucinations in animals and man. In R. K. Siegel & L. J. West (Eds.), *Hallucinations: Behavior, experience, and theory* (pp. 81–161). New York: John Wiley & Sons.

Singer, J. L., & Antrobus, J. S. (1972). Daydreaming, imaginal processes, and personality: A normative study. In P. W. Sheehan (Ed.), *The function and nature of imagery* (pp. 175–202). New York: Academic Press.

Smith, A. L., & Tart, C. T. (1998). Cosmic consciousness experience and psychedelic experiences: A first person comparison. *Journal of Consciousness Studies, 5*(1), 97–107.

Smith, C. (1995). Sleep states and memory processes. *Behavioural Brain Research, 69,* 137–145.

Smith, C. (1996). Sleep states, memory processes and synaptic plasticity. *Behavioural Brain Research, 78,* 49–56.

Smith, C., & Lapp, L. (1991). Increases in number of REMS and REM density in humans following an intensive learning period. *Sleep, 14*(4), 325–330.

Smith, H. (2000). *Cleansing the doors of perception: The religious significance of entheogenic plants and chemicals.* New York: Jeremy P. Tarcher/Putnam.

Smith, J. C., Amutio, A., Anderson, J. P., & Aria, L. A. (1996). Relaxation: Mapping an uncharted world. *Biofeedback and Self-Regulation, 21*(1), 63–90.

Smith, J. T., Barabasz, A., & Barabasz, M. (1996). Comparison of hypnosis and distraction in severely ill children undergoing painful medical procedures. *Journal of Counseling Psychology, 43*(2), 187–195.

Smolensky, P. (1988). On the proper treatment of connectionism. *Behavioral and Brain Sciences, 11*(1), 1–23.

Spanos, N. P. (1982). Hypnotic behavior: A cognitive, social psychological perspective. *Research Communications in Psychology, Psychiatry and Behavior, 7*(2), 199–213.

Spanos, N. P. (1986). Hypnotic behavior: A social-psychological interpretation of amnesia, analgesia, and "trance logic." *The Behavioral and Brain Sciences, 9*(3), 449–467.

Spanos, N. P. (1991). A sociocognitive approach to hypnosis. In S. J. Lynn & J. W. Rhue (Eds.), *Theories of hypnosis: Current models and perspectives* (pp. 324–361). New York: Guilford Press.

Spanos, N. P., Cross, W. P., Menary, E. P., Brett, P. J., & de Groh, M. (1987). Attitudinal and imaginal ability predictors of social cognitive skill-training enhancements in hypnotic susceptibility. *Personality and Social Psychology Bulletin, 13*(3), 379–398.

Spanos, N. P., Menary, E., Gabora, N. J., DuBreuil, S. C., & Dewhirst, B. (1991). Secondary identity enactments during hypnotic past-life regression: A sociocognitive perspective. *Journal of Personality and Social Psychology, 61*(2), 308–320.

Spanos, N. P., Radtke, H. L., Hodgins, D. C., Bertrand, L. D., Stam, H. J., et al. (1983). The Carleton University Responsiveness to Suggestion Scale: Stability, reliability, and relationships with expectancy and "hypnotic experiences." *Psychological Reports, 53,* 555–563.

Spanos, N. P., Radtke, H. L., Hodgins, D. C., Stam, H. J., & Bertrand, L. D. (1983). The Carleton University Responsiveness to Suggestion Scale: Normative data and psychometric properties. *Psychological Reports, 53,* 523–535.

Spiegel, D., Bierre, P., & Rootenberg, J. (1989). Hypnotic alteration of somatosensory perception. *American Journal of Psychiatry, 146*(6), 749–754.

Spiegel, H., & Spiegel, D. (1978). *Trance and treatment: Clinical uses of hypnosis.* Washington, DC: American Psychiatric Press.

Spielman, A. J., Yang, C.-M., & Glovinsky, P. B. (2000). Assessment techniques for insomnia. In M. H. Kryger, T. Roth, & W. C. Dement (Eds.), *Principles and practice of sleep medicine* (3rd ed., pp. 1239–1250). Philadelphia: W. B. Saunders.

Stace, W. T. (1960). *Mysticism and philosophy.* Los Angeles: Jeremy P. Tarcher.

Steriade, M. (2000). Brain electrical activity and sensory processing during waking and sleep states. In M. H. Kryger, T. Roth, & W. C. Dement (Eds.), *Principles and practice of sleep medicine* (3rd ed., pp. 93–111). Philadelphia: W. B. Saunders.

Sternberg, R. J. (1995). *In search of the human mind.* Fort Worth, TX: Harcourt Brace.

Stevens, A. (1995). *Private myths: Dreams and dreaming.* Cambridge, MA: Harvard University Press.

Stevenson, I. (1990). Phobias in children who claim to remember previous lives. *Journal of Scientific Exploration, 4*(2), 243–254.

Stevenson, I. (1994). A case of the psychotherapist's fallacy: Hypnotic regression to "previous lives." *American Journal of Clinical Hypnosis, 36*(3), 188–193.

Stevenson, I. (1997a). *Reincarnation and biology: A contribution to the etiology of birthmarks and birth defects.* Westport, CT: Praeger.

Stevenson, I. (1997b). *Where reincarnation and biology intersect.* Westport, CT: Praeger.

Stevenson, I., Pasricha, S., & McClean-Rice, N. (1989). A case of the possession type in India with evidence of paranormal knowledge. *Journal of Scientific Exploration, 3*(1), 81–101.

Stickgold, R., Pace-Schott, E., & Hobson, J. A. (1994). A new paradigm for dream research: Mentation reports following spontaneous arousal from REM and NREM sleep recorded in a home setting. *Consciousness and Cognition, 3,* 16–29.

Stolaroff, M. J. (1993). Using psychedelics wisely. *Gnosis: A Journal of the Western Inner Traditions, 26,* 26–30.

Storm, L., & Ertel, S. (2001). Does psi exist? Comments on Milton and Wiseman's (1999) meta-analysis of ganzfeld research. *Psychological Bulletin, 127*(3), 424–433.

Strassman, R. J. (1996). Human psychopharmacology of N, N-dimethyltryptamine. *Behavioural Brain Research, 73,* 121–124.

Strassman, R. J. (1997). Biomedical research with psychedelics: Current models and future prospects. In R. Forte (Ed.), *Entheogens and the future of religion* (pp. 153–162). San Francisco: Council on Spiritual Practices.

Strassman, R. J. (2001). *DMT: The spirit molecule.* Rochester, VT: Park Street Press.

Strauch, I., & Meier, B. (1996). *In search of dreams: Results of experimental dream research.* Albany: State University of New York Press. (Original work published 1992)

Suedfeld, P., & Borrie, R. A. (1999). Health and therapeutic applications of chamber and flotation restricted environmental stimulation therapy (REST). *Psychology and Health, 14*, 545–566.

Suedfeld, P., & Coren, S. (1989). Perceptual isolation, sensory deprivation, and REST: Moving introductory psychology texts out of the 1950s. *Canadian Psychology/Psychologie Canadienne, 30(1)*, 17–29.

Suedfeld, P., & Mocellin, J. S. P. (1987). The "sensed presence" in unusual environments. *Environment and Behavior, 19*(1), 33–52.

Szechtman, H., Woody, E., Bowers, K. S., & Nahmias, C. (1998). Where the imaginal appears real: A positron emission tomography study of auditory hallucinations. *Proceedings of the National Academy of Sciences of the United States of America, 95*, 1956–1960.

Tarazi, L. (1990). An unusual case of hypnotic regression with some unexplained contents. *Journal of the American Society for Psychical Research, 84*(4), 309–344.

Tart, C. T. (1971). A psychologist's experience with transcendental meditation. *Journal of Transpersonal Psychology, 3*(2), 135–140.

Tart, C. T. (Ed.). (1972a). *Altered states of consciousness* (2nd ed.). Garden City, NY: Anchor.

Tart, C. T. (1972b). Introduction. In Charles T. Tart (Ed.), *Altered states of consciousness* (pp. 1–6). Garden City, NY: Anchor.

Tart, C. T. (1972c). States of consciousness and state-specific sciences. *Science, 176*(4038), 1203–1210.

Tart, C. T. (1975). *States of consciousness.* New York: E. P. Dutton.

Tart, C. T. (1988). Meditation and consciousness: A dialogue between a meditation teacher and a psychologist: An interview with Shinzen Young. *Noetic Sciences Review, 8*, 14–21.

Tart, C. T. (1991). Influences of previous psychedelic drug experiences on students of Tibetan Buddhism: A preliminary exploration. *Journal of Transpersonal Psychology, 23*(2), 139–173.

Tart, C. T. (1993). The structure and dynamics of waking sleep. *Journal of Transpersonal Psychology, 25*(2), 141–168.

Tart, C. T. (1998). Six studies of out-of-body experiences. *Journal of Near-Death Studies, 17*(2), 73–99.

Tart, C. T. (2000). Investigating altered states on their own terms: State-specific sciences. In M. Velmans (Ed.), *Investigating phenomenal consciousness: New methodologies and maps* (pp. 255–278). Amsterdam, The Netherlands: John Benjamins.

Taylor, E. (1981). The evolution of William James's definition of consciousness. *ReVision: Journal of Knowledge and Consciousness, 4*(2), 40–47.

Taylor, E. (1997). Introduction. In M. Murphy & S. Donovan (Authors) & E. Taylor (Ed.), *The physical and psychological effects of meditation: A review of contemporary research with a comprehensive bibliography 1931–1996.* Sausalito, CA: Institute of Noetic Sciences.

Taylor, E. (1999). *Shadow culture: Psychology and spirituality in America*. Washington, DC: Counterpoint.

Thalbourne, M. A. (1998). Transliminality: Further correlates and a short measure. *Journal of the American Society for Psychical Research, 92*, 402–419.

Thomas, L. E., & Cooper, P. E. (1980). Incidence and psychological correlates of intense spiritual experiences. *Journal of Transpersonal Psychology, 12*(1), 75–85.

Tompkins, P. (1990). *This tree grows out of hell: Mesoamerica and the search for the magical body*. New York: HarperSanFrancisco.

Turner, E. (1992a). The reality of spirits. *ReVision: A Journal of Consciousness and Transformation, 15*(1), 28–32.

Turner, E. (with Blodgett, W., Kahona, S., & Benwa, F.). (1992b). *Experiencing ritual: A new interpretation of African healing*. Philadelphia: University of Pennsylvania Press.

Ullman, M. (1986). Access to dreams. In B. B. Wolman & M. Ullman (Eds.), *Handbook of states of consciousness* (pp. 524–552). New York: Van Nostrand Reinhold.

Ullman, M. (1999). Dreaming consciousness: More than a bit player in the search for answers to the mind/body problem. *Journal of Scientific Exploration, 13*(1), 91–112.

Ullman, M., & Krippner, S. (with Vaughan, A.). (1973). *Dream telepathy*. New York: Macmillan.

Valkenburg, P. M., & van der Voort, T. H. A. (1995). The influence of television on children's daydreaming styles: A 1-year panel study. *Communication Research, 22*(3), 267–287.

Vallee, J. F. (1990). Five arguments against the extraterrestrial origin of unidentified flying objects. *Journal of Scientific Exploration, 4*(1), 105–117.

Vallee, J. (1991). *Revelations: Alien contact and human deception*. New York: Ballantine.

van der Kolk, B. A. (1996). Trauma and memory. In B. A. van der Kolk, A. C. McFarlane, & L. Weisaeth (Eds.), *Traumatic stress: The effects of overwhelming experience on mind, body, and society* (pp. 279–302). New York: Guilford Press.

van Eeden, F. (1913). A study of dreams. *Proceedings of the Society for Psychical Research, 26* (Pt. 67), 431–461.

van Lommel, P., van Wees, R., Meyers, V., & Elfferich, I. (2001). Near-death experience in survivors of cardiac arrest: A prospective study in the Netherlands. *The Lancet, 358*, 2039–2045.

van Quekelberghe, R., Göbel, P., & Hertweck, E. (1995). Simulation of near-death and out-of-body experiences under hypnosis. *Imagination, Cognition and Personality, 14*(2), 151–164.

Venn, J. (1986). Hypnosis and the reincarnation hypothesis: A critical review and intensive case study. *Journal of the American Society for Psychical Research, 80*, 409–425.

Vollenweider, F. X., Gamma, A., Liechti, M., & Huber, T. (1998). Psychological and cardiovascular effects and short-term sequelae of MDMA ("ecstasy") in MDMA-naïve healthy volunteers. *Neuropsychopharmacology, 19*(4), 241–251.

Vollenweider, F. X., Leenders, K. L., Scharfetter, C., Maguire, P., Stadelmann, O., et al. (1997). Positron emission tomography and fluorodeoxyglucose studies of metabolic hyperfrontality and psychopathology in the psilocybin model of psychosis. *Neuropsychopharmacology, 16*(5), 357–372.

Vollenweider, F. X., Vollenweider-Scherpenhuyzen, M. F. I., Bäbler, A., Vogel, H., & Hell, D. (1998). Psilocybin induces schizophrenia-like psychosis in humans via a serotonin-2 agonist action. *NeuroReport, 9*(17), 3897–3902.

Wagaman, J., & Barabasz, A. (1993). Flotation REST and imagery in the improvement of collegiate athletic performance: Basketball. In A. F. Barabasz & M. Barabasz (Eds.), *Clinical and experimental restricted environmental stimulation: New developments and perspectives* (pp. 87–92). New York: Springer-Verlag.

Wagaman, J. D., Barabasz, A. F., & Barabasz, M. (1991). Flotation REST and imagery in the improvement of collegiate basketball performance. *Perceptual and Motor Skills, 72,* 119–122.

Waldron, J. L. (1998). The life impact of transcendent experiences with a pronounced quality of noesis. *Journal of Transpersonal Psychology, 30*(2), 103–134.

Walker, E. H. (1970). The nature of consciousness. *Mathematical Biosciences, 7,* 131–178.

Walker, E. H. (1977). Quantum mechanical tunneling in synaptic and ephaptic transmission. *International Journal of Quantum Chemistry, 11,* 103–127.

Walker, E. H. (2000). *The physics of consciousness: Quantum minds and the meaning of life.* Cambridge, MA: Perseus.

Wallace, B. A. (1998). *The bridge of quiescence: Experiencing Tibetan Buddhist meditation.* Chicago: Open Court.

Walling, D. P., & Baker, J. M. (1996). Hypnosis training in psychology intern programs. *American Journal of Clinical Hypnosis, 38*(3), 219–223.

Walsh, R. (1989). What is a shaman? Definition, origin and distribution. *Journal of Transpersonal Psychology, 21*(1), 1–11.

Walsh, R. (1995). Phenomenological mapping: A method for describing and comparing states of consciousness. *Journal of Transpersonal Psychology, 27*(1), 25-56.

Walsh, R. N., & Vaughan, F. (1992). Lucid dreaming: Some transpersonal implications. *Journal of Transpersonal Psychology, 24*(2), 193–200.

Walter, W. G., & Dovey, V. J. (1944). Electro-encephalography in cases of subcortical tumour. *Journal of Neurology, Neurosurgery and Psychiatry, 7*(3 & 4), 57–65.

Ward, C. A. (1989). Possession and exorcism: Psychopathology and psychotherapy in a magico-religious context. In C. A. Ward (Ed.), *Altered states of consciousness and mental health: A cross-cultural perspective* (pp. 125–144). Newbury Park, CA: Sage.

Ware, J. C., & Hirshkowitz, M. (2000). Assessment of sleep-related erections. In M. H. Kryger, T. Roth, & W. C. Dement (Eds.), *Principles and practice of sleep medicine* (3rd ed., pp. 1231–1237). Philadelphia: W. B. Saunders.

Watkins, J. G., & Watkins, H. H. (1986). Hypnosis, multiple personality, and ego states as altered states of consciousness. In B. B. Wolman & M. Ullman (Eds.), *Handbook of states of consciousness* (pp. 133–158). New York: Van Nostrand Reinhold.

Watson, J. B. (1919). *Psychology from the standpoint of a behaviorist.* Philadelphia: J. B. Lippincott.

Weil, A., & Rosen, W. (1993). *From chocolate to morphine: Everything you need to know about mind-altering drugs* (Rev. ed.). Boston, MA: Houghton Mifflin.

Weiss, B. L. (1992). *Through time into healing.* New York: Simon & Schuster.

Weitzenhoffer, A. M., & Hilgard, E. R. (1962). *Stanford Hypnotic Susceptibility Scale: Form C.* Palo Alto, CA: Consulting Psychologists Press.

Wenzlaff, R. M., & Wegner, D. M. (2000). Thought suppression. *Annual Review of Psychology, 51,* 59–91.

West, V., Fellows, B., & Easton, S. (1995). The British Society of Experimental and Clinical Hypnosis: A national survey. *Contemporary Hypnosis, 12*(2), 143–147.

White, P. A. (1988). Knowing more about what we can tell: "Introspective access" and causal report accuracy 10 years later. *British Journal of Psychology, 79,* 13–45.

Wilbur, C. B., & Kluft, R. P. (1989). Multiple personality disorder. In *Treatments of psychiatric disorders: A task force report of the American Psychiatric Association* (pp. 2197–2216). Washington, DC: American Psychiatric Association.

Wilson, C. (1990). Glimpses of a wider reality. In G. Doore (Ed.), *What survives? Contemporary explorations of life after death.* Los Angeles: Jeremy P. Tarcher.

Wilson, J. (1992). Are memories of alien abductions recollections of surgical experiences? *Journal of Scientific Exploration, 6*(3), 291–294.

Wilson, M. A., & McNaughton, B. L. (1994). Reactivation of hippocampal ensemble memories during sleep. *Science, 265,* 676–679.

Wilson, S. C., & Barber, T. X. (1981). Vivid fantasy and hallucinatory abilities in the life histories of excellent hypnotic subjects ("somnambules"): Preliminary report with female subjects. In E. Klinger (Ed.), *Imagery (Vol. 2): Concepts, results, and applications* (pp. 133–149). New York: Plenum Press.

Winkelman, M. (2000). *Shamanism: The neural ecology of consciousness and healing.* Westport, CT: Bergin & Garvey.

Wolf, F. A. (1991). *The eagle's quest: A physicist's search for truth in the heart of the shamanic world.* New York: Summit.

Wood, D. P., & Sexton, J. L. (1997). Self-hypnosis training and captivity survival. *American Journal of Clinical Hypnosis, 39*(3), 201–211.

Woody, E. Z. (1997). Have the hypnotic susceptibility scales outlived their usefulness? *International Journal of Clinical and Experimental Hypnosis, 45*(3), 226–238.

Woody, E. Z., & Bowers, K. S. (1994). A frontal assault on dissociated control. In S. J. Lynn & J. W. Rhue (Eds.), *Dissociation: Clinical and theoretical perspectives* (pp. 52–79). New York: Guilford Press.

Woody, E. Z., Drugovic, M., & Oakman, J. M. (1997). A reexamination of the role of nonhypnotic suggestibility in hypnotic responding. *Journal of Personality and Social Psychology, 72*(2), 399–407.

Woody, E., & Sadler, P. (1998). On reintegrating dissociated theories: Comment on Kirsch and Lynn (1998). *Psychological Bulletin, 123*(2), 192–197.

Wren-Lewis, J. (1988). The darkness of God: A personal report on consciousness transformation through an encounter with death. *Journal of Humanistic Psychology, 28*(2), 105–122.

Wren-Lewis, J. (1991). A reluctant mystic: God-consciousness not guru worship. *Self and Society, 19*(2), 4–11.

Wren-Lewis, J. (1994). Aftereffects of near-death experiences: A survival mechanism hypothesis. *Journal of Transpersonal Psychology, 26*(2), 107–115.

Wulff, D. M. (2000). Mystical experience. In E. Cardeña, S. J. Lynn, & S. Krippner (Eds.), *Varieties of anomalous experience: Examining the scientific evidence* (pp. 397–440). Washington, DC: American Psychological Association.

Wuthnow, R. (1998). *After heaven: Spirituality in America since the 1950s.* Berkeley: University of California Press.

Wuthnow, R. (1999). Returning to practice. *Noetic Sciences Review, 49*, 32–38.

Wyatt, J. K., Bootzin, R. R., Anthony, J., & Stevenson, S. (1992). Does sleep onset produce retrograde amnesia? *Sleep Research, 21*, 113.

Yang, E. H., Hla, K. M., McHorney, C. A., Havighurst, T., Badr, M. S., et al. (2000). Sleep apnea and quality of life. *Sleep, 23*(4), 535–541.

Younger, J., Adriance, W., & Berger, R. J. (1975). Sleep during transcendental meditation. *Perceptual and Motor Skills, 40*, 953–954.

Zarcone, V. P., Jr. (2000). Sleep hygiene. In M. H. Kryger, T. Roth, & W. C. Dement (Eds.), *Principles and practice of sleep medicine* (3rd ed., pp. 657–661). Philadelphia: W. B. Saunders.

Zhiyan, T., & Singer, J. L. (1997). Daydreaming styles, emotionality and the big five personality dimensions. *Imagination, Cognition and Personality, 16*(4), 399–414.

Zubek, J. P., Bayer, L., Milstein, S., & Shephard, J. M. (1969). Behavioral and physiological changes during prolonged immobilization plus perceptual deprivation. *Journal of Abnormal Psychology, 74*(2), 230–236.

Zuckerman, M. (1969). Variables affecting deprivation results. In J. P. Zubek (Ed.), *Sensory deprivation: Fifteen years of research* (pp. 47–84). New York: Appleton-Century-Crofts.

Zusne, L., & Jones, W. H. (1989). *Anomalistic psychology: A study of magical thinking* (2nd ed.). Hillsdale, NJ: Erlbaum.

INDEX

Absorption and transcendence, 188
Acetylcholine, 66, 68
Activation during REM sleep, 80
Activation–synthesis hypothesis, 80–81, 82
Adherence and neutrophils, 42, 131–132
Age and sleep stages, 54, 57–58, 63
Agreeableness, 39
Akinetic mutism, 59
Alcohol and alcoholism, 68
    psychedelic psychotherapy for alcoholism, 179–180
Alien abduction experiences, 152–159
    absence of mental illness among reporters, 157
    characteristics of, 152–154
    children reporting, 157–158
    compared to shamanism, 158–159
    corroborative physical evidence, 157
    critical features of, 156–158
    and DMT use, 170
    ET hypothesis, 158
    explanations of, 155–156
    intensity of emotion of reporters, 155, 157
    narrative consistency among reports, 157
    sincerity of reporters, 156
Alpert, Richard, 165, 166, 194
Alpha-delta sleep, 55
Alpha waves, 53, 54, 56
Alterations of consciousness, 9–10
    and emotions, 36
    framework for, 4–11
Altered state of consciousness, 7–8. *See also* Coma
    dangerous versus beneficial, 23, 236–237
    defined, 8
    difference from alterations of consciousness, 4–5, 9–10
    example of, 3–4
    and psychopathology, 10–11

Amnesia
    hypnotic amnesia, 112–113
    for personal information in dissociative identity disorder, 150
Amnesia-prone persons, 123
Amphetamine, 67
Analgesic effects, 237
    of hypnosis, 111–112, 130–131
    of psychedelic drugs, 180, 237
Anandamide, 174
Anomalous information transfer, 13–15
Anomalous phenomena, 15–16
    and past-life therapy, 228
Archetypes, 85–86
Aserinksy, Eugene, 59
Assagioli, Roberto, 40, 91, 92
Athletic performance and use of REST, 47
Attenuation of self concerns and transcendence, 188
Attitude change after mystical experiences, 184
Auditory phenomena in dreams, 89, 90
Axon, 52
Ayahuasca, 170–172

Baker, Douglas, 94, 194
Banisteriopsis, 170–171
Barabasz, Arreed, 118–119
Barber, Theodore, 121, 123, 124
Barrett, Deirdre, 122
Behavioral consciousness$_2$, 6
Behavior change after mystical experiences, 184
Behaviorism, 27
Benson, Herbert, 196
Benzodiazepine receptors, 68
Benzodiazepines, 68
Bessent, Malcolm, 104–105
Beta-cabolines, 171
    neuropharmacology of, 172–173
Beta waves, 53, 54, 197, 198
Bhirendra (shaman). *See* Tamang of Nepal

Birth, memories of, 129
Blackmore, Susan, 215, 218–219
Blind persons' near-death experiences,
    220–221
Bowers, Kenneth, 123
Brain
    activation during REM sleep, 80
    coherence of brain waves, 197–
        198
    during dreaming, 65–66
    left and right hemispheres, 52
    nerve cells in, 51–52, 66
    processing by, 52
    resting during sleep, 51–52, 63
    self-organizing system of, 81–82
    stochastic resonance, 81
    synaptic homeostasis, 177
Brainstem, 52, 66
Breathing-related sleep disorder, 72
    smoking and, 74
Brentano, Franz, 26
Bucke, Richard Maurice, 209
Buddhism, 166, 194, 198, 223

Caffeine, 68
Cancer and administration of psychedelic
        drugs, 180
Cannabinoid receptors, 174
Çapar, Süleyman, 225–226
Cardeña, Etzel, 139–140
Carleton University Responsiveness to
        Suggestion Scale (CURSS),
        114
Cataplexy, 71, 72
Cerebral cortex, 52, 66
Chamber REST, 45, 46–47
Channeling, 142–144
    and dissociative identity disorder,
        150–151
Chaos theory, 81
Child abuse
    and alien abduction experiences,
        155
    dissociative identity disorder and,
        147–148
    and paranormal experiences among
        victims of, 16
    repressed memories of sexual abuse
        surfacing in dreams, 88
        surfacing under hypnosis, 126

Children. See also Infants
    abuse. See Child abuse
    alien abduction experiences reported
        by, 157–158
    past-life experiences of, 224
    sleep. See Age and sleep stages
Christos technique, 227
Circadian rhythms, 62–63, 66, 74
Closed psyche. See Open versus closed
        psyche
Cocaine, 67
Coconsciousness, 150
Cognitive–experiential theory, 82
Cognitive perspective on consciousness,
        5, 22, 233–234
    and emotions, 36
    out-of-body experiences, 215
    purpose of sleep and, 64
Cognitive theories of dreams, 82–83
    lucid dreams, 98
Coherence of brain waves, 197–198
Collective unconscious, 85
Color, ability to see, 209
Coma, 59
Comprehensive Drug Abuse Prevention
        and Control Act of 1970, 166
Computational approach to mental pro-
        cesses, 27–28
Computerized polysomnography, 54
Concentrative meditation, 198–199,
        201
Confabulation, 127, 148
Confusional arousals, 76
Conscientiousness, 39
Conscious channeling, 143
Consciousness. See also Introspection
    beliefs about, 11–16
    cosmic consciousness, 191, 209
    daydreaming, 37–43
    defined, 6–7
    evidence for survival after death,
        231–232
    evolved consciousness, 209
    perspectives on, 5–6
    scientific study of, 16–21
    stream of, 31–34
    thinking, 31–37
    transcendent state of. See Transcen-
        dence
Consistency seeker and self-knowledge,
        30

Continuous positive airway pressure, 73
Control and transcendence, 188
Controllability, 34
Convictions, 30
Core sleep, 63
Cosmic consciousness, 191, 209, 221
Counterculture and psychedelic drugs, 165–166
Cross-cultural studies of near-death experiences, 222–223
Csikszentmihalyi, Mihaly, 187–188
CURSS. *See* Carleton University Responsiveness to Suggestion Scale

Daydreaming, 9, 37–43
    about current concerns, 38
    imagination, 40–41
    styles of, 38–39
Death, 211–232. *See also* Near-death experiences
Deliberate thinking, 34, 35
Delta waves, 53, 55, 56, 60, 63
Delusions
    and alterations of consciousness, 22, 234–235
    defined, 137
Dendrites, 52
Depression, drugs used in treatment of, 69
Deterministic conceptualization, 12
Dextromethorphan, 162
Diagnostic and Statistical Manual of Mental Disorders (DSM-IV-TR) on sleep disorders, 70
DID. *See* Dissociative identity disorder
N,N-dimethyltryptamine. *See* DMT
Disaggregation, 123
Discursive meditation, 199
Dissociated control, theory of, 123
Dissociaters, 122–123
Dissociation, 123–124, 132
Dissociative identity disorder, 144–151
    absence of restorative experiences, 148
    amnesia for personal information, 150
    biological potential for dissociation, 148

and channeling, 150–151
characteristics of, 144–145
coconsciousness, 150
description of alternate personalities, 145–147
distinguished from schizophrenia, 144–145
dynamics of alternate personalities, 149–150
four-factor theory, 148
fragments, 149
host personality, 149
inner self-helpers, 149
overwhelming experiences and, 148
and past-life experience, 226
and possession, 150–151
shaping influences, 148
suicide rates, 150
switching of alternate personalities, 146–147
trauma as etiological factor, 147–148
treatment, 150
DMT, 169–170, 171
    neuropharmacology of, 172–173
Doblin, Rick, 181, 182, 183
Dopamine, 67
Dream analysis, 79
Dream interpretation, 79, 83–86, 92–94
Dream lag effect, 87
DreamLight, 100
Dreams, 59–61, 79–106. *See also* Nightmares
    and anomalous phenomena, 16
    brain functioning during, 65–66
    cerebral blood flow during, 65
    characteristics of, 80
    content of, 86–95
    control of events occurring, 96
    culmination, 84
    development of plot, 84
    discrimination of state in which person finds self, 96
    exposition, 84
    heightened reality in, 89
    hypnagogic images, 71–72, 88–90
    hypnopompic images, 71–72, 90
    lag effect, 87
    latent content of, 83

Dreams, *continued*
    lucid dreaming, 95–102
        characteristics of, 96–98
        development of, 97
        implications of, 101–102
        induction of, 98–101
        meditation and, 197
        modified mnemonic method for
            induction of, 99
        prelucid dreams, 100
    manifest content of, 83
    meaningfulness of, 91–92
    methods of gathering data on, 86,
        89, 97
    precognitive dreams, 102–106
        empirical studies of, 103–106
        example of, 102–103
    problem solving during, 90, 94–95
    recall of, 60
    recurrent in posttraumatic stress
        disorder, 88
    sensations associated with, 89,
        90
    sense of reality during, 96
    sexual content of dreams, 83, 85,
        101
    solution or result phase, 84–85
    stimulus incorporation in, 86–88
    structure of, 84–85
    switching of alternate personalities
        in, 147
    symbolism of images in, 85
    theories, 79–86
        cognitive theories, 82–83
        Jungian theory, 84–86
        physiological theories, 80–82
        psychoanalytic theory, 83–84
    as thinking, 82
    traumatic events and, 87–88
    as wish-fulfillment, 83–84
Dream work, 83
Drugs. *See also* Psychedelics
    Comprehensive Drug Abuse Preven-
        tion and Control Act of 1970,
        166
    effects on sleep, 67–70
    illicit drugs, 161
    narcolepsy treatment, 72
    psychoactive drugs, 161
    sleeping pills, 73
Dualists, 11–12

Dying of cancer and administration of
    psychedelic drugs, 180
Dyssomnias, 70

Ecstasy, 161–162, 173–174
EEG (electroencephalograph), 53, 54,
    57
    event-related potentials (ERPs) as
        waveforms, 118
    during meditation, 197
Egoist metaphor and self-knowledge, 30
Electrooculogram. *See* EOG
EMG (electromyograph), 53–54, 55
Emotions, 36
Endorphins, 218, 219, 220
Engagement in challenge and transcen-
    dence, 188
Entactogen, 173
Entheogens, 164, 194
Environment
    identification with and transcen-
        dence, 188
    setting in which psychedelic drug is
        taken, 167, 184
EOG (electro-oculograph), 53, 54
Escalating self, 202–203
Event-related potentials (ERPs), 118–
    119
Evolved consciousness, 209
Existential coherence, 81
Exosomatic experiences, 72
Experience sampling method, 29–30
Experiential perspective on conscious-
    ness, 5–6, 22, 233–234
Experimental versus control groups,
    19–20
Externally focused thinking, 35
External unity within mystical experi-
    ences, 183
Extroversion, 39
Eye movements, measurement during
    sleep, 53, 54, 55, 56
    and fluoxetine, 69

False memories, 127
Fanciful versus realistic thoughts, 35
Fantasy-prone persons, 121–122
Feedback and transcendence, 188
Flashbacks, 176

Flotation REST, 45, 46
Flow and transcendence, 187–188
Fluoxetine, 69–70, 72
Foulkes, David, 82, 94
Freud, Sigmund, 37, 84, 91
    on dreams, 83–84, 92

Gamma-aminobutyric acid (GABA),
    68
Ganzfeld studies, 13–15, 23, 130
Gender differences and insomnia, 73
Glossolalia, 142
Goal setting and transcendence, 188
Good Friday experiment with psychedel-
    ics, 180–184
Greyson, Bruce, 221
Grof, Stanislav, 180
Growth hormone and sleep, 63
Guided imagery, 40–41
Guilty-Dysphoric Daydreaming, 38
    and neuroticism, 39
Gustatory phenomena in dreams, 89

Habit modification, 45, 46–47
Hallucinations
    defined, 4
    drug-induced by hallucinogens,
        164
    positive hallucinations, 111, 115
    and sleep deprivation, 61
Hallucinogen persisting perception
    disorder, 176–177
Harvard Group Scale of Hypnotic
    Susceptibility, 113
Hilgard, Ernest, 113, 114, 123
Hill, Clara, 82
Hobson, Allan, 80, 81, 94
Hofmann, Albert, 162–163
Hypnagogic images, 71–72, 88–90
    autosymbolic imagery, 89
    meditation and, 197
    psychedelic drugs inducing, 176
    during shaman ritual, 142
Hypnopompic images, 71–72, 90
Hypnosis, 9, 107–133
    active-alert hypnosis, 110
    amnesia, hypnotic, 112–113
    analgesic effects of, 111–112,
        130–131

    and anomalous phenomena, 16
    applications of, 125–133
        clinical applications, 130–132
        hypnotically recalled memories,
            125–128
        hypnotic regression, extent of,
            128–130
        problems with, 132–133
    classic suggestion effect, 119
    complexity of experiences, 124–
        125
    derivation of term, 107
    dissociaters, 122–123
    dissociation, 123–124, 132
    domain of, 108
    explanations of, 117–125
    fantasy-prone persons and, 121–122
    hidden observer during, 123
    hypnotic subject, 109
    hypnotist, 109
    induction of, 109–110
    involuntary volition, 119–121
    past-life regression and, 226–227
    phenomena of, 108–113
    physiology during, 118
    positive hallucination, 111
    positively set persons and, 121
    posthypnotic suggestions, 111, 112,
        115
    REST, use in conjunction with, 46,
        131
    self-hypnosis, 109
    shamanism and, 139–140
    similarities to sleep, 107–108
    sociocognitive theory of, 117–119
    stage hypnosis, 132–133
    suggestions, hypnotic, 110–113
    susceptibility, 110, 113–117
        differences in responding,
            115–117
        measurement scales, 113–115
    trance, 110
    traumatic events, recall of, 126,
        127–128
    tripartite theory of, 121–123
Hypnotic amnesia, 112–113
Hypnotic induction, 109–110
Hypnotic regression, extent of, 128–
    130
Hypnotics, 68–69
Hypnotic suggestions, 110–113

Hypnotic susceptibility, 110, 113–117
Hypnotic virtuosos, 107, 114, 139
Hypopnea, 73

Idiopathic insomnia, 75
Illicit drugs, 161
Imagery. See Hypnagogic images; Hypno-
    pompic images; Symbolic imagery
Imagination, 40–41
Indigenous cultures and shamanism, 136
Induction, hypnotic, 109–110
Induction of lucid dreaming, 98–101
Ineffability of mystical experiences, 184
Infantile amnesia, 128–129
Infants
    memory processing of, 128–129
    and sleep cycles, 57, 64
Inner observation, 26
Inner perception, 26
Insight, 200
Insomnia, 73–75. See also Sleep: disorders
    drug-induced, 67–69, 74
    idiopathic insomnia, 75
    psychophysiological insomnia, 75
Institute of Noetic Sciences, 191
Internally focused thinking, 35
Internal unity within mystical experi-
    ences, 183, 184
Introspection, 18, 26–31
    computational approach to, 27–28
    inner observation, 26
    inner perception, 26
    modern beginnings of, 26–27
    practical applications, 28–31
Intuition, 91
Involuntary volition and hypnosis,
    119–121

James, William, 7, 31
    on daydreaming, 37
    on introspection, 26–27, 29
    on thinking, 31–34, 48
Jewish mysticism, 208
Jung, Carl, 84–86, 91
Jungian theory, 84–86, 88, 92

K complexes, 55, 58
Kekulé's discovery of benzene's structure,
    90, 94

Klinger, Eric, 34–37, 38, 48
Kluft, Richard, 148
Krippner, Stanley, 104, 151

LaBerge, Stephen, 97, 99, 101
Latent content of dreams, 83
Leary, Timothy, 164–165
Life after death, 211, 216, 229–232
    evidence for survival of conscious-
        ness, 231–232
    mediumship, 229–231
Lilly, John, 43–44, 45, 47, 53, 163
Lindbergh, Charles, 48
Loss of self-awareness and transcendence,
    188
LSD, 161, 167–168
    CIA experiments with, 170
    flashbacks, 176
    invention of, 162–164
    neuropharmacology of, 172–173
    physiological effects of, 167
    in the psychedelic sixties, 164–167
    therapeutic value of, 178–180
    used for psychotherapy for alcohol-
        ism, 179–180
Lucid dreaming, 95–102, 197. See also
    Dreams
Ludwig, Arnold, 179–180
Lysergic acid diethylamide. See LSD

MacDonald, Douglas, 204–206
Mack, John, 156, 159
Magic mushrooms. See Psilocybin
Maimonides Medical Center (Brooklyn,
    NY) and precognitive dream ex-
    periments, 103–105, 130
Manifest content of dreams, 83
Mantra, 195
Marijuana, 5–6, 161, 174–175
Maslow, Abraham, 189
Materialist theory
    James on material reality, 33
    problems presented by, 20–21
    versus transcendent beliefs, 11–13,
        22, 234
Mathematical yoga, 203–204
Mavromatis, Andreas, 88–90
McCarley, Robert, 80, 81
McKenna, Terence, 3–4, 9, 168

MDMA (Ecstasy), 161–162, 173–174
Meaningful versus meaningless phenomenon, 22, 235
    dreams, meaningfulness of, 91–92
Mechanistic conceptualization, 12
Meditation, 195–204
    and anomalous phenomena, 16
    concentrative meditation, 198–199, 201
    and control of the mind, 37
    defined, 195
    dimensions of spirituality, 204–206
    discursive meditation, 199
    physiology of, 196–198
    reflexive meditation, 201
    spiritual aspiration, 204–206
    styles of, 198–201
    transcendental meditation (TM), 195–196, 197, 198
    witnessing meditation, 199–200, 201
Mediumship, 229–231
Memory
    birth, memories of, 129
    confabulation, 127
    false memories, 127
    hypnotically recalled memories, 125–128
    and sleep, 64–65, 82
    womb memories, 130
Mental processes and computational approach, 27–28
Merrell-Wolff, F., 201–204, 236
Mescaline, 161, 169
    neuropharmacology of, 172–173
Mesmer, Franz Anton, 108
Mesmerism, 111
Methadone, 67
4-methoxyamphetamine, 161
3,4-methylenedioxymethamphetamine. See MDMA
Military use of self-hypnosis, 132
Mindfulness, 200
Mitchell, Edgar, 190–191
Modified mnemonic method for induction of lucid dreaming, 99
Monroe, Robert, 213
Mood
    in mystical experiences, 183
    and sleep deprivation, 61
Moody, Raymond, 216

Moore, Robert, 11–12, 190, 205, 208, 211
Multiple personalities. See Dissociative identity disorder
Mundane versus extraordinary phenomena, 235
Muscle activity, measurement during sleep, 53–54, 55, 56
Mushrooms containing psilocybin. See Psilocybin
Mystical experiences, 189–190. See also Transcendence
    contextual or constructivist explanation for, 208
    as erroneous attribution, 208
    explanation for, 207–208
    Jewish mysticism, 208
    peak experiences, 189
    and psychedelics, 183–185

Narcolepsy, 71–72
Nature of self. See Self, nature of
Ndembu healing ritual, 140
Near-death experiences (NDEs), 11, 215–224
    of blind persons, 220–221
    characteristics of, 216–217
    cross-cultural studies, 222–223
    distressing NDEs, 221–222
    example of, 217–218
    logical considerations, 223–224
    reductionist explanations of, 218–220
    subsequent transcendence, 192
Neodissociation theory, 123
Nerve cells. See Brain
Nervous system, 51–53
Neurons, 52
Neuropharmacology of psychedelics, 172–173
Neuroticism, 39
Neurotransmitters, 52, 66, 67, 68
Neutrophils, 42, 131–132
Nicotine, 74
Nightmares, 75–76
    and induction of lucid dreams, 99
    posttraumatic stress disorder, 88
    relief from, via lucid dreams, 101
    switching of alternate personalities in, 147

Noetic quality of mystical experiences, 183, 209–210
Noradrenalin, 66, 67, 68
NovaDreamer, 100
NREM (Non-REM) sleep, 56, 57
    alcohol and, 68
    and day residues, 87
    dream reports from, 59–61
    physiology of, 66
    sleep terrors during, 76

OBEs. See Out-of-body experiences
Obstructive sleep apnea syndrome, 72
Olfactory phenomena in dreams, 89
Oneirology, 79. See also Dreams
Openness, 39
Open versus closed psyche, 23, 135, 151, 159, 237
Opiate receptors, 67
Opioids, 67
Optional sleep, 63
Orloff, Judith, 95
Orne, M. T., 114–115, 120
Osmond, Humphry, 164
Out-of-body experiences (OBEs), 138, 212–215
    characteristics of, 212–213
    cognitive theory of, 215
    during NDEs, 11, 216, 217–219, 220, 221
    perceptions during, 213–214

Pacemakers, 53
Pahnke, Walter, 181–184, 192, 208
Paradoxicality of mystical experiences, 183–184
Paradoxical sleep, 56
Paranormal Beliefs, 205, 206
Parasomnias, 75–78
Past-life experiences, 224–229
    children's, 224–226
    example of, 225–226
    past-life regression, 226–228
    past-life therapy, 228–229
PCI (Phenomenology of Consciousness Inventory), 124
PCP, 161
Peak experiences, 189
Pekala, Ronald, 124

Pentacostalism, 142
Perennial philosophy, 208–209
Periodic limb movements, 69–70
Persinger, Michael, 206–207
Persistent vegetative state, 59
Peters, Larry, 141–142
Peyote cactus, 169
Phantasticum, 164
Phasic REM sleep, 56
Phenomenological mapping, 138–139
Phenomenology of Consciousness Inventory (PCI), 124
Phobias, treatment of, 47
    past-life therapy, 228–229
Physicalists, 12
Physical mediums, 230
Physiological effects of psychedelics
    ayahuasca, 171
    LSD, 167
    marijuana, 174
    MDMA, 173–174
Physiological perspective on consciousness, 5–6, 22, 51, 233–234
Physiological theories of dreams, 80–82
Physiology during hypnosis, 118–119
Physiology during sleep, 51–58, 65–67
    NREM sleep, 66
Physiology of meditation, 196–198
Politician metaphor and self-knowledge, 30
Politics of science, 20–21
Polysomnography, 53–54
    measuring stages of sleep, 54–56
Poor Attentional Control, and Neuroticism, 39
Portable computerized polysomnography, 54, 59
Positive-Constructive Daydreaming, 38
    and Openness, 39
Positive hallucinations, 111, 115
Positively set persons, 121
Positron emission tomography, 198
Possession, 136–137, 141–144. See also Shamanism
    and dissociative identity disorder, 150–151
Possession trance, 141
Posthypnotic suggestions, 111, 112–113, 115
Posttraumatic stress disorder, 87–88, 179

Precognitive dreams, 102–106
Prelucid dreams, 100
Problem solving during dreams, 90,
        94–95
Psilocybin, 161, 168–169
    Good Friday experiment with,
        180–185
    neuropharmacology of, 172–173
Psychedelic psychotherapy, 179
Psychedelics, 161–185. See also LSD
    cross-tolerance of, 172
    flashbacks, 176
    Good Friday experiment, 180–185
    hallucinogens, 164
    long-term effects of, 175–180
    modern beginnings of, 162–167
    mystical experiences and, 183–185
    neuropharmacology of, 172–173
    perceptual effects of, 176–177
    psychotic effects of, 177–178
    psychotropic nature of, 164
    set at time of taking, 167, 184
    setting in which drug is taken, 167,
        184
    shaman's experiences induced by, 137
    therapeutic effects of, 178–180
    tolerance of, 172
    transcendental effects of, 180–185,
        194
    types of, 167–175
Psychoactive drugs, 161
Psychoanalytic theory of dreams, 83–84
Psychodysleptic drugs, 164
Psycholytic psychotherapy, 178–179
Psychoneuroimmunology, 41–43
Psychopathology
    and altered states, 10–11
    versus well-being, 23, 236
Psychophysiological insomnia, 75
Psychosomatic problems and past-life ther-
        apy, 228
Psychosynthesis, 40
Psychotic effects of psychedelics, 177–178
Psychotomimetic drugs, 164, 178

Quantum mechanics, 140

Rapid eye movement (REM), 56. See also
        REM sleep

Reality
    alternative explanations of, 238–239
    conventional ways of thinking
        about, 12
    fanciful versus realistic thoughts, 35
    James on material reality, 33
    of near-death experiences, 223–224
    in transcendent state, 202
Receptor sites, 52
Recurrent dreams in posttraumatic stress
        disorder, 88
Reductionism, 12
    as explanations of NDEs, 218–220
    as explanations of transcendence,
        206–208
Reflexive meditation, 201
Relaxation response, 196, 198
Religion. See also Buddhism; Mystical ex-
        periences; Shamanism
    and near-death experiences,
        222–223
    and possession, 142, 143
    spiritual aspiration, 204–206
REM sleep, 56, 57
    activation during, 80
    deprivation of, 62
    dream reports from, 59–61, 97–98
    drugs' effects on, 67–70
    and learning, 64
    lucid dreams during, 97, 98
    physiology of, 65–67
    rebound, 62
    waking someone from, 58
Restricted environmental stimulation
        technique/therapy (REST), 45–
        47, 131
Reynolds, Pam, 217–220
Ring, Kenneth, 220, 221
Roberts, Bernadette, 208
Roberts, Jane, 143

Sabom, Michael, 217
Sawtooth waves, 56
Schizophrenia
    defined, 137
    delusions and hallucinations, similar-
        ity to international myths and
        fairy tales, 85
    DID compared with, 144–145
    negative symptoms, 137

Schizophrenia, *continued*
  positive symptoms, 137
  psychedelics and, 177–178
  shamanism/soul journeying compared
    to, 10, 137–139
Schneider, John, 42
Scientific study of consciousness, 16–21
  authentic mode of science, 17
  experimental versus control groups,
    19–20
  methodological flexibility, 18–20
  nature of science, 17–18
Scientism, 17
Scientist metaphor and self-knowledge,
  30
Selective serotonin reuptake inhibitors
  (SSRIs), 69
  and flashbacks, 176
Self-hypnosis, 109, 132
Self, nature of, 23, 31–32, 237
Self-talk, 35–36
Self-transformation in study of conscious-
    ness, 19
Sensed presences, 47–49
Sense of sacredness in mystical experi-
    ences, 183
Sensory restriction, 43–49
  early research on, 43–45
  effects of, 46–47
  and sensed presences, 47–49
  types of, 45–46
Serotonin, 66, 67, 68, 69
Sexual abuse. *See* Child abuse
Sexual content of dreams, 83–84, 101
Shamanism, 136–141
  ayahuasca use, 170–172
  characteristics of, 136–137
  compared to alien abduction experi-
    ences, 158–159
  compared with schizophrenia, 10,
    137–139
  hypnosis and, 139–140
  initiation as shaman, 137
  mentoring, 137
  possession, 136–137, 141–144
    channeling, 142–144
    characteristics of, 141–142
    trance, 141
  soul journeying. *See* Soul journeying
  world view of, 140–141
Shanon, Benny, 171

SHSS. *See* Stanford Hypnotic Susceptibil-
    ity Scale
Singer, Jerome, 37, 38
Sleep, 51–78
  arousal, 58–59
  brain activity during, 52–53
  core sleep, 63
  disorders, 70–78
    insomnia, 73–75
    narcolepsy, 71–72
    parasomnias, 75–78
    sleep apnea, 72–73
    sleepwalking, 76–77
  drugs' effects on, 67–70
  explanations for, 63–65
  insights and problem solving during,
    90
  measuring of, 53–54
  memory and, 64–65, 82
  mentation, 58–61
  need for, 61–63
  neural mechanisms of, 65–67
  neurobiology of, 65–70
  non-REM (NREM) sleep, 56, 57
  optional sleep, 63
  patterns of stages, 57–58
  physiology and behavior during,
    51–58
  purpose of, 61–65
  REM sleep, 56, 57
  stages of, 54–56
  TM, falling asleep during, 196–197
Sleep apnea, 72–73
Sleep continuity, 57
Sleep deprivation, 61–62
Sleep efficiency, 57
Sleepiness, 73
Sleeping pills, 73
Sleep latency, 57
Sleep paralysis, 71
Sleep spindles, 55, 58
Sleep state misperception, 74
Sleep terrors, 76
Sleepwalking, 76–77
Slow-wave sleep (SWS), 55, 57
  brain during, 63
  dream recall from, 59–61
  need for, 62–63
  sleep terrors during, 76
Smith, Allan, 191, 209
Smith, Huston, 169, 182–183, 193

Smoking cessation programs, 46
Smoking's effect on sleep, 74
Snoring, 72–73
Sociocognitive theory of hypnosis, 117–119
Somatic phenomena in dreams, 89
Soul journeying, 136–137
    affect during, 138
    compared with schizophrenia, 10, 137–139
    concentration during, 138
Spanos, Nicholas, 117
Speaking in tongues, 142
Spinal cord, 52
Spiritual aspiration, 204–206
Spontaneous thinking, 34
Stage hypnosis, 132–133
Stanford Hypnotic Susceptibility Scale (SHSS), 113–114
Stevens, Anthony, 91
Stevenson, Ian, 224, 227
Stimulus hunger, 47
Stimulus incorporation in dreams, 86–88
Stochastic resonance, 81
Strassman, Rick, 170
Stream of consciousness, 31–34
Subjective consciousness$_2$, 6
Substance-induced sleep disorders, 70. See also Drugs
Suicide rates and dissociative identity disorder, 150
Superconscious, 40
SWS. See Slow-wave sleep
Symbolic imagery, 41
    archetypes, 85–86
    in dreams, 85
Synaptic homeostasis, 177
Synthesis. See Activation–synthesis hypothesis

Tamang of Nepal, 136, 137, 140, 141–142, 168
Tarazi, Linda, 228
Tart, Charles, 7–8, 9, 195–196, 213–214
Thalmus, 52, 66
THC, 174–175
Therapeutic effects, 236–237
    of meditation, 196
    of psychedelics, 178–180
Theta waves, 53, 54, 55, 197

Thinking, 31–37
    controllability, 34
    degenerated nature of thoughts, 35
    deliberate thinking, 34
    dimensions of, 34–37
    disconnected nature of thoughts, 35
    dreaming as, 82
    emotions, 36
    externally focused, 35
    fanciful versus realistic thoughts, 35
    internally focused, 35
    self-talk, 35–36
    spontaneous thinking, 34
    stream of consciousness, 31–34
    thought suppression, 36–37
    well-integrated nature of thoughts, 35
Thought suppression, 36–37
Tibetan Buddhism, 166
Time, freedom from, and transcendence, 188
TM. See Transcendental meditation
Tobacco smoking and sleep, 74
Tonic REM sleep, 56
Trance, 135–159
    alien abduction experiences, 152–159. See also Alien abduction experiences
    defined, 135
    dissociative identity disorder, 144–151. See also Dissociative identity disorder
    hypnosis and, 110
    shamanism, 136–141. See also Shamanism
Trance channeling, 143
Trance logic, 111
Transcendence, 187–210
    examples of spontaneous transcendence, 190–194
    as exceptional functioning, 208–210
    explanations of, 206–210
    flow, 187–188
    versus material beliefs, 11–13, 234
    and methodological flexibility, 18
    meditation, 195–204. See also Meditation
    of mystical experiences, 183, 184, 187, 189–190, 191
    peak experiences, 189

Transcendence, *continued*
    psychedelics' effects and, 180–185,
        194
    reductionist theories, 206–208
    transcendental philosophy of
        Merrell-Wolff, 201–204, 235–
        236
    types of experiences, 187–190
Transcendental awareness, 221, 238
Transcendental meditation (TM), 195–
    197, 198, 199
Transiency of mystical experiences, 184
Transliminality, 16
Traumatic events
    dissociative identity disorder and,
        147–148
    and dreams, 87–88
    and hypnotically recalled memories,
        126, 127–128
    meditation and, 198
Tungus of Siberia, 136

UFOs. *See* Alien abduction experiences
Ullman, Montague, 104
Unity within mystical experiences,
    183

Veridical events, 22, 234–235
Vertex sharp waves, 54–55, 56

Wakefulness, 25–49. *See also* Con-
        sciousness
    daydreaming, 37–43
    imagination, 40–41
    introspection, 18, 26–31
    sensory restriction, 43–49
    thinking, 31–37
Walsh, Roger, 138, 139
Watson, John, 27
Weiss, Brian, 226, 228
Weitzenhoffer, A. M., 114
Wish-fulfillment and dreams, 83–84
Witnessing meditation, 199–200, 201
Wolf, Fred Alan, 140
Womb memories, 130
Wren-Lewis, John, 9, 192–193, 194, 202,
    210
Wundt, Wilhelm, 26, 29

Yagé, 170–172
Young, Mike, 182, 194

ABOUT THE AUTHOR

Imants Baruss, PhD, is a professor of psychology at King's College, University of Western Ontario, where he has been teaching undergraduate courses in consciousness for more than 15 years. His research focuses on fundamental questions concerning the nature of consciousness, with academic papers having appeared in psychology, philosophy, anthropology, and science journals. He is the author of two previous books, *The Personal Nature of Notions of Consciousness* and *Authentic Knowing*.